CARPING RE-CUT

ISBN NUMBER 978-0-9926839-0-0

The first edition of Carping Re-Cut is limited to 3000 copies.
There are 40 leather-bound collector's editions.

Printed and bound in the UK by CPI Colour.

First published in November 2013 by Jim Shelley
Carping Re-Cut is a registered trademark

A copy of this book is held by the British Library.

Acknowledgements

Rich Stewart
Bradley Sharp
Jane Shelley
Mark Shave
Steve Allcott
Sean Leverett
Darrell Stile
Ben Finlay
Mark Willcocks
Rob Gillespie
Sam Pavitt of Fruitful Media
Craig Stannard
Andy Stafford
Cyril Rogers & Family
Rob Shanks
Martin Pick
David Slowen
Gary Lewis
Michael Krassos
Matt Gosling
Dave Tudor

Lee Yateman
Mark Dean
Paul Nelhams
Dave Mallin
James Turner
Tom Anderson of Sticky Baits
Daniel Wildbore
Jamie Russell
Phil Rust
Helen Laird
Ben Dowers
Paul Harrison
Max Whittred
Nathan Highley
David Hall Publications
Godman Angling
Vision Ultimate Angling

Last but not least to all of my many mates.

Contents

Foreword

Steve Allcott

Jim Shelley has written Carping Re-Cut from start to finish, as it happened, with not much left to the imagination. His name is known to most anglers, so notorious is he for his continued success in catching big carp. I have spent four decades in the company of the greatest anglers in our sport; more than a carp-angling lifetime you could say.

So, I feel my assessment of Jim's Carping Re-Cut will be as close to as it happened. There are few carp hunters that have Jim's rare gift. He has both passion and obsession all the way to his core, showing conciseness in his movements and mannerisms. If anyone or anything is in his path it may as well move aside because Jim's coming through, all the way to the carp getting caught.

Along the winding paths Jim has followed he has made hundreds of friends and, as in all walks of life and in any sports, several enemies. Oh and they've tried so hard to bring him down, the same faces time and time again, even anonymous vendettas bouncing around the World Wide Web. It's a shame really; it's just the way they are and I'm sure Jim is not their only target. Some were friends in past times; I hope they will be again. Some will be mentioned in this book but don't choose sides, read the whole story of what Jim has achieved and in the end you can't help but be inspired with his impressive continued success. If you don't want to read Jim's Carping Re-Cut then that's OK, just browse through 400 plus pictures and drool in envy! Most are eagerly waiting for Jim's series of adventures and you will be shown by example what can be achieved. Clearly, none of us are Jim Shelley, but we can all gain something from this book.

I have analysed his style and it seems not too dissimilar to my own and that of many other anglers, yet Jim always catches more… why? He is hotwired, fully tuned, his head carries no clutter and he is just fully focused on hunting carp.

Maybe some of you think differently, and if just a few of you change your mind after reading this book then more power to Jim. I get how he quickly tops up all the percentages to be fully loaded; his honed rigs are always the best traps on the best spots and that in itself is key. Jim gives them the best food and as much as they want to eat when and where necessary, that again is key. I have stood with Jim watching the

water, Jim points at a carp that has showed yet I never see it and I don't miss much! Therefore, I know he has the edge, so now I look harder. Are you with me?
We used to call it watercraft. Jim is beyond that, the success in this book will show you clues, how he located them; often a common-sense approach is a benchmark to how we could re-cut our own angling style. The pages before you are full of the most beautiful, iconic carp with the purest pedigree that most desire. The photography will astound and absorb you so much that it will appear almost fiction, but it is very real, and human nature will show a tad of envy. Jim has been lucky enough to catch many of our old English monsters before they passed away. We could all be an alarm call away from holding one ourselves. I could go on and on repetitively pushing Jim Shelley and Carping Re-Cut but the book will do that itself. Fasten your seatbelts, this is a high-octane white-knuckle ride of carp annihilation.

Keep it real, Steve Allcott.

Introduction

My life has changed so much for the better since my last book. Meeting Jane, who I later married in Mauritius, has changed my world in so many ways. She has kept me on the straight and narrow and during our time together, I have learnt how to communicate, teaching myself how to read and write, initially on the internet and my mobile phone! This seemingly simple thing has helped me hugely, as I can now deal positively with most things that life throws at me, instead of getting somewhat frustrated at times, as I have in the past.

After spending a couple of years of learning how to string words together into sentences, and memorising hundreds of words and their meanings, I felt I could now start on the journey that has resulted in my second book, which you have in your hands. It took me many hundreds of hours across two winters, sitting in my van and bivvy with the rods out, to put this long-awaited book together.

I decided to take the plunge and publish the book myself. Trust me, at times I did wonder if I hadn't taken on a little bit too much, but with continued help from my darling wife I can now stand proud and say that I caught all of these fantastic old English carp, took most of the pictures, wrote the words, financed it and published the mammoth book that you are about to read. I hope you enjoy the journey as much as I did in putting this book together. Of course, without the help of many friends and my sponsors I wouldn't have been able to dedicate as much time to the pursuit of the carp that you're about to read about, so huge thanks to them.

Finally and most importantly, this book is dedicated equally to my best friend the late Marky Mark Shave, God I miss you so much, and my wife Jane Shelley; love you lots. xx

Jim Shelley, Lowestoft, August 2013.

The Road Lake

Back On The Road

As you pass between Wraysbury Village and Staines, as I often did during my time in that area, you might notice bright water flickering between the roadside trees in places. I occasionally got that same tantalising glimpse while driving to the Indian or KFC from the mighty Wraysbury One or Horton Church Lake. Occasional visits to see my mate Dave Mallin, as he targeted The Pet from the Priory, led me to become more familiar with the historic lakes scattered along that famous stretch of road. Of course, I knew the history of the Longfield lakes and had been fortunate enough to catch a few of its ex-residents during my time on Horton Church Lake. I wasn't sure what was left, but I knew that a fish called Scaly had been moved to Horton long after the rest of its cohort. Two syndicates had taken over Fox Pool and The Road Lake and had stocked them with new fish. A new era had begun for Longfield. It wasn't too long before the grapevine hummed with talk of The Road Lake producing a forty, called The Big Dink. The phoenix had well and truly risen from the ashes.

I had other targets at the time and the lake drifted from my thoughts for a few years until talk was rife on the internet that The Road Lake and Fox Pool were coming back under RMC control, now this was interesting. A call to RMC Angling boss Ian Welch and the rumours were confirmed, which must have thoroughly pissed the old syndicate off. With Ian's say so, I started to make plans to fish the lakes as soon as I could. Although I'd heard about The Dink, I was more interested in Fox Pool initially, because it too held big carp once more, although I didn't set foot on there until my second season on the famous, old complex.

When June 1st came around I found myself once again in the Staines area, a place that had been a second home to me at times. At that time, I'd have the odd social at Wraysbury and Horton, drawing inspiration from simply being around the lakes, in the company of like-minded anglers and an underarm cast from some awesome carp. Apart from that though, I'd been in limbo somewhat, unable to commit to a water after banking Two Tone from Conningbrook. Dave Mallin had tried to persuade me to go straight onto The Mere, in pursuit of 'the ultimate goal' but I just didn't have the time due to major upheaval in my life. So, Longfield it was to be. I swung the car off the

I swung the car off the road and up to an imposing set of black gates.

perilously fast road and up to the big set of gates, which fascinated me, reminding me of a prison. Yep, these were serious gates and I was having serious problems getting through them. I tried all the RMC keys that I had as a gold-card holder, but none of them worked. I phoned Ian Welch to find out what the crack was and laughed as he told me that the lakes didn't open until the 16th!

I was a little unsure of what I'd find at the end of the potholed track on the other side of the prison gates when I finally got inside for my first look. However, you just can't be disappointed with The Road Lake. The small, quiet pool is fringed with loads of dead and overhanging trees and I even managed to find a few fish on my first circuit. I left the car park and arrived in the swim called The Launch, noticing loads of tall, thin trees, many of them crisscrossed where they'd crashed down and rotted. I looked left and I could see an inviting line of snags, snaking out of the clear pool. I walked through to Peg One and along behind the snags. I couldn't believe that I was seeing fish straight away. They were just happily lying up but I was anything but happy to stop; I wanted to get on to the next corner and see what else was about. I proceeded along the House Bank, stopping in the corner nearest the road where there's a big snag in the water. Sitting in the snag was this f'ing great thing that I later found out hadn't been banked since it was 27lb. The syndicate had dubbed it The Block and it had attitude. I couldn't put a name to this brooding giant at the time, but I described it to people afterwards and they identified it for me. I put it at 43lb to 45lb - it was that big.

I didn't see much at the other end but, on re-entering the main snags, I saw another big fish with a line of gold-sovereign scales along its back. It was The Dink and in that instant I knew that I had to have him. Details of the rest of the stock were hard to come by and much of my information was based on rumour, but Ian had told me about a zip linear that he reckoned was one of the best in the country. I found this hard to take in at the time, because I'd just landed Mary's Mate from Wraysbury, a fish that I considered to be one of the ultimate linears. When I did finally see the zip, it was indeed a perfect linear, but it did nothing for me. Don't get me wrong though, I still wanted to catch it! I spent time with Rick on that opening night as he described the characters of the lake to me. Someone had given me a bottle of pink champagne after I caught Two Tone and I told Rick that I had it in the van but I wasn't going to drink it. He quickly piped up, saying, "I'll have it then." I had a couple of glasses and he polished off the rest as we toasted the capture of the UK's biggest carp. Rick told me that there were maybe 30 or 35 fish in the lake, but The Dink was my target, all I could think of were those big scales. It looked like someone had embossed them along its back – it reminded me of The Causeway Fish.

Soon enough I was able to set my watch by the fish, they'd turn up in certain spots at certain times of day, allowing me to watch them and build a picture of the stock. The fish seemed to spend most of the main part of the day in the snags and moved out into

I found Ian's opinion hard to accept as I felt that I'd landed a fish that I considered to be one of the ultimate linears.

Someone had given me a bottle of pink champagne after I'd landed Two Tone; Rick offered to drink it for me!

the open water at night. Because I couldn't always get in different swims for the day and night, I had to sit out long periods when I knew that the fish simply weren't going to be in my water.

I was using Dynamite at the time and pretty quickly I decided to team up with a few of the other lads on the lake, who were also using the bait…big mistake. Within two weeks the back stabbing that I thought I'd long-since left behind had started again in earnest. These so-called mates were soon putting in calls to Ian Welch claiming that I'd been doing more than my allotted time on the lake. Ian even told me that I'd been accused of soaping my particles to ruin other anglers' chances. All this and I hadn't even caught a fish at this stage! With two losses to my name I turned my back on the water because this definitely wasn't what I signed up for, no way. As it turned out, I was to be away from the lake for eight months, although I did carry out a few baitings on the quiet. I was parking in the sailing club gates, crossing the road and pushing through the trees by a gap in the Road Lake fence. I spent my time in the wilderness flitting between waters, unable to settle because of major upheavals in my personal life. It wasn't pretty, but I ended up living on the bank and emerged from that period having kicked the drink and desperate to get back into my serious carp fishing.

I timed my return to the real world to coincide with what I thought would be the quietest time, March. The thought of those great big chunks creeping up into the snags, through the cool, dark water and beginning to rub themselves up after a quiet winter spent unmolested out in the lake, got the old juices flowing. I pulled into the tight area in front of the prison gates, although this time I was going to shut myself away willingly. I bounced down the potholed lane scattering rabbits to either side, trying hard not to bottom out the wagon – what a nightmare! On reaching the third gate I could see that the car park was empty, just how I like it. I coasted the car into the car park and grabbed the big puffa jacket off the seat next to me. I gave the trusty glasses a clean and headed straight to the main snags for a look. I passed swim one and had to force myself to slow up and take more deliberate paces as I neared the holding area. The weather had turned mild and I was expecting them to be at home, especially considering Nigel Sharp had bagged Clover out of The Launch and Terry Hearn had banked The Big Dink, all within the last six weeks. They'd now both gone, having caught the two biggest carp in the pond. Good angling!

I peered into the snags and I could quite clearly see that the crust had been worn away from the main rubbing spot. Although there are probably thirty yards of snags in this tree line, there's one raised area that has a special significance. During the winter, when the fish aren't rubbing up, nature comes back and reclaims these spots. The debris that collects on top forms a crust and I was delighted to see that the gravel was glowing through. On closer inspection, I could see that not only had this crust been removed,

There was a tiny little swim just to the left, in a tight corner, and I planned to catch The Dink from there.

This was going to be up-close-and-personal fishing!

but the stones had been turned. In among these stones was fine yellow sand, which told me that it had been in and out of carp's mouths – birds couldn't be responsible. Birds might pick up the odd stone, but not sand. However, carp love passing sand through their gill rakers – I reckon that it almost gives them a little tone-up. This whole process of elimination took a matter of seconds and my hunting instinct screamed CARP!

I always carry a few baits in my pocket in case I can get in front of a few carp at close quarters. I crumbed up what I had, saving seven whole ones, and chucked the crumb in. As it fluttered down into the snags, I tucked my hands away into my pockets and pulled my hood over my head – something that I always do when I'm observing marginal spots. I'm sure they can get spooked from the white skin at close quarters. Five minutes passed and I caught sight of what I thought was a movement out of the corner of my eye. There's always an element of disbelief about that first sighting of the year and I had to pinch myself as this shape emerged from the abyss and began sliding up the shelf. I was running through the stock in my head and this carp just kept getting bigger as it moved into three and a half feet of water in the main snags. The sharp profile as it moved over the light-coloured gravel left me in no doubt – this was a big fish. Its identity wasn't difficult to pin down when I saw the huge sovereign scales along the dorsal line; it was The Dink, the queen of the lake. I'd finally seen a picture of the great fish, with Terry in the Angling Times, and it looked every bit as impressive in the flesh. Pretty soon it was clear that The Dink wasn't alone. Within twenty minutes

I'd seen seven different fish, including The Scattered Linear. This was the chance I was looking for; the fish were awake early.

The Dink almost seemed to have her own aura. I don't know why, but I just wanted to catch that carp, it looked like those scales had been chiselled out of a block of wood and splashed with colour. She dropped onto the crumb and made sure that she got her share. The Dink was the most aggressive feeder there and she was having it. She was plainly back on the munch just a month or so after Tel had nailed her at just under forty. To catch her, I needed to move her from where she was feeding, to somewhere I could land her safely. This was much easier than I thought. I plopped a few baits out in a line toward a fishable spot and she just followed them! Unbelievably, I'd managed to isolate the one I wanted, straight away. There was a tiny little swim just to the left, in a tight corner, and I planned to catch her from there. This was going to be up-close-and-personal fishing, so I'd have to be mega quiet in the swim. I'd fished in snaggy spots on Toll Pits so I'd got the right kit and I knew exactly what to do. Bullet Braid is a huge edge in these tight spots. It gives you unparalleled indication even though it's nailed hard along the bottom. It's do or die in these situations; there's no point using a small hook, it'll just pop out under pressure.

Twigs were removed from the path and I laid old, dead leaves over the gravel to deaden the crunch - nothing was left to chance. With the bedchair in the swim and the bivvy squeezed over the top there was no room for manoeuvre and I didn't want to move

There was a fallen tree projecting 20ft out into the lake between The Dink and me.

an inch, I was right where I wanted to be. Even in the new position, there was a fallen tree projecting 20ft out into the lake between The Dink and me. A cunning plan was hatched. I cut the leader off a rod, tied on a little lead and flicked it hard round to the right, just over the tree. I then walked along the bank and slowly inched my way down to the base of the tree to collect the lead. Then, I carefully shimmied along the trunk a little and passed the lead under the tree, so that the line was now running beneath it. I got up, cut the lead off and tied my leader and baited rig back on. Understandably, the fish had disappeared into the snags because I was so close to them. Unsteadily, I lowered the rig onto the gravel hump, using a landing net handle to get the distance. While getting the lead into position, I'd noticed that the bait had gone so I chewed up some that I'd popped into my pocket and dropped them in. I watched the cloud descend through the water and, just as the fragments of Monster Pursuit (I'd now signed for Nashbait) hit the deck, The Dink flew over and went straight down on the bait, circling with her gills flaring as she sucked up the particles. I quickly dropped in seven whole barrels and backed off to the swim where I teased the slack line back slightly and gingerly slid a 2oz back lead down it.

I eased another bank stick into the gravel, just in front of the alarm and tight to the rod blank to stop the rod being pulled off the rests. Everything was then locked up solid. Despite the proximity of the big 'un, I couldn't resist having a quick look on the spot. I had a little chuckle to myself when I saw The Dink, all on her own, nailed to the lake bed, munching away. I got the impression that she was getting into a bit of a tizz because she couldn't get all of the crumb. I heard a couple of muted bleeps so, as quickly as I could, I retreated the few feet to the swim. I thought that it was going to be a liner but, as I set foot in the swim, the tip whacked round to the right. I pulled into it immediately and it surged off to the right in unstoppable fashion. The fish was running hard out into the lake, away from the snags but well under the fallen tree. The 13ft Pursuit rod was bent double – I really had to stop this beast before it found sanctuary. I held on hard and she came to a complete halt. Knowing that the carp was some 20 to 25 yards out, I pumped him back and she came straight back towards me, sweet. I told myself that I'd ease off as soon as I saw the fish. She gave a final big kick and slowed to a stop. Acting quickly, I dropped the rod tip and started to pump her back to me. All this time I was just praying that everything would hold firm because I was 99 per cent sure what I was attached to.

My immediate concern lay with the snags to the right and the tree to my left, but the fish kept coming and kept coming. All of a sudden she was right there, close in. A twisting row of sovereign scales hit the surface as the fish half-rolled. A second later it was coughing water, ready for the net. "Easy Uncle Jim," I muttered, sliding the net out and under The Dink's long frame. Relief coursed through me. The fish went mad in the net, foaming up the margin before calming and slowly dropping into the dark folds. Moments before I'd netted her I'd had a strange experience; I'd made eye contact with The Dink, just like I had with Mary, years before. I notice this eye contact with a few of the fish I catch; it's weird, almost like a feeling of respect from both parties. Maybe

The things that I find important when choosing my targets are the water that they live in, who's caught them before, how old they are and where they've travelled.

The carp gods had awarded me an early spring present in the shape of my target fish.

it's an inbuilt animal thing, connected with hunting and long lost to most people. Now there's another chapter!

I struggle to explain the surge of emotions that ran through me as I admired my prize stirring slowly in the net. The carp gods had awarded me an early spring present in the shape of my target fish. I just stood there, taking it all in like I always do; savouring the moment – a piece if time logged forever inside my mind…for my eyes only. It's an odd moment when your target fish lies defeated, finally. I feel sorry for them sometimes, mixed with the more obvious feelings of joy. I made a few calls and arranged my mat and scales as the lads made their way over from Horton. Looking down at the long, scaly beast in the net, I knew that she would be 39lb plus. When it came time to get her out, I broke the net down and rolled it up, drawing the fish to the surface. As I touched her for the first time I whispered a few words of respect and told her that I'd look after her – the respect of the hunt. As I carefully laid the queen of the lake down on the wet mat, I paused for a moment to take in her beauty. Hoisted on Marky's scales she went 40lb 4oz. The weight didn't matter to me. The things that I find important when choosing my targets are the water that they live in, who's caught them before, how old they are and where they've travelled.

After the last shutter had clicked, I took her back to the swim and gently lowered her back. Straight away, she took some big gulps of water and began to move, showing me that she was ready to go back home. I got one last glance as she swam off down the shelf, back into the inky abyss.

I would be away from the lake for the best part of a year after the capture of The Dink. I did pop in a few times during the warmer months but it was always too busy for my liking. The return was planned for the colder months again, as many of the lads with the most time would have moved on. I spent the early part of the winter fishing close to my Suffolk home, on Waveney Valley Lakes. It was a busy period as I caught mega amounts of fish, giving me loads of confidence in the way I was angling. Although the fishing was good and I love getting bites, by the time we'd celebrated the New Year, my mind was starting to wander back around the banks of The Road Lake. I was fully aware that these big-fish waters tend to come alive around the end of January and I wanted to get something going. Because it's 167 miles from my house to The Road Lake, I had to plan my baiting campaign with military precision and carry it out with discipline. My baitings would have to be kept 'under the radar' for the time being, because I didn't want anyone else getting the same ideas. I knew that those fish would be starting to look for food and I wanted to be in pole position. During the winter, you can see the lake from the road and I didn't want to risk someone seeing my bivvy while I started to bait, so I generally fished at places like Camelot Lake in Norfolk and set off to The Road Lake at midnight. As I drove through the cold early hours, passing sleeping towns, I wondered if the carp would be about yet. It had been a mild winter so far and I'd been giving them plenty of my bait, so there had to be a good chance that one or two of those old warriors had switched onto it. Once at the lake, I'd drop plenty of the White Nash Amber Attract with Strawberry Oil Palatant into the snags and be on my way in twenty minutes, arriving back at the local lake at first light.

Just as important as the physical act of baiting up was the bait itself. Since getting on board with Nash, I was in the fortunate position that I was able to have a winter bait made to my specifications. The White Amber was the result. I'd been using the Strawberry Oil Palatant for many years and here I was, signed up with the company that made it. I was confident that the Amber Attract base mix was sound, because I'd seen people like Terry Hearn and Nigel Sharp using it to good effect. I was chuffed that, finally, someone had listened to me and put together my winter bait with all of its tweaks. Six years on and I'm still using the same recipe!

At the end of January, I was ready for my first trip. I fired up the carp wagon in the early hours, pointed it south and let my mind wander deep into those sheltered, cold waters. Would they be in the snags? Would they feed? Time would tell. I pulled off the M25 at junction 14 and wound my way through carp fishing's golden mile, along the side of the big ressies. Around that time, I regularly used to see foxes in my headlights near the bridge next to Wraysbury Two. It was like they'd been on a feeding raid somewhere and they were going back to their camp. I cruised into Staines around 6:30am and headed straight to the local café. It was still dark, so there was no need to hurry to the lake just yet. As I munched the full English breakfast I let the quiet anticipation build inside, confident that my little baiting missions would have had the desired effect. Deep inside, I knew that I'd see them in the snags, just as I had the year before.

A week previous, I'd spoken to Rick, to see how he was getting on down on the Road. He said that he'd seen nothing, not even in the snags. I was careful not to say that I'd been down to bait up but, to be fair, I hadn't seen anything on the bait yet anyway, because I'd been there at night. I didn't like holding out on Rick, because he was a sound geezer back then and I committed to telling him everything when I got back on the lake. You know who you can tell without getting your swim jumped! Feeling pumped with enthusiasm, I got back into the carp wagon and headed out along the waking streets. I drove down the road that runs alongside the North Lake of Wraysbury One. Passing the great lake I was overcome with nostalgia, remembering the lake as it was; an awe-inspiring water. Gone, but never forgotten. Further on into Wraysbury village you come to a junction where you can go left to Wraysbury's South Lake. This time, I swung the car right, on towards The Road Lake. A minute or so out of the village, the windswept Priory Lake came into view on my left. I remembered seeing the huge Pet in there while my mate Dave Mallin was fishing for it. At the time, it was a lake that I had in mind for a future campaign, but the great fish sadly died before I cast a rod in there. As The Priory receded in the rear-view mirror, I glimpsed The Road Lake in daylight for once, snaggy and intimate through the trees.

Brakes on, indicate and keep your eyes on the mirror just in case some idiot is speeding and not looking! It amazes me that no one has had a crash there yet, pulling into the tight slot in the muddy verge. With the gates dealt with, I bounced into the car park to find it empty again. As soon as I got out of the car I could tell that the weather was milder down here. I pulled on my coat as a flock of absurd green parakeets flew

I'd never seen birds in the snags before, so it had to be carp that had disturbed the winter crust.

Watching and learning.

Swim One gave me the best chance to hit the bar along the snag line.

overhead, squawking, it felt good to be back. The cries of these noisy aliens will be all-too familiar to those of you fishing in the Colne Valley and it felt like I was being welcomed home and reassured that nothing had changed. Before leaving the car park I noticed that I'd not quite pulled the car in behind the bushes. Remember, I didn't want the locals to know that I was back in the area so I hid it nicely.

I went through my usual routine, clearing the twigs off the path and pulled my hood up as I entered the snags. A quick look revealed that the winter crust had once again been removed from the rubbing spot. I quickly shuffled behind a tree to break up my outline. Rick had mentioned that the crust had been intact the week before and I'd never seen birds in the snags before, so it had to be carp, it had to be. Ten minutes had passed when I saw something move deep down, behind the shallow spot. I strained to make out its shape as it got bigger and bigger. Hell, it was Clover; very much one of the A-Team and a fish that I definitely wanted in my portfolio. It's a pale, chunky fish that I later found out originates from Wellington Country Park. Seeing that fish made me think that it was going to happen all over again. Breathlessly, I phoned Rick to tell him what I'd seen and he couldn't believe it, but I could. I chewed up a few baits and dropped them in, getting a reaction straight away. Five fish came straight up the shelf, onto the shallow table and started feeding. I steadily increased the size of the boilie bits, until I was feeding whole 10mm by 20mm barrels. They were demolishing them, all apart from Clover, which seemed to hang back. Clover aside, I could identify

I knew I'd got Orange Spot, thanks to his colour and pronounced hump.

I'd chalked off another Road Lake jewel.

The long, dark, hard-fighting animal was later identified as The Pug.

Clover, it just wasn't meant to be!

Orange Spot and a long dark fish that I assumed was The Pug. I couldn't get them to feed on the hump that I'd had The Dink from, but I liked the look of a clay bar that ran out from the snags. I flicked a few baits out to the end of the bar, where it drops away into deeper water and considered my options. I couldn't fish from the swim that I caught The Dink from as that was now shut, but Swim One gave me a good shot at hitting the bar, along the snag line. It's not my favourite Road Lake swim, because you're right above the water, on a built-up pontoon and your lines are right out of the water, but the fish were there. I told myself, "No messing Jim, you know they've been eating the white lovelies, get your gear and get those rods out." The car was less than 100 yards from the swim, so it was easy fishing.

I was shaking with excitement as I removed the rods from their sleeves. As I pushed the sections together, I quickly checked that the braid and leadcore weren't damaged, as there is no room for error in swims like this one. I attached a long, coated-braid hook link and size-eight Wide Gape with a barrel threaded onto a long hair. Then, I slipped the hair stop through the weave of a PVA-mesh bag of boilies to stop it tangling around the hook on the cast. I flicked the first rod close to the snags and the second ten to twelve feet away, on the end of the bar. I let loads of slack out on the rod away from the snags, to allow the Bullet braid to hug the contours of the bottom. With the line out of the way, I hoped that I wouldn't cut off access to the spot closer to the snags. The snag rod was fished on a tight line, with a six-inch drop on the bobbin. Now for

It had to be The Scattered Linear, another jewel.

CEMEX Angling

Dear Sim

After careful scrutiny of the amount of Gold Card permits given out free gratis in the last angling year, it has been decided to severely limit the allocation.

Your Gold Card fishing permit was unfortunately one of the cards that will not be renewed. Your current permit lasts until the 31st of May 2007 and you are free to use it until that date.

The allocation of complimentary tickets is done on an individual basis and is based on the contribution to CEMEX Angling's profile in the angling press during the last year.

If you wish to participate in a magazine feature on CEMEX Angling's waters in the coming year, then phone the office with all the details and we will do our best to accommodate you.

CEMEX Angling thanks you for your support in the past and wish you all the best in the coming year.

Mick Barnes
General Manager
CEMEX Angling

the third rod. Swims One and Two are a matter of feet apart so, because there was no-one else on, I decided to fish the third rod out of Swim Two. There's a little gravel hump just ten yards out from the swim and I was just flicking the lead out, to have a feel around, when I heard two bleeps from my left-hand rod. There was no movement where the line entered the water, so I put it down to a liner, which was encouraging nonetheless. On the second cast, the lead thumped down bang on the money and I drew it back across a lovely smooth area. The line was clipped and marked against a far-bank tree. I tied the same bottom-bait presentation to this rod, flicked it to the mark and slackened the line right off. As is my way, I then flicked seven free offerings out onto the hump. Why seven, you ask? Well, it's my lucky number and I always bait with multiples of seven.

Just as I walked back to the plot, the flaming left-hand rod pulled up tight. With the clutch screwed up as far as it'd go, all I had to do was steer him away from the snags. The braid was singing as the fish ran along the snag line – I offered a quick prayer to the carp gods, "Please, please; I will be a good boy," with my fingers firmly crossed! After running away from me along the snags, the fish then turned right, away from danger. I immediately eased off, as there was now no need to put the fish under so much pressure. Just like The Dink had, this fish then surfaced in front, giving me a good look at its orangey colour and pronounced hump, which put me in mind of The Dustbin from Yateley Car Park Lake. On seeing this, I knew which one I'd got - Orange Spot. With a slight sense of déjà vu, I netted him as soon as he'd hit the surface. Pulling the net into the bank, I could see him, laying still, gills pumping the little barrel hook bait in and out of his mouth. I leant down and snipped the hook link, which I always tend to do. Once again, the Horton phones were ringing and K1 Scott was soon on his way down to do the honours. I think that both the fish and I needed a breather at this point so I left him to chill in the net. The orange spot on his flank confirmed that I'd chalked off another Road Lake jewel.

While Scott was on his way down, the unthinkable happened, I got another take! Flaming hell, could this be real? Two takes in less than twenty minutes, in January? There was no way that I could be dreaming though, because this thing was pulling back pretty hard, trying to get me into the snags to the left. This time it came away easily, telling me that it was a smaller fish. Once into safe water, he put up a better performance under the rod tip. Eventually, the pressure told and up came this long, dark, fighting animal that was later identified as The Pug, which weighed 29lb plus. I always have two nets set up, which is lucky, because I had 36lb plus of angry male mirror sitting in the other one! As he slid over the cord, I looked skywards and said my thanks to those lucky carp gods of mine.

As Scott Bennett turned up, I walked over to him with a big smile on my face. He said, "Nice one mate," to which I replied, "I've got two now fella!" I swore him to secrecy because it didn't take a genius to tell that there were more to come from this swim and there were a few armchair anglers, just waiting for news. After the pictures were done I set up camp for the night but, apart from a few liners, all was quiet. You could hardly blame them for being a bit spooky, because I'd just had two so quickly. I was packed up by midday and I made sure to bait up my little area off the snags with 20kg of boilies for my return next week. The plan was to give them a bit of free food and hope that no one went in there, so that they'd have a week to eat it all with no lines in the water. I thought that the other guys would steer clear anyway, because they all 'knew' that I 'filled it in'. Whether I do or not, the reputation works for me sometimes! I couldn't get back to the lake until the following Tuesday because I had a meeting at Nash Tackle and when the boss calls, you've gotta go. I wish I hadn't though, as you'll find out shortly. Right in the middle of the meeting I had a call telling me that Little Rob had banked Clover at over 40lb from The Hump Swim and in the snow as well – good angling fella. Even though the one I wanted had been out, I decided still to go, because I had a feature to do with Angler's Mail journalist Gary 'Garfield' Newman.

I got down to the lake early and met Gary at the gates. We shot the feature and I was able to show him the fish in the snags. Suitably impressed, Gary left for the office and I was left to contemplate my session. I reckoned that if they were on the move, then I could bait 'em, then catch 'em… simple really. I decided to change the line angles to my spot by fishing The Hump Swim, in the hope that I could keep the bites coming. As I struggled my way round the tight, muddy path with the barrow, Garfield's words were ringing in my ears, "You'll have 'em tonight son." As it happened, he couldn't have got more than 30 minutes down the road before I was in. As I turned to see which rod was away, I could see the right-hand rod, which had been fished to the base of the bar, bent round alarmingly. I ran over and pulled into an angry carp, which was hell bent on getting into the snags. There was no way that Uncle Jim was letting him have any more line, however. The pressure took its toll and as he began to kite away from danger I eased off again.

I caught sight of this scaly creature, twisting and turning deep in the clear margins. I let him slowly wear himself out under the rod tip and started to see the end of the leadcore emerge at reassuringly frequent intervals. I now knew that he was a maximum of 8ft down. Finally, a mirror rolled on top and I saw these massive gold scales all over its body. It had to be The Scattered Linear, another jewel. At that moment, I eased right off, because I REALLY didn't want to lose this one.

Knowing that I had a mega-rare one that doesn't like visiting the bank much, I briefly lost it, but quickly calmed myself, as I wanted it in the net. I only play fish as hard as I have to and now that this one was in close, I was happy to take my time. After all, why compromise the hook hold? He rolled one more time and I positioned the net, ready to do its job. A massive head came up and I saw right down his mouth as he coughed water. In that moment, I knew that he was mine. The next second, he was in the net. I dropped the rod and rolled the fish to take my first look at this most awesome carp. Gathering my senses, I quickly called Gary, but he was back in London by now, he just said, "I told you, mate." I wondered if Scott was still in the area, so I called him and luckily he was. Twenty minutes later, I could hear the faint clang of the prison gates being opened, so I started to get the equipment together. I hadn't told Scott which fish I'd got, just that I had a mid-thirty mirror. I think that he was as blown away as I was when he saw he him. All he could manage was, "Bloody hell Jim, that's an awesome carp." I walked the fish, safely cradled in the mat, to my chosen spot. It was lit up perfectly, as if the carp gods had painted it. Unbelievably, this was the Scattered's first capture in over two and a half years and he slammed the scales round to 35lb 12oz. As I lifted him up for the camera his massive apple-slice scales lit up in the low, winter sun. It was well and truly job done, another winter whacker for my collection. I didn't return to the lake before the season's end because Little Rob had caught the one I wanted. On a sad note though, Ian Welch had left RMC Angling, paving the way for Barney to come in as fishery manager. It seemed an odd appointment because this guy had not run a fishery before, nor did he have any fisheries qualifications. Things were to change for me quickly; I received a letter from Barney telling me that they were not going to renew my honorary gold card. His letter explained that I hadn't been promoting the venues, but telling me that I could buy a gold card if I wanted! I rang Barney up to try to reason with him, but it soon became clear that he had a personal problem with me, because some of those in his circle of close friends had stuck the knife in. I know this because Mike, Barney's number two later told me what went on behind the scenes.

However, this is where I must thank Barney because, thanks to this act, he unwittingly furthered my angling, forcing me to spread my wings and fish elsewhere, outside the RMC portfolio. Unfortunately, Barney later left his position at CEMEX, and when I heard the news I opened a bottle of Lanson Champagne to toast him. Sometimes, it's best not to react at the time, but to let fate play its part.

Horton

The Return

Floating around the Wraysbury area of the Colne Valley, I realised that there was still an itch that I really needed to scratch. Certain fish just draw you back and I couldn't consign Horton to the past until I'd evened the score with my old mate The Parrot. The term 'history fish' could have been invented for this one – every line on his wrinkled body told of his age and prestige. I laid a plan to catch him by design, hopefully off the top as he's been partial to slurping down a mixer in his own inimitable way since his days in Fox Pool. I wouldn't leave it there either, at night I could lay traps in 'his' areas, spots that I knew he favoured. He was an easy carp to recognise when he showed because of that distinctive round head. As a hunter, I had several vital signs to look for if I were to complete my Horton album.

Along the way I hoped to meet a few of the better stockies that the lake now held, topped by a clean-looking carp called The Lodger, which conveniently also loved a floater! In fact, most of the stock of this historic pool loved floaters, apart from the two biggest commons, The Thorpe Park and the enigmatic Tet's, although I'm sure even they had a few on the quiet, never quite slipping up. As on most waters though, you had your hardcore floater hit squad, fish that looked upwards for their food. Of course, my old mate Shoulders was in that group, but I hoped to be able to avoid him by spotting his bulky shoulders barging through the surface; there was no way that I wanted to catch him again.

So, all I had to do was put my plan into action. To put it into perspective, even back then the lake held an outstanding stock. The Parrot had been 45lb plus, as had The Lodger; Tet's was 40lb plus and The Thorpe Park was 39lb. All the Fisher's Pond carp were stacking it on, so you never quite knew what would be out at what weight. I know that some people just don't get on with floater fishing but, over a couple of years, I had perfected an approach that the fish just hadn't seen before. However, even I couldn't have known just how devastating this method would turn out to be. Most anglers creep around trying to stalk their targets, stealthily plinking out little bags of mixers. I found all that a bit slow and boring so I went the other way, tactically speaking. I'd noticed that I could often find signs of fish holding up on the surface at range. I'd walk and walk until I spotted fish cruising, or the water rocking subtly, gentle swirls, dorsals sticking out or any signs really. Much of the time these signs would be at long range, where most people accept that things become a lot harder on the top. Sorry, but that just didn't wash with Uncle Jim, there's always a way, and I wanted to be the first to really exploit long-range floater fishing. I remembered Ian Pullinger spodding mixers at Fen Drayton a few years previously. At the time I'd wondered why I hadn't thought of it, but it was logged in the memory and now it looked like I had the place to try it out.

It had taken me a couple of years, but I'd come up with the perfect smash-and-grab floater kit. The rods were 12ft 3.75lb Nash Pursuits that could punch a 4oz Nash Bolt Machine controller 120 yards with 10lb Bullet XT mono. Now, the Bullet is a sinking mono, which you might think is an odd choice for floater work, but it's exactly what I wanted. When it sunk, the weight and drag on the line really helped to exaggerate the bolt effect at the hook end – the carp hadn't seen the likes before. I settled on 6ft Drennan Double Strength hook links in 8lb, 10lb and 12lb. This material is the best I've found and I usually use it in the 10lb version because I want to be able to impose myself on a big fish, not have it taking me around the lake all day long. I do play around with hooks but I keep coming back to Wide Gapes in size 12 and 10.

I tend to set the hairs nice and long on my floater rigs, say 1.25in or 2in – none of this tight to the hook stuff – I'm looking for nice positive hook holds. If the hair is set short

I'd refined my floater kit so I had the perfect smash-and-grab outfit.

The crucial Bolt Machine.

I find that you can end up with lightly hooked fish, which tend to fall off – not good for the head! Mind you, you always do seem to lose a few off the top, you just have to accept that and get another one hooked up. It might not be so fashionable, but I use greyhound pellets from a pet shop as my freebies. They're cheap, dark and oily and their small size makes it easy to pick out the hook bait. Seeing the hook bait is key to my approach because I like to actually strike at all signs, twitcher hitting, as I call it. I use coloured hook baits so I can watch the bait like a hawk. If it turns from orange to black, I'll hit it. I decided that I'd use two rods for my surface fishing, constantly working one and leaving the other static. I'd set one up with double 10mm orange Scopex Airball pop-ups and a different one on the other rod, perhaps a single. The static rod has the bigger Bolt Machine on it and the 'twitcher' rod is set up with a 2oz version on it. I'd use this one to rove, pulling it into the path of cruisers to make a chance. Sometimes they'd even take a bait that was gently teased into their field of vision.

My Emblem Pro reels turned out to be the best tools for the job. They have awesome line lay and a quick retrieve so you can pick up loads of line instantly. My spod rod was an old cut-down Extreme Pursuit, which is just right for firing a spod of mixers out to where I need them. One problem that I encountered was that the spod floats and so do the mixers, which means that they won't come out of the spod easily. To combat this, as soon as the spod touched down, I'd whip the rod back, causing the spod to cartwheel back, spraying mixers around. This actually had another benefit as well. I'm

My floater terminal tackle pouch, complete with trusty Drennan Double Strength.

I prefer a longer hair than most for my floater fishing, sometimes up to two inches.

sure that the fish came to recognise the crash of the spod and responded like it was a dinner bell. Even if the fish stopped taking, I wouldn't stop spodding because they'd tune back in eventually; they just don't seem to be able to help themselves!

I was dosing my freebies in Nash Crustacean Oil, which I likened to sea anglers laying a chum line. This oily slick would travel far and wide, pulling fish from all over the lake – they ended up coming to me! It was around this time that I learned the importance of having a few floater waters at my disposal close to each other. If I couldn't interest the fish at a given lake, then I'd take advantage of my gold card and hop over to another where I'd usually find a few fish that were willing to look upwards for their food.

I went in for the draw on opening day but I came out well back, so I decided to pull out and let one of the new members fish instead, as there were quite a few that year. I thought that I'd give it a miss for a few weeks and just float around on the lookout for chances. By the second week there really hadn't been much out, plus it was getting nice and quiet. I had a feature to do for Advanced Carp Fishing with James Harrison, so I arranged to meet him at Horton for a spot of floater fishing. I guess that I must have been getting a bit of a name for myself, pioneering this radical style of floater fishing. We knocked the feature off and James left me to it shortly before sunset. With the light going I needed to come up with somewhere to pitch up for the night and fast. As I was walking back along the causeway between Horton and the Boat Pool I glimpsed some movement just to the side of The Plateau. What was more, I could see that the plot was empty so I practically ran down the bank to stake my claim! As I set foot in the swim I noticed a few fish floating about and, all of a sudden, The Parrot stuck her head out, right at the back of the swim. The water out there was pretty much debatable territory so I made my mind up to go round and set up in The Spindly Tree opposite because it was deeper in front and there was less weed than at the shallow Plateau side.

As I wandered round I marvelled at the sheer lack of anglers down at this end. Usually The Plateau was the domain of the 'bucket campers' and the number of buckets piled on top of each other behind the swim indicated how many people were waiting for their moment in the sun; funny really. As soon as I feathered the first spod of mixers down it seemed to push the carp further over, back towards The Plateau. Within half an hour I had to admit defeat and head back to The Plateau to get some bottom baits out for the night. As I clumsily fumbled around, unlocking and locking the gate again, I offered up a silent prayer that no one had noticed what I'd seen and that the swim would still be free. Would the carp gods be on my side once again?

I walked around, trying not to run and draw attention to myself. If I was looking calm on the surface then I was anything but beneath; adrenaline coursed through my veins – I really didn't want to lose this swim. Plus, I was kicking myself for not putting a bucket in the swim because you have then 90 minutes to play with, silly boy Jim. It was that old Parrot getting me all hot and bothered. It's unreal; sometimes I have to work really hard to control myself when I spot my target fish. I was desperately trying to make the right decision on a water where that choice is sometimes taken out of your hands. You see, these waters can often have some very good anglers on them, so you

Horton's lodge, it was lovely to have the home comforts so close by. Christ, you even had an awesome TV, kitchen, even an armchair and settee!

have to be smart to stay ahead of the game.

I was in luck again and dumped my floater gear right in the middle of the swim, defiantly stating to all that could see that I was in there. With the swim secured I wandered up to the lodge and popped some alcohol-free beers into the fridge to chill for later. I also offloaded some milk, food and spare bait – it was lovely to have the home comforts so close by. Christ, you even had an awesome TV, kitchen, even an armchair and settee, what more could you want?

I made sure that I was signed in as I'd forgotten to do it again. I must admit that I didn't much like all this because it was awfully easy for people to work out what was coming from where and what time you were turning up to fish. It was even worse in the winter, with people just turning up to check if anything had been out and buggering off again, rules are rules though! I loaded my gear onto the barrow for the short trip to the swim. As I got to the plot, fish started topping all over the swim, no more than 60 yards out. The sun was dropping fast so I had to get my two made-up rods out first – this was no time to be messing about because I had an absolute load of Horton chunks showing all over me! I slid the rods out of their sleeves, rigged-up and ready to go. I always have them ready to rock and I can't believe it when I see others wasting time setting rods up or even, god forbid, setting the bivvy up first!

While getting everything sorted I kept an eye on the water, noting where the fish kept

The bag rig, complete with 5oz lead.

I kept my eyes glued to the area that was bubbling as I set up the rods.

showing. One spot in particular, towards the right-hand side of the Scooter swim at about 55 yards was looking particularly good with fish repeatedly rolling over it. That was definitely getting a bait! Luckily, I could clearly see the weed beds in this area, in between two blatant, gravel high spots. Unlike most people in this situation, I didn't want to fish the gravel humps. I could see bubbling going on out over the area that they were showing in so I knew that it had to be dirty and silty out there… my sort of spot! So I could keep my eyes on the area while I changed rigs, I leant the rod up against a tree at the front of the swim. Keeping my eyes glued to the water, I ran my hands down the 8ft of leadcore, taking hold of the 5oz, inline square lead so that I could cut the old rig off. I'd doctored the lead system by removing the hard plastic inner and replacing it with a rubber shockleader sleeve. The resulting rig just held the swivel firmly enough to hook the carp, after which it would pop out and turn the setup into a running rig. I was, and always have been, adamant that the safety of carp should come first – after all we really don't want tethered fish.

The spectacular show was generating a bit of attention but with the light fading fast, I imagined that plans were being hatched for a move down to this area in the morning, if the fish were still in residence. In some ways, it was academic really, because the fish were well and truly in my water; I was happy with that and implored the carp gods to keep them there. I opted to keep the rigs simple in weed, all I needed of them was to be able to handle a big carp charging off, if I were lucky enough to hook one. I was a big fan of 20lb Nash Ultrasilk, which is a lovely, supple material but very strong. I coupled this with the new Wide Gape hooks in size eight, which I had every confidence in. Hook baits were to be barrel-shaped and were mounted onto long, two-inch hairs. Finally, shrink tube was used to create a nice curve off the eye of the hook, giving the setup good hooking qualities. Because the hook link was braided, I needed to use a PVA mesh bag to prevent tangles. So, I filled one with barrel baits, nicked the hook through and then popped the hair stop into the weave to prevent it tangling around the shank on the cast.

With the rod ready, I leant it up against the tree and placed my bag of freebies and catapult at the front of the swim, ready to dispatch some baits into the rings once the lead had landed. While I waited for a carp to show over the spot I got to work getting my second rod ready. As I was tying the rig on, a big 'un, well over thirty, rolled gently over the most active spot at 55 yards. I quickly left that rod, grabbed the other and cast straight into the ripples, pukka. I placed the rod on the ground, with the line semi slack and the clutch set to give line so that the fast-sinking braid could sink back on itself. I started firing out a mixture of small different sized/shaped baits plus a scattering of 15mm Scopex Squid freebies over the top to keep them guessing which one was dangerous. I guess I put out about 100 in total. Now this might come as a shock to some people, because I only ever fill it in, right? Yeah right! There really was no need to do this in this situation because the fish were clearly feeding already. Little and often would be more than sufficient, just enough to keep the zone active. After setting the landing net up I turned my attentions back to the other rod, as it was now nearly dark.

With the rigs in place, I popped the rod onto the deck and fired out around 100 baits.

The barrel-shaped baits that I was so fond of.

With that sorted, I turned my back to set up the house. While I pushed the pegs into the ground I could hear carp pushing out in the darkness concentrated out in front of my swim, so things were looking very promising for a visit by morning.

When I finally laid back on the bed I was close to collapse after chasing them around the pond all day – who says that carp fishing's easy? Well, it is if you're a camper I suppose and that sure ain't me! When I go to sleep it's because I'm genuinely knackered; like the old saying goes, you get out what you're willing to put in. Lying there listening to the muffled splashes as the sky turned from deep blue, to dark blue and finally black, I started to think that the fish were gathering for their once-a-year bash, and I was right up 'em. Surely there was a chance of one of the rarer Horton jewels as they just might be craving some of Uncle Jim's Scopex Squid before the bash of the Horton giants.

The next thing that I remember is jumping up, with the blue LED from a screaming buzzer lighting my way to the rods. I picked the rod up and it was instantly slammed down again as an angry carp legged it at high speed. The bright moon picked out a silvery bow-wave cleaving the water, travelling away from the back of the spot. Even as I battled the carp, others were showing over the spot. I smiled to myself; there really could be a big hit on the cards. My attention was drawn back to the matter in hand as the fish neared the pontoon down to my right. I thought that it was high time that I showed him who was boss, tightening the clutch and lowering the rod tip down to my left. He dropped in the water and slowed up considerably, sweeping in

The dull beam lit up this long, black animal with a row of gold sovereigns running along his back. "Christ," I said to myself, "That looks like Merlin!"

along the margins towards me. The pressure had turned him into a slow, plodding weight on the end and I was just wondering which one he might be when he surfaced under the tip, sending out big, oily swirls. The moonlight allowed me to keep close control of his lunges as the fight neared its conclusion. The silver light picked out this great long beast as his frame broke surface, allowing me to slide the net under him. He gave one last burst, but it was in vain as he powered into the walls of my net.

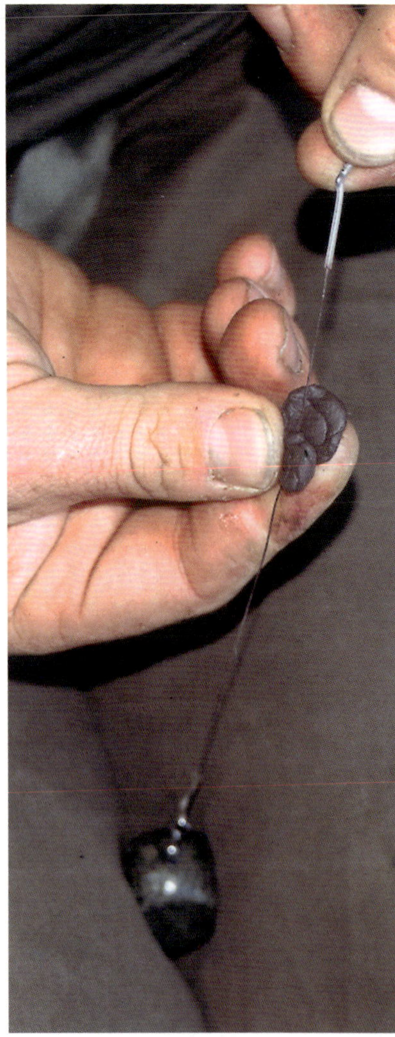

Rubbing the Ultrasilk with Heavy Metal helped to pin the rig hard to the deck and darken it off.

Laying the rod down, I pulled the net in so that I could pop the spreader block to secure the fish while I grabbed my torch and some clothes. I was a bit worried that, as Beadle had just come back from Thailand, he'd see me and offer 10 dollar! Walking back to the front of the swim, I flicked the torch on and the dull beam lit up this long, black animal with a row of gold sovereigns running along his back. "Christ," I said to myself, "that looks like Merlin… no way!" I plunged the kettle into the margins and thoroughly wetted the mat before carefully breaking the net down. I centred the fish in the mesh, and checked that his pecs were flat to his sides before hoisting him up onto dry land. Upon lifting, I was sure that he was a good thirty. Placing him gently on the mat, I popped the hook out and took a moment to admire Merlin, one of the jewels on my most-wanted list!

I popped him back into the net and dashed up to the lodge to get Beadle because I wanted pics doing immediately. As I bustled in through the door, I could see Beadle wrapped up all snug, probably dreaming about those Thai girls! "Oi oi," I said, "Wake up!" Dopey with sleep, he asked what was up and I simply pointed to a picture of Merlin on the wall. He sat up and I thrust the camera towards him. Back in the swim, I lifted Merlin out and placed him safely in the carp cot, before carrying him to where we'd do the honours. As I put the mat down and pulled the mesh away Beadle said, "Yep, that's Merlin," confirming my identification. Ever alert I could still hear carp boshing around while all this was going on. I made sure to keep Merlin well wetted down because the night was a typical warm June affair. After zeroing the scales, I slipped him into the sling and recorded a weight of 38lb 12oz. As you can see from the pictures, this is one awesome-looking creature and as I slid him home I quietly thanked him for the moment we'd shared. Beadle snapped me back into the here and now by shaking my hand and reminding me that The Parrot was well and truly on the cards. Beadle knew that I'd seen him in the area and also knew exactly how much I wanted the king of the ugly ones! As I turned to pick the rod up Beadle said that he was off back up to the lodge to catch up on his beauty sleep. I thanked him for his help and told him that I'd see him in the morning.

Leaning the rod against the bivvy, I tied a new rig and bag on that I'd kept in a sealed bucket to protect it from the damp. Running my fingers along the leadcore and lead, I picked off the slimy bits of silkweed that had accumulated and checked that everything was in working order. One thing that I always made sure to do after attaching a new braided rig was to rub some Heavy Metal putty up and down the link so that the tiny granules of putty catch among the fibres of the braid. This darkens the hook link and, along with a couple of mouse-droppings of putty, adds considerable weight to keep it pinned down among the straggly weed. Once the rod was back out, I fired out some 15mm boilies and barrels into the area to refresh the trap. As I was sinking the line I could pause to appreciate just how many fish were showing out there; I imagined that most of the stock were in front of me – a mad feeling I can tell you. With the bits all sorted, I popped the net back together and had a little tidy up, ready for the next one

Thai girls "ten dollar"

A young chap set up next to me… Mick The Greek.

that would surely come. I plopped back onto the bed, taking a big, deep swig of water. Just musing about what could be out there put a smile on my face.

Just after first light my right-hand bobbin pulled up tight to the rod. As I made contact with this fish I could tell that it was a smaller one. He came in quite easily, turning out to be a common called Stella, which weighed 27lb. I now had a young chap set up next to me in Waiting Man's, he was called Mick The Greek and also, I later found out, went by the name of Melon Head, God knows why! Mick agreed to come up and do the photos for me, a job that he was about to become used to, thanks mate! The carpy activity out in front showed no sign of stopping just yet so I decided to re-do the other rod, ready for their next bait-raiding assault. With that done, I sat back, having a little chat with The Greek, speculating about what was going on out in front of me. Without any warning, I was in again. The fish ploughed off through the weed and this time I had a gallery behind me because word seemed to have spread that most of the 'Horton Hit Squad' were out in front of Uncle Jim. Even as I stood, centre stage, bent into a carp I couldn't help but wonder when the backstabbing would begin! The fish had quickly put clear water between us and was in danger of grounding out in the Scooter swim on the far side! I had to stop him and applied determined finger pressure to the spool, which caused him to slow and begin a sweeping kite to my left. On seeing this change of tack, Mick ran up to his swim and dropped the lines, out of harm's way. Thankfully, there were no hairy moments and the fish came in quite quickly.

The gallery behind me had grown in size and was getting noisier. As I got the fish in close, Del came down, just in time to see it surface. He said, "You're gonna like this one Jim," as I slid the net under it. I peered into the folds and replied, "Too right," because I could see that it was a cracking, long, zip linear called Wallace. I couldn't believe how long and wide he was. I carried him over to the spot to have his picture taken and, as you can see, he's another stunner. His shape reminded me of the old Crayfish Pool big 'un, Scar – another right old croc! Weighing in at 35lb 14oz. Once he was returned Mick pointed out that it hadn't taken long after casting out, in fact, it couldn't have been more than twenty minutes. I was now sure that the fish were having their big, pre-spawning feed right in front of me! Of course, if they did start to spawn properly, I'd reel in as it's unfair to angle for them as they go through their annual ritual. As I got my rod back out Mick said, "Twenty minutes," and I laughed and sat back down. I guess that you're getting the gist of this now but that same rod was away straight away and I pulled into another Horton carp with a smirk on my face. The crowd reappeared, as if by magic in time to see me net a fish, which turned out to be a stockie mirror of 29lb 4oz. I wasted no time in getting him back because there were whackers flaunting themselves out there and I had to wonder how long it would take before someone tried their luck with a long cast from the far bank.

The left-hand rod seemed dead after Merlin, so I picked the right-hander up and attached a new rig to get it back out there. Surely it just couldn't keep happening every

Del said, "You're gonna like this one Jim," he was right! Wallace at 35lb 14oz.

This fish was one of the oldest that swam in Horton and a right old character to boot.

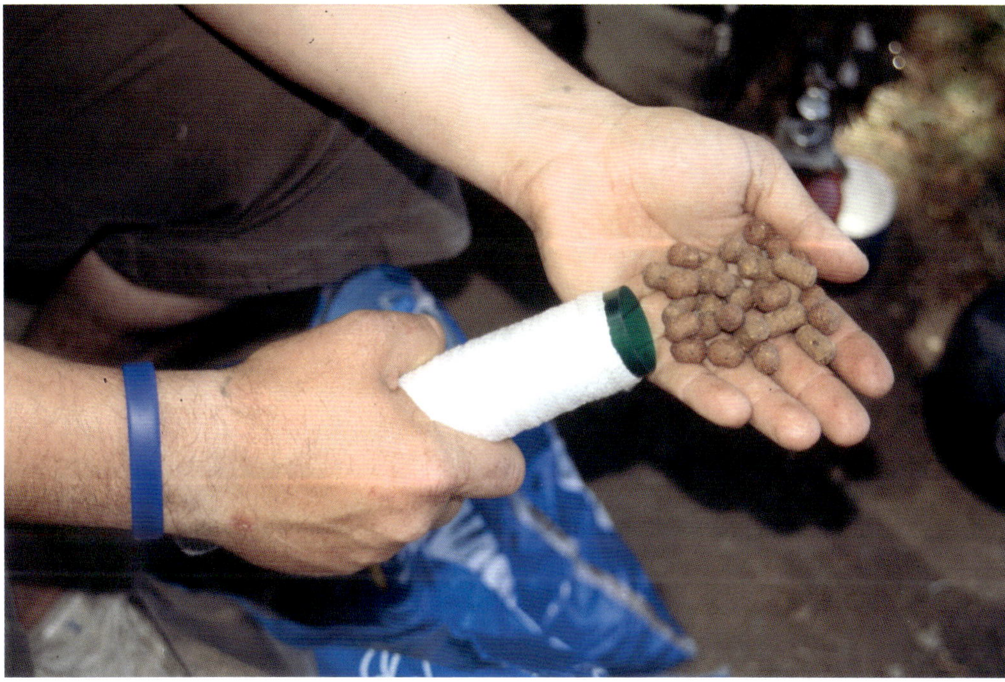

I loaded some fresh PVA bags with a mixture of barrels and 15mm boilies.

20-25 minutes, could it? The Greek and I were enjoying it now though, and the twenty-minute countdown started again. While Mick kept an eye on the time, I decided to move the left-hand rod closer to the action zone. I had a few bleeps on the right-hand buzzer as I readied the other rod. Some of the crowd had stayed this time, watching. I bet that it did their heads in that I wasn't using a carp-scaring marker rod. A few more bleeps registered… this was weird. With the rod out to the left of the going area, Mick informed me that the 25 minutes were up. Those bleeps were playing on my mind – I honestly thought that I'd probably got a big, old bream on, pulling me into the weed. With the fan club behind me, I decided to leave it out there until they drifted off. A few more bleeps marked the bobbin pulling up to the top and the line began to pick up – it didn't look like I was going to get the chance to leave it. I walked down to the rod and said, "Bream on." Pulling into it, I felt a lot of resistance. All of a sudden, something surfaced as I pumped it in. I was pretty sure that I was attached to a bream, but the thing that surfaced looked more like a carp! The piss-taking stopped as it went into the net and Mick muttered the word "Fantail". I looked and laughed as I knew this fish from years ago when I'd stitched his huge tail up after it got damaged. This fish was one of the oldest that swam in Horton and a right old character to boot. I was simply made up to have caught another original weighing in at 30lb. Now, Fantail is known to play up big time but he gave me no trouble at all. I often wonder why he didn't give me a full-blown take; he must have been sat out there shaking his head, determined not to

Roger The Dodger at 36lb 12oz. I hadn't heard of him, but I wasn't complaining!

give the game away, the crafty old stager!

With Fantail safely back to fight another day I began to wonder if this was really happening to me because Horton just isn't that easy! Daydreaming aside, I really needed that rod back out there because I really had The Parrot in my head. I'd wanted to catch him ever since I'd seen Steve Allcott holding it as part of his Longfield brace all those years ago. Although I hadn't seen him show again Beadle reckoned that he was still about; I bloody hoped so. Mick the timekeeper was getting close to twenty minutes and this was all getting a bit silly! Thirty minutes went by without action so I decided to give them an hour out there before rechucking. That flew by and I was soon skipping the right-hand rod in. The left-hander hadn't even bleeped, even in its new position nearer to the zone. So close yet so far! It just goes to show just how tight productive spots can be. I can only guess that the size of these areas depends on how widely distributed the stuff that they're looking for is. I had noticed a lot of silkweed coming in on the rigs so perhaps there was something in the green stuff that they wanted. The shows were becoming less frequent – perhaps they were doing the offski? I did think that perhaps the noise from the crowd had scared the fish off.

Anyway, I slid fresh hook baits onto the hairs and loaded some new PVA bags with a mixture of 15mm boilies and barrels. Once they were out there, I topped the swim up with some more Scopex Squids. Mick had gone back to his swim so I had a moment to sit back and take in what had just happened to me. I was snatched from my daydreaming

I was now getting a lot of liners, so I clipped the bobbins onto the line behind the buzzers to eliminate false bleeps.

by a screaming alarm; Mick came scrambling into the swim, saying that it was 20 minutes again! This fish had shot off miles to my left but Mick had already slackened off the other rod so it wouldn't give me any problems close in. All of a sudden, the line pinged slack; it'd fallen off. I absolutely hate that feeling and wondered what I'd lost. The feeling always stays with me and always takes a while to put behind me. Mick knew that I was pissed off and legged it! When I got the rig back and checked it over, there was nothing wrong with it at all. However, I still cut it off and tied a new one on. I couldn't have it let me down again, plus what does a bit of braid and a hook cost?

I didn't have too long to dwell on the loss before the same rod was away with a fast take again. I jumped down to it and picked the rod up, which was immediately slammed down hard as another Horton carp made off with my rig. "Only twelve minutes this time Jim," Mick said. Christ, the crowd was back as well, in fact, looking at the size of the gathered throng, there couldn't have been many people actually left fishing on the pond! This fish had taken fifty yards of line off me pretty quickly before a huge bounce transmitted down the rod. For a split second I thought that he was off again but in fact he'd just started to kite towards Waiting Man's and I was gaining line fast. Mick reassured me that his lines were mega slack, because he just knew that I'd get another bite. The fish was now charging around close in under my other line but all was sweet in the end as Mick got him first time with the net. Del had a quick look and pronounced that I'd got Roger The Dodger; "You what?" I asked, having not heard of that one. Just for the record he weighed 36lb 12oz. It turned out that it was one of the newer stockies that RMC had introduced to replace the ones that died in the Horton fish kill. The new fish were OK, but I was there for the Longfield beauties and The Parrot in particular. I knew that I was close because I'd seen him stick his head out in the swim and with all those fish in residence surely he had to come to Uncle Jim? Plus, I was in constant contact with the carp gods, imploring them to surrender the king of the ugly ones.

With Roger returned I was told by a mate that some members of the crowd had begun to slag me off, saying that I was fishing for spawning carp. At this point I can categorically state that those fish were not spawning. It just seems that the backbiting is a part of life on some of these circuit waters – there's nothing like slagging off the guy who is catching, eh lads? I was now getting quite a few liners so I clipped the bobbins onto the line on the other side of the buzzers, which eliminated the single bleeps and little pulls. Of course, you still get indication, especially if you get a screamer! As far as I was concerned these were feeding fish, judging from the sheer amount of action I was receiving. Just after the magic 20-minute mark again the bobbin on my faithful right-hander pulled up tight. As soon as I made contact the carp went mental and started stripping line off the reel. All the while it stayed deep and headed for the pontoon to my right. I whipped the rod down to my left and hung on in an attempt to stop this animal. This seemed to have the desired effect, although I'm not sure that it hadn't simply got its head down in some weed deep down the shelf. I lifted the rod into the vertical, tightened the clutch and began to pull hard. All of a sudden, with the line creaking through the rings, things started to move again. Steady pressure brought the dead weight slowly but surely in front of me. When it was twenty feet out I finally got some movement; the tip pulled down, indicating that the fish was still there… I just wondered which one. After that he just plodded up and down the margins – obviously the burst of power had drained his energy reserves.

All of a sudden the Greek said "Common", which made me consider just which Longfield bar of gold I was attached to. Then I saw him; short, wide and deep – a right chunk. Up he came and Mick did the honours, slipping the net under my latest victim. Mick inspected the fish, looked up and said, "I think that it's the Humpy Backed Common," now, I knew this kiddy and he was one that didn't come out a lot. It was soon confirmed as the Humpy Backed Common weighing in at 32lb12oz – another ex-Longfield carp ticked off the list. As I held him up for the cameras a wide grin spread across my face – this was the way to silence the knockers, Uncle Jim style. Just as I laid the mat in the water for a few returners he must have sensed that freedom was near as he powered off the mat with all the anger that he'd shown me before. I could only watch him glide away from me into the clear depths. At the time of writing that fish hasn't graced the bank for the best part of five years!

Without wishing to rush on too much at the expense of detail, I banked a further three fish to 33lb. They were all stockies and the last one, a 29lb mirror, was banked fully

Another Longfield original ticked off the list in the form of the elusive Humpy Backed Common.

two hours after casting out. I was getting lazy, but after all 10 takes and 9 landed was a right result for Horton so you can't really blame me, can you? The liners had slowed down but there was still no sign of spawning – they had gathered but not shagged… yet. After a quiet night I woke early to watch the sun climb slowly before me. A strong cup of coffee had the old grey matter working again. I quickly answered the call of nature and begin to get ready to recast the rods. Just then, Beadle walked up for a chat – probably on the ponce. Perhaps he'd already raided my supplies in the lodge fridge? I made him a cup of coffee to keep him happy and got the rods back out. Surely there would still be one or two around after all the carnage of yesterday? Beadle was straight on about The Parrot, although I hadn't seen a sign of him since he'd showed the previous day. Beadle was adamant, however, that he was out there, hiding in the weed. I hoped so. As I was baiting up The Greek came round and started on about the 20-minute rule again. It's funny how things go, I just wanted one or two more – but I could hardly complain. I hoped that rebaiting would help to pull the fish back into the area as I hadn't seen a sign yet. An hour and twenty minutes had passed with the odd liner to reassure me that something was out there.

A few of the crowd from yesterday enquired about my fortunes as they headed to and from the bog. It's funny really because I'm sure that there were more carp in their swims than mine right about then. However, not long afterwards I caught a movement just out of the corner of my eye, coming from the left. "So," I thought, "It looks like some are coming back this way." I decided to recast, baiting the rigs with new barrel hook baits and nipping the hair stops into the mesh of the PVA bags. I cast the first rod out, then dropped it, leaving the semi-slack line to sink while I chucked the other one out. This way disturbance is kept to a minimum. Happy once more, I settled back to chat with Beadle and Mick, this time with the bobbins my side of the buzzers because I was getting sod all liners! Around midday I started to get a few odd bleeps. Beadle and Mick said, "They're back!" I turned the buzzers down and clipped the bobbins back around the back of the heads because I really didn't want to alert any of the backstabbing crowd. A quick check revealed that the 20 minutes were up. Thirty minutes later and beeeeeeeeeee – I was away. I ran down and pulled into a carp that immediately felt like a smaller one because he was kicking far too vigorously. As I stood there, rod in hand, I noticed that people were watching me. I chuckled to myself; number ten was near. This fish came in quickly and darted about in the edge before Beadle netted him. As he lifted the net the fish exploded into life, thrashing the water to foam and soaking Beadle in the process. I got a few quick snaps of the 25lb mirror responsible, all the while thinking that I really needed that rod back out there.

The right-hand rod was rocking big time and we'd noticed big patches of bubbles fizzing to the surface around the area. Beadle still reckoned that The Parrot was out there. As the words left his lips, we clearly saw the bulbous head of The Parrot push silently out over the spot. I eventually decided to put both rods on the productive area, 6ft apart. A scattering of 50 or 60 15mm baits completed the trap. Just five or ten minutes later, patches of bubbles started coming up over the spot! 'Bosh', The Parrot came out again,

The king of the ugly ones; my on-and-off, four-year itch had finally been scratched.

Word had got around after I'd given the shout, so the crowd had swelled somewhat.

right over the rods. I was now praying to the carp gods constantly, promising that I'd be a good boy! Again, a few minutes later he lifted out and Beadle said, "Look, he's there son." For some reason, I went down to the rods and reeled the left-hander in. As I did that he came out again. Beadle looked incredulous, "Why the hell did you do that?" he asked. I wasn't sure myself but I had a feeling that by taking the other rod out he might pick up the right-hand bait more readily. As I swung the lead in to hand Beadle shouted, "Oi oi Uncle, your line's tightening up." Because the bobbins were on the other side of the buzzer it hadn't registered yet. I dropped the rod that I was holding and got to the other one just as the buzzer started its battle cry. Straight away the fish took an untold amount of line off me. It felt really big, continually powering off uncontrollably. At least it had run straight out and not down towards the pontoon. Beadle said "I bet you've got The Parrot on," but I didn't need telling, I'd already started to think that as this fish was leading me on a right merry old dance.

Mick must have been watching from his swim because he arrived and told me that he'd wound his rod in. This turned out to be good angling on his part as the fish was now kiting well to my left. I dropped the rod to the right to give him some heavy side strain and he started to come in. All of a sudden, he swam past us and Beadle turned to Mick and quietly whispered, "Parrot". Deep down I already knew that it was him – the one I really wanted. I turned him and he went deep down, which I was happy with as I thought that it'd slow him. As he chugged about a rod-length out I just told myself to take it easy. Suddenly, up he came, showing his face and the incredible boxy bulk of his body. "Oh my God Beadle, that's him – the king of the ugly ones," was all I could muster. The Parrot was almost mine. He turned and took a gulp of air and I led him to the waiting net, whereupon Beadle got him first go. Beadle turned and said, "Oi oi Uncle, you've got him, The Parrot." I simply looked skywards and shouted "PARROT!"

Dropping the rod I rushed forwards and looked at him nestled in the bottom of my net. My on-and-off, four-year itch had finally been scratched. I left him with Beadle and asked him to look after him for a minute as I just wanted to walk (to nowhere in particular) and take it in. Five minutes later I was back to have another look. The crowd had swelled by now as word had got around after I'd shouted. As I peered down into the net I could see just how ridiculously wide he was for such a short fish. I gently touched him for the first time – there was no need to unhook him as Beadle had done it. We readied everything so that I could have my moment with him. The scales thumped round to 44lb 12oz, but the weight was largely irrelevant compared to the journey that this fish had been on. The age and history of a fish are the most important things to me, along with the hunt itself, and these final, precious closing moments. As I held him up all these things were going through my mind. With a cheeky smile it was job done and pressure off. What's more…they never did spawn!

When I got back home the weather picked up, the skies cleared and the temperatures

Pulling through the big Horton gates, I could see that there were a few cars parked up.

The beauty of a Horton sunrise.

Out of the corner of my eye, I caught sight of fish taking mixers already.

climbed, which meant hardcore floater fishing was on the menu. I decided on a return trip to Horton over the weekend to bag a few off the top. On the Saturday I popped down to the local pet shop to buy five sacks of greyhound pellets. The alarm was set for 2am on the Sunday and I was soon splashing my face with plenty of cold water in the bathroom, to shake the last vestiges of sleep from my body for the 170-mile journey. I gulped down a strong coffee, loaded the Focus ST 170 and thirty minutes later I was racing down the A12, bound for some floater-fishing carnage down south. Pulling through the big Horton gates, I could see that there were a few cars present. I loaded the barrow with the floater gear, went through a quick mental checklist, grabbed the food and soft drink and pushed off towards the pontoon. It was 5am by that point and I looked out across the misty lake as the sun rose. There was a slight ripple, which was pushing the scum down the lake and I realised that I was already starting to sweat. I could make out some movement already, long out in front of The Blank, so I rushed to get signed in, before legging it round there. I unlocked the gate near RIP corner and pushed the barrow through, before locking it again and heading towards The Blank. As I reached The Scooter I could see some very slight dimples on the surface, as the fish touched the surface ever so slightly, no more than thirty yards out.
I quickly unsheathed the spod rod, put the big bag of mixers (which were soaked in Nash Crustacean Oil) on the floor and rolled the top down to allow easy access. The fish seemed a little too far out for the catapult, so I loaded the spod, dipped it into the

Gary Lewis with Shoulders. Luckily, he offered to help me net Uno.

In the midst of another epic battle!

The fish broke free of the weed and Gary snapped a few pictures off on my camera.

water and fired it 35 yards out into the pond. As usual, I snatched the spod back just as it hit the surface, sending a good spread of mixers across the immediate area. As the spod impacted, there was a massive eruption as I disturbed the carp from their sunbathing – game on. Most people would be gutted to have disturbed them but not me; I've found that this turns them on even more! I propped the spod rod against a tree, reached for a fishing rod and started unzipping the sleeve when, out of the corner of my eye, I caught sight of fish taking the mixers already. Shaking with excitement, I quickly hair-rigged a 10mm fluoro orange Scopex pop-up before sending it out well beyond the fish with the help of a 2oz Bolt Machine. I tweaked the controller back towards the feeding fish and as soon as it was in the zone I set the clutch and put the rod down to spod some more out. Just as I laid my hands on the spod rod the clutch started ticking, I was in straight away! I swung round and grabbed the rod, which pulled round to the right. I knew that I was going to have to play the fish hard because there was a band of weed extending 15 yards out from my margin and I didn't want any last-minute dramas. I heard someone approach behind me and ask if I needed any help. It was Gary Lewis and he offered to man the net to help me get the fish in safely despite the heavy weed in the edge. The fish didn't give me too many problems in the open water, just hanging low, feeling like a good 'un. As he came closer, I started to feel a vibration coming down the line and I knew that I'd have to give him all I could on the 10lb hook link. Bending into the fish, I offered a little prayer to the carp gods that my tactics would work. The line went dead and I couldn't feel the fish any more, but applying as much pressure as I dared, I started to feel big jolts on the rod as something came in, slowly but surely. I wasn't sure that he was still on, but soon enough the controller broke the surface. I knew that the fish could only be 5ft behind the float and all of a sudden, a big ball of weed hit the top. I could make out a small movement in there and said, "Christ Gary, it's still on!" What I could now see was a big mirror broke free of the weed and powered away. I piled on the pressure as Gary snapped a few pics off with the camera but the fish soon found the weed again. I was able to free him again and with the weed around his head, he seemed much calmer and went straight into the net.

I secured the net and immediately picked up the spod rod and gave them a few more spods of mixers. The noise of that spod hitting the water was just like a dinner bell to them. I quickly found a spot to do the photos in, laid the mat down, zeroed the scales and wetted the weigh sling. I leant over the front of the swim to take a closer look at him and thought, "Christ that looks like a good thirty." I carefully transferred him to the mat, where Gary was waiting with the camera. Once on the mat, we could see a lovely darkish mirror, which Gary recognised as Uno. I knew of this fish, but, thankfully, I hadn't caught him. We weighed him in at 37lb, pukka; less than an hour's fishing and I'd had one. I looked up and could see that the fish were still well up for it, so we needed to get this one photographed and back ASAP. As I watched him disappear into the weed I knew that I was going to catch more fish. Gary headed off in the direction of the lodge and I retackled the rod with a fresh hook link and pop-up before adding a couple more spodfuls of mixers to the swim. They were having it big time as I picked the rod up to make a cast. I knew that there was a good chance of another, but I had to be alive to the possibility that they'd move off, especially if I did manage a second fish.

I made a cast to an area where I could see several sets of lips scoffing mixers. I slowed the controller as it neared them, but it still managed to touch one, causing panic among the fish – they know the difference between a spod and a controller! They all sped off, leaving me to wonder if they'd be back. Things were quiet for a bit until, out of the blue, my line pulled tight. Straight away it felt like a smaller fish, given how it was darting about in the swim. I had to show him who was boss as he was a lively so and so, messing up my swim by charging around in the upper layers. Once more the fish weeded me solid just out from the swim and I was gaining line in sharp jolts. "You in again Uncle?" said Gary, as he appeared behind me on his way back from the lodge. "It's only a pup," I replied, but I was still grateful of a hand. The fish hit the top amongst a ball of weed and I was able to guide him into the net at the first time of asking. We could see that he was clearly a smaller fish and I looked up to see the hit squad on the move to my right – a change of swim was on the cards. I bit the hook link and carried him up to the mat. It was one of the leathers and Gary reckoned that it was the small one. The scales proved him right, registering 25lb 4oz. As soon as the fish was back, I was on the move, because you really do have to be on the ball when fishing places like this or you will get jumped as the followers watch you. Mind you, I find that I'm usually ahead of most in this type of fishing and I was packed up and gone in five minutes! I pulled up in The Blank and there they were none the wiser.

The fish started taking mixers before I'd even had chance to get the spod back to the bank this time, something that happens oh so many times! Because I'd put them on edge with the two previous captures, I decided to give them ten spods of mixers. I wanted to get both rods in the game, which can work really well as they often move away from the line that you're casting about, right onto the one that's been left quietly to do its own thing. Pretty quickly, it was clear that these fish weren't happy and although they hit the mixers hard, they soon moved off to my right again. I leapfrogged them and went two swims up into The Ski Slope. I spodded some mixers out straight away to intercept the fish that were still moving up from the left. They started taking straight away and I got a rod out quickly. Then, I noticed a cheeky fish taking the spod-spill mixers just 15 yards out, so I quickly reeled the hook bait towards this fish. As it got closer, I gently teased the pop-up into position and dropped the rod, grabbed the catapult and pinged a few freebies out to keep him interested. This fish started pac-manning the mixers but as he was on his own I didn't hold out too much hope of hooking him. However, I was proved wrong as a big bow-wave went up and the line shot tight. He shot off on a powerful run along the left-hand margin, forcing me to plunge the rod tip deep into the water to stop him from snagging me under the overhanging branches. Even so, I still felt that horrible grating feeling coming up the line. I decided that this was shit or bust and clamped down to stop the fish in its tracks. I feared that the line would

A lovely, darkish mirror that Gary recognised as Uno.

A rarely caught stockie called Spotty at 37lb.

simply cut, but stop him I did, and I was soon pumping him back along the margin. It seemed to take an eternity, but soon the line was entering the water close to me and, as I watched, a grey shape swam past me really close in. I think that he saw me too as he turned and headed out into the lake. He went deep and started just plodding around, which told me that now I had more control and could adjust the clutch accordingly; I didn't need to give him any more grief and I just prayed that the hook hold was good. After five minutes he started to tire and came up from Horton's depths. He just got bigger and bigger as he came up in the water and I started to lead him towards the net. He went in first time and I had another Horton chunk in the bag. This one was lighter than Uno, but he looked like another good thirty – Christ, this was floater trawling at its best!

It seemed that the carp gods had truly blessed me because this fish weighed 37lb as well, and Gary was happy to do some more pics for me. I later found out that the fish was called Spotty, a rarely caught stockie. With Spotty returned, I was aware that the fish had moved right again and I caught a glimpse of some movement just as a gust of wind hit the water. It had turned quite humid all of a sudden and the skies darkened as a big low-pressure front started to build. There was now a bit of a chop on the water, blowing from left to right. I've found it very hard to get the fish interested in floaters when the water starts to get choppy, but this time they carried on regardless and it was fascinating watching them creating these big flat spots among the waves as they fed in the increasingly choppy water. I knew that I wouldn't get much time to capitalise, as there was a clap of thunder away in the distance, so I quickly introduced a couple of spods of mixers out to my left. The fish were going mad but the rumblings of thunder were getting closer and it looked like we were in the path of a storm. Thankfully, the rig was still good, so I quickly cast well out to the left. As soon as the controller hit the water I dipped the tip and reeled like mad to get the main line sunk to stop it from drifting. With the 1oz controller bobbing about 10ft from the main pod of mixer munchers I could only watch the line for movement. As soon as the rig drifted over the feeding carp there was an inspection of sorts, which manifested itself as a big swirl on the surface. I hadn't seen any movement of the line but then, all of a sudden, the line pulled tight in my hand as an angry carp legged it right, taking line off me at a fair old rate. It was kiting right, heading for Church Bay and if it got there, I'd have big problems! I laid the rod over to the left and gave him some heavy side strain. This seemed to work, either that, or he'd run out of water on the corner of the bay. I could now see the line heading out into the lake, over very deep water. I tweaked the clutch, as there was now no need to play him so hard. I had to stay on top of this beast as he clearly wasn't happy about the way that his day was unfolding. He stayed close in and showed immense power, leading me to think that he was a real big 'un. After about ten minutes of me hanging on, not really making much of an impression the tip started to come back a bit, indicating that he was tiring a bit. I placed the net at the ready and watched as a dark shape started to materialise. Once more, the fish seemed to grow in size as if by magic and I could see that it was a common, which meant that it was

He looked every inch a thirty pounder as he slid over the net cord.

The telltale pimple gave him away.

likely to be an original. Horton's originals are tricky to outwit at the best of times, let alone the original commons. Now I was praying big style, promising to be a good boy. There was no need to worry though as he soon surfaced and looked every inch a thirty pounder as he slid over the net cord.

Once on the mat, Mike identified him as Pimple, checking his head for the telltale pimple. On the scales he went 34lb; one of the bigger commons in the lake. The storm was nearly upon us, so I lowered the mat into the edge and gave him his first gulp of water to let him know that he was about to be released. I watched through my polarised glasses as Pimple drifted off into the depths, none the worse for his experience. I looked towards the skies and thanked the carp gods for granting me four Horton carp in a day, off the top too! Just as I thought about packing up the heavens opened; a quick retreat to the lodge was in order as it was late anyway. I fancied rewarding myself with a nice meal and a bottle of alcohol-free lager. I planned to tie a few spare floater rigs for the next day's action. The swims that controlled the shallow areas that I would have wanted to be in were all taken, so I decided not to fish the night. I put the bedchair up in the lodge and set the alarm for 6am and was soon out for the count – this type of fishing really does take it out of you! Typically, it felt like I'd been asleep for about five minutes when the alarm went off to wake me. I made a big mistake by not getting straight up and was soon back in the land of nod when I should have been out there fishing. Luckily, something clicked inside me and I sat bolt upright, ready for my last day's floater fishing. I grabbed the phone… shit it was 8:30am! I popped the kettle on to get my caffeine hit then grabbed my packed lunch from the fridge and headed outside. I'd left the loaded barrow under the veranda, so it was just a case of pushing off towards the pond. As I walked I was worried that the followers would have swooped in on my floater fishing action. I made my way along the Church bank and came upon one such angler in The Sick Swim. I decided to wait and watch from The Blank because I was sure that if this guy was on them, he would push the fish to the left, which would mean that they'd bump into the master! After five minutes I thought that I may as well spod out a few mixers as I knew that the noise and the Crustacean Oil would draw them to me. I kept looking up while getting the rods ready but saw nothing. Once the rods were done, I propped them against a tree and scanned the surface. This time there was a slight dimpling, not much, but for a hunter like me it was the sign I needed. No sooner had I seen that, than the fish were hitting the mixers in a frenzied attack.

I didn't waste any time as these fish could move so fast. The fish were around 85 yards out, so I whacked the controller 100 yards into the pond and slowly reeled it back. As soon as it settled behind a cluster of mixers there was a huge swirl and a bow wave and the line tightened across the surface. Straight away I knew I wasn't in control of this battle as this lump shot off, ripping line from the clutch. It crossed my mind that I was attached to a grassy. I'm not exaggerating when I say that this fish took 80 to 100 yards of line off me in this one surge and was now heading towards Weedy Bay. Dan The Man appeared behind me, asking, "You in mate?" I told him that the fish was now well over the other side of the pond and was probably a grassy. Finally, the line

When it finally came up neither of us could believe it as this huge, bulbous head emerged from the gloom.

stopped leaving the spool and the bend started to come out of the rod slightly. Fearing that I'd lost the fish, I started to reel like mad, but the line was cutting to the left – this bastard was kiting at a pace! This was all happening so quickly that we felt that it must have been one of the grassies, which can be explosive, fast fighters. Soon, the fish was in close and I was hopeful of gaining control now, I had to wonder just what was on the other end? I had my glasses on and we caught a glimpse in the clear water, but it was hard to make it out. I asked Dan to man the net for me as we waited for the fish to show itself again. When it finally came up neither of us could believe it as this huge, bulbous head emerged from the gloom – it was the king of the ugly ones, The Parrot, a fish that I'd been four years trying to catch and had finally netted just seven days before! Here he was though, tripped up on a floater, just like I'd originally wanted to catch him. He was clearly tired now, after that mad dash across the lake, and Dan was able to scoop him up at the first time of asking. I turned to Dan and said, "Just think mate, if I'd lost him I'd have put it down to a grassy!" In his usual way, Dan took the piss and we laughed.

He still looked big and had clearly not spawned yet, which just goes to show what a load of bull some were spouting about me fishing for spawning carp the week before. In fact, he weighed in at 44lb 12oz, the same weight as the week before. As Dan clicked away, I couldn't help but smile because I'd had the king of the ugly ones twice in a week, off the bottom and the top – that should ruffle a few feathers. Dan shook my hand and headed off on his own pursuit. I decided that because it was still early, I'd head off home as the M25 would still be clear, unless someone had decided to play Wacky Races. I phoned my girlfriend, Jane, telling her that I'd be home early for dinner! As I pushed the barrow round I pondered on the fact that I'd now had 17 from Horton in less than four days' fishing. This is just the way that I liked to hit back at the backstabbers. When they're worrying about what I'm doing, they're not paying enough attention to their own angling, which is just how I like it. I loaded the car and signed out after putting my catches in the log. On the way home it started to sink in just how much of an edge this style of fishing could be on most waters, especially as most haven't got the bollocks to do it! I simply see it as the more you put into your fishing, the more you'll get back, and I was putting an awful lot into my floater fishing.

Back home, I got back into the swing of family life, but I was already planning a day session back at Horton. It was to be an early start as usual and Jane had made me a packed lunch. I blasted along the single-lane roads for the first 50 miles of my journey, with the hardcore trance cranked right up. A couple of Red Bulls kept me buzzing and I was soon pulling up to the first set of three gates that allowed access to Fort Knox. The sun was rising fast as I signed in and loaded the barrow. I could see the fish cruising in the middle section of the lake, but I knew that the Boat Pool side was busy, so I headed round to the Church side. I could see that there was someone plotted up in The Blank but I fancied the Sick area, as the fish seemed to be using Church Bay a lot. As I pushed my gear along, I muttered a quick prayer to the carp gods, imploring them to grant me a swim. There was no need to worry though, as both The Ski Slope and Sick swims

Scar looked big, close to 40lb for sure.

I couldn't help but think that I'd made the most of my time after the long drive.

After we'd snapped off a few shots, I held him in the clear margin and stroked his head.

were free, but there was someone fishing in Church Bay. I parked my barrow in The Sick and I could see loads of fish, gagging for some Uncle Jim therapy. It seemed that everyone was still asleep, so with no time to waste I got the spod out and whacked a few spodfuls out there. After three spods some of the fish decided that it was breakfast time and I had plenty more to give them! A couple of mates had told me that there had been some moaning about me turning up and spodding mixers out. Apparently, I was spodding too much in the early hours and the fish weren't feeding because they were full up of floaters! Well, sorry boys, you pays your money and you makes your choice. If I had seen someone doing something new and catching I'd be interested in doing it for myself. Too many are set in their ways though, which is fine by me – it makes my job easier! The fish were having it, big time, so I punched the controller out into the middle. Someone shouted from the swim opposite, Captors. I've seen loads fish well past halfway, thinking that's their water, so bollocks to that, I was halfway out and they were fishing on the bottom in 18ft of water. I started to reel the controller back towards the feeding fish and put the rod down to launch another spod out there. As it landed, this twat started up again so I shouted across that it was my water and if he was over halfway then he should move his baits. As I was retrieving the spod, the rod on the floor bounced and the line pulled tight. I upped the pace, reeling the spod out of the way as the clutch whizzed on the floor. I chucked the spod rod into the reeds then applied finger pressure to the spool to try to slow this fish down.

The fish had kited well to the left and as I tried to gain line quickly, I knew that he would be swinging in tight to my margin. I figured that he was at least 50 yards down the bank towards The Ski Slope. This area is heavily tree-lined and I had lost a fish in that margin before. I thrust the rod into the water up to the spigot and tightened the clutch. As I clamped down, I could feel that old, familiar grating sensation transmitting up the rod. I really didn't want to lose this one, as he felt like a right chunk. I pumped him along the margin and I couldn't feel any grating now, which was a result. I started to think that he must be close just as a chunk swam past me from left to right. I thought, "No way mate," and laid the rod left to pile on the pressure. It seemed to work as he headed off into the depths, allowing me to relax a little. I played him gently, worrying about the damage that could have been caused to the hook link during the margin battle. I knew that given time, he'd be mine if I was careful not to put too much pressure on that hook. I started to see huge oily swirls on the surface as the battle reached its climax. I saw him again and realised that he looked even bigger than I'd thought. He was really broad across his back, which made me think he might be close to 40lb. He made one more lunge along the margins, but didn't take much line, which told me that he'd soon be mine. His great bulk surfaced and I led him over the net, where he could rest for a few minutes. Boy, he looked close to 40lb. After admiring my prize, Scar, I turned around just as a new member came walking into the swim. He agreed

Floater time again!

to help me with the pictures and I prepared everything while he took a look into the net. "That's a big 'un," he said, and I replied, "You know it mate, I've only been fishing for 25 minutes!" I showed the guy how to use the camera, before carefully lifting the fish from that water… Christ he was heavy! I gently laid him down in the big cradle mat and poured some water over him as it was hot already. Once I'd removed the hook I rolled him into the sling and recorded a weight of 40lb 4oz! Happy days! As I lifted him up for photos I couldn't help but think that I'd made the most of my time after the long drive and made the idiot on the far bank look like a fool.

I decided that I wanted to get some water shots of this baby, so I stripped off and gave my privates a cool dunking. After we'd snapped off a few shots, I held him in the clear margin and stroked his head. I put my finger in his mouth, which made him back off with his pecs and when I removed it he bolted off in defiance, sending a bow wave out into Church Bay. The fish seemed to disappear after this and I eventually found them sitting safely in front of the campers! I couldn't get on them and with one under my belt already, I thought that I'd head for home. I pushed the barrow back down the side of K1 and alongside the Boat Pool towards the lodge. Just as I was nearing the lodge, Del came out to tell me that the bloke in Captors had complained that I was spodding too many mixers. "Look Del," I said, "I can tell you that I was fishing my half of the

They were still spawning by the pontoon and I watched in awe as these old jewels danced in their annual ritual.

Oli told me, "You haven't got anything to worry about Uncle, your ticket's Teflon coated!"

lake, it's not my problem if he's fishing further than he should be." It started to get a bit heated so I just said, "I'll tell you what Del, I'm going to ring Ian Welch and you can tell him, because I'm not going to waste time arguing with someone who clearly doesn't have his facts right." Mind you, I wasn't surprised, because there are more politics down at Horton than at Prime Minister's Question Time in Westminster.

I loaded the car, signed out and put my capture in the log before ringing Jane to tell her that I'd be home earlier than I thought. I turned the tunes up and started on my long journey home, happy that I'd added another floater-caught forty to my tally. I returned the following week for more floater fishing, but they were in full spawning mode, so I thought that I'd load the barrow up and head off to K1 to see what I could find floating around. This is where having a gold card was useful, because it gave me so many options. If one lake wasn't fishing, then all you had to do was to go and have a look around. I knew the combination for the lock on a gate that led onto the road that runs past the dog kennels, next to Horton, so I headed out that way with the barrow. As I was passing the kennels, the dogs started barking, making me jump! I thought that it must be a nightmare fishing the Dog Kennel swims on K1. On a bend in the track I passed the entrance for The Crayfish Pool and Kingsmead Islands. I had fond memories of The Crayfish Pool, which is where I'd caught the mighty Scar a couple of Novembers previously. Once inside the K1 gates, I was surprised to find that the

Kennels swims were empty, because you can fish out of your motor here, ideal for the campers. I could see most of the lake from here and there was a slight ripple blowing from right to left. The calm water was right next to where the big, old green bridge spanned the channel that joined the two Kingsmead lakes. There was a net stopping the fish from travelling back and forth and I had occasionally looked off the bridge, although I hadn't fished the Island side. I caught a glimpse of a slight flat spot among the ripples out from where I was standing, so I quickly readied my spod rod and loaded it with oily mixers, which would create a nice flat spot of their own among the ripples. I realised that I was in the wrong spot to actually fish from, because I would get bad line drag thanks to the ripple. I put a few more spods out to get them interested and headed off round to the Helipad swim, which luckily was vacant. This put me on the back of the wind, which would allow me to keep a chum line going thanks to the inevitable spod spill and a few mixers that I'd trickle in by hand to let them drift over the fish.

By the time I got my gear installed in the swim, they were well and truly munching those mixers and there were quite a few carp present, judging from the number of flat spots and swirls out there. I put the spod rod back together and launched a spod right among the feeding fish. As the spod touched down, I snatched it back, spooking some fish, as bow waves went up leaving the area. However, by the time I had the spod back in my hand the fish were in a frenzy, attacking the mixers. I resisted casting as they were clearly up for it and I had a big bag of mixers to give them. I had told Bullaboss that I was heading over to K1 and he'd said to give him a shout if I needed any pictures taking. That was nice of him, mind you, I still had to actually catch one! I told Bulla what was going on and he assured me that I was about to have one! I put the phone in my pocket and assembled the floater rod as quickly as possible. Adrenalin was surging through my body as I prepared everything; I was almost shaking at the thought of the K1 hit squad smashing the floaters out there. I whacked the controller out 70 yards or so, and reeled it back 10 yards or so. As the controller neared them, I set the clutch and put the rod down so I could get more floaters out there. As I swung the spod back, the line from the rod on the deck shot tight. I was amazed by the number of takes that I was getting like this, so quickly after casting out. The fish was swinging well left, trying to gain the sanctuary of a big tree that had fallen into the water in the corner to my left. It's funny how fish know exactly where these sanctuaries are. With a 10lb hook link on, I had to stop him, and sharpish. I started to load the 3.5lb Pursuit and clamped down as much as I dared to get this fish turned. The rod took on an alarming bend but I'd managed to stop him and I soon had him coming back towards me, away from the danger zone. I remember thinking that I had to keep the pressure on until he was well away from the snags, because laying off too soon can allow them to charge back again. As he came to within thirty yards, I eased off and he swung out into the lake. It was looking like I'd got him to safety and I knew that the fight would be much slower out in the deep water. I let him chug about, out of sight, in the depths to tire him out. He came in quickly and, as he surfaced he looked like a good twenty. As he came closer, he kept growing, "Christ, that chunk looks thirty-plus," I thought. I noticed that he seemed to have a badly damaged tail but I didn't know these fish well at all so I was none the wiser as to his identity. All I knew was that he was one of the big 'uns. Finally, he surrendered and floated over the net cord. As he sank into the mesh, I looked up and smiled.

I made sure that he was safe then phoned Bulla to see if he could help me with the pics. He answered, saying, "Christ, that was quick, have you got one?" I told him that it was a chunk with part of the top of its tail missing. Bulla knew the K1 fish, as he'd fished there and he told me that it was probably Dean's Fish and promised to be round in a few minutes. I bit off the hook link and took a closer look at him; I just couldn't think that he was much less than an upper thirty. While I waited for Bulla, I picked a spot to weigh and photograph him. I heard the chain clang in the distance and a minute or so later I could see Bulla en route with someone else in tow, which turned out to be K1's head bailiff Oli Davies. "Stand to attention and be on your best behaviour," I thought, and as he walked in I bowed! Oli laughed and asked why I'd done that, "Gaffer alert," I told him, and he replied, "You haven't got anything to worry about Uncle, your ticket's Teflon coated!" We all laughed and took the piss. I took the fish out and the lads confirmed that it was Dean's, commenting that the broken tail had started to repair well. Up on the scales, the big mirror banged the needle round to 38lb 12oz, adding another floater-caught chunk to my ever-growing list. As I held him up for pictures,

My first floater-caught Road Lake carp at 30lb 4oz.

I told the boys that this was the way forward in these conditions, rather than sitting, vegetating behind motionless bobbins, hoping for something to happen.
Once I'd returned Dean's Fish, I noticed that the bulk of the stock seemed to have moved over to the other side, where there were more anglers. I barrowed my gear back round Horton, to the lodge, and stopped off to see if they were still spawning, which they were, by the pontoon. I watched in awe as these old jewels danced in their annual ritual. I could clearly see Shoulders, The Woodcarving, The Big Grey, Wallace and The Parrot, Christ, they were nearly all here along with the stockies. I tried to photograph them individually, but it wasn't happening and it was clear that I'd have to look elsewhere. If I didn't find anything, I'd head home for some brownie points. First stop was the Road Lake, as I still wanted Clover from there before I could say goodbye to it for good. As I neared the Road Lake I passed Silverwings and I couldn't help but wish that The Pet was still around. My thoughts inevitably also turned to the Black Mirror… definitely a target one day soon! I diced with death on the familiar bend in the road, before pulling up at the black prison gates. I couldn't help feeling that a few years earlier and I'd have been fishing Longfield in its heyday, just one of those things that you have to swallow. I was just too late, but you can't win them all and I had caught some of them in their new home at least. There were no cars in the car park, so I grabbed my bucket, catapult and glasses before setting off in search of the carp. I'd usually have taken my floater rods too, but the Road Lake isn't the easiest place to

The rig was that close that several feet of leadcore poked out of the water!

get them taking mixers. The Launch swim would give me a good chunk of the central portion of the lake, especially as there was nobody else there. It seemed mad; the place was usually quite busy.

I scanned the water and could make out a few carp sunning themselves out in the middle, well out of catapult range. I was going to need the spod after all and turned to head back to the car when a flock of green parakeets flew overhead, as they do twice daily in these parts. The bits were already stowed in my carp cradle, so I grabbed a couple of rods and headed back to the swim. I cast the spod over the fish as usual, eliciting a few swirls from the sunbathing carp, which made me think that I'd get a good feeding reaction. As I swung the spod to hand one fish took a floater. I knew that the others wouldn't be far behind, as they don't want to miss out and the greed factor takes over. Seeing their reaction always makes me wonder how they react to normal sinking baits falling from a spod; I bet they always take it on the drop! I spodded another patch of mixers out to the left, so I could position my hook baits in among them before the fish finished the first batch off and moved in. I flicked a rod out 10 yards past the freebies but didn't reel it back, instead I opted to wait until they were having it so I could easily keep tabs on my orange hook bait. The fish finished their meal and began searching for more, which were only 18ft away. I watched intently, gently tweaking the line to stop it snaking. There was a boil and a snout poked through the oily surface. "Here we go," I thought, as big pair of lips engulfed a mixer. I eased the controller back towards the fish and one tried to take the Bolt Machine! The greedy git – I bet he thought it was a big bait, food for thought perhaps? As the ripples subsided, I knew that the fish were only five feet behind the hook bait and I watched the fluoro hook bait, waiting for my chance. By now, the water was boiling, indicating that several fish were close. One fish started pac-manning towards my bait and the hook bait went black. I struck and all hell let loose as the carp bolted off. The Road Lake is very weedy, but it hadn't made the surface yet and I could feel the fish boring very hard, trying to make the weed. The rod whipped back straight, indicating that he'd cut me off; I was gutted. As I reeled it back I realised that it was 10lb Double Strength, not 12lb and I kicked myself as in my haste to cast out I hadn't weighed up the situation fully. What was clear was that it was Road Lake 1, Jim 0.

I spodded some more mixers out to the right and set up the rod with 12lb Double Strength on and a size-10 Wide Gape. This time I mounted two 10mm pop-ups onto the hair, which is something that I usually do on the static rod. They really have to suck at this bait to take it and I'm sure that the shape of the bait prevents them from ejecting it easily. The fish were still having it, even after the loss, so I sent the controller out past the several that were in residence. They had pretty much cleared up the other mixers and were now boiling up under the new patch. I tweaked the hook bait back into the zone and in the blink of an eye it had gone black. I pulled into that fish, which ploughed off and went deep, so I wound the clutch up and held on tight. I could tell that this one just didn't have the same power as the one I'd lost, but rather than mope about it, I had to concentrate on getting this one in. The fish had bogged me down, but

Kingsmead One's Thorpe Park Common at 37lb 12oz from right in the edge.

I just kept the rod high and the pressure on. I started to get the weed on the move, but I couldn't feel if the fish was still attached. I just kept it moving and a weed bed hit the surface 20 yards out. All of a sudden, there was a kick, indicating that the fish was still on. As the weed bed neared, I sunk the net deep and just scooped the whole lot up. I dropped the rod and started ripping weed from the net, hoping to find a carp in there. After a few handfuls, I started to reveal my first floater-caught Road Lake carp, and he looked to be a mirror in the low thirties. I weighed him at 30lb 4oz and luckily one of the Fox Pool syndicate members was about, so I was able to get him to help with the pictures. When I got back to the swim, I couldn't see any signs of feeding carp, so I decided that I'd have to do a lap once we'd done the pictures. The fish was a long, dark one; a right old character that I was delighted to add to my Road Lake collection. I still wanted Clover above all else though! I gathered up the mesh and carried him ashore for a few pictures. As I unrolled him on the mat, matey said, "Wow, that's a cracker!" and I said, "You know it mate." I poured some water over him, which made his flanks shine, before lifting him up and admiring my prize. I laid him back down and covered him in water again as it was hot, before hoisting him for a few final shots. Once we were finished, I carried him back to the water's edge in the cradle and let him slip back into the lake. I thanked the Fox Pool angler and wished him good luck before scanning the lake for signs. I decided to go for that lap, but in my heart of hearts I knew where they would be, so I made my way round to the snags.

As expected, most of the stock was there; they'd clearly legged it to the safety of the snags after a bit of Uncle Jim therapee. Where next then? I decided that I'd head back to K1, but rather than heading for the Dog Kennels end, I decided to park up at Horton and walk round the Boat Pool to the car park at the other end. I let myself in through a small gate and headed along the causeway between the Boat Pool and K1. After about 100 yards or so, I came to a small ditch that linked the two lakes, which was flowing into Kingsmead. I quietly followed the ditch down to where it flowed into K1 and noticed that the water was coloured. As I peered into the water I could make out the outline of a carp. He saw me and lifted slightly off the shelf he was feeding on. I carefully backed away and half-turned my head so he couldn't see the white of my face as I already had a hoodie on. I tried to hide myself behind a bush to my right but all I could see out the corner of my eye was this mirror lifting off the bottom, getting bigger and bigger. I recognised him as Starrie's, the biggest fish in the pond. I could see that he wasn't happy and had sensed that something was wrong; I had overstepped the mark and I told myself off. He gently slipped away and I could see his pec twitching, he definitely wasn't happy! I had a couple of baits in my pocket and crunched them up in my mouth before scattering them over the silkweed covering the shelf. As I watched the bits flutter down I saw a common of around 20lb come up the shelf and sample the bait. As my eyes became accustomed to the light conditions down there, I could make out other fish down at the foot of the shelf – I had to make a decision quickly. I decided to put some more bait in and leg it back to Horton for my kit ASAP, as it was clear that there were a few about. As I rushed back, I was praying that no one else found the feeding fish. I was going to have to barrow all the way back because I wanted to leave the car in the Horton car park rather than the K1 one, because it would be safer there with the rest of my kit in it. The whole area was constantly being done over, there were always too many robbings in this bandit zone!

I loaded the barrow up with food and night gear so I could do the night on K1, as it was evening by now. As I barrowed round I was hatching a plan to tackle the swim because I didn't want to scare these fish, they were so close it was going to be easy to overstep the mark. When I reached the gate I was relieved to see that the swim was still free. Once inside, I parked the barrow up well back from the water's edge. One showed not more than 5ft out as I stood there, which was incentive enough to get on with setting up. I cut the old rig off the double-barrelled swivel; I was using a light running lead on 10ft of leadcore and the new hook link was 14 inches of Ultrasilk tied to a size-10 Longshank X. I was using a ¾ inch piece of curved shrink tube at the eye to help turn the hook and a smaller piece on the shank to hold the long hair in place. I rubbed some putty along the link, which both dyes and weights the hook link. I finished the rig with a 20mm barrel hook bait, which was PVA taped tight to a PVA mesh bag that I'd nicked the hook though to prevent the hair from tangling. I now had to get into place without being sussed and lower the rig onto the shelf.

As I started to make my way down to the water's edge, a fish pushed out just off the shelf and I watched it sink back down, sending up a plume of bubbles, which headed towards the spot. I carefully moved closer and I could see fine bubbles popping on the surface. The culprit was a 20lb common and I planned to lower the rig in and touch him with the lead to semi-spook him because there were definitely other, bigger fish around and I didn't want him messing it up! The plan worked perfectly and the common moved off slowly, probably thinking that another carp had nudged him. As the lead touched down, I gently lifted it to open the hook link up so it sat better on the shelf. As I did this, a long fish glided past and I withdrew carefully, playing out line so that the leadcore laid flat on the shelf. In fact, I was fishing that close that several feet of the leadcore poked out of the water and lay on the bank. I pulled the rod tip back away from the water and set the clutch, positioning the reel handle so the reel wasn't in contact with the ground. Before making my way back, I double-checked the clutch, because I didn't want to lose the rod. I positioned myself well away from the edge and got all worked up as several fish showed; I was going to catch, it was just a matter of time! I had to resist the temptation to go and have a look because I knew that the rig was sitting as well as I could get it. At one point, three fish slid out of the water together, making me think that there must be several about. On a few occasions there were slight movements of the line that must have been liners, which nearly had me running for the rod. Twenty minutes later, I was getting impatient with this lack of action. I rang Dan The Man to tell him what was going on in front of me. After a few minutes, Dan said, "I bet you have The Thorpe Park Common," and I said, "Yeah right!" All the time I was talking, tiny pin-prick bubbles were breaking the surface. All of a sudden, the rod tip bounced, the line pulled tight and a huge bow-wave exited

As I approached the biggest area of snags to the left of Phil's Corner, I could clearly see several carp sunning themselves in the last rays of summer.

Phil's Corner.

the margin as a carp legged it hard and fast. The 20lb braided main line was leaving the spool at quite a rate as I picked the rod up and I could see it cutting through the water to the right. There was no need to strike and I gently pulled into the fish. The rod took on its battle curve as the fish motored away from me. The power of this carp was unreal and soon he was over 70 yards out and still going. I simply couldn't stop him and he fought like he was possessed.

I reckon that he reached 100 yards out on his first run before I could stop him, he was kiting left and there was no way that I was in control just yet. All through the fight I just couldn't believe the power that this fish exerted on my rod and arm. Ten minutes later, he was getting closer, but powering all over the swim. Three minutes later, it was charging around under the rod tip and making powerful surges to rid itself of the rig. Only after another five minutes or so did he finally stop making the power surges and slow down a bit. Only then did I think that I was beginning to win. Now I could see him and Christ, it was a long common – I wondered if it was the fish that I'd seen when I went to place the rig? Next, he surfaced and was shaking his head; this fish was well and truly hacked off with me! I knew that I had to net him quick and I duly lifted the net around him. He kicked hard against the mesh, nearly pulling the net out of my hands. It was then that I began to wonder whether this could be The Thorpey. I called Dan to see if he could come and take the pictures for me, but he had just got his rods out and was on fish. He suggested that I try Bulla, who thankfully agreed to help. I found a suitable spot to take the pictures and I kept checking on the common to make sure that he was OK. About 15 minutes later, I heard voices and Bulla and Oli appeared. I told them that I wasn't sure what I had, but that Dan had told me that it was most likely to be The Thorpe Park at that sort of weight. They both went over to the net for a look and confirmed that it was indeed the Thorpe Park Common. As I carried him up the bank I could tell that he was a mid-thirty or bigger. He actually weighed 37lb 12oz and Bulla said, "Christ Jim, you've had two of K1's big 'uns in a day!" I replied, "Yeah man, I bet the jungle drums are going to start beating now!" Oli reckoned that my Teflon card would keep me safe though! With the beast returned, Oli and Bulla shook my hand and departed for Horton. It was evening so there was no way that I was leaving just yet, I'd let the M25 quieten down first. Understandably, the fish had legged it and I packed up at 6:30pm. I signed out and headed off on the three-hour drive home.

After that spring madness I flitted about all over the place catching untold carp from a variety of waters, including Horton, and mostly off the top. There are just too many to list here but around September time, after the summer holidays, I returned southwards for some rich pickings leading into autumn. After signing in again at Horton, I walked out from the front of the lodge and carefully made my way out onto the pontoon to look for signs of carp in between the weed and cabbages. There was nothing about so I walked back round and up to the RIP Corner but couldn't look in there as someone was fishing. Moving on, I made my way up to Church Bay. There were no signs of carp along this bank either, so I carried on into the mouth of the bay, scanning the water

A small amount of hemp had the swim fizzing like a Jacuzzi.

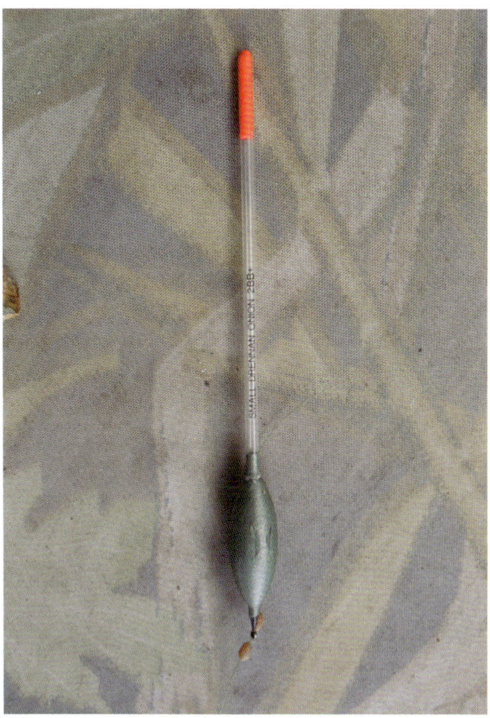

Simple but effective.

The hair was baited with half a 20mm barrel.

as I went. I thought I could see some bubbles in the corner, and quickly made my way round there. I dropped down off the path towards the snaggy tree line, putting my hood up as I approached to hide the white of my face. I slowly made my way along the margin, looking into the water under the snags for signs of carp. The water was quite clear and I could see six to eight feet down into it with my polarising sunglasses on. As I approached the biggest area of snags to the left of Phil's Corner, I could clearly see several carp sunning themselves in the last rays of summer. As I got close I made sure my hands were in my pockets as I didn't want them to spot me. I got myself hidden behind several bushes and counted seven rather large carp sitting there. All of a sudden two more glided in and disturbed the others, then it was a mass of swirls and chunks bombing around. I decided to get out and hatch a plan. I crumbled up 50 baits and gently threw them in, along with seven whole ones, just off the overhanging bushes to the left of the swim. I took my hoodie off and placed it down along with my glasses to reserve the swim, and legged to get my gear from the motor. I prayed that no-one would find the fish in the meantime and hoped the sweatshirt would put them off as it was there to mark my intention to set up in there. I could feel myself getting excited as I loaded up the barrow. I grabbed my phone from the car charger, saw a float and something made me grab it. I put it in my mouth so I knew it was safe and then made my way back to the swim with the barrow. As I neared Phil's Corner I could see foam-like bubbles which weren't there before. It wasn't over the area I had baited but had drifted right into the edge, however there was no fizzing going on now. A quick look in the bushes revealed the fish were settled sunning themselves and I spent a few minutes trying to make out which ones were in residence. The only one I could identify for sure was Merlin, an awesome fish that I had caught earlier in the year at 38lbs 12oz. I decided to introduce some more crushed baits onto the spot, along with yet another seven whole baits. Upon returning to the bush, the fish were gone, had I messed it up again? Actually, the opposite was true, as pin-prick bubbles now rose to the surface over the baited area, cheeky fcukers. I had some hemp so I grabbed a jar, opened it and poured a small amount into the palm of my hand, around 50 to 60 grains. I threw a few grains at a time over the area to increase the attraction, and watched as they started fizzing like a Jacuzzi. This was something that I'd never seen before right in the edge and I just kept tossing in more hemp, broken boilies and the odd 20mm barrel. All this time I was wondering how to tackle the situation and remembered the float as it was still in my mouth. I decided to set up the float rig on my floater gear, lift-method style. I used some rig putty, moulded around a four-turn grinner knot three inches from the hook bait to weight the setup. Should a fish mouth the bait, I'd get indication in the form of a lift on the float as it picked the putty off the bottom. I was using 10lb main line and simply carried it through for the hair – nice and simple. All I had to do now was get the depth right, this would mean carefully casting behind the spot, then drawing the float up onto it. I started at about 8ft but I quickly found that I was way too shallow – I'd forgotten just how deep the margins are at Horton. My second cast saw the float sitting just two or three inches under so I knew that I was close. I adjusted it

Bulla crept into the swim.

I was hanging on for dear life as the fish tested the tackle to its limit.

again, baited the hair with half a 20mm barrel and nicked on a bag of crumb and it was ready to rock. All this time, the fish had been feeding hard still and I was really excited that I was about to catch a Horton carp on the float!
Just as I was about to make the cast, Bulla crept into the swim, seeing that I was up to some kind of stalking, he'd kept a low profile, cheers mate! I flicked the setup out well past the spot and quickly drew it back as it sank. The float initially disappeared, but I let out some slack and it popped up, just 8ft out. I sunk the line and set the float just how I wanted it, with a small amount of orange tip visible. I'd strike if the float rose or slid away, but I wouldn't act until it was taking line from the clutch should the float dip as I certainly didn't want to foul hook one. I crept away to have a chat with Bulla, all the time keeping my eyes on the float. After about ten minutes the fizzing stopped and we couldn't believe that I hadn't had a bite. I went to have a quick look in the bush and there they were, the cheeky scaly backs. I wasn't happy that I hadn't had a bite, so I decided to replace the rig. As I lifted the bait off the bottom I could feel something attached and reeled in a twig. I quickly put on another bag and reset the trap, "Come on carp gods, no more therapee," I prayed. I topped the swim up and settled back in to chat with Paul, watching the float like a hawk. I could hardly believe it when, just two minutes later, the float flew out of the water and lay flat. I ran down and pulled into a lump that I'm sure had no idea what was going on. As it felt the rod, it went on a mental charge across the surface. I just held on, praying to the carp gods to let me catch this animal. Before I knew it, it was 70 yards away and heading for the corner of

Finally, the float rose from the depths and the big mirror wasn't far behind.

Yes, it was a recapture, but to catch an original out of the edge on the float made it a moment to savour.

After a short, spirited fight I had this stunning mid-twenty common in the net.

I couldn't see anyone in Springate's, so I barrowed round there with everything crossed.

The Sick Swim – the fish was in total control and I was just hanging on for dear life. I lowered the rod to give him some side strain that I hoped might stop him; I could hear Paul talking to me about the fight, but I had switched off and was focused only on getting him in. He responded by kiting at an alarming speed to the right and was heading towards the overhangs down the margin. I didn't want him getting caught up there, so I decided to let him know who was boss and walked back, pumping him along the margin. I could feel that he was getting closer so I started to lay off the pressure. Paul clicked off some action shots with my camera as he came close in along a reed line to my right. I could feel that there was something on the line and this seemed to calm him down a bit, making him drop slowly into the deep water in the margins. The float rose from the depths and just kept coming until I saw a long, dark mirror with weed round his head, which looked ready for netting. I knew that I was attached to an original so as I slid the net out and lifted it round him I let out the cry; it was Blacktail.

Bulla walked over to congratulate me, shaking my hand and telling me that it had been awesome to watch and one of the best bits of angling that he'd seen. It dawned on me that he'd taken some shots of me playing the fish, so I had a quick look after getting the necessaries together. Yes, I had caught this fish before, but he looked a lot bigger now and I was delighted that I'd managed to catch him out of the edge on a float! As I laid him down on the mat Paul said, "Jesus Jim, he's awesome." I rolled the mesh away and he kicked and played up a bit, so I spoke to him, telling him that he was safe here, and that he'd be home soon. With the scales zeroed we recorded a weight of 37lb and I laid him back down and poured cold water over him. As I held him for the pictures in the last of the autumn sunlight, I couldn't help but think that this would probably be one of the last chances to see them up close and personal this season. I carried him down to the edge in the mat and splashed water into the cradle, pushing the front down to let the water pour in. He told me that he was ready to go and I watched him slide off the mat and away into the deep margins, always a special moment. We sat and relived the capture for a while, before Paul departed and I decided to set up for the night because I was sure that they'd be back at some point. I dropped two rods close in and set the bivvy up round the side of the bushes so I wouldn't disturb the margins with my head torch, etc. Sometime after midnight my left-hand rod bleeped and I went down to investigate, feeling the line to establish whether there was a fish on. It seemed that there was, and he must have been kiting right because I was able to pull loads of line back, indicating that he'd gone that way. I picked the rod up and reeled the slack up, making contact with a fish that felt a little smaller than the previous one. After a short, spirited fight, I slipped a mid-twenty common into the net. I weighed him at 24lb 12oz and took a couple of shots on the mat before slipping him back. After returning him I sat up listening in awe as the fish showed all over Church Bay, but mainly further out than I was, towards Springate's Point. I decided to scatter some baits around this area before first light for my next trip. I watched them fizzing up out there as dark turned to light, could I float fish out there? I wasn't sure that I could. I packed up at about 9am,

I watched as a chunky mirror twisted and turned in the clear water.

so I could get back to Jane. I was preoccupied with planning for the next session on the drive home and I realised that a float called the Polaris would indeed allow me to fish out in those depths. I stopped off at Angling Direct in Beccles and picked up four of the floats, sorted.

My next session was planned for the Monday, and I was soon eating up the motorways on my way down south. Getting close, I wondered if I would be able to get back into the area. I really fancied Springate's Point, because the weather had turned colder. I signed in and quickly made my way round to Church Bay, where I found one of the punishers set up in the mouth of the bay, just round from The Sick Swim. I couldn't see anyone in Springate's, so I then barrowed my gear round there with my conkers crossed, so to speak. I was just pushing my gear through the gate when I heard one jump. I practically ran round there and as I got as far as the Church Bay Steps I could see that the fish had shown between the Heart Tail and Springate's. I prepared a rod with my new Polaris setup, which featured a stop knot set at about ten feet, to keep the float away from the putty, which was now about half an ounce in weight to help get the setup fishing correctly in 20ft of water. I propped the rod up, ready to cast at any signs and made the net up. I sat on my mat on the staging to watch the water and cracked open a Red Bull to keep me alert and awake. I then unwrapped my packed lunch that Jane had made me; you've got to keep well fuelled! As the Red Bull kicked in I could see big patches of bubbles out to my left, in the zone where I'd scattered baits the previous trip. It looked like this plan was coming together and I had to stay one step ahead of the rest! I flicked the float out 30ft behind the fizzers and drew it back over the area before opening the bait arm and letting the line run through the base of the float until the putty hit the deck. I let the line go slack so that the float could rise up and set itself, which takes a while in 20ft of water. A minute or so later, the 10-inch float popped through the surface and I gently tightened down to sink the line and set the float with just the tip showing. I sat down to eat my sandwich and a few minutes later, completely without warning, the float disappeared. "Christ, this is unreal," I thought, as I pulled into the fish. It shot off to my right, into the centre of the lake. I could see the dopey punisher looking out and I smiled to myself, thinking, "You're too late son. You're now getting some Uncle Jim magic; that should fcuk you up for a few days!" The fish felt bigger than the 24lb common last week, but there was no way that it was fighting as hard as Blacktail. He was using his weight to stay deep, but as long as he didn't run round to the right, he was mine. I watched as a chunky mirror twisted and turned in the clear water. He looked like a thirty, so I just kept the pressure on and he was soon on the top. I grabbed the net and he went in first time, sweet!

When I turned around, there was an angler who I didn't know standing behind me. Thankfully, he agreed to help me with the pictures of this mirror, which we weighed in at 33lb. It just goes to show that simple tactics, coupled with a will to move will always pay dividends. I later moved into Dog Bay and in the early hours I had another 24lb common on my 10lb Maxima running rig. This was to be my last fish from the historic lake as Ian Welch moved on and some other muppet took control.

Longfield

A Brush With Carp Fishing History

This venue is steeped in carp-angling history and it was somewhere I dearly wanted to fish after reading about the exploits of my good friend Steve Allcott. However, before I had a chance to go there, the lake was drained down and netted, with the fish being transferred down the road to Horton Church Lake. It was a great shame that such an iconic fishery was lost, but after a bit of digging around I found where these fish were now residing, and added my name to the Horton list. I guess that this would be around 1991 and after a couple of years checking where I was on the waiting list, the RMC office informed me they were abolishing the old list. I was told that I needed to phone up on a certain date if I wanted to add my name to the new list. Thinking to myself, "Too right I do!" I mentally logged the date and when that day came along it took me over an hour to get through. Luckily, I finally did get through and I was now number 47, which gave me a better chance of fishing for these awesome old history carp; gems like Shoulders, Jack the Net Ripper, Heart Tail and of course the king of the ugly ones, The Parrot, to name but a few. Of course, in the fullness of time, I had the pleasure of catching some of these special fish, but listening to some of Steve Allcott's stories, I felt the need to walk the banks of their original home. The chance presented itself while I was fishing the lake next door, The Road Lake, some years later.

Like The Road Lake, Fox Pool had been controlled by a small syndicate, which had restocked both venues. Stories started circulating that the Road Lake fish had thrived and RMC Angling had not let the two syndicates renew their leases, which meant both venues were to be added back to the RMC portfolio of waters. On a winter's night, while I was fishing The Road Lake, with no-one about I decided to take a look at Fox Pool. Opening and closing the gate it hit me that this was the place I had wanted to fish and I could even picture Steve's tales unfolding when I stood in certain swims. As I walked back up to the gate following my clandestine lap, I felt honoured to have walked its banks but more importantly, I now wanted to fish there. That evening I rang Steve to tell him I had walked round and that I now planned to fish there. By that point it was common knowledge that the lake contained some awesome chunks and several more undercover walk-rounds were done when no-one was about. They

My first look at Fox Pool, I could picture Steve Allcott's tales unfolding as I walked round.

simply reinforced my desire to fish it before the season ended.

After my target, Clover, came out of The Road Lake, I drifted over to Horton for a few trips, waiting for spring to arrive. The thinking was that I might be able to relive my end-of-season hit in the RIP corner, when I nailed Shoulders for the third time that season, just after 3:15am at a weight of 45lb 2oz. Spring did hit but like all good plans I was camping in the RIP on a big, bad southwesterly wind. The problem was, it was bloody freezing… and I mean freezing… and like an idiot I stayed put because I was still targeting The Parrot. With the knowledge I had of this zone, I was sure he would turn up if only the bloody wind got milder. However, after two days I decided enough was enough and packed up, with most of Horton being stitched on the back of the wind I thought better of camping with that lot. Lost, with nowhere to go, I sat in the lodge pondering where I could head. Then a brainwave hit me. Fox Pool came back into my mind because being a smallish, square lake it would be sheltered from this cold wind somewhat. Now I had a direction and as I drove out of Horton's gates it felt great to get away from the rat race. I had to wonder if this could be the start of a new adventure for me, after Fox had dropped from my thoughts.

After closing the gates behind me I was finally free of the Horton way, far too much backstabbing, typical of today's circuit-water fishing and something I find myself hating more and more. Turning left, I drove through Horton village and down through bandit country. Turning left again at a mini roundabout, the road took me past one of

I was back in Wraysbury, the scene of Marky Mark's death. Losing him was like losing a brother.

I headed straight for the snaggy Common Corner.

the Kingsmead entrances with the Projects lake just before it. Over the railway bridge and Wraysbury One loomed up on my left. I followed the road that skirted the lake and memories of Mary, Mary's Mate, Mallins and The Pug came flooding back. They were happy times but later these memories were to be replaced somewhat with the very sad loss of the two Marks in a boating tragedy just before New Year's Eve. I knew both of these anglers but Marky Mark was one of my best friends and his death was to leave me lost, it was like losing a brother. If it wasn't for my darling wife Jane, who kept me sane, I am sure I would have taken my own life, it hurt me that much. As I write this, just over eight years after, it still brings tears to my eyes. This was a bloke I could ring at any time when things were shit but when this happened it was a major turning point in my life and with the help of Jane, I have rebuilt my life and now have a balance where I work, fish and then go home and play hard. It hasn't changed the fact that the same old wankers are out there, stirring the shit, but I have now learned how to deal with it by letting my angling do my talking. I know that I've got to keep living the dream and life to the max; Marky mate, you still drive me forward to the extent that I catch everything for you my friend and I will never forget the good times we shared over the years. RIP mate, I hope you've caught Mallins in the big pond in the sky.

A left turn at the crossroads took me past a massive expense of water, The Priory, home of The Pet, which sadly passed away. The lake still has hidden secrets… one day, hopefully. As The Priory ended, on my right I saw The Road Lake, then it was that

Walking through the mature surroundings. I wished I could have fished there when the A-Team lived and swam in this magical oasis.

I positioned myself behind a bush and watched the shallower shelf for signs. Straight away I noticed that the clay shelf looked cleaned off and polished.

old game of Russian roulette with the traffic on the tight bend. Parking the car on the other side outside the gates, I had to open two gates before I could even get the car in. I nearly came a cropper several times over the years, trying to get inside, but thankfully there have been no mishaps yet. Closing the gates, I drove down the track, noticing that the Road Lake car park was busy, with some of the lake's bitches in residence. I carried on round the bend and was greeted by an empty Fox Pool car park. Happy days. Parking up, I grabbed my glasses and on getting out of the car I noticed a posse of anglers, several of which were the arse-licking bitches that had tried to get me banned a couple of years back. I just ignored them but I knew they would spread the word to the Fox bailiffs that Uncle Jim was in town. With inside information I knew that one of them, Snowy, the lake's jobsworth, was one to watch out for, but at least he was easy to spot with his hair dyed white!

As soon as I opened the gate that strange feeling I'd experienced over a month ago came flooding back. This place had so much history and in daylight I was blown away by its beauty as it pulled me in. I followed the path straight on, heading for Common Corner. Walking through the mature surroundings, I wished I could have fished there when the A-Team lived and swam in this magical oasis. It felt a lot milder here and as I approached the snags, I put my glasses on. I slowly moved closer to the water and noticed immediately that it was flaming clear. I positioned myself behind a bush on the right of the swim and watched the shallower shelf for signs. Straight away I noticed that the clay shelf looked cleaned off and polished; it was amazing because I reckon I could see down through the water to a depth of ten or twelve feet. I was just considering how perfect it looked here, behind the snags, when suddenly I saw a group of five fish swim down past the shelf in about ten feet of water. This was the sign I was looking for and more fish appeared from the right again, but this lot were only just under the surface. Not long after, others appeared but there was one, a big mirror with a dark back, that took my attention. I decided to watch for a little while longer, even though I was gagging to get the rods out, because I just wanted to see what else turned up. There were fish of all shapes and sizes in this lake and most seemed to be around the low to mid-twenty mark, but every now and again you would see a bigger one. Hiding behind the bush watching this, I was aware of just how warm it was compared to Horton, so this move and a jackpot find had the juices flowing. I had seen around thirty fish and it seemed as if I had turned up just as they were arriving. This was all too much, I laid my glasses in the swim to reserve it but on turning round I noticed a small, white, laminated sign stapled to the trunk saying, "Daylight fishing, two rods only" along with other stuff. "Different," I thought, backing off and quietly creeping away, pushing any twigs that lay on the path to one side at the same time. I didn't want to spook the fish, but once I was away I legged it back to the car to get my gear and once the barrow was loaded it was a quick march back to the swim. As you can imagine, I was like a dog with two dicks. The day swim was tight and the little area you had to put a chair in was cut away into the high bank. Everything was kept mega-quiet because though they were near a snag, vibrations would scare them and make

The place had all these laminated signs dotted around the trees…

…Different, I thought.

them move deep into the sanctuary of the snags that festooned this corner.

I was going to fish one rod only, thinking that two would only hinder things, plus it was another line to worry about should I hook one. I made my way to the edge of the swim and pushed two single banksticks in but set at an angle so the rod tip was parallel to the bank, facing straight at this tiny cleared-off area by an overhanging bush just in front of the snags. I was going to fish totally locked up, with a simple running rig on a leadcore leader, with a 12-inch braided hook length tied to a Longshank hook, with a bag to stop it tangling. While I was setting up I kept low and several more fish ghosted past on their way into the snag. I was buzzing off my head; all I had to do now was get the rig in without scaring them on my first attempt. While I got the rod ready I watched the area of the overhanging bush and tiny bubbles popped on the surface; that was definitely the spot I had to get this rig on! Hiding behind the bush, I checked that the coast was clear before I broke cover. All was clear and I quietly walked to the front of the swim and under-armed the rig out to the spot of the overhanging branches. The mesh bag clipped the branches and cushioned the impact of the lead, which was bang on; I couldn't have done it any better if I'd tried. The lead donked on the hard, polished-off hump and I threw in a few crumbed up baits that I had in my pocket over the top. I slackened off and backed away from view before I was spotted, laying the rod on the rest and making sure that the line was semi-slack and running along the edge, out of the way of the carp as they went back and forth along the shelf. Before I retreated to the back of the swim I made sure the clutch was done up tight. With a rock-solid setup I had to be on the ball if I got a take.

Creeping to the barrow at the back of the swim, I set the net up ready and decided to sit on a bucket and watch for any telltale signs over the spot. I had a few hours left here before I would have to move into a night swim, which would be something I would worry about later on. I watched the spot, ready to pounce on the rod. Around fifteen minutes later I noticed the tiny pinprick bubbles pop to the surface, bang over the spot; this had to be the chance. Suddenly, the rod burst into life and the line pulled tight, as something had made a mistake. Grabbing the rod, I applied maximum side strain, keeping the rod low as he ran straight. I had to keep the pressure on because at any second he could swing back and try to gain sanctuary in those snags. So, he had to be played hard, which soon had him in close, whereupon I got a real good look at a long common, twisting and turning in the clear water. Suddenly, several others ghosted in for a look to see what all the commotion was about and they darted off, heading back into the snags and probably scaring everything in the vicinity, which meant I had been rumbled. He was soon on the surface and I scooped him straight up. Looking in the net the common that I saw was long with massive diamond scales, which gave him a unique coat of armour. As I slightly tipped him onto his side I could see that he had a double belly. Leaving him in the net I then rang one of the boys asking if one of them could pop over from Horton to do the pictures for me. I weighed him at 23lb 10oz in the meantime and after the pictures were taken I walked him further down the bank and released him well away from the zone. I didn't want an unhappy carp bolting into

The common in the net was long with massive diamond scales, which gave him a unique coat of armour.

those snags and upsetting the others any more.

Once matey had left I decided to bait the spot but not put a rod out because I wanted to watch and see if any fish appeared like before. After an hour nothing was seen so I ventured further along into the snags. Looking into the back of this forest of snags I could clearly see them well tucked in and it didn't look like they were coming out for a while. Their state is commonly known in the trade as 'spooked to hell'. I heard a twig snap as someone approached, he just walked up all blatant and said, "You should be on your rod, can I see your ticket?" Thinking, "Here we go, another jobsworth twat," I replied, "OK, no problem but if you care to have a look you will see the rod isn't in the water." He said "You know this swim is days only?" Keeping calm I said, "Yes, well, I could hardly miss it with a tiny sign stapled to the tree!" He checked my ticket and walked off, making a phone call. I thought, "I bet one of those Road Lake bods has informed him." One thing was for sure, he wasn't happy seeing me on his little lake, he was probably worried that if I caught anything I would probably publicise it or tell others what I'd seen. Mind you, I hadn't told him that I had caught one and everything was put away so hopefully my secret was safe.

With the swim being closed for night fishing I had eyed up the next swim along as a possible place to fish for the night, before moving back into the day swim in the morning. Walking up to the swim, I looked out and saw the bailiff over the other side

Because the swim in Common Corner was closed at night, I eyed up the next swim along.

of the pond bending someone's ear, probably about me. More importantly, as I looked out from this tight swim there was a small bar that ran out from the margin and on seeing this, a plan was hatched. It was a bit naughty, because there was a no-wading rule but trust me; there weren't many areas you could wade anyway, because most of the margins dropped away into fifteen to twenty feet of water. However, this swim had this little bar running out and I was sure that with the help of my waders I would be able to walk out a little way and execute one of my mega side casts down into the corner. It was going to be tight to get this past the bush to my left and land the rig in the tight area before the snags in the corner, plus if I was caught wading it could mean me losing my ticket! Sometimes, rules have to be broken but more importantly, if I could pull it off this would mean Uncle would have a rod in the zone!

Because it was such a tall order to get this rig in place given several casts, let alone just one, I decided to tie up a few spare PVA bags. Then an idea popped into my head while I was sorting everything out. No, it wasn't me using a boat or swimming out but I decided use the line clip to ensure an accurate cast. It takes a bit of faffing about, but it'd be worth it. With the spare bag in place and scissors at the ready I waded out as far as I could and with the thirteen foot rod and me at full stretch, and standing on the right side of the bar I swung the bare lead out. The rod hit the bush but thankfully the lead fell around eight feet short, so I pulled off the extra line and clipped it. I hastily fumbled around, trying to get this rig tied on, fearing I was going to get caught at any moment. I realised this was going to be even harder with the added weight of the bag but if anyone could nail it, Uncle could. Before I entered the water, I popped my head round the bush to see if it was all clear, fcuk knows why because if I was caught in the act I had no chance. I waded back out and just as I had the rod out to the right, the mesh bag touched the water! It didn't melt though, so I just gave it the big cast and as the rod whacked against the bush, the line hit the line clip and the rig touched the branches of the overhanging bush. "Pukka," I thought, "That's a one-in-a-million cast," while sinking the line out past the bush so I knew the line was away from it. I then attached a 1oz back lead, letting it go and watching it slide down under the branches of the bush; this would keep the line out of harm's way. If it became snagged up it would pull apart, which was good because I didn't fancy this lead swinging round the rod tip as I played a carp with a lot of side strain. I slackened the clutch off, laid the rod down and got out of the water as quickly as possible because I was shitting myself even more so now, as I had a rod bang on a rocking spot.

With the waders off and hidden, I grabbed the sticks and angled the left-hand setup so it was pointing slightly towards the spot, but not too much so as not to indicate that I was up to no good. You know me; I'd never take the pee by breaking any rules! With the rod on the rest I slowly retrieved the slack line back, pulling the bobbin up and letting it fall back, this was repeated several times slowly and gently because I didn't want to mess up the rig's presentation. With the bobbin sitting near the top and the tip slightly bent round and loaded up I would get immediate indication if something picked the rig up. With the landing net in place, I quickly legged it down to the spot and chucked in several handfuls of crumb over a bigger area this time to get them moving about. The other rod was placed at the bottom of the wading bar but this rod was used mainly to draw attention away from the naughty rod. All I had to do now was set up the house for the night. This swim was also cut into the bank but was a lot bigger than the other and around twenty minutes later I was dug in with my waders at the ready, just inside the door. If I got a bite I would have to be on it to the max. Several hours passed as I watched for signs, but the left-hand rod, fished quiver tip style, didn't move. I had a feeling that they had done the off after the capture of the common, but I hoped they might return at some point soon, especially if the sun came out to play again the next day. I was sure they were using this area on the back of the wind to sun themselves.

I sat on the bedchair, watching the zone until it was dark. With it being mild, the first bats hovered overhead gathering what spring had to offer after their winter slumber. It's amazing what some creatures go through, hibernating through nature's worst weather. Their emergence is one of the signs I look for, as well as frogs and birds singing their hearts out for a mate. I love being at one with nature and my surroundings and I smiled as I heard a fox screaming somewhere close by. With everything quiet and the trap set, it was time to turn in. Because it was dark I placed my waders at the side of my bed, ready for me to jump in if anything occurred. It was magic to finally be fishing at Fox, reliving Steve's stories. The atmosphere must have been unreal all those years ago, knowing what gems they were hunting. Although I was lucky enough to catch some of them in their new home, this was as close to it as I could get now; I was fishing the great venue.

I must have drifted off to sleep because the next thing I knew I had a single bleep, which woke me. I pulled my chesties on and legged it towards the blue LED out in the darkness. It was the left-hand rod, but nothing else happened, which meant one thing – a liner. This was a good sign and the bait robbers were probably back in residence. As I sat there watching, the rod bleeped again and in the moonlight I saw the rod tip ping back. Surely something was going to happen? After fifteen minutes all was quiet and I headed back to my bivvy for a coffee. Looking at my mobile I could see that the time was 5am. With first light just around the corner, I decided to sit by the rods in my chesties, ready if anything were to happen. I was drinking my coffee, taking in the atmosphere while listening and watching for carpy signs, when I had another bleep. Now I knew 100 per cent that they were about. By now the first signs of morning started to appear and out of the corner of my eye I noticed the rod plucking. The scene was set, all I needed now was Mr Carp to play the game. I had a problem though, because I couldn't sit out here much longer with chest waders on with the no-wading rule in case I was spotted by someone on an early morning mission to try to catch Uncle up to no good. I thought I would give it a little longer and keep an ear out for the gate.

I decided to sit by the rods in my chesties, ready if anything were to happen.

I had another bleep but because I was watching I saw the tip pull round, which had me hovering over the rod thinking it was a take. The tip sprang back and I sat back down again. I watched the tiny plucks, thinking to myself, "It can't be much longer," when suddenly the alarm bleeped, the tip went right round and the rod was nearly pulled in! I held on, giving no line because I couldn't let him get into that forest of snags. The pressure was unreal as I edged out into the pond as far as I could. One of us had to give and it sure wasn't going to be me. I managed to get a couple of turns on the spool, which was a good thing and thankfully he hadn't found sanctuary in those snags. The power this beast had shown had me thinking he might be a kipper because it sure felt heavy on the other end. The pressure must have taken its toll though, as he finally kited out into the pond. He went deep and everything went solid. "What the hell?" I thought, after keeping him away from the snags it was still stalemate. I slackened off and watched the line on the surface for movement. Nothing moved after a few seconds so I tightened up again and gave him the butt. Suddenly, the rod jolted back slightly and we were back in contact, sweet. I kept the pressure on as inch by inch, I gained line. It felt heavy, like I had a lot of weed on the line, but I could still feel something else. A massive weed bed surfaced, but more importantly there was a swirl behind it; he was still on! I reeled this dead weight back towards me, dropping the net into the water, ready to scoop the lot up. I looked for signs of life but saw nothing and not long afterwards I had this floating mass in front of me. In the middle the weed moved slightly, telling me he was there. I sunk the net and pushed it underneath the mass and lifted. Everything went in so I pulled the net towards me, dropped the rod and began ripping the weed away, looking for a carp. Several handfuls were thrown out before I saw some living thing move! A few more handfuls revealed my prize, a massive beast laid in front of me. As I took away more, it just got bigger and bigger, revealing a right chunk of a mirror with a black back, which faded down its flanks, into a creamy chestnut belly, with a massive scale on one side. I unhooked him and made a phone call to Mike over at Horton to see if he could pop over and do the pictures for me. I decided to leave him in the net while I sorted things out for the pictures.

I reeled the other rod in because there was no point taking a chance and getting caught off the rods. Grabbing my glasses, I went for a look in the snags to see if I could see any. I checked the area for signs but it looked like I had spooked them once again. However, I thought I would give it a couple of hours and if nothing was seen, I would pack up and head home for some brownie points. I hung around watching the snags for signs but it was clear that these fish don't like seeing one of their mates being caught. Hearing the gate go I headed back to my swim. With everything ready, I handed Mike the camera; it was now time to get that fish sorted and returned. As I began to lift him out of the lake I realised how heavy he was! Turning to Mike I said, "I think he might be an upper thirty!" because I thought he was around 34lb in the net.

As I gently laid him down on the mat it was clear that he was a bit bigger than 34lb. I then carefully got him in Marky's sling and the scales thumped round to 37lb 6oz. He was a lovely mirror with an awesome array of colours and this massive scale in

He was a lovely mirror with an awesome array of colours and this massive scale in the middle on one flank. I reckoned that he had the frame to get a lot bigger too.

the middle on one side. I reckoned that he had the frame to get a lot bigger too. As I held him up I felt somewhat honoured to have caught such a big carp on my first visit to this historic lake. After I watched him waddle off into the deep margins, I climbed out and Mike shook my hand, but then he pointed to the waders saying, "There is no wading on RMC venues Jim." I replied "I know Mike, I was drying them from a previous session elsewhere!" Not long after, he left me to it so I got my arse back in the snags to see if anything had turned up. I carefully checked all of the snags but saw nothing. After an hour my gut feeling was to leg it. Around an hour later, after putting 10kg on the spot, I departed for home but before hitting the M25 I decided to pop into 'Boss-man's' at Horton for some chicken samosas, which his missus makes, they're unreal!

Whilst on the motorway, dodging the traffic on the way back home, I tucked into Boss-man's Indian delights, which got me thinking about the fish I had seen in Common Corner; I vowed to return and have another look next week. This didn't happen though, as I ended up getting sidetracked somewhere else, but that's another story. I did visit the lakes several times through the summer, so it was a water that was on my mind, and a plan was hatched to fish it sometime in the late autumn and winter to unlock more of Fox's secrets.

I was back in the area, checking many lakes when Fox Pool popped into my head and I decided to go and check it out. It was unusually mild for the end of November and driving down the lane I got a really good gut feeling. Looking over to the right, there weren't any cars in that car park and nor were there any in the Fox car park, so I had the whole complex to myself! Grabbing my glasses, I walked over to the Fox Pool gate and as I opened it I noticed the birds were singing. This gave me a sense of wellbeing and reassured me that I was in the right place.

After closing the gate I headed straight for Common Corner covering my head with the sweater hood. As I came close to the zone I went into hunting mode, thinking this would be the zone from my previous observations. I peered through the foliage, looking into the water, which was once again gin-clear but the spot was dirty. This was not a good sign so I moved further along the snags, being careful not to make any noise. I searched the snags for signs of carp but saw nothing. As you can imagine, I was stunned that nothing was about in those snags but to be fair it was nearly December and the chances of me just walking on and finding them in the same place were a bit remote. Sometimes luck plays a part, especially if you know the lake a bit though, just not this time. I looked out across the lake thinking that I had a few more snaggy areas to check out and that surely they had to be in one of those sets of snags. Many of these areas had deep water close by, so they were perfect hiding places for the carp, plus being gin-clear they would quickly benefit from any sun and with bright conditions and it being a fairly mild winter so far, I felt there was a good chance of spotting one if I looked hard enough.

Not long after, I came to another forest of snags where the lake bed dropped away into the abyss, unlike the other two main sets, which had slightly shallower areas

There were no fish in Common Corner this time, so I headed up the path to Goose Pool instead.

underneath. This set didn't feel right so unless I saw them in here this wouldn't be an area that I would consider pre-baiting. However, right at the back of this savage set of snags was a shallow area that looked slightly cleaned off. I positioned myself behind a tree and watched for any signs. After half an hour I saw nothing so I headed along the path towards Goose Pool. Nearing the zone I once again covered my head and put my hands in my pockets to hide as much white as possible. I watched where I walked as I neared the zone and I peered down on the marginal shelf, which looked like it had been turned over about 6ft down. To the trained eye this was a mega find; all I needed now was to see one. This zone felt right with the sun beaming straight into the corner; if I were a carp this is where I would have been, as the sun warmed my face.

Back on the path, I walked down another twenty feet to another clearing that looked like an area anglers watched from. As I approached, I inched my way in as I had to clear the trail, which told me no one had been in there for a while. The shelf here was trashed too, the stones were all shiny and the sand clean and sifted; this was 100 per cent fresh too. My eyes scanned further out when suddenly a dark shape ghosted past. He was not spooked so I was hidden enough, thankfully, as I looked down into this aquarium, which was just how I like it, up close and personal. With one spotted there had to be others about, so getting myself comfortable against the trunk of a tree, I watched the zone like a hawk and planned my attack. Suddenly, the phone went and

I covered up as much white skin as possible and crept into position.

I carefully fumbled about for it in my pocket and answered it. It was Rich Stewart from Advanced Carp Fishing magazine asking if he could book in a date for my next monthly feature. He asked why I was whispering, so I told him of my find and where I was. "You kept that quiet!" he replied, "Mate, I have only just got here," I said, as another chunk swam past. "You want to see this," I whispered, as a group glided past on their way into the bay, not eight feet out and six feet below the surface. Rich listened as I relayed what I was watching over the next few minutes and I spotted several more. I was buzzing with my find because you can't beat finding them, and in my fishing location is a massive piece of the jigsaw.

I noticed that the chunky, deep-bellied mirror, which was the first one I saw, had a lump on his side. He looked around mid-thirty and also had a distinctive scar on his side that was healing. I was to see this fish many times over my few sessions here and he sure was one of the greediest residents in the pond. After several more minutes I said to Rich, "I must go and focus on this find, I'll ring you after dark mate." I slowly backed off and went back to the first swim that fished into Goose Pool, where once again there were small, laminated signs on the trunk of a tree. Reading it I laughed, as I had never fished a place with these day-only, dawn 'til dusk swims. I walked up to the next swim to see if it was possible for me to do one of my side casts from this tight swim, which would mean a twenty to twenty five yard side chuck. Standing in

Reading yet another laminated sign I laughed, as I had never fished a place with these day-only, dawn 'til dusk swims.

the swim I eyed it up, it was tight but do-able, although it was going to be tough to get enough momentum for a cast. The swim didn't look like it had been fished for a while but before I left I laid my coat in the swim so it was mine.

Walking round the back of the bay I had a little look in the snags and straight away I saw a big mirror sitting right at the back of the snags. I couldn't ID the fish but its shape reminded me of the fish that I caught back in March at 37lb, which I found out was called The Video Fish. I wondered why it didn't have a more fitting name? With so many fish in the zone this quiet little bay it seemed to be the place they were going to overwinter, being sheltered behind the cold winds and warmed by the sun when it was up. The mirror was the only one I saw on this spot and after a while I backed off and went for my gear. I was pumped up and gagging to get the rods out after my find.

The excitement was unreal and while I loaded my barrow I wondered what else was in Goose Pool. Around twenty minutes later I had my gear in the swim and I went for another look to gain more info. Over the next few minutes I only saw one small one but it was deep down, but I also saw the odd bubble popping on the surface where a fallen tree lay across the bay, just before the snags started. This had to be the place to have a hook bait but I had to drag a lead across it to see if it was fishable first. With only a couple of hours of daylight left, it was time to have that feel about. This was not going to be an easy side cast let alone with a rig and bag setup on. I decided to use a small, dumpy, 2oz lead because there was no way I could get enough of a cast to use anything bigger. Standing to the left of the swim, it took three attempts before the lead went in the right direction but as I looked round the bush I could see that I had cast it too far and the rig pulled up to the snag as I tightened up. With a lead it just pulled free, plopping off the snag and dropping down on my side. I felt the lead touch down and as I dragged it I could feel the line rubbing on that fallen tree that laid across the bay, so all I had to now do was gently tease the lead to the top and let it drop my side of the tree. It thudded down hard roughly where I had seen some bubbles. I pulled the lead around six feet and the bottom was smooth, sweet. I then put the line in the spool clip so it was ready and tied a marker to the line for later casts. I carried on dragging the lead and the bottom got dirtier and dirtier as it came towards me, but more importantly, there were no snags after the fallen tree, which I had hoped would be the case.

Now, this sounds easy, but what I had to do now was cast the rig to the clip, which in this tight swim, using a dodgy side cast, was not going to be simple. I was determined to get a rig there though, no matter how many casts it took. Rig-wise, I was going to use a leadcore leader, a braided hook length of around 14 inches, a Longshank hook, with a 20mm barrel hook bait on a two-inch hair, coupled with a small mesh bag for presentation. I was more worried about the angle of this side cast in such a tight swim than watching the rig in flight. Standing out as far as possible I started to practice the swing until I had the momentum and angle, then I let it go and surprisingly the rig hit the clip and landed bang on the spot. Trust me, I was a tad lucky with that. I took the line out of the clip and opened the bale arm, paying out line so I didn't move the rig.

I had seen several shows to my left, so as darkness fell and everything went black, the scene was set.

I then put the rod on the rest, clipped the bobbin on and gently teased the line back with the weight of the bobbin. Once this was done, I screwed the clutch up tight with the bobbin now sitting halfway up to the rod; any movement on the line would result in a bleep. With the rig in place it was time to bait it up. I was going to bait up with two different-sized, barrel-shaped White Amber boilies. I love these because they sit on the silt better instead of sinking in, they're good for anti-ejection when used on the hair, especially the 20mm versions, and they look like carp poos!

Standing in the day-only swim it was much easier to bait up and several catapults full of bait were fired out over the area where the rig was sitting, just off the snag. These barrels don't go out as far as round ones, but you get a better spread with them. I had a good feeling about this spot, with the cleaner bottom and a few bubbles spotted. The other rod would be a rover and I would randomly move this one about, fishing it with a single bag setup. Luckily, I had a brolly and sides because the swim was another tight one, although it was muddy and I don't really like carting mud into where I'm living, so out came the doormat. I would be better sorted next time. With light levels dropping it was time to watch the lake for any signs. The anticipation was unreal, plus I wasn't fishing blind, because I had seen several to my left, so as darkness fell and everything went black the scene was set and I was sure Mr Carp would visit me at some point. Leaning against a tree trunk my other senses kicked in because sight was lost tonight. Heavy cloud had moved in which would keep the temperatures up so I listened, waiting and hoping that something might show itself. About an hour later, sure enough one rolled over to the left. Straight away I made my way into the bay, trying not to make any noise. As I approached the day-only swim sure enough the telltale ripples rolled in from over the other side, near the rod I had seen fizzing. This added to my confidence big time, because they were still there. I reckoned that they were checking the spot out and hopefully it would only be a matter of time. I listened for a while longer but heard nothing more. Hunger was kicking in, so it was time to treat myself to a rib-eye steak.

I phoned Paul Nelhams, AKA Bullaboss, and told him that I was in the area. After a long chat and before I hung up, I swore him to secrecy about my whereabouts and he wished me good luck and told me that if I needed any pictures doing he was at Horton. After our conversation I went for another listen but all I heard was a fox howling like a wolf somewhere out over the back. I was knackered and it was now time to get some much-needed shuteye. It was hard to sleep properly because I knew that as soon as that buzzer sounded I'd need to be on it. Several times I turned over and lay awake before drifting off back to sleep. All was quiet, apart from a possible show in the night. I was too knackered from lack of sleep to investigate it and before I knew it birds were singing, which was a bit strange at this time of the year. It was still twilight, so I lay in the bag knackered and watched an awesome sunrise develop in front of me. Before

I lay in the bag and watched a truly awesome sunrise develop on the eastern horizon.

I put the kettle on I took a few pictures to remember this moment. I hoped a strong coffee would sort me out, as I hated feeling like that.

I didn't want to get out of the bag until I noticed a set of ripples rolling past me from the left. I sat up and pulled on my boots before carefully making my way towards the bay, carefully pushing twigs to the side as usual. I didn't want to draw attention to myself by snapping one. Every trip I was cleaning the path and area where I watched them, at close quarters it would be covered in leaves I'd gathered to soften the footfall. These are the sorts of things you would do if you were a hunter and over many years I have become a hunter of carp, learning and mastering this art form. This is something you learn over many hours spent observing and being at one with nature. The only thing I change in the hunt is replacing the kill with a trophy shot. The hunt is the biggest buzz for me now in carping and it results in many targets and their mates being caught; even more so now that I have other edges like hook sharpening and of course my perfected chod rig. God knows what I would have caught years ago if I had these few edges, coupled with my watercraft skills. It's a deadly combination for me, along with the right mindset.

Scanning the area, I soon located some bubbles, which just happened to be near the zone in which I had now seen a lot of carpy activity. Several minutes later I saw some

Scanning the area, I soon located some bubbles, which just happened to be near the zone in which I had now seen a lot of carpy activity.

Several minutes later I saw some discreet fizzing in that area near the fallen tree.

discreet fizzing in that area near the fallen tree. Seeing this and knowing how close it was to the rod, I backed off and went and stood by the rods, buzzing because I was now even closer. Suddenly there was a bleep. "That's weird," I thought. I looked down and the rod pulled tight. I picked the rod up and pulled into something that felt heavy, but was trying its best to get into the snags. All I could do was hang on and give no line as the rod bent double. I gave it maximum side strain and suddenly it bounced, which momentarily made me think he had come off. Thankfully he hadn't, as I now gained several turns on the reel. At this point he kited to the right, along the overhangs, so I lifted the rod, keeping the pressure on, watching the line, which was well clear of the bay by now. I eased off because he was around halfway out in open water, so unless something went wrong I was close to another fish that had some weight behind him as he chugged around deep down. Several plumes of bubbles hit the surface as he tried to rid himself of the hook. All I had to do was play him out. He stayed well down and five minutes later I was still yet to get a glimpse of what I was attached to. With the depth of the lake it seemed to take ages but my steady pressure was taking its toll. He ran along the right-hand margin but I was able to contain this short burst of power and he came straight back, whereupon I saw him for the first time; he was a really chunky-looking common. I chucked the net into the margin so I was ready as the long leadcore leader rose out of the water. He was getting close now, plus I got a really good look at him; he had a dark back and in the clear water I could see a light-coloured belly with

Knowing how close the fish were to the baits, I backed off to go and stand by the rods.

a mismatched patch of scales on his side. Suddenly, he wallowed on the surface and momentarily I was mesmerised by this carp as I gazed at his intense colours. Snapping out of it, I quickly scooped him up. He sure was a unique-looking specimen with a very up-front, chesty appearance. I leant down and popped the hook out, leaving him in the net while I phoned Bulla up to see if he could come over and do the honours. He said he would pop down within the hour.

This gave me time to get the rod back in position and get things ready. He soon arrived, on his own as well, which was good angling. Shaking my hand he said, "Nice one brother." The fish weighed 32lb 12oz, and after giving this awesome character the once-over I named him the Upfront Common. He was very tricky to hold because of his shape and bulk down at the front end. Once he was back home, I hid the evidence behind the bivvy because I wanted to keep this quiet. Before Bulla left I drilled him again, telling him not to breathe a word, especially to those town criers over at Horton with nothing better to do than gossiping. After Bulla went I was left with my thoughts and I sat watching the sunrise starting to light and warm up the zone. I wondered what I might see in residence that day. Perhaps thirty minutes later I heard a clank, someone had turned up. As I watched, this white-haired geezer appeared… enter Snowy the bailiff. He appeared opposite me and walked into a swim, before looking over and clocking where I was fishing. He then turned and stood at the back of the swim he was in and after several minutes I wondered what he was up to. The thought had crossed

Shaking my hand, Bulla said, "Nice one brother!"

my mind he might be pulling his leg if you know what I mean! When I next looked up he had disappeared, but I knew he was on his way round because he was one of Stoney's bitches. As I watched him walk round the bay, his first words were, "Can I see your ticket?" but he then clocked me and his face was a picture, like it was his worst nightmare as I handed him my honorary gold card. I knew full well that the bollocks would start at some point and that would be sooner rather than later with this bunch. They weren't happy with Welchy taking back their lake and adding it to the RMC Angling portfolio of waters. Handing my ticket back he then proceeded to tell me the do's and don'ts in certain swims. I just listened but in my head I was telling him to fcuk off, which he did eventually. But before he left he asked "Anything happening?" "Same old crap," I thought as I said, "Shit here." With him gone I could once again revel in the capture.

The funny thing was, he went back to that swim and faced the back of the swim again. All sorts of things were running through my head and it was something I was going to investigate when he was gone! After a few minutes he walked off. Hearing the clank of the gate I quickly popped next door to the day-only swim and checked out the snags where I had seen them; I reckoned that my capture had spooked them into hiding. With it being a nice day I thought I would get some much-needed shuteye and as I lay down I knew the drums would be beating overtime now they knew 'Mr

Once he was back home, I hid the evidence behind the bivvy because I wanted to keep this quiet.

The paths were waterlogged, so this would be a slip-and-slide mission to get the barrow back to the new carpmobile.

Mag-It' was here again. I soon fell asleep with the warm sunshine beating down on my bivvy, dreaming about all things carpy but several hours later I woke up shivering. Looking out, the weather conditions had changed drastically and it now looked like it was going to rain. As I climbed in the bag to warm up it started spitting. This carried on all night and when it did stop the rain dripping from the trees was a nightmare! All I hoped was that it stopped by morning so I could pack up without getting soaked through. Thankfully, by the morning it had indeed cleared away but the paths were waterlogged, so this would be a slip-and-slide mission to get the barrow back to the Focus ST 170, the new carpmobile. Now I had their location, I wanted to get a hit of bait in to keep them on it in the zone until I returned. I decided to put in a mixture of two sizes of barrels and 20mm round baits with the baiting spoon. This does seem a lot but there were plenty of tufted ducks on here and I knew they would hit the area once I was gone. The main thing was that I knew Mr Carp was there, so this filler would let them feast with no lines in the water as long as no one went in the zone. I knew it would only be a matter of time until this happened though, because the armchair anglers are always ready to swoop on people's hard work.

Driving home, all I could think about was the jackpot I had found and wondered what other secrets this lake had in store for me. Over the weekend my mind relived my first trip, seeing those other fish. I trawled the Internet, looking for pictures of the lake's

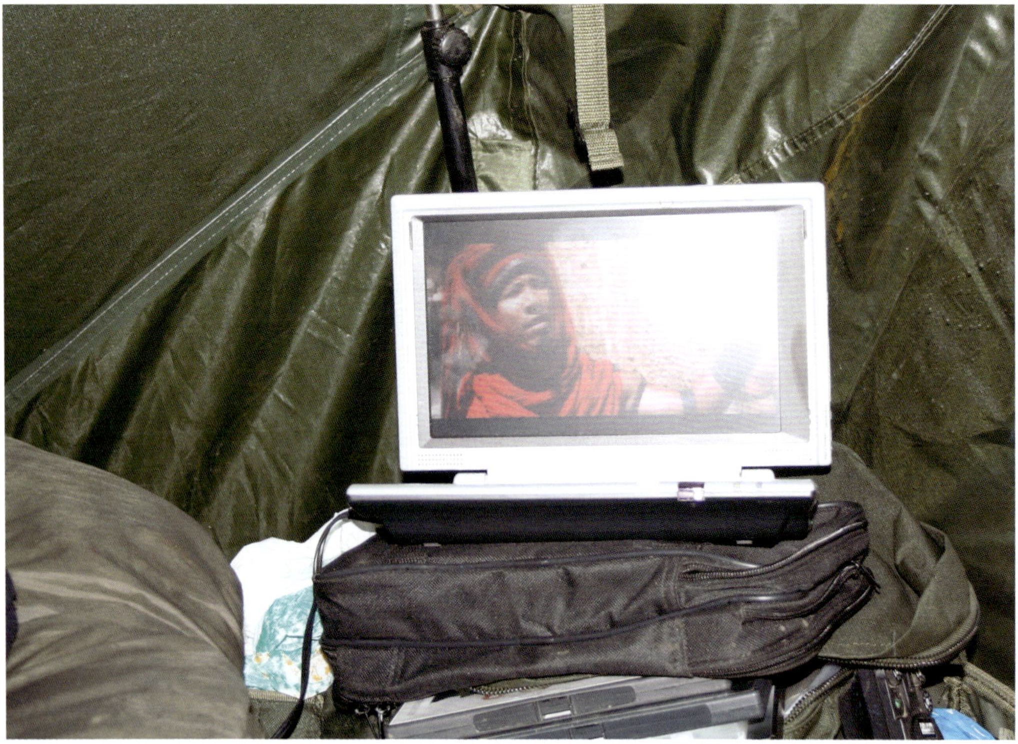

This time I was to get into full camping mode so I had brought the DVD player and a leisure battery.

inhabitants. Several were found like The Patch Common, The Winter Mirror and one referred to as Bazil, so there were several other targets, plus all the backups and ones I didn't know of yet. This winter was going to be interesting, as long as the fish stayed and I was left alone. The next trip saw me flying down in the Focus in the early hours of Monday morning. I was buzzing with excitement and gagging to get the rods back out, plus I did have a mag feature to do as Mr Stewart had put it off the previous week to see if I caught, because he wanted to do the feature on Fox Pool. Yes, I knew it meant the word would be out then but this feature would not hit the shelves until February or March and the season would nearly be over by then.

The car park was empty, so that was the first good sign. This time I was to get into full camping mode so I had brought the DVD player and a leisure battery so I had loads of power to watch film after film. I decided to lug these round first with a hit of films. The battery would be left hidden for a few trips until it needed recharging. As I neared the back of the bay where I had baited, I quietly put everything down and moving closer, I peered through the bushes. There was a patch of bubbles over the zone… they were on it. As you can imagine, I was now gagging to get fishing but before I backed off, I noticed the water was slightly cloudy after the rain the other night. I was now on a mission and once the bits were dropped off in the swim I quietly legged it back to the car to get the barrow loaded and round to the swim. I was like a mad, possessed animal getting the rods ready and while I was doing this I kept an eye on the spot, which was getting bigger in size. Luckily for me, that rod was clipped up ready… nothing like forward thinking Uncle!

Now, with everything set and ready to go all I had to do was repeat last week's cast, which was easier said than done. I then let rip and no word of a lie, it landed bang on the money! I felt the lead thud down, as my old mate Jon Mac would say, "I love it when a plan comes together." I then walked down to the day-only swim and catapulted out some sweeties for the boys. This noise would stir them up and reactivate the zone. The other rod was cast straight out this time on a bag setup. With the traps set it was time to get the house up, settle down and start the waiting game.

I was knackered so I thought it best to use the time before Rich turned up to regain the lost sleep, so I hit the sack and drifted off dreaming of all things carpy. The next thing I knew, the phone went and it was Rich asking if I needed anything. "No mate, I'm sorted," I replied. Rich said that he'd be there in 30 minutes but I was now fcuked and my head was pounding after being woken up. Grabbing the kettle, I hoped one of my super-charged coffees would sort me out. While I waited for it to boil I walked to the edge of the lake, cupping my hands I filled them with cold lake water and threw it

With the traps set it was time to get the house up, settle down and start the waiting game.

over my face. Trust me, three of those soon had me refreshed! After a sip of the coffee I was soon feeling a lot better and not long after Big Rich appeared. As he entered the swim I was swigging the coffee, giving him therapee for waking me up! He just laughed, knowing me of old. I brought him up to date in between swigs of coffee then said, "Once I've finished this I'll take you for a look fella." I read him the riot act, telling him to keep covered up and watch where he stepped and with glasses on we proceeded into the zone to a spot just before the back of the snaggy bay. I went in first and saw one straight away. I whispered, "Come in slowly mate." Rich saw the fish and I could tell in his voice that he was blown away by it. This was December, not exactly the best time to be seeing fish up close and personal. Rich quickly got some pictures done, after which, I informed him that we weren't going in there again as there were carp about and I had every chance of a bite.

With the rest of the pictures done, it was time to get the taping done. While we were working, Snowy turned up asking if Rich had permission to be there. I answered, "Of course, speak to Ian Welch at RMC." He grunted and scurried away from whence he came. I pointed over to the swim, telling Rich, "Watch Snowy do his thing over there mate." He looked at me a bit funny so I told him the tale as he watched Snowy in action. The problem was, I kept forgetting to have a look, which was probably because my inner self didn't know what to expect plus, looking at Rich, I could tell he was also

Rich quickly got the pictures done and we got on with taping my article.

Up there, nestled in the ivy, was a box. Intriguing!

confused by what he was seeing. After I heard the gate go I said, "Watch my rods while I go and investigate what the score is with the back of that swim." On the way round I had several ideas running though my mind like a blow-up doll, a stack of porn mags or some shrine praying for forgiveness. When I got there I couldn't find anything, which then threw me somewhat. However, I looked up there, nestled in the ivy, was a box. I had to know what this was all about. It was locked, so I broke into it. There was a book with messages written down. "Weirdo," I thought. I thought better of reading them because they might have been too explicit for Uncle Jim. Back at the swim I told Rich of my findings, trying to keep a straight face. I failed and burst into uncontrollable tears of laughter. That was the mag feature up the spout for a while because we couldn't stop talking about it. Suddenly, one of my rods screamed into life and after a spirited fight I landed a mirror of 26lb 12oz with a deformed mouth, meaning that it probably couldn't feed normally, Rich then released him several swims down. With the rod back in position and a sprinkling of bait, we continued on with the feature, vowing not to talk about Snowy's corner, because it was hurting so much; I hadn't laughed like that for ages. With the feature in the bag Rich said he would give it another hour just in case I was luckily enough to get another bite. The bite didn't materialise so Rich headed off so he could beat the M25 traffic. Shaking my hand and wishing me good luck he departed, leaving me to mull over the day's events, so to speak!

With Rich gone, I decided to lie down and chill out. I must have fallen asleep because

After a spirited fight I landed a mirror, which had a deformed mouth.

He weighed in at 26lb 12oz.

Rich released him down the bank so he wouldn't put the rest on edge.

the next thing I knew, I was standing doing a Snowy, with my rod in my hand. It was bent double into something that was trying its best to gain the sanctuary of the snags. Keeping the pressure on with the rod over to one side I soon had him kiting out on a long line and once he was clear I laid off with the pressure, which seemed to calm him. He then went deep, plodding about shaking his head in defiance. This one felt bigger than the last, plus the rod had a fair old bend in it. Five minutes later he was close in so it was only a matter of playing him out, but suddenly he went on a mental run along the right-hand margin, stripping line off the spool at a fair old rate before going solid. Straight away I slackened off, hoping this would make him think he was off but nothing happened. I watched the line as it entered the water and after a minute or so it twitched. I reeled into it and thankfully he was free. I played him heavily, until he was back in front of the swim and then set the clutch. The leadcore leader appeared and I could now see a nice, dark shape rise from the depths. He had a lovely chestnut complexion to him with a massive scale that I sort of recognised. As he slid into the net it dawned on me that he looked like my old mate The Video Fish, which I thought was such a sad name for a carp. As I looked into the net I did think to myself, "I bet that was the one I saw in the back of the snags a few weeks back." As I gently removed the hook I whispered, "I have a better name for you my friend, Big Scale." This seemed more of a fitting name, but once the person who first named him found out, he tried to get me dropped from ACF. Later on, he appeared at Fox after I had gone home. The

I betted the fish in the net was the one I'd seen in the back of the snags a few weeks back.

zone that I had been fishing had largely been left alone, but of course he or anyone else could have fished it. However, I found on my return that the swim had been filled in blatantly to fcuk over my fishing. Well, in my book that is bad angling and to top it all off, he then made several abusive calls and even sent a stupid text message while he was with Barney. This seems to be the nature of today's angler; they have no respect. They just get the knives out to get people off the lake no matter what, very shameful if you ask me.

With the fish left in the net, I phoned Bulla to see if he could do me a few pictures and sure enough, he soon appeared and asked, "What have you got brother?" "He's in the net mate, it looks like Big Scale; the one I had last March." The fish looked pumped up and with the light levels starting to drop and everything in place it was time to get the fish sorted. He weighed 39lb 6oz and was 100 per cent The Video Fish, AKA Big Scale and looked awesome. I was so close to a winter forty, but never mind. I held him up for the camera while Bulla clicked away, cheers for your help, I owe you one mate! Next, I lowered the mat into the margin and covered him in water. He knew it was time to go as he kicked off and disappeared back into the darkness to fight another day. Nothing else happened that night and I saw no signs in the morning. As I was having a slow pack up Darrell Stile phoned as he was in the area, so he popped over for a chat and a look about before I legged it. With family things happening as well as Christmas, I

I thought Big Scale was a more fitting name, but renaming him didn't go down well with a few people.

couldn't make it back until the New Year, so before I left I filled the zone in with 32kg of 20mm Ambers, one jar of hemp and milk pellets to hopefully keep the carp happy while I was away, as well as the armada of tufted ducks that were becoming a pain, especially at night. During the day they mostly kept away because I cast the marker rod across the entrance of the bay, but at night the fcukers dived under it. These days it is much easier with the use of the laser pen.

Once the gear was loaded into the van, Darius helped me with the hit of bait. Once the bait was in, he got up the tree and started laughing, "Jim you want to see the bottom, it's all lit up white!" I shouted, "I know mate," laughing at the power of the white while I started getting the salty hemp and pellet mixture out. The birds help to bury the seeds while diving for the bigger items. This means that there is always a food signal in the zone, hidden in the silt. Once this was done I legged it off home for Christmas with the family. I even managed to get out for a 24-hour trip over the festive period but nothing happened and it looked dead in the cold conditions. More importantly though, I could top the zone up with more bait. The spot was primed ready for my return in the first week of January, but as you can imagine all the time I was away I was thinking about who had fished there and whether he had fcuked it for me. If the fish were still there and if it had been left alone they should be up for it after their big feast.

In the New Year the car was loaded and I set off early. All I could think about was that area, hoping and praying that no-one was in there. It was hard not to dwell on it; I just turned the trance tunes up louder to try to chill me out. I sped across the country, breaking all speed limits. Luckily, no cops tugged me; maybe I was going so fast I was off the radar and gone before they knew it? Before I knew it I was there and there were no cars in the car park. Grabbing a few items I legged it round to see what the coup was. As I approached the back of the snags there was more fizzing going on over the spot than I had ever seen in January. It was nearly as big as a brolly, an unbelievable sight to behold. I then carried on round to the swim, and it looked like no one had been in here since me. Standing at the front of the swim, I looked left and the fizzing was still going on, which got me all excited. I was now gagging to get the rods out so I carefully and quietly walked off, but once I was away I was legging it back to the car to get my gear. I was pumped up and confident that I was going to catch this trip. With rain forecast for the evening, I needed to get everything sorted and get settled in. This time it took several casts to get the rig in position on the spot but with the amount of fizzing there, I knew they would be back. I watched the area like a heron hunting his dinner but nothing else was seen and I hoped I hadn't spooked them off with too many casts. After dark I listened for signs but heard nothing. I decided to cook dinner and have an early night but before I went to sleep I set the alarm for 1am to see if they were showing late at night. Climbing into the bag I was soon asleep, but before I knew it the alarm was banging out its tune. I dragged myself from the warmth of my bag and turned it off, wondering what the hell I was thinking, as I was shattered. I popped the kettle on, hoping that a strong coffee would bring me back into the land of the living. While I was sitting on the edge of the bedchair, drinking my coffee, I heard one go

While I was sitting on the edge of the bedchair, drinking my coffee, I heard one go over out in the blackness.

over out in the blackness so I stood straight up and walked down to the next swim to investigate. Lo and behold the ripples started to roll in from the zone, so things were now looking good because if there was one about then there would be others with him.

After five minutes I was getting cold so I went back for my coat and turned the cooker off. I went back to listen for more signs and looking at the phone it was now 3am. With no more signs it was time to get my head back down. Before I got in I turned the cooker on so it warmed me up before I got back into the bag. Once in I turned it off and drifted off back to sleep. A bleep on one of the buzzers woke me and as I unzipped the bag I had several more bleeps. Pulling on my boots, I jumped out and grabbed the offending rod but it seemed that there was nothing attached. I was furiously reeling in the slack, thinking that it must have been a liner when I connected with a fish close in. It was a drop back and this crafty carp had tried her best, but the running lead setup had given me indication. She was slow moving and felt heavy on the other end but she pretty much swam straight towards me, not really doing much, which was a bit different from my other captures from the venue. I made sure the clutch was set because I thought she might suddenly wake up and shoot off. However, the next thing I knew, there was a fat mirror laying on the surface. Grabbing my net, I scooped her up and the water in the net exploded as she tried to get away. "Easy tiger," I said, as she

Bulla said, "No wonder she's so fat!"

tried again to escape my net.

When she had calmed down I tipped her over in the net to get a look at her. I had seen a mark on her side, which was thankfully healing, but by the size of her belly she had been feasting on a larder big time! I unhooked her and before I texted Bulla I made sure the net was safe so she couldn't get out after her last couple of attempts. I covered the top of it with my unhooking mat, which I hoped would calm her. I then sent that text to Bulla to see if he was about. Straight away he texted back so I rang him to inform him that I had caught another. He promised to be over in an hour to help me out. While I waited for him, I got that rod back on the spot and served it up with some more sweeties. In reality though, it seemed that once you bagged one that was it for the trip, apart from once when I had two in a session. With everything sorted, it was not long after that I heard the chain go on the gate and Bulla once again walked round to help me with the pictures. The lake was quiet, which I thought was a bit weird; not even Snowy had been about. Bulla then walked up and shook my hand saying, "Good angling!" I thanked him and told him to come and have a look at the fat bitch! I removed the mat and lifted her so we could get a better look. Thankfully, she had calmed down by now and by turning her on her side Bulla could now see how fat she was, along with the scar, which I said that I'd treat shortly.

I broke down the net and carefully gathered up the mesh, but before I lifted her clear of the water I made sure the pecs were folded flat along her body. Bulla grabbed the camera off my bed and as I placed her in the weigh sling she was excreting bait from her rear end. Bulla said, "No wonder she's so fat!" The scales read 37lb and as you can see in the pictures she sure is a fat bitch! After I slipped her back and thanked Paul for taking time out of his fishing again and before he left I received another take which resulted in 20lb 4oz mirror. After the pictures were done I then wished him good luck as he headed off back to Horton. Even though I was well confident over the next two days nothing else was seen; it's like they had disappeared. I decided that next time, if or when I caught one, I would pack up and head off elsewhere. Before I left I baited the zone again and as I closed the gate I thought it strange that no one had been round, that was indeed a first. As I locked the gate I heard something and before I had a chance to get into my car, two teenagers appeared. One of them had a gun and the other said, "You're Jim Shelley," and pulled a pocket pen knife out and proceeded to wave it in my face, really close, which wasn't good. Several threats were fired at me and I was a bit stunned by it all. I did think about giving him a smack, but that would have put paid to me fishing the area again and deep down I still wanted to fish The Mere, so this all had to be taken into account, plus I had done nothing wrong! To this day I reckon this was all down to those jealous twats that thought they still owned Fox Pool. As quick as they had appeared, they walked off, turning round once to fire the airgun at me, shouting abuse. I must admit this didn't go down too well, and they damaged my Focus. After that, I didn't return until 2013 when I started to write this chapter, some six or seven years later. It was such a shame because I did enjoy my few sessions fishing there…

Kingfisher

The Jewels of the Wensum Valley

For more than a while, it looked like my attempts to gain access to Kingfisher Lakes, or Kingy, would come to nothing. Shut on the outside, I had to sit back and watch as Norfolk's answer to Wellington Country Park produced a succession of forties to 47lb 12oz, along with loads of thirties. It seemed that some northern lads, who had a way of keeping things the way that they wanted, had blacklisted me. After a while, Kingy faded from my consciousness and I found myself down south, smashing the famous big-fish waters.

Kingy is situated deep in the heart of the Norfolk wilderness, just outside Lenwade, a place that I was to become pretty familiar with. Apart from the lake, Kingy is a lakeside social and bowls club, owned by Cyril Rogers. Several years passed and, out of the blue, I had a call from a colourful chap called Mike 'Spug' Redfern. Spug told me that he had been talking with his mate 'Hogg', who knew Cyril rather well and it transpired that there was a good chance that between them, they could get me in. I remember Spug telling me to keep it quiet and to keep my fingers crossed; I crossed everything!

The previous clique had long since moved on and Spug reckoned that there would be a good chance of success, so I prayed secretly to the carp gods once again. Six weeks passed before I got the call that I was praying for. A long-held dream was now within touching distance, my first Norfolk forty. I was told that I'd hear from Hogg in due course but not to breathe a word until that ticket was in my hand. I was so excited, which made it hard not to talk to my mates who already had tickets. I was out fishing when Jane phoned to tell me that my application form had landed on the doormat that morning. It looked as if it would finally happen after all… yes!

Still I didn't breathe a word, until finally, in May, the ticket arrived. As soon as I had it I phoned everyone up to get the grapevine pumping – Uncle Jim was coming to Kingy! Soon after, I phoned the office to see when I could take my first look around. They told me to hold off for a few days as they were hosting a big do. Mollusc and I headed over as soon as we could – I had the pedal pushed to the floor as the Focus ST170 melted across Norfolk. Mol showed me the best way to navigate across via the back roads and as we came into Lyng the red-hot brakes slowed us safely into the 30mph zone. I eased

The bridge that leads to Kingy's island, an area that I was to become rather familiar with over the coming sessions.

A moody weather front rolls in over the Wensum Valley.

the car along the potholed track that Mollusc had led us to, trying not to damage the suspension! I made sure to stick to the 5mph speed limit as we swung past the club, before passing the hotel where I got my first glimpse of water between the big willows that line the banks in that area.

As we walked towards the lake, Mol was pumping my head full of information. Crossing a bridge over a small ditch, he pointed towards a small hut, telling me that there were toilets and a shower in there, as well as a book that had to be used for signing in and out and recording captures. "Nice setup," I thought, but I was more interested in seeing the lake. Walking to the right, we soon came to the dam end. This had loads of open water out in front, with a large bay further round to the right. It all looked nice and I kept an eye out for showing fish as we walked. The back of the bay was lined with overhanging bushes that looked really carpy. Not only that, it looked like an area that wasn't seeing much pressure, which made it very much my sort of a spot, being easy to prime up on the quiet.

The next swim we encountered after leaving the bay was Two Trees, which looked like it was fished a lot. By analysing each swim as we passed through it, I was able to build up a picture of the favoured swims during what was the close season. We passed the Climbing Tree swim, then circumnavigated the Back Bay, before eventually coming within sight of a steel bridge that spanned a small channel, linking the big island to the mainland. From the very tip of this island, a swim called The Tins, the main body

Mollusc with a Kingy gem.

The Jib Bay was a one of the features that made Kingy so unique.

of Kingy opened up in front and I gazed right down to the dam end. God this lake was interesting and the fish had real freedom to rove its 25 acres. It turned out that the lake bed was every bit as interesting as the surface, as Mol filled me in on its egg-box nature.

We passed the Hide swim before crossing the bridge once more and turning left, towards a swim called Ringside, after a fight that had happened in there! Next, we entered a swim called The Willow. Mol reckoned that this was a good winter zone. There was a small island close by and I could see that the water shallowed up, running up to some big overhanging trees that guarded the island margins. These inviting overhangs were around 35 to 40 yards out from the next swim, The Jib. Looking out across the area, I got the feeling that I could nail the fish as they passed through. The most striking feature in this area was a metal jib that linked the island to the bank. "Yes, before you ask, they do go out there to bait up," Mol told me, "Just don't let Wally catch you." "Who the fcuk is Wally?" I retorted. Mol told me that he was the bailiff and explained that I'd know him because he looked like a weeble and because he was a dirty old bastard! Christ, my mind was whirring to conjure up an image of this character – it wasn't a pretty sight!

As we neared the hut to sign out, I bumped into an old friend, Paul Mallows aka Gismo le Claw, from my Weybred Pit days. We chatted for a while before hunger got the better of me and I offered to treat Mol to a McDonald's.

We spoke more about the inhabitants of the lake on the way home. Several of the big 'uns had died, including the 47lb Norfolk record mirror. That still left four or five forties swimming around though and the 47 miles that I'd have to travel seemed a lot less than the 150-180 that it took to get me down south. Plus, Jane could visit and we could have the occasional meal together in the bar – pukka! So, plans were made to start that year and I hoped that the Norfolk forty that I'd desired for so long would soon be coming my way.

I couldn't fish the first day because the existing members have a draw for swims and it sounded like it was rammed anyway. Instead, I stayed in contact with Mol, keeping tabs on when anglers were leaving. Mol actually had an awesome result himself that week, bagging several fish, topped off by Mega-Tail at 42lb, a new PB for him and the one I wanted most. This was good news; I now knew that Mega-Tail was still about.

I decided to make my Kingy debut on the third day of the season, once most of the members had departed. Not a lot had been out other than Mol's hit. I got up at 3am to make sure that I gave myself every chance of seeing where they were showing and get on those Norfolk scalybacks.

I made sure to pack plenty of floaters because the weather was settled and hot. I had been told that the fish didn't like floaters, but that seemed like a real opening for me; I'd teach 'em what a floater was! I had heard that Laney was down there, which was going to be interesting after his banning from Fen. I raced through the early morning mist

Wally the weeble!

across Norfolk, slowing a little for the country lanes, and finally dropping to 30mph as my headlights lit up the speed limit signs in Lyng. Swinging into the car park, my headlights revealed that only a handful of members remained, sweet. I gathered my senses, fired a quick text off to the missus to tell her that I'd arrived safely and loaded up the barrow. As I had to sign in, I decided to leave my barrow parked up by the hut and wander around until I found the fish.

I took a 4kg bag of bait with me, so I could use it to reserve the swim if I found the fish, plus it saved 4kg on the barrow trip.

Looking across the waking lake, I swigged a can of Red Bull and grabbed a sandwich that Jane had made for me. I don't know why it is, but you always seem to be hungrier if you're up and about early. It looked like it was going to be hot, and knowing that the fish hadn't spawned yet, I was sure that they wouldn't be far from shallow water. Location wise, I had a few ideas from what Mol had told me and what had unfolded over the previous few days. The lake was packed with bars and could be very weedy, which, coupled with the large number of bait-robbing swans on the water, could make life difficult. Mol had told me to fish the gullies during the night and the tops of the bars during the day. Everyone was asleep, so if or when I found the fish it would be just me, ready to pounce.

After completing the first lap, I decided to sit down on the wall by the bog to watch the big expanse of water that you can see from there. This gave me the chance to tuck

Sunset over a flat-calm Kingy. Moments like this make fishing all the more enjoyable.

The barrel hook baits, long braided links and bags of salmon fry crumb that I used to such good effect.

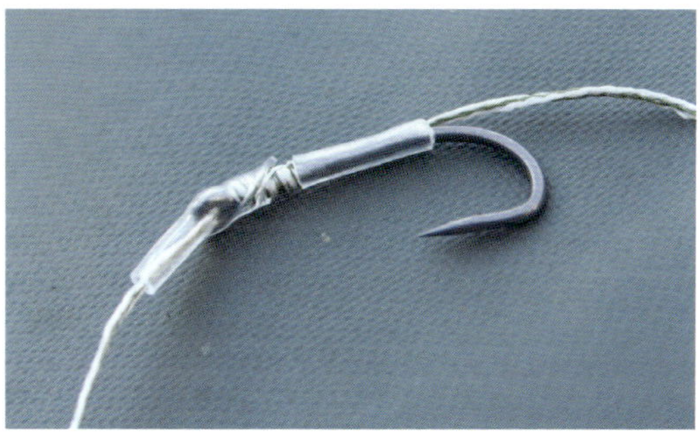

I was, and still am, a big advocate of longshank hooks for bottom-bait fishing.

into the sandwich that I'd been clutching all the way round. Mol had told me that the fish could be difficult to find at times, but it only takes a second to find them and the resolve not to give up is strong within me. As the day drew on, I still hadn't found any fish and I was beginning to think that they were lying low in preparation for their once-yearly leg-over. I know that I'd focus on that event if I were a carp!

After three laps I started to see some of the locals beginning to stir and wondered if I was going to get collared and have to exchange pleasantries. By the afternoon, I began to get a feeling for the Island. I could bait and fish loads of areas and keep an eye on them. Sometimes, you just have to use your gut instinct and watercraft, once mastered, is one of the biggest edges in fishing. I decided to set up in The Hide for my first night, which gave me loads of water to fish and watch. Mol had caught just 180 yards up to my left, so I knew that the fish had been in the rough area.

The channel between the bank and the island that I was on led down to the right,

My first from the lake was this 31lb 12oz mirror.

towards the bridge that I'd crossed. This seemed like the ideal ambush point. I quickly spotted a small bar running up to a plateau 20 yards out to my left. This looked like the sort of spot that the fish would visit once the sun was up to warm their bodies in the shallow water. I put a rod together so that I could have a feel around to see what was in front of me. I don't use a plumbing rod, preferring to use the rods that I actually fish with and use the most. You see, I'm used to the feel of these rods and I'm not concerned about how deep the water is as long as the carp are there – I just want to get the rods out as quickly as possible.

Pretty soon I managed to find a nice area at about fifty yards range. The lake bed was smooth and silty and felt clean, however, it was weedy just behind. I quickly clipped the line up and lined it up with a tree on the horizon. I planned to fish the gullies for the night, pulling two rods up onto the shallow area close in if the fish showed on top.

The rigs were simple running setups with a 14 to 16 inch 20lb braided hook link with a 2.5inch hair baited with a 20mm by 10mm barrel hook bait. To prevent tangles, I clipped on a large PVA mesh bag of crushed and crumbed baits, mixed with some salmon fry crumb. Once I'd cast to the area, I laid the rod down to allow the 20lb Bullet Braid to sink on its own. While the line was sinking, I baited the area with 15mm boilies and barrels. As usual, I spread the bait over a large area. I popped the rod onto the buzzer before quickly flicking the other two rods into the area because I was losing the light fast. Although it was early days, I felt strangely confident of action at some stage. I settled in, cooked a nice meal and downed a couple of alcohol-free beers before it was time to get some sleep. My sleep was broken as my middle rod screamed off; evidently something wasn't happy with the situation, flaming night-time bait robber!

The fish went on a mental run and shot all over the swim in its bid for freedom. After what seemed like an eternity I had him close in to the right of the swim; I really didn't want to lose my first fish from Kingy. After the fish ploughed up and down the margins I finally netted him. In my haste to get to the rod, I hadn't put my headtorch on, so I made the net safe and grabbed the torch. Upon flicking the headtorch on I couldn't believe what I was seeing; a long, dark-backed mirror that looked as if he'd go 30lb plus. I sorted the mat out and wetted a sack to house him for a few hours until dawn. Placing him reverently on the wet mat, the torchlight picked out an awesome creature with several big, apple-slice scales on his flanks. I weighed him at 31lb 12oz before slipping him into the sack and gently lowering him into the margin. My first fish and it's a thirty – happy days!

I got the rod back on the area before sticking the kettle on for a nice strong milky coffee. Cup in hand, I sat back to watch a new day unfold. As the glow emerged over the Eastern horizon, painting the sky with subtle pinks, purples and peach, I thought to myself, "This is what carp fishing is all about." I got a lad to come round to take the pictures as soon as it was light enough and as you can see, the fish was an awesome chestnut mirror. I phoned Jane to tell her the good news before positioning two rods on the shallow marks, as I could see that it was going to be a hot day and fish were

Pale in colour, with a lump on one flank, one that the poacher didn't get at just over 30lb.

Sunrise off the island; one of my favourite shots.

Base camp in the High Bank.

already starting to cruise around in the upper layers. The shallow water on top of the plateau was gin-clear, so I could see the fish as they ghosted over the spot. With the trusty glasses on, I could even see the contents of the dissolved bag on the gravel bed. It quickly became clear that I'd done the right thing by reacting quickly because more and more fish turned up in the area, loving the warm sun. I knew that they could see the baits that were dotted over the plateau, and watched as a big mirror upended over the bag then it righted itself sharply before bolting off, accompanied by my screaming buzzer – unreal! I picked the rod up and began to play the fish while the others continued to swim around it! As I coaxed him closer, I could see that he was pale in colour, with a lump on one flank. Soon he was mine and I'd banked another Kingy thirty at 30lb 4oz. Once we'd done the pictures, I looked out to find that most of the fish had legged it. "Don't worry boys," I thought, "I'll find you!"

Within thirty minutes the area was totally dead and most of the fish that I could see were hanging to the left of the swim. There was someone in The Tins swim, which fishes the water off the very end of the finger of land that I was set up on, so I cut across to The High Bank swim, and there they were, sunning themselves in the really shallow water. As I looked closer, I could see that some of the fish were ones that I'd seen in front of my swim just 30 minutes earlier.

I didn't need telling twice, I ran back to The Hide, grabbed the rods and scooted back to The High Bank, to confirm my ownership of the swim – I didn't want to lose it while packing up. Looking up, I could see that there were loads of fish in residence… "Christ, hurry up Uncle Jim!" I thought. My gear was packed and loaded onto the

I got the rods straight out…

… and was soon in action – there's a 39lb mirror on the end!

barrow in double-quick time. The new swim was a bit exposed, so I parked the barrow well back from the edge and used a bramble bush for cover as I set up. There must have been 35 fish about and I could feel a hit coming!

I put two rods together and got them ready, just as before. The mesh bags were already made so I simply had to check the rigs and slide fresh baits onto the hairs before clipping the bags on and firing them out. As I crept towards the front of the swim, I could see dozens of fish in a shallow, weedyish bay to my right. This area had to have a rod on it and I could just make out an area of sparser weed; probably where the fish had dug it up while feeding. I flicked the rig out the 25 yards to the spot and it landed smack on, first time, sweet. I laid the rod down to catapult a few carp sweeties out. When I picked the rod back up, I was pleased to see that the line had sunk nicely. I pulled the rod back a little further before putting it down again, I wanted the tip well back because the fish were coming in really close at times and I didn't want to

"What you caught mate?" Mol asked. "God knows, but he looks real big," I replied.

A stunning 18lb common.

spook them if I could help it.

The next rod went straight out, where it looked clear and a bit deeper. After carefully sinking the line, I set the clutch, laid that rod next to the other one and retreated. Literally, as I was setting the buzzers up I could hear a whizzing sound and thought, "Christ, that's a clutch!" The right-hand rod was off already! The rod was nearly dragged in by the force of the take. As I pulled into a fast-moving lump, a massive bow-wave exited the bay at a fair old rate. Thankfully, the braided main line cut through the weed so I was now in direct contact with the carp. The bow wave soon disappeared as the carp dropped into a gully and started heading towards me. I was worried that the fish might get around one of the islands and snags that sat on a certain shallow spot, so I must admit I played him a little harder than usual until I got him in close. The strategy worked; I managed to keep the fish under control and soon had him close, in shallow water. He looked big as he chugged around over the rod tip sending up big swirls that made oily patterns on the surface. I let some of the pressure off, as there was no need for it now and went to grab the net but found that the mesh was caught up in the brambles. Next thing, I saw the fish was on the top out of the corner of my eye, Christ, I was now in a pickle. I had to rip it from the grasp of the brambles. Thankfully, the mesh started to free itself, so I gave it the big yank, and it came free. I pushed the net out and scooped this lump of a mirror up.

I laid the rod down so I could get a better look at what was sitting in my net. He

Mol was summoned again to do the pictures.

looked close to forty but I was now on my own as Mol and Quicky had gone up to the clubhouse for a bite to eat and a pint. I wasn't drinking then so I declined the offer as I was on fish. I tried to call the lads but the signal was crap so I dropped them a text instead. I soon had word that they were on their way so I decided to remove the hook and wait until they arrived before getting him out. Ten minutes later I could hear voices as people approached. Mol walked in with Quicky in tow. "What you caught mate?" Mol asked. "God knows, but he looks real big," I replied. They grabbed the net for a look, but couldn't identify the fish, so my head was spinning as I thought that I might have caught a rare one.

It was hot, so I wanted to get the pictures done straight away, so before we got him out I covered the mat in cold water straight from the lake as the water on the mat heats up quickly on summer days. Up on the scales, he pulled the needle round to 39lb 8oz, happy days, Uncle's first big 'un from Kingy! As I peeled the sling back, both Quicky and Mol repeated that they didn't recognise the fish (which was later named 007). As Mol did the pictures, Quicky made sure lake water was poured over the fish to keep him cool and comfortable. I must admit that I wanted him back in the lake ASAP, so we snapped off a few quick water shots before letting him swim back into his watery home. As soon as he felt the embrace of the cool lake water, he shot from between my hands in a blast of power, sending up a huge cloud of silt and pushing a bow-wave some twenty yards out into the lake.

I was now buzzing as everything was rockin' nicely on the fishing front for Uncle Jim at Kingy, and more importantly, I'd had no real 'therapy' as of yet. Unfortunately, this looked set to change as Terry Hearn's 'spot poacher' moved in to my right in The Tins swim. I hoped his angling ethics, which are mentioned in Terry's book, didn't affect my fishing! I had to be on my guard and plan ahead now, as I had two spots rocking in The Hide and The High Bank swims, and I knew he would be aware of my captures and the take times. I knew that I would need to have my rods in The Hide well before he thought of 'sheeping' me up in the early morning as the fish passed through on their way to the weedy bay in my swim. My base camp in The High Bank swim was safe, so I could be elsewhere and be in position well before he might turn up, and I had a chance of a bite as they passed through on their way round.

As I sorted out the recast, I could see he was watching my every move. I must admit, he kept to his water, but I made my presence known. The fish were still in the area and I watched them moving, mostly in the weedy bay, but later that evening the fish activity increased, like they were on the move elsewhere for the night. As the carp began to pass in front of me, my middle rod started bouncing on the floor as one of those fish picked up the bait presented in slightly deeper water. The fish stripped ten yards of line off me before I managed to stop it; I didn't want him getting around one of the obstructions that littered this little swim. He rolled on the surface as the pressure took its toll, and I soon had him under my rod tip. Not long after, I lifted the net around a long, golden common that weighed 18lb 12oz. After photographing the fish, I decided to take him for a little walk and return him away from the other carp, as they were really close and I didn't want to risk spooking them further as they fed in the shallow water. I soon had a new rig back in position and quickly got back out of the way, behind a bush where I could watch what they were up to. All I had to do was keep an eye on the rods as they were still on the floor.

I love watching them at close quarters, going about their business and I guess that they must have completely captivated me because I suddenly heard a clutch screaming as another fish made a mistake. I was on it quickly and this fish kited left, heading towards an island at high speed. I clamped down hard to prevent him making the sanctuary of the island, which clearly worked, as I watched him kite away. Now however, he was heading quickly towards my left-hand margin, trying to get down the channel. I couldn't let him reach the end of the channel as it led around another island! I needn't have worried though, as he was now tired and mustering the last burst of power had taken its toll. I carefully drew him up the margin where I'd been watching them from behind the bush, and suddenly he was in front of me, looking like I could net him. I pushed the net out and scooped up a chunky mirror that looked a mid-twenty.

Four fish landed in just over 24 hours fishing, from two different swims, showed me that they were well and truly on the salty, 20mm, squid barrels. The salmon fry crumb mesh bags coupled with long, braided hook lengths and running leads were also doing the business, so there was no need to change anything, meaning that all I had to do was concentrate on finding them and baiting areas.

Mol was summoned once again to do the pictures and my guess was right as the chunky mirror weighed in at 24lb 12oz. Once again, I took him for a little walk to release him away from the fish, and as I set foot back in the swim, Mol gestured towards my left-hand rod, saying, "There's one on boy!" As I looked at the rod the line pulled tight and then fell slack, which immediately made me think, tench or bream. I calmly picked the rod up, commenting to Mol, "Its a wrong 'un on the end," but as I tightened up I felt a satisfying weight as this 'wrong 'un' suddenly turned into a carp! It must have been sitting there, trying to get rid of the rig it was pricked on.

When this tricky fellow felt the pressure from my Pursuit, he put in a surge of power, aiming for that left-hand island. As braid was stripped from the clutch I applied steady finger pressure on the spool to try and slow this bugger down. Such was his power that I couldn't dictate to him and as he made the island, I had no choice but to let the line fall slack. I wanted the fish to think that he was free and I intently watched the braid where it entered the water for signs of movement. It seemed that he'd stopped moving, so I reeled up the slack. As the braid tightened I could see that the line angle had changed and it was now well away from the island and kiting left. I applied as much pressure as I dared, as I wanted to get this carp nearer to me as soon as possible. As soon as I got him away from danger, I laid off the pressure and let him tire himself a rod length out. When it came, my first glimpse was of another mirror, except this one looked a little bit bigger than the last one. As I watched him slowly tire in the shallow

It had been a mental fight, but thanks to the carp gods I won that battle.

I needed to be in position at first light before the poacher got in the swim.

water, Mol handed me the net as he'd just put it back together for me; if he hadn't been around I would have been in a right two-and-eight sorting that out. I sunk the net and watched as his back broke the surface and he took a few gulps of air. I took the chance, pushed the net out and lifted… he was mine. It had been a mental fight, but thanks to the carp gods I won that battle. Just for the record, he weighed 27lb 12oz and was in perfect condition.

After that, I got the rod back out on the spot but noticed that they had done the off, probably heading for their night feeding zones. Mind you, I had just pulled four out in a few hours so they probably didn't like Uncle Jim's therapy! I was hoping that they would come back by late the next afternoon, so I decided to get the rods set up on buzzers for the night, and get my base camp set up well back from the rods; I wanted to keep the area quiet and keep myself hidden from view. Just before dark, I decided to pop over to The Hide to get some bait in, ready for their arrival. That way, I only had to cast my rigs back to the shallow area that produced the thirty that morning. I grabbed a bag of 20mm squids and a catapult, and walked to the back of the swim. As I turned the corner and looked out across the peninsula I saw a ghostly shape. Straining my eyes, I knew that it was the poacher, watching and making plans from what he'd seen. I watched him for five minutes before he headed back to his swim.

With the ghostly poacher ready to do his dirty deed, I changed my plans and decided to bait up in the early hours, under the cover of darkness, but now I also needed to be in position at first light before he got in there. So, just before I got my head down, I set my alarm for 1am. Soon, I was pulled from my deep sleep as the alarm was singing its song. I quickly reset the alarm and headed out into the misty, spooky darkness to pre-bait The Hide for the morning's stalking manoeuvres. With that done, I slipped back into the bag and slipped into a fitful sleep. It seemed like seconds before that flaming alarm was ringing in my head again. I leaned over and turned it off, then popped the kettle on. I sat on the edge of the bedchair, drinking a nice warm cup of coffee as the sun started to creep above the trees. Soon, the sun started burn through it and a scene of beauty took shape in front of me. I quickly grabbed the camera and took some pictures so I could save this moment forever.

Snapping back to reality, I gathered my stalking bits, reeled the rods in and made my way to The Hide to see if the poacher had sheeped me up yet. I looked across to the swim and was pleased to see that it was free. I instinctively quickened my step through the fading mist, worried that I could still miss out. As soon as I entered the swim I got straight to work. I had rigs ready to go in a re-sealable bag, so all I had to do was to cut off the old ones and tie them on. I soon had three rods rockin' on the zone, no more than fifteen yards out over that shallow hump.

I relaxed behind the hide, waiting for events to unfold. Not long after, I heard someone approach and as I popped my head round the corner, there was the poacher, rods in one hand and bits in the other! As soon as he saw me he turned round and headed back; I just laughed and thought, "You'll have to do better than that if you are going to sheep Uncle Jim!" As the morning progressed nothing was seen, maybe I was asking too much? It seemed that way because nothing happened, but before I left the swim I put a few kilo of squids in. Back in The High Bank I dropped my rigs on the spots I caught from the day before as I had a few hours left before I had to pack up. I saw the odd fish, but nothing occurred and before I left I filled the swim in with a few kilos for them to feast on.

As you can imagine, I was gagging to get back after taking a six-fish hit on my first visit! Luckily, I didn't have to wait long and as I drove into the entrance to the clubhouse, I wondered who would be about. Pulling up in the car park, I was pleased to see that there were only two cars there; time to go and check where the two anglers were. I did fancy getting back into the area where I caught the previous week, so I walked to the right so I could have a look and see if anyone was fishing off The Tins. I couldn't see anyone and just to the right of where I was standing an angler was plotted up in the Car Park swim. With one more to find, I decided to load the barrow and get it up to the bridge. On my way I found the second angler plotted up in The Willows. I stopped for a quick chat and he informed me that they had been showing off The Tins area and told me that he was packing up soon. So, I knew where I wanted to be and while I was standing in The Willows I saw a fish push out close in off the end of the island. Seeing that show, I was now in full 'mission' mode and I bade him farewell before pushing my barrow towards the bridge so I could get over onto the island. Once I got across I had to push my barrow along this peaty track, certain parts of which were boggy, so you can imagine what it would be like after it had rained. I dodged the potholes along this spongy track and after a few minutes I parked my barrow in The Tins on the end

of the island.
I stood and watched the area where I saw the fish show from The Willows when, suddenly, straight out in front of me, around forty to fifty yards out a carp pushed his head out. I didn't need to see any more, so I was now in machine mode and got straight to work, with location sorted all that was needed was to spread the rods across the area that fish had shown in, as they normally go around in some sort of group.
I had baited rigs ready to go, sitting in a bucket of salmon fry crumb so everything stayed dry, so it was on with the new rigs and out they go. The first rod was going to be cast to where I saw the carp show and luckily, the humid wind was blowing over my head, making it easier to chuck out the big bags. I whacked the rig out and it landed in the general area I wanted, and as I sunk the braid a nice flat spot appeared as the mesh bag of salmon fry crumb melted. I could imagine some of these tiny pellets rising up in the water and dropping back down. It's a great method for drawing attention to the area of your hook bait and the tiny, oily pellets keep them digging around for ages.
I laid the rod on the deck, slackened off the clutch and then went to work on another rod. As I was attaching a new rig a tortured squeal from the clutch grabbed my attention. I legged it over to the rod and pulled into another bait robber. The fish tore off on a 25-yard run, travelling straight out over the deep water, so there was no chance of this carp getting behind one of the many brick-wall bars in certain areas of the lake. The nearest bars were well to my left and this fish was kiting well right now, so all I had to do was to keep steady pressure on him. I suddenly became aware of someone standing in the swim and as I looked round, there stood Wally, wobbling around, spitting dribble, with half of his dinner splattered down his dirty old jumper, spouting "Shelley boy," as I tried to play the fish. Cyril Rodgers, the owner, had made him walk the lake once a day for exercise from the clubhouse to the bridge, but he never crossed onto the island. As you can imagine, I was concerned as to whether he could make it back, so the therapy started, "For fcuks sake," I said, "Looks like I'll have to barrow you back as you're well out of your comfort zone! Plus, you're banned from going past the bridge!" He then shouted something incomprehensible at me in the local 'yokel' dialect while I was trying to play this carp. I just switched off to all his drivel and carried on playing the fish. After a few minutes I caught a glimpse of a chunky mirror in the clear water, twisting and turning, trying to free himself. Next, I raised him and saw a massive mouth break surface, gulping air. I didn't need asking twice, and netted the fat mirror. Now, I was worried about Wally offering to do the pictures, in fact, there was no way he was taking them! Thankfully, Mollusc walked into my swim while I was sorting things out and he and Wally started ripping into each other. Mol's heartless when he gets into full swing, dishing out the therapy, but at least that kept Wally off me and more importantly, I now had someone who could take a decent picture.
I called Mol over to have a look to see if he recognised him, and soon as he saw it he said, "That's The Prehistoric," and went on to tell me that it was a rare visitor to the bank. I unhooked him in the net and while I was getting everything ready I could still hear the other two at it! It was hilarious to hear these two wrong 'uns ripping into each

As soon as Mol saw the fish, he said, "That's The Prehistoric!" a rare visitor to the bank as it turned out.

other. When I was ready I said, "Come on you two, let's sort this fish out." Wally walked off muttering something I best not repeat, and as Mol walked over I shouted, "Keep the fcuk off the island!" I was glad that he had gone and I never saw him on the island again! This fish was a very old-looking warrior, hence his name, with a very dark back and a pale belly with a few big scales in the middle of his flank. His mouth was massive and I pointed it out, "Look at this Mol, I bet that's why he doesn't come out much; a prehistoric rig specialist!" Mol just laughed and commented in his own inimitable, eloquent style, "BOY!" We carefully weighed The Prehistoric in at 34lb 12oz, another chunk for Uncle Jim! As I had a little cuddle with the carp, Mol took a few pictures for me and, for some reason, they were loads of uprights and I didn't notice. God knows what was going on in his head doing that, oh well that's another story! He kicked out of my hands, sending out a bow-wave as he powered off with his back out of the water. I pointed it out to Mol saying, "Christ Mol, he was in a rush to get back." He just muttered, "Yeah boy".

Later that evening, after setting up my house, I was sitting back and watching several fish pushing their heads out in front of my swim. I was well confident of another take at some point. All this watching carp had made me hungry so it was time to cook myself a rib-eye steak with mushrooms, tomatoes and onion to stop the hunger pains. I saved cooking the steak until the other stuff was ready, which I tipped out on to a plate so I could cook the steak as I like it cooked rare. I wanted it nice and bloody, so it only needed two minutes, maximum. As I popped the pan back onto the flame, my middle rod let out its battle cry! I pulled the pan off and legged it over to the rod as line was being ripped off the clutch at a fair old rate.

The rod took on its battle curve as I lifted into the fish and all I could do was let the clutch do its job, then try to slow it down with finger pressure on the spool. It took fifty yards on that first dash and was now kiting towards the area where the bars started in this part of the lake. This was not good; if I let it get behind one of these then I could be cut off. I decided to clamp down to try and get this fish into the upper layers. This seemed to work as an angry swirl appeared on the top. I kept the pressure on and he kited well left, diving into the weedy bay where I'd banked the 007 fish. It was very shallow in there, with a lot of weed, so I climbed the high bank beside the swim to get a better angle. As I stood there playing this carp Mol appeared opposite, in The High Bank swim. I shouted, "BOY!" but he disappeared from view and I just carried on with the job in hand as I finally had the carp under control. It had picked up some weed so I was just reeling in a dead weight. Bang on time, Mol appeared, giving it large that I was taking the piss. "Oi oi, get the net and net that fish, boy!" I told him, which he did, and in fine style too, wading out and engulfing it, weed and all, on his first attempt. He then started ripping the weed out and then shouted, "Boy, you have a nice common!" "Sweet," I thought, shouting back, "How big boy?" When the reply came back, "Mid-thirty boy!" I thought that he was on the windup. Either way, I was gagging to see the beast.

Mol waded around to the front of the swim, where he popped the hook out and handed me the rig. I had a look in the net and exclaimed, "Bloody hell boy, that's a corker; definitely a mid-thirty." Mol broke the net down, rolled it up then handed it to me. I placed him on the mat, pointing Mol in the direction of the camera, which was on the bed. I was like a kid in a sweet shop as I unfolded the mesh and my gaze was met by the most beautiful, black common. Mol told me that I'd caught one of the really tough ones; "That's the Black Common boy, it's been over two years since he was last banked!" I seem to have a knack of catching the hard ones; I've even been known to bank some of them twice. This common was simply stunning in every way; one of Kingy's finest. For the record he weighed 35lb 12oz. After the common, I just seemed to lose them and couldn't find them again. They must have been running scared and keeping their heads down so, the following day, I retreated back home for some more brownie points.

After a few days sitting at home, the weather forecast indicated that some adverse conditions were to roll in the next day on southerly winds. I felt that this was likely to stir things up a little, so I planned an early start for the next morning to try to get on the scalybacks again, before the wind and rain hit.

When I set off the sky was full of low cloud and things were looking really moody. Not long into the 45-mile journey it started to spit with rain and as I turned off the A47 and then cut across country to the lake, I noticed the trees were blowing all over the

The Black Common, simply breathtaking.

place. As I drove through the village and down the short lane to the lake I was already interested in the dam wall area as this is where this fresh new wind would be pumping into. I honestly thought that, in light of the conditions, there would be several anglers already there but as I neared the car park I could see that it was empty. I later found out that Kingy normally ends up like a ghost lake in the summer, as people hate the weed. Okay, there was weed, but it wasn't that bad yet. After I had parked the car, I trotted off to see if they were showing on the wind.

As soon as I sat down on the dam wall I began to see fish showing round an old staging at around eighty yards range. Bang on them again. The skies started to darken as the storm started to build before it rolled down and through the Wensum Valley. Thankfully, it was only a short trip with the barrow and, as per usual, I had several rigs pre-tied with mesh bags clipped on ready. It was off with the old and on with the new and within twenty minutes I had three rods out on the spots. I had cast two rods onto shallow water and one into slightly deeper water to the left. With the rods out, I needed to get the brolly up quickly as black clouds loomed on the horizon and the wind had increased in strength, indicating that it was going to chuck it down imminently. As I was pushing the bed under the brolly, one of my buzzers burst into life as another carp made its mistake. Before I picked the rod up I grabbed my rolled-up sleeping bag and chucked it under the brolly as it looked like the heavens were going to open shortly.

The bite had come to the rod in the deeper water and the fish ran to the left, where I knew he was safe in the deep water. The fish soon surrendered ground and kited in closer before just coming in, along some reeds. All the way through the fight I was thinking that it was unreal here, as I was catching every trip and quickly too. This increased my confidence and also indicated that the rig and bait were spot on. As soon as they saw it they were on it, so all I had to do was to keep putting myself on the fish, which was second nature to me. It might have looked like I was making Kingy look like a runs water, but fishing like that is very hard work! I had the fish ready for the net when I heard something behind me and turned around, hoping it wasn't Wally the Weeble! Thank God, it was just one of the old boys that worked on site. I nodded a greeting then turned around to slide the net under another one. The old boy then approached me and said in a deep, Norfolk voice, "You got one then." He then said "You're that carp catcher called Jim," I laughed and said, "Some say that, amongst other things." I thrust my hand out and he said "I'm Mick Moor." The name rang a bell and I asked, "You're the gamekeeper that works for Cyril then?" "Yes Jim," he replied, and from that very day until this one, we have remained good friends and he's one of the nicest blokes you could ever wish to meet; sound as a pound with a heart of gold.

I asked him whether he'd be happy to take some pictures for me but he was unsure. "Don't worry Mick," I said, "I'll show you how to use the camera." We weighed the grey mirror, which turned out to be another thirty at 30lb 3oz, and Mick did a great job with the pictures, cheers mate! I slipped him back just before the monsoon swept in and with rumblings of thunder off in the distance, Mick wished me good luck as he legged it before the heavens opened. The skies soon darkened further and the wind started to swirl about as the eye of the storm approached. Five minutes later it started to lash it down and I was hanging on to the brolly for dear life.

The fish had stopped showing, but I think this time it was down to the adverse conditions, rather than me trawling them out! Huge winds, combined with massive downpours, continued to batter the lake for the next few hours. Thankfully I didn't get a take while this was all going on because, trust me, I didn't fancy playing a fish in that. Finally, things started to brighten up and with a rainbow setting the scene the fish started to show again, but this time well over in front of The Tins swim. It was time to pack up and get my gear round there while it was still dry. I was in The Tins within thirty minutes and I soon had three rods cast out at various ranges between thirty and seventy yards, roughly where I had seen fish showing from opposite. It was still moody, so I needed to get the house up quickly and I had got away with the move without getting soaked, apart from my trainers, which were saturated after I walked the gear round through the wet grass. Over the next few hours I had mirrors of 21lb, 23lb 12oz and 24lb 12oz, all of which were males. I was soaked through to the skin and tried to keep and get myself warm and dry by zipping the door down and leaving the cooker on full bore. As the takes kept coming, I just kept on with the job in hand; tying new rigs, but the hardest thing was to keep a fresh supply of mesh bags as I couldn't make these until my hands were dry. Thankfully, someone had turned up and

A distinctive, grey mirror that nudged into the thirties.

Cookie; I hope I'm still at it at his age!

was fishing next door and he very kindly did the pictures for me in the short breaks in the rain. Mind you, I had photographed an unusual 21lb mirror on the mat before he turned up. It had strange red spots on it! It seemed that a few other anglers had noticed the weather conditions and decided to fish, but they turned up as the weather started to calm down.

I could see bivvies in the Car Park, Willows and Ringside swims. The rain finally eased right off but it was still awesome fishing conditions. I hadn't seen anything show for a couple of hours, since the last fish, and wondered if they were still in the area. Later that evening, as I scanned the water for signs, they started showing off a swim called Two Trees. This would be a mental walk, even for me, as I was wet, cold and mentally drained, but I dug deep for this last push as I was off in the morning. I even decided to go the long way round so I could get some dry clothes, a waterproof coat and two spare gas canisters. As I made way round to Two Trees, I could see them sticking their heads out, which made me push the barrow faster as I was now on a mission. When I entered the swim it started to rain, and as I looked out I could see fish all over this very shallow area. This time, I had to get my house up first as it started to rain and there was no way I wanted a wet sleeping bag as I needed that to keep me warm. After that job was done, it was time to get the rods out quickly as it had now stopped raining. Everything was done at speed because I wanted to get into the dry and didn't fancy getting soaked

Huge winds, combined with massive downpours continued to batter the lake for the next few hours.

through again! Once I was done, the door was zipped down and I fired the cooker up in an attempt to get everything dry and, more importantly, get me warm.

The odd fish was seen, but things had definitely quietened down and the conditions were worsening by the minute with driving rain and lightning, which was making it really scary. I was shitting myself thinking about what could happen if I got a take with all of this going on above me. The storm raged on for most of the night and the winds increased, battering the bivvy. It was hard to sleep but sometime in the early hours I fell asleep and, the next thing I knew, one of my buzzers was screaming at me. I must admit it was hard for me to get up, as I was totally knackered due to lack of sleep. I planned to play the fish in my pants to save my clothes getting wet, so I unzipped the door to see the left-hand rod, still screaming at me, through the rain. I legged it out in my pants and the cold rain on my body took my breath away! There I was, out there, disco dancing while playing a carp in the pissing rain, with thunder and lightning all around me! Mercifully, the fish didn't do much after its first run and I soon had it in the net.

While sorting the weighing kit, I heard a noise and popped my head out of the door. There stood someone I hadn't seen for ages, a fella called Cookie. I got out (before you gasp, I had put some clothes on by now) and greeted him, "Oi oi mate, how the hell are you? Been a few years..." As we were talking, my net moved and he noticed that I'd got one in there. Cookie agreed to do pictures for me but he was another old codger I had to show how to use the camera! I later found out that several pensioners fished Kingy, the oldest being Old Man Sparky and he still pushed his barrow round; I did hope that I would be able to do that at his age. Anyway, the fish was unreal, with a dark back and a very pale, glossy complexion underneath with little red dots towards his back end. He pulled the needle round to a thumping 35lb; another Kingy jewel was mine. Because of this thick, glossy sheen I only got a couple of pictures that came out pukka. He went back to fight another day and my quest continued for that elusive Norfolk forty. Encouragingly, Mega-Tail still had not been banked that season. Later that morning the sun came out and the fish had done the off. After a good look around the area, nothing was spotted apart from a very friendly pheasant that had a taste for boilies! I was to bump into him loads; I even thought he was on the lookout for me, as most trips he came over for lunch and in the end he was even taking food from my hand. It was time to leg it home as I had caught my quota again that trip. I was enjoying it on Kingy; everything was spot on and my mobile approach was paying off big time, as these fish seemed to get about the pond a lot. I was starting to think that it would only be a matter of time before I bumped into Mega-Tail, and hopefully he would be the Norfolk forty that I desired.

Over the next few weeks a savage heatwave saw me doing a lot of floater fishing.

The pick of the burst of smaller males that I took after the rain.

The little linear heads home, powering out of my arms.

Kingy was another of these venues where they apparently didn't like floaters! I ended up teaching them a lesson and the other anglers followed like sheep. The problem however, wasn't the sheep; it was the swans! There were well over fifty on the lake and in the end they would follow me around, which meant that I had to carry forty to sixty kilos of floaters per trip as I had to feed them off somewhere else, well away from where I found the fish on top. This meant that I adopted a mobile, day-only approach with the floater fishing as it seemed a waste of time fishing on the bottom with the carp spending so much time on the top. I found an old, unused barrow in the car park, which I adopted as my floater wagon. I don't want to dwell too much on the floater captures, as a lot of them were run-of-mill twenties. I battered Kingy on the floaters but lost a lot due to cut-offs on the bars, so in the end I used 15lb Big Game hook lengths in those areas of the lake, and stuck to 12lb Double Strength in the deeper parts of the lake. When I found them on the top they were often at range and it just happened that Nash had brought out a new controller called the Bolt Machine around this time. This four-ounce missile allowed me to put a tangle-free setup well over hundred yards, which was very often extremely necessary. One of these occasions was a very misty, humid morning in midsummer. I stood in the Car Park swim, watching for signs as I waited for the mist to clear. I began to see movements way out in the centre of the lake but I wasn't sure if it was one of the big shoals of roach just flicking their dorsals on the surface over hundred yards out. I decided to get the spod out and get some mixers

out near this disturbance to see what occurred. As the spod touched down there was a movement. I wasn't sure what it was but as I started to retrieve the spod, I saw a back pushing; it was now quite clear carp, not roach, were responsible for the subtle signs.
I carried on retrieving the spod until it was halfway back, dropped the spod rod and grabbed the rod sleeve that held the floater rod. Luckily, the rig was still good and I put the rod together with shaking hands. By this time, the carp were going mental on the oily, greyhound pellets that I was using, and I really needed a bait out there! I watched as the controller landed just behind the activity, allowing me to tweak gently into the feeding activity. I laid the rod down and set the clutch, before starting to reel in the spod; I certainly didn't want that braid floating around if I hooked one. As I started to reel it in I caught the line shooting tight out of the corner of my eye. The spools started to scream, but I had to get the braid in before I could play the carp. Before I eventually picked the rod up, the carp had stripped more than thirty yards off the reel. As soon as this fish felt tension it kited left, but I couldn't allow it to go too far left on a long line, as there were some bars and another wooden structure sitting out there. I piled on as much pressure as I dared with 12lb Double Strength, thinking that at least I had a lot of stretch in the line as there was now well over 100 yards of it out there. Suddenly, I began to gain a lot of line as the fish turned and started to run towards me at a fair old rate. It was hard for me to keep up with this beast but that didn't really matter as he was now well away from those dangers, thank the carp gods, in the deep bowl. I laid off because I didn't want to over-pressure a bad hook hold, especially as I was now thinking that this could be one of the few big 'uns that I still needed.
Cookie appeared next to me and I just remained silent – he knew something special was just about to happen. I realised that my net was not set up and asked Cookie if he could do it for me. He put it together and laid it down next to me and left me to it. I got a glimpse of pink and white edging to a huge tail. My mind went into overdrive; there was only handful of fish that had that sort of marking and this fish was clearly big, so that left one fish on the list. I didn't say anything to Cookie as this fish scrapped very hard under the rod tip and it was another four or five minutes before he came up. When he did, a great, dark back broke the surface and then I knew one hundred per cent that it was the fish I had desperately desired after being blocked from having a ticket for so many years.

The friendly pheasant that had a taste for boilies!

One that I really wanted to meet, weighing a thumping 35lb.

Mega-Tail was soon on the surface and in a split second I had pushed the net under this old character. As I looked into the net, time seemed to draw out; he was finally mine. Cookie brought me back into the present saying, "Well done mate!" Years ago Mega-Tail's distinctive tail was mint, but something had happened to it more recently. It was well healed now though, and apart from that he was in fine fettle, sporting a very dark complexion. He was very similar to Mallin's from Wraysbury. I was totally blown away by the whole thing. The one I wanted so much was now mine, mainly thanks to Cyril Rodgers for being so noble and letting me fish this most awesome Norfolk venue. He later drove round in his Range Rover Vogue and we shook hands through the open window. For now though, Cookie was in charge of the camera and he was shitting himself as he knew how much this fish meant to me! First, we weighed the old fish at 39lb 6oz, a little down, but I didn't care as I'd just caught one of Norfolk's finest. After I slipped him back, I carried on feeding the floaters, but the swans and seagulls moved in and after a few hours I left and headed back home to celebrate by taking Jane out for a meal.

The heatwave carried on and the weed grew with it, almost taking over the whole lake. This meant that the fish were mainly hiding in the thickest weed beds, so floater fishing wasn't worth trying. Instead, I flitted around on other waters for the rest of the summer, but I planned to return for the autumn and resume my quest for a Norfolk forty. While I was away I kept in touch with Cookie and Mick the gamekeeper.

Simply... awesome!

The mighty Mega-Tail was very similar to Mallin's from Wraysbury. I was totally blown away by the whole thing.

The one I wanted so much was now mine, mainly thanks to Cyril Rodgers.

The nightmare scenario when you're floater fishing!

My first session back was a very windy affair and on the second day I found them showing over the bars out in the middle, to the right of The Front area again. They seemed to like this zone a lot and there were several swims you could hit this area from, The Front, The Car Park and The Dam Wall. I preferred fishing it from The Front but that was a mental walk and once over the bridge, the peat-bog path was worse than ever; you had to unload some of the gear and walk half of it to the swim! This meant that I would only fish the area from The Front if I had a few days fishing, I'd fish it from the Car Park or Dam Wall on shorter sessions. Before I packed up, I spodded a lot of boilies onto the area that the fish showed, which took me over an hour to complete. The only person around was Cookie, and he was doing his own thing in the Willows swim, which was another good area that they used a lot. Before I reeled the rods in, I clipped

Mick the gamekeeper, one of the good guys.

them up ready for next time because I was intending to get back into the swim again. I then made my way back to the car, stopping at Cookie's to rest and see how he was doing, as well as to ask him not to say anything about me filling the middle in!
I didn't hang around as I didn't want people to know that I was back, so I didn't sign in or out as I wanted to keep a low profile. That was the reason I'd packed up early on the Friday morning; if any weekend anglers turned up I would already be gone. All weekend I was worried about anyone getting on the zone, but Cookie kept me informed and eased my mind. Only one angler turned up and he fished The Car Park. Cookie told me that he was fishing straight along the island, well off my area. This was all good news, as they would surely have feasted in peace on the food that I had put out. My plan was to turn up at midday when, hopefully, The Front would be free. As you can imagine, I was gagging to get back onto the baited zone and was pleased to find that I had the lake to myself when I turned up. I got straight to work and loaded the barrow for the long march to The Front. I decided to set the house up first as it was windy and spitting with rain and I didn't fancy my gear getting wet. The rigs were the same apart from two aspects. Because I'd be fishing at over 100 yards, I was using smaller bags and I had upped the lead size. I knew that it was going to be a cold night as the weather forecast had predicted that the wind and rain would clear, leaving clear skies for the night, with a chance of the first frost of the year. However, by mid morning the next day more wind and rain was forecast. Knowing all this, and knowing

Looking towards the spot that was about to produce a very special fish indeed.

Not C-Scale was my first Norfolk forty, finally!

Cookie read the scales, stuttering, "40lb 4oz, Jim."

that I had located the carp and had baited up, I felt very confident of action over the next three days.
All three rods were positioned and baited lightly. They were spread along the bottom of a brick wall in a very smooth, silty gully. There was a 10ft smooth pull before it locked up at the bottom of the bar. Weed growing on the top of this bar would help protect the line if I was luckily enough to hook one up too.
I sat on my bedchair and watched the water for any signs. I saw nothing, but I expected that after all the disturbance. I wasn't worried though, because the rods were staying in position until I left. It was soon time to cook dinner before lying back on my bed to watch a film on my DVD player. By 9pm I was knackered and turned the DVD player off. I popped out for a leak and noticed that the skies had cleared; it was time to get into the bag for an early night.
Several bleeps roused me from my slumber. It was dark in the bivvy and I thought it was still night as I didn't feel like I'd been asleep for long. Another bleep had me climbing out of the bed to investigate. As I unzipped the door I was staggered to see that it was daylight! Looking over to the rods, I could see that my right-hand bobbin had pulled up tight. As I ran over towards it, I could see the line slowly tightening. Upon picking up the rod, I thought it might be one of the few bream in the lake. All of a sudden though, the rod slammed down… this was no bream! Everything went solid so I started to apply pressure to try and tease this carp from its weedy sanctuary. As the pressure increased, I started to feel a horrible grating sensation transmitting back up the braid. Inch by inch, I started to gain some braid back. I knew that if this kept happening, I would need to use the boat. Mind you, it was round the other side of the lake anyway.
I looked up at the fully compressed rod, and out into the lake just in time to see a flat spot appear around the top of the bar as a massive weed bed surfaced. I kept the pressure on but felt no movement. As this gargantuan weed bed approached I thought that I could see movement in the weed. Something was still there and as the weed bed got close it became clear that there was no way that I could get it all in the net. I steered it into the margin and started ripping some of the weed away. The carp, which had been motionless until this point, started to move when I'd ripped half of the weed away. I plunged the net under what was left and scooped the whole lot in one go. The water in the net exploded, indicating that it wasn't a pastie!
I couldn't really see how big it was, so I started to lift the weed away to see what I had landed. As I pulled more and more away this carp just kept on getting bigger and bigger, until suddenly there it was. It looked massive, could it be my first Norfolk forty? Cookie was soon in the swim and he had a look, as I didn't recognise it. He said, "That's Not C-Scale, the one I had two weeks ago at 38lb 12oz." I unhooked him in the net and commented to Cookie about how fat it looked. I laughed and said, "He's been feasting on all that bait I had put in," and as if to confirm it, he was venting red Scopex Squid all over the mat.
Cookie read the scales, stuttering, "40lb 4oz, Jim." "You what mate?" I replied,

incredulous. I turned them round for a look myself and confirmed that Cookie's eyes weren't deceiving him! As you can imagine, I was buzzing as finally, there lay my first Norfolk forty, a dream come true. Once again, Cookie did the honours for me, so thanks very much for your help, mate.

I packed up the next day as nothing else happened and didn't return until the last two days of the season, when I landed one of the two most beautiful carp that inhabit the lake, one which weighed 27lb 4oz, and his sister which I caught earlier in the season and weighed 27lb. He was covered in tiny, pearly scales and came from The Car Park swim. The following season Cyril very kindly gave Jane and I a free ticket to fish Kingy, but I had moved on. We did have the odd trip during the kid's holidays; Jane loved it down there as it was nice and quiet and she liked visiting the clubhouse for a meal and a beer. Later that year the carp were to be safe for six weeks, as we got married in Mauritius and spent fifteen days in paradise. It was funny really, because I was halfway round the world and as I came off a charter boat, I noticed two blokes pointing at me. I turned to Jane and said, "I can't even go halfway round the world without being noticed!"

This geezer later came up to me in the gents, and asked me if I would take him fishing! I told him that it was funny he'd asked, as I'd just set up a tuition business and the adverts were hitting the magazines when I got back. We decided that we'd probably

I was lucky enough to capture two of the most beautiful carp that the lake held, in the shape of this starburst mirror…

...and his sister, both of which were 27lb plus.

I'd look back on my time in the Wensum Valley with real contentment – it was a stunning lake, with fish to match.

I was delighted to sign off with this distinctive mirror, unsurprisingly called The White Tipped Mirror.

spent too long together in the gent's toilets, so he shook my hand and introduced himself as Mark Lemmon. When we got home Mark rang me, booked up a trip and we are still good friends to this very day. Mind you, I still like to give him some therapy on the toilet thing! After six weeks with no carp fishing, I was gagging to get out, so I decided to have a trip to Kingy for an overnighter. Well, that night I had the good fortune of landing 007 again, spawned out at 37lb and, before packing up I banked another, The White-Tipped Mirror at 32lb 12oz.

In closing this chapter, I would like to thank Mr Cyril Rodgers for letting me fish his water. On a sadder note, while my darling wife was recovering from a major operation in hospital, I heard Cyril was in there himself, so I went and visited him on several occasions while Jane was getting well. After several weeks of illness, Mick the gamekeeper rang me with the sad news that Cyril had passed away. RIP mate.

I owe this man a lot, cheers Cyril. RIP.

A fitting tribute to the lake's great benefactor.

Lenwade

Searching for Norfolk's biggest

The grapevine was humming with talk of a big Norfolk carp that I hadn't even heard about, let alone caught. Now, big thirties and forties are very thin on the ground in the Norfolk area and I was hearing about a venue called The Charities, in the village of Lenwade. Over the years I'd come to know that it had a low-thirty mirror in it but all of a sudden I heard this fish had been out at just over forty. As I had been fishing Kingy, which was just down the road, this venue grabbed my attention. I asked several mates of its whereabouts and how to obtain a ticket. Well on its case, I was soon pointed in the right direction and had the ticket.

There were three lakes on the ticket, The Main Lake, The Tench Lake and The Long Lake. All contained carp but not a lot was known about the Tench and Long Lake residents. They weren't fished for a great deal by carp anglers but the odd capture of fish to low thirties on tench gear had been recorded. This meant that I had three lakes to play with on the same ticket, plus, that January I had purchased a ticket for another water on the opposite side of the same village called Bolton's. I had poached this water the year before on the way back from Fen after catching Big Scale. I had decided to pop in for a look after mates told me of its whereabouts. No-one was fishing it back then because it was up for sale. I just wanted to have a look and as I walked onto the venue, I was hit square between the eyes by one of the most beautiful lakes I had ever seen. It was set in a very old wood and its surface was studded with lily pads. I found a group of fish milling about in the lilies right where I'd walked up to the lake. I knew someone kept an eye on the place but I just had to have a go for one of the jewels that I had heard lived in this secret lake. It was in fact very hard to obtain a ticket unless you were very lucky indeed as it too held fish to forty pounds. During a two-hour period I hooked two carp but only landed one, which was a 34lb leathery mirror and as I popped back to the van for the tripod and camera to do self-takes I bumped into a postman sitting in his van next to mine having a tea break. I thought, "Fcuk it", and asked him if he would kindly do me some pictures. After that I thought it was best to get out of there, as I didn't want a cross against my name if tickets became available. I didn't visit it again until I knew the score with tickets, as several rumours were flying

Bolton's was set in a very old wood and its surface was studded with lily pads.

During a two-hour period I hooked two carp and landed one, this 34lb leathery mirror.

about. Not long after, a bloke called Mo purchased it and Uncle Jim got a ticket, which started on January 1st. This meant I now had four lakes to play with in Lenwade!

When Mo took over the lake, he started work on it, and mates informed me that it now looked like a bomb had hit it. I was fishing hard over at The Charities for the big one and I hadn't been over Bolton's for a while so I decided to have a look for myself. As I drove through the entrance I was gobsmacked at what I was looking at because it looked like the place had been raped, big time. I got out of the car shaking my head; the magic had gone and all I had to remember my first impression by was a picture I had taken on my phone. I didn't return until the following January after I renewed my ticket in the hope that the lake would regain some of its former beauty.

Anyway, back to The Charities, or Lenwade as I called it. On my first trip I pulled into the lane and drove down the long, potholed track that lead into the woods. Once through the gate I pulled into the car park, where I met some friends of mine, Caz and Dave, who had offered to give me a guided tour of the lakes. We walked straight into the main car park swim so I could have my first look at the lake. As I looked out I could see an army of caravans, motorhomes and bivvies on the opposite side. Seeing my surprise, Caz informed me that they were basically the old, regular campers that fished the same old swims. They told me that there was a bay just round to the left with a great viewing spot where we'd stand a good chance of seeing some. Suddenly,

Stunning, but not for long!

The fish presented me with a chance to get the floater kit out on my first visit.

I saw some movement on the surface to my left, just out from the out-of-bounds safe area. My eyes fixated on the zone as several more bobbed up in between the odd bits of weed on the surface. I wasn't quite expecting to walk straight onto the lake and be in with a chance, but maybe the carp gods had rolled their dice in my favour?

I legged it back to the van to fetch my floater kit and within a few minutes I was back in the swim and firing out some oily floaters over the zone. Nothing showed an interest but sometimes you just have to be patient, because once you get one taking the rest follow like sheep. Suddenly there was a swirl, then several more joined in and the excitement kicked in as I fumbled about, trying to get the floater rod set up. I kept looking up and there were even more in the mix. Once I had the 10lb hook link tied to the swivel I oiled it up and checked that the dog mixer hook bait floated. I fired more mixers out and the anticipation and excitement built as I made the twenty-yard cast with a small surface controller. Backs pushed about all over the surface, as they hunted out every last floater. The controller landed behind them and I teased it back towards all the swirling, as they fought over what was left. I fired just enough mixers out to keep them on it and inched the controller back a bit more; the scene was set. I focused on the hook bait as it bobbed in all among the feasting carp and, inevitably, a mouth came up and engulfed the bait. I struck quickly, making contact. The rod took on its battle curve and the water's surface exploded as the fish dived down into its weedy home. It carried on surging through the jungle of weed, taking a few yards off me before everything went solid. I just kept the pressure on; after hooking one so quickly and this being the first fish, I wanted it on the bank. Putting on the maximum pressure I could with a 10lb hook length, I started to feel those vibrations through the rod, as inch by inch I got the carp moving. I couldn't feel anything on the end apart from a dead weight but when a weed bed surfaced I could see slight swirl behind it. As everything got closer I reduced the pressure and slid the net under the whole lot. The fish still had plenty of energy because it went mad, thrashing the water in the confines of the net. I looked out and could see that the odd carp was still taking mixers, so I grabbed the catapult and fired some more out to keep them happy while I dealt with this fish.

The fish was calm now as I lifted the net for a look at my first fish from the lake. I'd opened my account within ten minutes of casting out, and it seemed that it hadn't gone unnoticed as there was a gathering over the other side; at least the campers now knew Uncle Jim had arrived. I ripped the weed away to reveal a very long, old-looking fish with a dark back. I tilted him slightly to get a better look; he had a creamy body and looked to be around 30lb. I was buzzing at having banked one of the lake's proper ones off the top so quick. Dave said, "I don't know what fish that is Jim," and he had fished the lake over many years, so it was now looking that Uncle might have caught a rare one from a water where the locals will tell you they don't like floaters! I love it

I found out that it was a complete unknown for the lake and, to my knowledge, it hasn't been caught since!

when I hear this on a new venue because I know it will be carnage and this was a prime example what can be done with the right mindset. When starting on a new water, don't listen to the bollocks, just do your own thing, which will normally out-fish the locals who are at best stuck in a rut doing the same old thing.

While they kept an eye on the fish in the net, I legged it back to the van for the camera and scales. The spot was picked and I handed the camera to Dave. As I lifted my prize up Dave took the shots but I had a feeling from the way he was taking them that they weren't right. I laid the fish down and asked him to show me. They were shocking and I ripped into him saying, "Would you like me to take pictures like that for you?!" I was just a dot in the distance! God knows what he was looking at but he smirked at me, knowing I was dishing him up some therapee! I asked Caz if she would have a go for me and she did me proud, so cheers! As for your other half… he needs glasses. For the record, the fish weighed in at 31lb 8oz and I later found out that it was a complete unknown for the lake and to my knowledge it hasn't been caught since; a very rare visitor to the bank. As I slipped him back I could see that there were still odd ones kicking about so I catapulted some more mixers out and they started taking them straight away. I kept my eyes on the zone while tying up a new hook length; I was gagging to get back out there in the mix because I could smell another chance.

Before tying the hook length on I decided to give them some more freebies to keep them interested because they were going crazy out there. My cast landed bang in the middle of them, which wasn't what I'd wanted at all. I wasn't too happy with what I had just done and the action had stopped. As I watched, thinking about how I'd just ruined it, the water seemed to dip, telling me that a big fish was just under the surface. Straight away I thought was this her, the big 'un, when suddenly a mouth appeared and slurped the hook bait down. I struck into something solid that momentarily did nothing, then the water opened, as something big powered off the shallow, reedy area, stripping line off the clutch at a fair old rate. It reminded me of the Jaws scene when they pour water on the smoking reel. All I could do was hold on as this beast took me along the length of the pond. Suddenly it stopped and kited round to the right on what was now a very long line.

It must have been at least a 100 yards from where I had first hooked it and now I was reeling in what felt like nothing. I knew what this crafty old beast was up to, dropping back on me. I thought that he was going to try something, like turning suddenly and trying to smash me up but no, the animal came in close and dived just before it reached the shallow weedy area that I'd hooked it from. I knew now what this crafty fish was up to as a horrible grating sensation transmitted up the line, as it buried its head in the weed. I honestly thought I would win the battle though, because the line kept coming a lot easier than the last fish and surely I had a decent hook hold after such a hard and testing fight? Suddenly, 'bang', the rod tip flew back and that sickening feeling ran through my body because I'd pulled out of a big and very powerful carp. In my heart of hearts I knew it was her. I threw the rod into the bushes shouting, "Fcuking hell!" That loss still hurts to this very day; it's always the pain of the losses that you remember!

Suddenly, a mouth appeared and slurped the hook bait down – it was the big 'un!

The next day I was told that the big 'un had been seen acting weirdly in the safe area. To be honest, I'd already worked that out for myself! Dave and Caz walked off because they could see I wasn't too happy. I packed up as there was no point in carrying on. I was too pissed off to carry on for a walk round. They understood and I threw my gear in the van, vowing to return the following week; this bitch was now under my skin and there was no way I was walking away from this battle even if she now had the upper hand on me.

As I left the lake I decided to go over to Kingy for a look. During the short drive over to Kingy I kept reliving the events of the day. No matter how I looked at it, I had done nothing wrong and it was down to bad luck. That said, perhaps the carp gods had something else in mind for me? Only time would tell. Kingy was flat calm and as I looked out from the van I noticed several bivvies from the Car Park swim to the Dam Wall and round to Two Trees. I scanned the water for signs of carp and spotted a disturbance that looked like it was in front of Ringside. By the way it pushed water it was a big 'un. While I watched, I heard a motor. Looking up, I could see that it was Cyril in his Vogue. The engine roared as he drove up and leaned out asking me how I was getting on. I told Cyril what I had just seen and he smiled, saying, "That will do Jim." After a few minutes spent chatting he headed off for his daily drive round the lake. I headed off the other way to investigate what I had seen, walking up the long,

After the loss, she was seen acting weirdly in the safe area.

straight narrow bank towards Ringside. As I walked one popped his head out so I ran up to pinpoint the exact spot. The ripples were rolling straight into the front of the swim and I spotted a plume of bubbles popping in a line on the surface. As I watched I noticed some patches of fizzing too; this was it! As I pushed my gear towards the swim from the carp park I saw some ripples telling me another had shown. This was looking bang on for a bite and as soon as I arrived back at Ringside I positioned the barrow so I could watch the water while I got the rods ready. I had never fished the swim before but the fish had given away areas for me to cast to.

I didn't see any carp show while I sorted the rods, but I did see random fizzing around the swim, which told me they were on the munch. The rods were cast to the spots in which I had seen fish and I scattered a few freebies over the top. It was very warm but with odd rumbles of thunder in the distance I thought I'd better get the house up. Once I was installed, I laid down on the bedchair, watching the water, and started to drift off. Apart from the odd bleep nothing disturbed me and I zonked out from lack of sleep. It was nearly dark when I woke from my slumber. This wasn't good, as I'd been crashed out for hours! I hadn't even spoken to Jane but first thing I needed was a leak, as I was bursting! After speaking with the missus I settled back down on the bedchair to watch for signs. In the distance lightning lit up the sky and thunder rumbled, what a setting! One went over out in the darkness as I cooked my dinner. I watched as the ripples came in from the right of the swim, so things looked bang on for a bite in what were simply electric conditions. Seemingly from nowhere, the swim came alive, as carp rolled out in front of my swim while my buzzers bleeped and my bobbins danced. Some of these liners were so savage that they had me going down to the rods to investigate. The carpy activity carried on for a few hours, after which it died away, leaving me hoping that they hadn't gone elsewhere. Hoping I would get a visit from Mr Carp by the morning, I drifted off to sleep. Sometime later the liners started up again and every time I fell back to sleep, one of the buzzers would momentarily wake me. This wasn't funny, as I was still knackered from the night before and I simply couldn't believe I still hadn't had a take yet.

It was getting light when the next flurry of bleeps woke me. I was listening to the birds singing when suddenly a rod roared off as something finally succumbed. I was using braided main line and the fish banged the rod over, stripping line off me in a fierce run. After belting all over the swim in a frankly uncontrollable manner, he calmed down, allowing me to gain some control. He was soon under the rod tip and huge swirls boiled on the surface. I got a glimpse of a long common that wallowed up on top and I took my chance, sliding the net out and underneath it. By the way he had fought I thought he was going to go mental, but when I looked in to get a better look at this long, solid common, it just sat there quiet as a mouse. Placing him on the mat,

It was nearly dark when I awoke from my slumber; this wasn't good!

It was coloured like a highly polished bar of gold!

I carefully removed the hook that was firmly embedded in his bottom lip and was never coming out. He looked awesome, covered in massive diamond-shaped scales and coloured like a highly polished bar of gold. I was sure he was a thirty but scales told another story, settling at 29lb. I popped him into a sack and sent Cookie a text to see if he was awake and willing to do the honours for me. Luckily he was and promised to be round soon.

With all the funny liners I decided not to put the rod back out because I thought it might ruin the chance of another bite. I was just making a strong coffee when the left-hand alarm bleeped and the bobbin slowly pulled up tight. I commenced battle with another one, which came in like a dog on a lead and I landed a chunky common just as Cookie turned up. This common looked awesome, apart from slight tail damage that was probably caused by an otter. It was an old wound that had now healed and when I lifted him up for the trophy shots Cookie noted that the sun had lit up an area of metallic scales on his belly. He was covered in chestnut-coloured scales and weighed in at 24lb 12oz. I returned him, wishing him good luck, and we prepared the first fish for his turn. He glistened in the early morning sun and thankfully he didn't play up, until I put him back, when I got a soaking. Later that morning I packed up and shot off home to see Jane and spend some time with the family. Even at home I couldn't shake the thought of the fish that I'd lost and I knew exactly where I was going next week… Lenwade.

My next session soon came around and upon arriving I could see that the car park swim was free. Well, after last week I drove straight into the swim because I thought it would be a good starting point, especially as conditions were exactly the same as last week. I could see the old boys camped up in their usual swims over the other side of pond but more importantly the carp were still in residence where I had left them last time. No-one was along this bank at all, which I found a bit weird because they weren't that hard to spot. This amused me greatly because it isn't hard to have a little look around before setting up! I put so much into my angling that I tend to get the work done quickly and this place would be no different once I started trawling, as you will find out. I had to dig in and play the game though because several factors would make this target a tricky one to nail. Grabbing my floater kit from the van I proceeded to fire some mixers out but this time they just moved further back, which wasn't a problem because no-one was fishing next door. With the wind blowing away from me I just kept feeding mixers, throwing them out by hand. I have to admit that I was thinking that it would only be a matter of time before they started taking them again but after around 30 minutes they had ignored them completely, which I thought was a bit weird after last week's observations.

I decided to stir them up with the oxygenator, or the spod as you might know it! This weapon is my main tool for floater fishing because the noise of the spod hitting

Cookie noted that the sun had lit up an area of metallic scales on his belly.

the water stirs the carp up and gets them investigating what's going on; it's amazing to watch! Spodding floaters at long range is a tactic that my mate Ian Pullinger first showed me. This spodding method allowed me to get over a hundred freebies out but I soon found that it had another use, the splash attracted carp. Anyway, I loaded the spod with mixers and then poured oil in to add to the food signal and flatten the ripple out. Out went the spod and it impacted in among them, this sure stirred them up and the water exploded. As I swung the spod in a fish started taking and several of his mates joined in. Mouths started popping out all over the shop, fighting over a spodful of mixers. It's hard to believe that they had ignored them before the spodding. I whacked another at them, which now sent the shoal on a mental rampage, hunting like a pack of wolves.

My cast landed out behind the ravenous pack and I inched it back. One even had a go at the moving target, spooking off at the last moment! As the water settled he had another go but this time he got nailed! I got a glimpse of an orangey coloured fish as the rod took on its battle curve. The fish dived down into the weed, and all I could do was to keep the rod bent and hope that the pressure would get him moving. I was able to tease him from his weedy sanctuary but then he shot off, trying to get out into open water. I didn't want him to do this as I could imagine him diving down the back edge of the weed and doing me like the big 'un had done, so I laid the rod to the left to

I got a glimpse of an orangey coloured fish as the rod took on its battle curve.

The kid just couldn't believe how easy I made it all look!

make him kite and go down in the water. This worked and I coaxed him slowly back, keeping the rod low until he was close. When he was in my margin I lifted the rod up and played him out under the rod tip. Eventually, I was able to slide the net under a chunky, orangey mirror. I tipped him slightly onto his side to reveal a fantastically coloured carp. His overriding colour was orange and he had a creamy belly with a nick in the top part of his tail. While I was getting the mat and scales sorted, a young lad turned up so I asked him if he would be kind enough to take a few shots for me. He agreed, asking me, "Are you Jim Shelley?" I laughed and said, "No," before admitting it; he looked puzzled as I handed him the camera! The young lad read the weight off as 26lb and before lifting the fish up for some pictures I noticed that he had a cute, chubby face – a right old-looking character. I thought it a fitting tribute to name him Chubby Chops because this fish didn't have a name. In fact, only one fish in the lake was named, and that was the big 'un, which had the undignified name The Mug, which I was definitely going to change when I caught her.

After I returned Chubby the young lad asked me if he could watch me fishing and over the next few hours I caught five more. Four of them were stockies up to 25lb 4oz, topped off by a mirror that was two-tone on one side, with a slightly deformed mouth on the same side. This kid couldn't believe how easy I made it all look but by the time he left the swim had gone dead. I packed up and decided to go for a mooch because I still hadn't walked around the pond yet and I thought it was about time I met this old motley crew of swim-hogging campers that were over the other side, watching first hand how to fish their water the Uncle Jim way.

Before leaving I tidied my swim up and set off for a look round the pond, walking to the right in between the Main Lake and the Tench Lake. I looked for any signs of carp but nothing showed itself. The posse was now splitting up and heading into their respective swims, knowing I was on my way round. The first old boy that I came across was called Albert, and it turned out that he was a bailiff. We chatted and Albert said, "Come and meet Martin in the next swim." Now these two blokes were quite pleasant to talk to; they then questioned me how I was doing so well and I played it all down by saying I had been a bit lucky. Martin then offered me a hot drink, which I declined by telling them that I only had one strong coffee in the morning to get me going. Martin was perched in his trailer bivvy, inside there was everything but the kitchen sink! I couldn't help but notice a crucifix on the wall and asked him what the hell it was all about! He then proceeded to preach to me! "Fcuking hell Jim, what have you started now?" I thought, when he asked if I was religious. I had to get out of there, fast. "Look Martin," I said, "I have my own beliefs and you have yours fella. I don't do this sort of thing and it's best we don't get into this on our first meeting because my views are a bit radical fella. I'm not up for conversion just yet!" He smiled, saying "No problem Jim," and we shook hands before I beat a hasty retreat, thinking, "Christ, I hope I'm not stuck on here for years… I could be converted into a believer!" With my chequered history I could be in confession for far too long begging for forgiveness!

I didn't want any more therapee so I didn't stop and speak to the others, just saying "Hello" and nodding as I passed. I stopped when I got to the swim called The Steps, just before the island. I was to notice over the next few trips that none of the trailer campers or other members fished up there. I found this bizarre because where they fished had depths of 13ft to 15ft but this other half of the lake was between 15ft and 22ft. OK, this wasn't really much of a change but this area of deeper water interested me greatly. I hoped that I could get something going there and be left alone. Carrying on round, I scanned the water for signs. There seemed to be only one swim along the bottom bank and there was a gentle breeze blowing in. There had to be some carp down here on this warm, well-oxygenated wind, hiding from Uncle Jim's floater carnage at the other end. Looking round to the right into a snaggy corner I noticed some fizzing in the edge and as I walked round the back of the snags I got a whiff of fish slime, as the wind blew off the water and through the bushes. I clocked this second sign and as I entered the swim there were loads of patches of fizz dotted around the swim. Looking at the size of the patches of bubbles, these had to be from carp. I sat down on a wooden seat beside the swim so I wouldn't draw attention to my find. In hindsight I don't know why I was worrying about the trailer boys because they wouldn't venture up into that alien part of the lake; they only drove past on their way in and out! I was sitting quietly, watching and planning how I was going to fish this zone when a massive, orangey carp rolled so discreetly in the ripple that if I hadn't seen it I would have thought it was a tench. I jumped, watching where she went down because I was near-on 100 per cent positive it was the big 'un. Fifteen to twenty seconds later she let out a line of bubbles, then a massive fizz hit the surface, so she was on the munch in near-on perfect conditions. Turning right, I headed off on the quickest route to my gear. I grabbed two rods from the van, put them together and checked the rigs, which were pukka. I tied on two fresh hook baits and leant the sticks up against the van, before putting all the bits I needed in the unhooking mat and getting my landing net. I slung the unhooking mat over my shoulder, grabbed the rods and net and set off in the direction of my new find. Walking down the long bank towards the corner I could feel eyes burning into me, but I didn't look round until I got to the seat. I was right, as the trailer boys were stood together facing towards me; it was funny really because I didn't really have anything to fear from most of them, as they were so stuck in their ways over there.

It was still going off in the zone and I was now gagging to get the rigs in place as quietly as possible. The plan was to cast one straight to where the big 'un had been seen and the other rod would be cast down along the margin to the right. Getting them in as quietly as I could would mean casting out further and reeling them back in before letting them gently drop down over the spots. I halved seven squid boilies and one at a time, threw them out, spreading them over the zone so it would add some attractiveness to get them searching. I planned to repeat this every thirty minutes to keep the area activated with food signals.

After that I sat down to keep quiet and watch the zone; the fizzing had slowed down a bit but after ten minutes they were back, fizzing in the mix. Out of the corner of my eye I noticed the line from the right-hand rod lift slightly with a piece of weed on it. Just as I was thinking it was a liner, that rod then bent round until the lightly clipped line was pulled from the clip and the clutch whizzed off. The carp surged off, taking a few yards of line before kiting from the margin out into the lake. While I was playing this fish the posse gathered over the other side and watched the whole fight. I heard a car pull up and looking round I discovered that it was my old mate Mollusc. "Boy, do you want a hand to net this one?" he asked. I said, "Don't fcuk about, of course I do!" He grabbed the net, trying to manoeuvre it between me and the rod that was on the floor. Thankfully, as I had the Mollusc on the net, this fish came in close without really doing a lot. Mol slid the net out moaning that it was tight, as he tried to reach out through this tiny poke hole between the reeds. "Come on Mol, net the fcuking thing for fcuk's sake!" I said. Mol wasn't happy, telling me to "Shut the fcuk up!" "Oi oi watch my rod, you're standing on it!" I told him, but he finally got the net through and scooped the fish up. "Good boy Mol," I said and he told me that it was a common. "I can see that, I'm not blind you know," I replied, which precipitated an outburst of banter, as we ripped into each other like we normally do. He pulled the net into the gap in the reeds and we both looked in. "Oi oi boy, that's a half decent common there son, it looks upper-twenty to thirty pounds." I said, "The trailer boys over there must be wondering what the hell's going on with all this trawling." We laughed and Mol waved at them, "Stop it!" I demanded, "That'll only stir 'em up!" I bit the line and got rid of the rod while Mol looked after the fish. It was bright now, with cloud building in the distance and

One in the net in the poke hole!

a nice breeze blowing down into this end of the lake. Little did we know what was in store for Mol and I that evening. I gently popped the hook out of a very pale common, which for the record weighed 29lb and was the biggest known common caught from the lake. As I held the fish up for the camera, the campers gathered in the background, watching, probably chewing over how the hell I was doing it. Mol clicked away taking good pictures this time but that's another story! With the fish safely returned there was no way that those carp would still be here, so it was time to find them again. Before leaving the swim I lightly baited the area in case they returned.

With Mol about fishing I had to be on the ball so I headed off to dump my tackle in the van. Mol had parked his van in The Oaks, one down from the Car Park swim but was on the mooch. The weather was changing with light rain in the air and big, black clouds moving in. We had been getting a hell of a lot of rain lately and with the river running very high things looked grim, but more importantly I had to locate some carp quick before the rough weather touched down. I just kept my head down praying for no more therapee, as I did a couple of laps. Bumping into Mol it seemed that neither of us had seen anything and I asked, "What do you think of that lot?" gesturing over to the campers. He replied, "I haven't really spoken to any of them." Seeing the chance to stitch him up I pointed over to Martin's gaff, "Next time you're passing pop in, he's sound as a pound and is an ideal pit stop." This was my ploy to hold him back, knowing

The biggest known common in the lake at 29lb.

With the fish safely returned, it was time to go looking for the rest of them.

We both noticed some foam in the opposite corner of the lake.

on his next walk round he would stop off for a drink. This would give me extra time to locate the carp! As I walked round I could see that he was in residence at the so-called pit stop so I smiled as I passed. Mol looked over with a pissed-off look and I started laughing. "How you doing mate?" I asked as I passed and he whispered, "Fcuk you!" I winked because he knew I'd done him up big time. Martin handed him a cuppa as I walked off on another circuit pissing myself. A few minutes later I gave him a little text for good measure.

Even with him out of the way I couldn't find the fish and it was now peeing down big time, so I headed off to the van to watch the lake in the dry once I'd parked up in an area with a good view of the lake. I was feeling a bit lost but I knew everything was going well as no one else was catching. I just had to push on for the bitch. It had been a while since I had targeted a big 'un; meeting Jane and flitting around a few venues saw to that. After an hour Mol knocked on the window. As I unwound it he proceeded to dish the therapee. I laughed saying, "Are you converted?" "You wanker Jim," he replied, "What is he all about?" I lost it in the van, laughing uncontrollably when Mol mentioned the cross hanging up. After we calmed down he asked, "What you seen?" "Nothing mate," I replied. I told him that I was going to fish somewhere up the deep end because I was sure they were hiding up near where I had caught that common. Looking out we both noticed some foam in the corner of the lake opposite us, so we went for a closer look. As we got close we could see the water breaching in from The

With a waterfall pouring across the bank, Mol opted to stay on high ground!

Long Lake. This inflow would attract everything in the lake and straight away I said, "I'm fishing here." Mol said, "You can have it," and pointed over near where my van was parked saying, "I'm staying on high ground!" As we watched, a massive eel flew up the waterfall and disappeared into The Long Lake, probably now on his way to his spawning grounds in the Sargasso Sea. More importantly, I was eyeing him up for grub because I loved fried and jellied eels. Mol thought it was gross but I told him, "Don't knock it until you've tried it son."

Mol walked off in disgust, leaving me to it because I was focused on this sudden change in the lake's dynamics. I was sure I was going to hit jackpot as they came to investigate. Not long after I saw one close to the bank in the murky water. I noticed the waterfall was getting worse so legged it back to the van and drove it over, parking near the swim. While sorting the rods I could hear the noise of the waterfall; it was unreal. I was soon ready to get the rods in place but the path was flooding with the intensity of the push of water, meaning that I needed boots on to get the rods in the swim. As I waded up to the swim, there was this massive eddy spinning round in front of the swim and the lake looked like it was rising quickly. This was mental! Pushing my bank sticks in by the waterfall a fish boshed out right in front of me; they were here and I was sure I was going to get a take. With the baits in position where the water was flowing in, surely it was only a matter of time before something happened? Over the next hour things got worse because water was now breaching further along the bank and the lake started to fill up. It seemed the lake had gone dead as darkness fell. I was going to bivvy up on a slightly higher spot on the road but Mol advised me to set up near him. I honestly didn't think things would get much worse; little did I know what was in store for me in the morning! The night was quiet and just one liner stirred me from my sleep until something woke me at first light. It was Mol wading through the water where I was bivvied up. Looking out there was a foot of water in the bivvy! Where were my boots? Searching around I located them in the back of my house. Mol was now getting his own back, laughing his head off at me saying, "I told you so." Suddenly, I realised that my van was in it as well. This wasn't good. I jumped up and walked over to the van, opening the door to find that the foot wells had water in them! Now I was panicking big time, worried my wheels wouldn't work. I jumped in turned the engine on and she turned over, thank God. As I pulled away, a surge of water pushed up in front of the van. Mol followed, pissing himself. I wasn't finding this funny, especially as my hard work hadn't paid off. Approaching Mol's pitch, I noticed his rods tips poking about a foot above the water. "Look you muppet," I shouted, it was now my turn to dish the grief! I had to bail the water out of the van while he jumped in to rescue his kit. I bet his privates disappeared from sight! Unsurprisingly, we packed up and headed for home after that!

Not long after the lakes were closed because the venue was totally flooded, apart from The Tench Lake, which was on slightly higher ground. Several big fish were seen in The Long Lake and I hoped the big girl wasn't one of them. I had to go elsewhere, so I played over at Linch Hill in Oxfordshire, which was a 430-mile round trip. It's not a place I want to dwell on because my time over there left a bitter taste in my mouth. The main place I turned over was Willow, but I was fishing Stoneacres at night and stalking with floaters. Some of the locals informed me that they didn't take floaters. Now, for the record, I've never known a water where carp will not take them at some point. Some of these locals later took it upon themselves to make things much harder for us. I started it all on one very hot, still morning with my floater gear on Willow. I passed Nigel Sharp and he winked saying, "I know where you're going." I carried on with a smile on my face he called after me, "Keep me posted." Straight away I found the fish basking on the surface, under the scum in a quiet corner. I fired some mixers out and not long after I got them taking with gusto. This was the moment. I overcast and reeled the bait back slowly towards the pack. I was watching the hook bait, as fish were taking all round it when suddenly it just disappeared. It was really weird, no lips or anything; the fish had just sucked it in and gone. Upon striking, several bow waves shot off and after a spirited fight I landed a long mirror that weighed 27lb 12oz. That was the only action of the day so I was soon heading back to my base-camp swim on Stoney. I went the other way round so Nigel couldn't question me about my day; I wanted to have a head start because I got the feeling the others boys might be up for a spot of floater fishing the next day! With darkness fast approaching I got my rods in position.

All I could think about that night was getting back on Willow because I knew there was a massive window of opportunity to be taken advantage of and I was buzzing for

Floater fun on a new venue, Linch Hill.

My first Willow carp in the net, and it's a long mirror.

It weighed in at 27lb 12oz.

With darkness approaching I got my rods sorted on Stoneacres.

it. In the morning I hurried to get everything sorted ready for my attack on Willow. At that point you were allowed to stalk and leave your gear on another lake but, as I mentioned, things were about to change for the worse. I went the long way round so the others didn't see me but not long after finding the fish, Beadle, Nigel, Terry Hearn, Nick Helleur and a couple of others arrived. Nigel came over smiled and said, "Thought you were going to pop in and tell us how you got on?" I replied, "You know the score; I bet the bloke who took my pictures told you?" Now, if you can imagine there were seven of us all in a line fishing like Noddy with a rod; we trawled like you don't want to know and Nick topped it off with a 40lb common. Over the next few weeks we emptied the lake floater fishing but from that day on the locals, led by a bloke called Colin, planned their attack. By the next morning I'd had a visit from Julie and she told me that I couldn't leave my gear set up on Stoneys and stalk elsewhere, but it was OK to be left in the van away from the swim. Over the next few weeks I landed over thirty carp off the surface, topped by mirrors of 33lb and a 35lb 10oz called Baby Basil but could not use the pictures because of poor quality, plus I caught a leathery one of 37lb. Alarmingly, the goal posts were being moved all the time, which seemed to be almost daily. This culminated in a new rule being introduced, which stated that you could only use 1kg of dry of mixers per day. Colin was at the centre of it all and you can imagine how I laughed when I saw him floater fishing over there in the end. By this time, I often found myself floater fishing on my own, just popping over for a

Over the next few weeks I landed over 30 carp off the surface. This one was 33lb.

few hours' fun and on one of those days Colin came running round and asked me if I could take some pictures for him! I shouted, "NO WAY!" Some people eh? The gall of it...

In the end I suppose I was there for about five weeks. Stoneys seemed to be very quiet after the early spring carnage and I did wangle one out from the disabled bay by the car park while stalking from a concrete swim. I found loads in there late one evening, ripping the whole area up. It was a massive chance I had to act on and I legged it back to the Pipe swim and grabbed two rods and the bits that I needed. This was the first session I started using the running chod rig actually, and I was unsure whether this rig was any good. With two underarm flicks I soon had two of these rigs in place with seven free offerings thrown in by hand around each hook bait. With the rods on the concrete, lines hanging slack with the clutches set, I was just thinking about how alien this fishing felt when the left-hand rod pulled tight and the rod tip bounced. Picking the rod up I connected with something that felt weird; it was a tench and soon had my first chod victim in the net. I unhooked him in the net then released him along the bank because I wasn't about to put him back in the bay and spook them again. Checking the rig, I found that it was sweet so I flicked it back out to the zone. Feeling the lead down onto soft ground, I slackened off the clutch, laid the rod down and threw seven more lucky ones out around it. I just hoped that the tench hadn't spooked them away. It all looked dead, but not long after I heard this scratching noise. Looking down to the right, that

At 37lb, this leathery one topped off the surface action nicely.

I legged it back to the Pipe swim for my kit.

Rod out on the concrete, and on the fish!

same rod was whizzing off. Whatever was on the other end stripped line off me and it was apparent that this was no tench. I was quaking in my boots as I played my first ever chod-caught carp; would this be the start of something special? I must confess I was surprised when I slid my first ever chod victim into the net. Looking in to get a better look I was blown away by this most awesome scaly carp. I gently popped the hook out, noticing how awesome the hook hold was. I belled Beadle to ask if he could do the honours for me and while I waited for him I noticed a bush in full bloom. This had to be the spot to capture the special moment because Uncle Jim was no longer a chod virgin. This was a rig I was going to bring into the forefront of my angling over the years that followed so this was a true turning point in my career. After five or six months of tweaking the rig, I had perfected the setup that has now become my long running chod. Beadle was soon on the scene and as soon as he clapped on eyes on this beast he agreed it was a stunner. It had a unique shape, which made him different. We got a better look at him on the mat, whereupon I turned to Beadle saying, "He looks like a tadpole," so I named him The Tadpole, which I thought was a fitting tribute but sometime later I was slagged off by some for naming him that. For the record, he weighed 30lb 12oz and as you can see in the pictures he is an awesome creature, and thanks to Beadle for taking the stunning pictures. After a few water shots he was returned to fight another day. After the capture I moved swims to cover the zone because the odd fish was still about. However, by the morning nothing else had happened, so before leaving I loaded it up with salty seeds of the gods for next time.

This was the first time that I used the running chod!

"He looks like a Tadpole."

Later that morning Nigel spotted all the bait I had dropped in on my way out and later on the bait was hit, culminating in several captures, but that's another story.
While on my next trip to Oxford, Lenwade reopened but it was busy, so I stayed put. I had a tuition booked in at Linear later on in the week so I decided that if she hadn't been caught by the time I was done, I might go back there, especially as all the politics at Linch were boring me somewhat. However, I was about to receive some disturbing news from Lenwade; an angler had caught the big 'un on the QT and re-homed her in The Long Lake. She'd been spotted in there and yes she could have gone across in the floods but one of his mates let the truth slip out, saying that this bloke did it to stop me from catching it. In the light of this new information I was now truly pissed off. Several calls to mates who were down there fishing confirmed this story and they were trying to get her out and back in her home. She was looking lost and agitated, charging around the lake and clearly mega stressed out. I was totally pissed off with this and got the angler's number. I phoned him up that evening and told him I knew what and why he had moved that fish. I ended up losing the plot and telling him fcuk off. The following evening a kid that was a friend of the twat who moved the fish caught her. A couple of mates, Graeme and Rob, were straight on the scene, as this kid tried to return the fish back into The Long Lake. Luckily, they acted quickly and decisively, taking the fish from him. Good angling boys and 100% respect because you saved her from certain death. She wasn't right as they carried her across the causeway back to

An old 36lb 8oz Hardwick common.

her home; she was bleeding from the gills and they got her straight into the lake and retained her until she was fit enough to swim off. I take my hat off to you both for a great job you did watching over her while she recovered. As soon as she swam off they walked over to her safe area in the bay and straight away they spotted her with several of the other residents. The other fish watched over her and they gently rubbed against her, knowing their queen was not well. I asked them to bait the bay to keep her in there for her safety, as several anglers carried on fishing there regardless. I didn't return for a while, except for several undercover night baiting campaigns to keep her in the bay and safe, so she could recover in peace and build herself back up. This worked because she wasn't caught while I was away and people started commenting on how big she looked in the bay… wink wink!

I did carry on a little longer at Linch, but some of the locals were after us 'names'. Most had left and in the end so did I. I flitted around over at Linear but it was far too busy for me there. I did manage to catch fish to 36lb 8oz from Hardwick off the top, but after several weeks flitting around I thought it was about time I got my arse back to Lenwade. I was getting the vibe as I drove down the lane through the woods and unlocked the gate. It sure was nice to get back and with the harvest moon and equinox fast approaching it was time to get serious. She hadn't been caught since that twat moved her, although she was seen quite regularly in the bay, looking pukka and plump. I wonder why? Looking out across the lake there were only the trailer boys

Sunset over Hardwick.

It was about time I got my arse back over to Lenwade.

camped in their normal swims, with no one else about. Parking the van I grabbed my polarising glasses and headed off to see if I could see her in the bay. As I approached the bay there were several fish milling about just under the surface. Closer inspection revealed that she was not with them. I carefully made my way along the edge of the bay, trying to keep myself concealed as much as possible, hoping to get a glimpse of the queen. I eventually came to the edge of the bay's entrance and noticed movement close in by the rope. The fish was gone, apart from a massive swirl on the surface. I hid behind a tiny bush, watching the area when suddenly the water rocked, as a carp slowly came into view. It just kept getting bigger and bigger until it dawned on me which one it was. There beneath me was my target, the queen of the lake. She looked awesome with massive, golden sovereign scales along her back. She had to be 45lb plus, this was meant to be surely? She looked perfect in every way. This was the first time I had seen her properly up close and personal, with eye contact. Maybe she was saying thanks for all the bait I had given her to see her right? Seeing her looking so good I knew I had made the right decision to come back for her. All I had to do now was catch her and this was a one of those chances. Backing off, it was time to get in position. With most of the fish in front of the Little Oaks, I decided to fish from that swim so I jumped into the van and drove into the swim. This was too good an opportunity to miss; with the bulk of the fish sunning themselves to the left of the swim and the big 'un mainly sitting by herself just off the rope, I was hoping I could feed the pack away from her and make my target easier to pick out. I decided to use a catapult because I felt if I used

I carefully made my way along the edge of the bay, hoping to get a glimpse of the queen.

a spod this might spread the pack, plus I didn't want to spook her back into the bay. I fired several pouchfuls of mixers over the pack and straight away they feasted but I had to stick to the plan of trying to single her out. The excitement was unreal and before I left I gave the pack some more mixers. I wanted to locate her and see her reaction to the floaters.

I was soon in position and looking down she was still sitting where I had left her. I threw some mixers in three or four feet away from her. As soon as they landed she knew something was up, her gills began to work; it looked like I had woken her up. Then, she simply sunk from view. I thought it was a bit strange but suddenly I heard a slurp and there she was, tucking into the floaters! I chucked some more in right on her head. This spooked her but not for long and before the swirl died she reappeared, taking the odd floater. I thought she looked uneasy and suddenly she just waddled off under the rope and well down into the bay, sitting just under the surface on her own. Over the next thirty minutes she didn't move. It looked like I had blown my chance. With her sulking I decided to go and try to catch one of the others, plus she might even turn up? I fired out some more floaters and grabbed my floater kit from the van. They were taking the floaters again and shortly after I tweaked the rig into the feasting pack. I knew it wasn't going to be long before I had a chance but suddenly I heard the gravel crunching behind me. It was Albert, one of the nice blokes who helped run the club, As soon as I saw him I whispered, "Shhh," pointing out into to the lake. He smiled and then quietly made his way down into the swim. I had a lot of time for him; he was a lovely gentleman who loved to pop in to say hello and occasionally fished himself. Unfortunately, he hadn't had time of late because he was looking after his poorly wife.

Not long after Albert arrived, I hooked a very powerful fish that surged off across the top, sending a massive bow wave up and stripping line off the clutch. I applied finger pressure to the spool and tried to slow this carp down as he shot off on a mental, 40-yard run. He finally stopped and kited round to the left, before diving down trying to get behind the weed bed in front of the swim. It was now do or die as I crammed on the pressure to try and stop him getting down the back of this weed and shedding the rig. Normally there's no way I would exert this much pressure on my tackle but it worked because I could see the controller, which told me the fish was around five feet behind it. The fish swirled as it came over the weed and I kept the pressure on as Albert sunk the net ready. He asked me if I wanted him to net it and I told him that I did. I was now playing him on the clutch and in the clear, shallow water he looked a right chunk. After a few more minutes he wallowed on the surface and Albert took his chance, netting the fish on his first attempt. Turning round he informed me "That's a big one Jim." I walked over for a better look and it certainly looked over 30lb. Albert shook my hand, saying, "Well done." It was time to weigh him and Albert confirmed a weight of 35lb 8oz, the second biggest in the pond. He had a very distinctive red colouration to

Albert was one of the nice blokes who helped run the club.

Albert confirmed a weight of 35lb 8oz, the second biggest in the pond.

his face so I named him Red Cheeks. So many of the fish in this lake were nameless and the big girl was no different. I didn't see it very fitting hearing her referred to as The Mug or The Pet, so when that special day came when I banked her I would christen her with a more fitting name for a fish that looked like it could be on its way to being one of the biggest in Norfolk. Over the next month I caught on each trip, with the biggest being a recapture of Red Cheeks at 36lb. I had booked in a lot of tuition work to pay for Christmas and the finer things in life, which I really should have put off until later in the year because September and October are big-fish months. These months are now booked in my diary as holiday because you've got to use your time wisely. During this period there was only one other fish out, to a guy called Jim The Punisher and with the best month of September gone, I was getting worried because it was only a matter of time before she slipped up to somebody. However, the longer she went uncaught, the bigger she would get and she did look bigger than ever when I got the odd sighting in the bay.

I knew that I had to pull out all the stops and fish the lake as much as possible until she came out. I had a lovely, long, creamy mirror of 28lb 12oz from The Steps swim on an overnighter while watching a movie called Blade, so that mirror got the name Blade! Loading the swim up with bait before I reeled in meant I wouldn't get in trouble for baiting up before I left. I had been working this particular zone a lot with undercover baiting going on, spreading the bait to the right of the swim where it dropped off into depths of over 20ft. This swim to the right was called The Oaks and it was rarely fished. I had first been drawn to the area after seeing subtle patches of bubbles, which made me think that it could be a natural food larder and a place they might visit at the right time, especially if it was baited. When it looked ripe I could use it as a backup plan, which all meant secret baiting up in the middle of the night with the spoon. Having kept an eye on the zone, I'd noticed that the fizzing was often no more than ten to fifteen yards out. When I first found this going on I dragged a lead through it late one night and the lead pulled through very smoothly, telling me the close-in baited area was being worked. Baiting with the spoon is a lot noisier but because 5kg corresponds to around ten to twelve spoonfuls, it'd be in quicker than a stick or catapult. So, before first light I filled the area in with 15kg of salty squids. Bite time had switched over to nights, so with the 28lb 12oz mirror coming off the edge of the zone cast down from The Steps it felt right to fish The Oaks swim on my next trip, which was to be the following week on a 48-hour tuition. I was feeling close, surely it was only a matter of time before the queen slipped up in advance of her winter slumber?

Luckily for me, Jane let me out on a quick overnighter because she knew how close things were getting. I was obsessed with the place, every minute I was thinking about her; it had been a while since I had let a target take over my every thought. As you can imagine I broke every speed limit on my way over, but to make the 40-mile journey all the sweeter I had the trance tunes pumping. My mind was racing, wondering where would she be. Deep down I had a good idea where she would be feeding but I didn't want to draw any attention to the baited zone by fishing it before the following week, so unless I saw her show in the zone, all I wanted to do was get some bait out in the middle of the night. By the morning I had 10kg on my close-in zone. When I packed up early in the morning to shoot over to Waveney for a tuition I stopped off at one of the new campers and woke him up saying, "Did you hear someone baiting up your end last night?" This was to sow the seeds of doubt in this head. He said he hadn't and I looked out from his swim with a smile on my face. I also noticed his lines were straight out and to the left now, sweet. I just hoped he wouldn't see anything in the zone to the right but before I left I asked him if he had seen or caught anything. He said, "Yes, I've seen some show to the left of the swim and I've caught a small common." Perfect.

We had a new full-time camper on the pond now, called Jan The Sheep. This guy had no angling morals, apart from taking what he could from whomever he could. He watched my every move and he would act on any captures and jump straight into sheeping mode. Things had got so bad that I would cast way past the distance I was fishing and reel back until the line marker appeared, letting the rig drop down to disguise the spots I was fishing. Other more productive spots would see me recasting after dark onto the real marks. I would even fish other swims to throw him off the scent. I do hate when the fishing becomes like this but in this day and age there's far too many anglers willing to rape your hard work. Walking off to the van, I hoped everything would stay the same until my return especially as I had another hit of bait in the zone. I had a really good feeling about the un-fished area in deep water that

A lovely, long, creamy mirror called Blade.

I knew that I had to pull out all the stops and fish the lake as much as possible until she came out.

I had been prepping for a while and before I got in the van I looked over the water and prayed all would be safe. More importantly, I noticed very small, discreet bubbles popping on the surface over the baited area close in. Christ they were already on it, but I had to go… work was calling me.

Over the weekend the weather turned a lot colder with the first frost of the winter forecast along with a full moon for Monday night, when I was due back. Surely she would be on the munch with her mates? All I could do was pray she'd wait for my return and, as you can probably imagine, I made several calls to check the score. She'd yet to be caught so I was pulling into the car park with a three-day session ahead of me. Two days were with a guest… or tuition, if you know what I mean. Speaking with others she hadn't been seen for over a week, I wondered where she was and hoped that it was my spot. Looking out from the car park I could see two anglers in the swim; my heart sunk. We took a walk around the lake and as we approached the swim I could see that they were pleasure anglers on a day session and after a quick chat they said they'd be off before dark. It was time to get on with the tuition, so we carried on in our search for carp. We located some hanging around in the roped-off safe area but closer inspection revealed some of them were leaving the area. However, once they went under the rope they dropped down and disappeared from view. After watching this for a few minutes I suggested that we should get round to The Oaks swim and get his rods in position ASAP. Not long after we had the rods fanned out over the weed off the rope. I only put one rod out as it was a double swim but still relatively tight. After we were all sorted we sat at the top of the swim out of the way and got on with the tuition. Over the course of the day he had several liners and several poked their heads out over his rods. By late afternoon things seemed dead and a quick look in and around the bay told us they had done the off. Shortly after, I had a take on my rod. After flying down the bank I pulled into something that felt a little strange. Suddenly, up popped a small fish that looked like a dead bait with a float behind it! It transpired that Mr Pike Angler had turned up next to me and had cast well right, in front of me. As he reeled in he'd caught me up. Looking left I could see him, "Hold on geezer, I'm fishing here and you've caught me up… open your bail arm." Now this is no word of a lie, as I swung this dead 'un in I saw that I'd chodded it fair and square in the mouth. I then turned to the client and said, "That's dinner sorted". As this piker had ruined my swim and I had caught his dead bait, I took its head off for a trophy before dropping his rig back in. I heard him moaning when he saw what was left of his dead bait but moments later the rig landed back in my swim! Turning to the client I said, "That's a sign from the carp gods to move over the other side." It's one of the ways I turn negativity into positivity. Time was getting on and the pleasure anglers were packing away, so we packed our gear up and checked the bay again. Nothing was at home, but we still spread a few baits over the weedy shelf for tomorrow if they returned.

When we got round to the zone a fish stuck its head out in the swim to the right of where the pleasure anglers were packing away. This was the sign we needed and he opted not to wait and get set up straight away in the swim where we had spotted that carp. This suited me fine as it meant I could get on my prepped zone. We soon had all our rods spread out no more than fifteen yards out in the deep silty gully. With the day being clear and sunny I knew it was going to be a cold night with these clear skies, but as darkness fell the lake seemed to come alive in front of us as carp started to dance in the moonlight. It was fascinating to watch the shows while we chatted in the dark under the trees over a few beers. I even put a snide fifth rod out later on in the night because one showed mega close in… naughty Uncle! Climbing into the bag I looked out over the water thinking, "Surely with all these carpy goings-on something has to happen for us tonight?" The full moon climbed higher in the sky and darkness nearly turned to daylight. Once this happened the activity died off dramatically, so I dropped the door and turned my back on the lake in disgust.

The next thing I knew, the birds were singing… shit it was first light and I had five rods out! As I moved I noticed that my bladder was killing me so first things first, I walked out to take a leak in the cold. Standing there, I was looking at the dying foliage covered by the first frost of winter, thinking, "Why the hell haven't we had a take?" I had to get that rod in before I got caught taking the pee and just as I was swinging the lead in one of the bobbins pulled up tight, the rod tip bent over and it screamed off! The clutch gave line as the rod took on its full battle curve and something solid moved slowly off to the right with immense power. It felt heavy and was taking line out to the right. The problem was, the previous night I'd found a snag close in running out from the shelf to the right when I leaded around before placing the snide. All of a sudden a massive grating sensation transmitted back up the line. Knowing this crafty beast was up to no good I decided to cram on the pressure. The rod took on an alarming bend, as the unseen beast tried in vain to gain its freedom by doing me in this snag. Suddenly there was a big jolt on the rod as it kicked away from the snag kiting left and away. Fearing possible damage to the main line I laid off the pressure just as my client appeared. "You got one Jim?" he asked. "Yes mate, I think it might be the big 'un," I replied, as it had now dawned on me what I might be attached to. He then grabbed my net, which was leant up against the trunk of a big old oak tree and as he sunk the net I said, "Please don't lift it until I tell you to." The fish stayed deep and plodded around just under the rod tip so all I had to do was keep my cool and play her out. After about four minutes she started to rise up from the depths. Upon seeing the leadcore I knew she was close and then this massive bulk turned on the surface. I clocked the big sovereign scales along her back and I shit myself, as I now knew that the queen, my target, was very close. She set off on a short run back down but it was nothing I couldn't handle. We did not talk throughout the fight, as we both knew the score. She came up again but this time she gulped some air and wallowed on the surface like a fat pig. This was the chance and my client pushed the net out. Taking his chance, he lifted and she was mine. My obsession was now over, I'd realised my dream and I screamed "Yessss!"

The next thing I knew, it was first light and the birds were singing.

across the lake.
I touched her for the first time as I popped the hook; she was really wide and very deep. She'd clearly benefited from all the bait I'd been putting in the lake. She looked mint and had got over her ordeal from earlier in the year. I made a call to Matiz to see if he was about to do the pictures for me and all I could do was stare at what was sitting in my net. She looked well over 45lb. Matt answered and I shouted down the phone, "Got her mate!" "I'll be over shortly" he replied. Now it was the moment of truth; I was gagging to get a better look at her and matey shook my hand, saying, "That's the biggest fish I will probably ever see." While he looked after my prize I got all the things ready before I had my first proper look at her. Taking my time, I gathered the net and lifted her from her watery home. I could feel how big she was as we safely transferred my prize to the mat. She behaved like a perfect queen but one thing we noticed was how far she sat off the mat and how plump she was; full and ripe in her polished autumn coat. On the mat she looked so impressive that I was in total awe of this majestic creature. We gently got her into the sling, which we'd already zeroed and lifted this baby just off the floor. The needle of the scales slammed round and we confirmed an unbelievable weight of 49lb 4oz. I knew she looked big but this was a massive weight gain for her and I wondered why? She had obviously prospered from all that bait I had been feeding her after that ordeal which nearly killed her, all to stop me from catching her. What the hell goes on

I was looking at the dying foliage covered by the first frost of winter, thinking, "Why the hell haven't we had a take?"

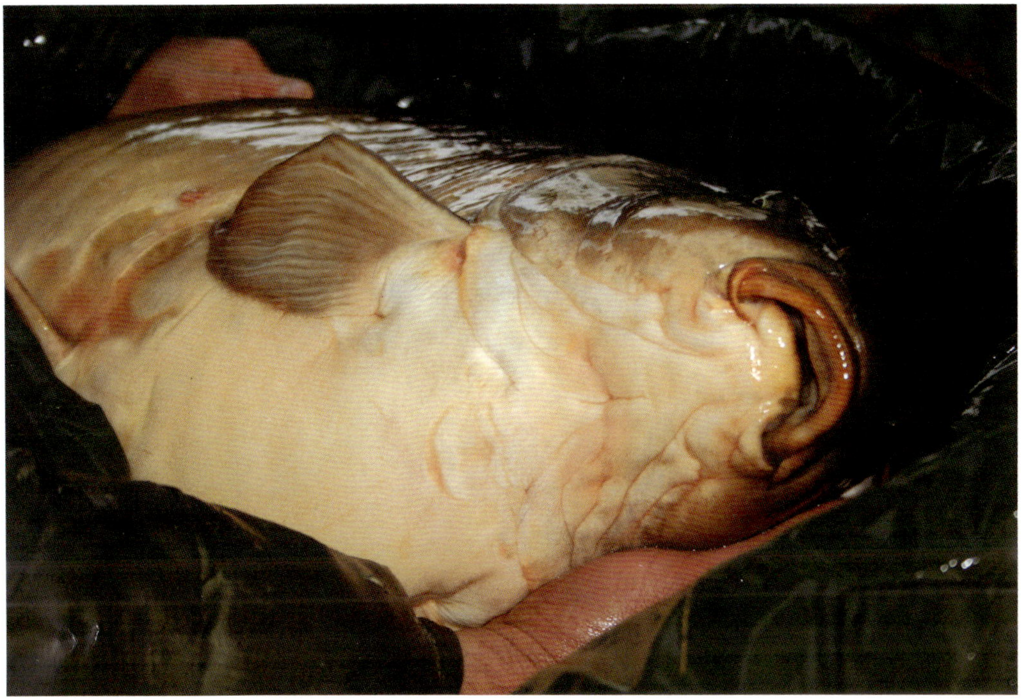

We noticed was how far she sat off the mat and how plump she was; full and ripe in her polished autumn coat.

in people's heads? The time had now come to give her a fitting name. Looking at her she had such a cute face and I had looked after her from her misfortune like she was my baby. Smiling, I whispered, "Hello Babyface." A more fitting tribute to Norfolk's biggest proper carp that looked destined for bigger things.

I popped her into a sack for a short period of time and while we waited for Matiz, Caz and Dave turned up. I stood over my prize while I waited, looking out over the misty lake, taking in the moment with a great big smile on my face. I knew that my time on there had come to a close. Matiz arrived and shook my hand, as I informed him how much she weighed. We chatted about the events of the morning and I said, "Watch this mate, I'm going to tell the camper next door." Walking into his swim I could hear him snoring, oblivious to what had happened next door. This was my time to get him back, "Oi oi Jan!" "What? Who's that?" he muttered, as I popped my head round the door and gave it to him both barrels. "Job done, I've caught the big girl!" "No you haven't!" he answered. "I have Jan. Ask yourself this question: why the hell else would I wake you up?" Walking off I told him that pictures were being done in five minutes if he wanted to come and see her.

The moment had come as the crowd gathered for a look; it was time for me to have a little cuddle with my prize. The spot had already been chosen with a backdrop of brambles, which were lightly covered in Jack Frost. Laying her gently on the mat, her

We confirmed an unbelievable weight of 49lb 4oz!

Smiling, I whispered, "Hello Babyface."

I was drawn to this sheltered area on the Tench Lake.

bulk was immense. I looked up and told those assembled, "Wait till you see her!" Undoing the sack, I revealed the queen of the pond and poured water over her. As I lifted her I told the crowd that I had named her Babyface. God she was cold. With a cheeky smile I posed with the queen; this was the moment I had waited for so long and all the time she was out of the water she behaved herself. After a few shots it was time to get her back into her world to fight another day. Matiz and I walked her over to the lake in the cradle and placed it in the margin. I covered her in water and she indicated that she was ready to go, so I tipped the mat and she slid in. I watched her gills blow bubbles, then she waddled off, disappearing from view and I punched the air shouting "Yessss!" Not long after returning her everyone had left and I was left alone with my thoughts. The feeling is magic after you bag a target but you also have a sense of being lost, as your mind starts to think, "Where next?" Before I could think about that I still had a tuition to finish, so I focused on that and after dark they danced again, mostly in front of the client. By morning nothing had happened though, and I would have put money of him getting a bite; funny old game this carp fishing.

After we said our goodbyes I decided to have a walk round the Tench Lake to try and get some inspiration. I thought that this lake and Bolton's over the road would be good options until it got really cold. I had heard that both waters fished better in the winter so things looked good for a new challenge, with the chance of more little known Norfolk gems before next spring. I was drawn to a sheltered area behind the island to the left of the only swim that allowed you to fish the area. The margin was lined with snags and after closer inspection from a high spot further round I could see a small, sunken plateau with odd tree stumps round it. This just screamed carp, so next thing was to get one of my rods and have a feel around with a light lead. This would tell me roughly how deep and how silty the bottom was. I spent several minutes leading around and this area just felt right with deep and shallow water with a soft, silty bottom. It was sheltered too, nestling behind an island flanked by massive willows. With no-one about, I wanted to get a hit of bait in for my return next week but there was a no pre-baiting rule so I had to play the game. I cast out three rods for an hour and before I reeled in I grabbed the baiting spoon and filled it in with 10kg of 15mm and 20mm squids. You might think that was a lot of bait for that time of the year but this lake had a massive population of bream and tench. I hoped they wouldn't be too much of a pest once the water cooled though.

The carp population seemed low; with around 20 to 25 carp present. There were several mirrors to 30lb and a mid-thirty common but most known captures came to tench anglers. These fish were scaly and black with several being fully scaled; the sort of old-English carp I crave. The fact that they were pretty much unknown added to the attractiveness too. After the hit went in I reeled the rods in and legged it. I knew I had got away with it and that no one saw the bait going in, so that would stop the tongues from wagging but more importantly it would keep the sheep from jumping the zone.

Graeme was an awesome ghillie!

Before leaving the village I popped into Bolton's for a look. As soon as I looked over the gate I realised that it was far too busy for me there. I didn't even go in, because sometimes it is best to stay away to keep the jungle drums quiet until I feel it is the right time for a look. While fishing over the road it would be easy to keep an eye on the venue for quieter times. I now had a plan and fishing off the back of the Babyface capture would keep me on a high for a while, without questioning what I was doing. I drove off and headed for home because the wife and I were going out for one of our special nights out. I had booked us into a very expensive restaurant called The Seafood Restaurant in Great Yarmouth that night. I like to fish hard and live life to the max, which is a part of my life people don't know about because it seems I'm known as a full-timer! I'm living the dream and long may it continue because all aspects of life are precious to me and trust me, fishing is only part of it.

Having the weekend and Monday off with Jane and the family was great but it was soon time to head back out and see if I could unlock some of the secrets of The Tench Lake. I bombed over with the tunes pumping out and before I knew it, the 45-mile journey was over and I drove down the lane to start my new challenge with a two-day session. I parked the van beside the swim that separated The Tench Lake from The Long Lake. Getting out of the van the cold hit me; winter was well and truly here now. I walked over to the swim and looked out over the water, wondering if the baited area had been visited beneath the calm, glassy surface; only time would tell. Because I had caught

I was greeted by the sight of a black-backed mirror with an orangey, chestnut belly.

Three rods fanned across the Back Bay.

Babyface, the lakes were a ghost town and I was the only person on the complex… just how I like it! This meant I could now fish in peace for a change. I soon had three rods fanned out over The Back Bay and with the traps set it was time to watch the lake for signs. Apart from a couple of bleeps, all was quiet. With darkness approaching fast I looked out across the bay wondering what was in store for the night ahead as the bats collected the last bugs of the autumn before they hibernated for the winter. The scene was set for a new challenge but I had taken on more tuition work to pay for Christmas and new tickets. The demand for my tuition trips went mental so I took the bookings, which meant that my time would be limited; but hey, you can't keep turning away the dollar! I just happened to have rib-eye steak with all the trimmings and a nice bottle of red to toast my new adventure so I was tucking into my dinner when I noticed a set of ripples rolling in from the left, then another. Standing out in the dark, I listened as an owl hooted over on the other side of the pond when suddenly one rolled out in the darkness. My senses kicked and I pinpointed the spot to the left again. I counted until I saw the ripples to gauge the distance and angle. I now knew roughly that it was over near the snags so I went for a walk round to watch over the top of the zone, so I could hopefully pinpoint the exact spot. Over the next twenty minutes I saw three more roughly in the same spot, which wasn't a million miles away from my left-hand rod. Things were looking good for a bite before I left. I wondered how much bait had been eaten but with the zone having been left natural for five days and the sightings so far,

After a spirited fight Graeme netted an awesome fully scaled mirror.

they were definitely in the mix. I thought it best to get back on the rods because things were looking good for a bite or two. In the darkness of my bivvy I soon fell asleep but sometime later I was woken by several bleeps on the left-hand rod. Watching the LED go out I felt cold, it was time to climb into the bag to get warm but before I closed my eyes, I sent Jane a message and then turned my phone off.

Suddenly, I was wide awake, pulling into the fish that I soon realised was a flaming tench. "Here we go," I thought, I hoped I wasn't going to get loads of tench therapee now because they should have been mostly asleep! I unhooked him in the net and then released him, watching the night robber dart off back into the darkness. I soon had that rig back out and topped up all the spots with a few freebies because it seemed a few robbers were on the prowl. I turned the phone on to see what the time was… flaming 2am, time to get back into the bag to warm up. Suddenly, I had a series of bleeps then nothing. Before the LED went out I had another bleep. I pulled my boots on and walked over to the rods, expecting more tench action. I could see the bobbin was well up and, as I pulled into whatever was on the other end, the rod kicked and took on a satisfying curve, telling me this was a carp after all. He kited out into the lake, heading right along the margin and within a few minutes I had him chugging around under the rod tip. Not along after that I had him in the net. I legged it back to the bivvy to grab my headtorch and peered in for a better look. I was greeted by the sight of a black-backed mirror with an orangey, chestnut belly and mismatched scale pattern on one side towards the back of his lateral line. Leaning down, I gently popped the hook and decided to leave him in the net until first light for a couple of pictures. With the rod back in the zone I rebaited them all again. I zipped the door shut but had a letterbox at the top unzipped so I could look out. I popped the kettle on and decided to watch the water as first light was only an hour away. Once the kettle boiled I left it on low, which warmed up the inside of the bivvy while I drunk my coffee. Looking out through my peephole I scanned for signs and kept an eye on the carp in my net. I heard the gate go, so someone was about and a few minutes later Graeme walked into my swim. He asked me how I was and if anything was happening. As I pointed at the net one of my rods screamed into life. I scrambled out of the bivvy and grabbed the right-hand rod, commencing battle with another Tench Lake carp. It felt like another small one, darting about the swim, but after a spirited fight Graeme netted an awesome fully scaled mirror. When you catch these pretty, rarely caught carp size does not matter in the slightest. I didn't bother weighing these fish but you can see from the pictures how unique they are, especially the fully who had black edging to his sovereign scales and a pinky-red underneath.

After I slipped him back I got the rod back out on its silty spot, which was just off the corner of the island. I thought that this would be a natural route in and out of the bay area. A few more baits went out with the throwing stick and Graeme disappeared over

He wallowed on the surface and we got a real good look at his armour-plated body.

to The Main Lake in his search for Babyface. I decided it was brekkie time and you cannot beat a nice bowl of porridge with jam or brown sugar to keep you fed. While I was tucking into it I had a few more bleeps and as I watched the line where it entered the water, it twitched several times. Putting the porridge down, I walked over to the rods and pulled the line. The line kept coming, which could only mean one thing… as Jeremy Wade would say, "Fish on!" I reeled in the slack until it started to tighten and I made contact with a crafty one. He turned and stripped several yards off me, which had me thinking that this might be a bigger one. One of the other rods started bleeping as he picked the line up. I turned the buzzer off and a few seconds later he dropped that line. He was plodding around deep down under the rod tip when Graeme appeared asking if I wanted him to land the fish for me. He grabbed the net and we watched the line cutting through the surface. I looked down into the gin-clear water to get my first glimpse and I saw a flash of scales. This was another scaly babe that looked bigger than the other two. A couple more minutes passed before he wallowed on the surface and we got a real good look at his armour-plated body. Graeme pushed the net out and he went in first time. Slackening off I let the fish sink to the bottom of the net and another scaly gem was mine. This session was unreal! I wasn't expecting to catch so many beautiful, scaly specimens in one trip, let alone the first! No one knew exactly what the lake's population was because only the odd carp had been caught, so there was the added buzz of unlocking its secrets. Lakes like this are very hard to find these days and

He was long, with perfect lines of scales, a unique creature.

keeping it quiet is even harder, unless you're poaching somewhere you shouldn't be. Suddenly, my worst nightmare walked into my swim in the form of Jim The Punisher AKA The Town Crier. I hoped he wouldn't clock what was in my net. "Any good Jim?" he asked, pointing at the net. I said, "No carp, just had a tench." I just had to hope that he wouldn't hang around and prayed the net didn't move, giving my secret away. If he rumbled me the news would spread fast. This bloke totally took the piss, sitting in my swim on The Main Lake for hours, just watching what I was doing, to the extent that I would go into the bivvy and shut the door. It all came to a head one evening and I told him straight to get lost and get on with his own fishing, because his behaviour was a bit abnormal and I felt like I was being stalked! Thankfully, he didn't hang around and, as he walked off, Graeme and I shrugged at each other. I knew he would probably sheep me up in some way though, and spread the news that I was on The Tench Lake now. We watched him disappear onto The Main Lake so this was the chance we needed to get the pictures done. We got the undercover exercise done before the Town Crier rumbled us! I weighed him while Graeme kept an eye out. Thankfully, we were fairly well hidden, so unless he walked past at the end of the track we should be OK. For the record, this beast weighed 26lb 12oz. He was another fine example of the lake's stock and was covered in big plate-like scales, which gave him an impressive, armour-plated body. He had a creamy underneath, which gave him a different look to the other two I'd caught. The pictures were done in double quick time and I slipped him back while Graeme kept watch. I watched him glide off from view and I wondered what other secrets the lake held for me. Before I got the rod back on the spot I thought I had better clear the swim up so there was no evidence, hiding the sling and mat from view. With everything sorted and the rod back out, I topped up the swim and finished off my porridge, which was cold. My philosophy is waste not, want not, so I tucked in to my cold grubus.

Throughout the day, several anglers walked round the pond. I knew that this was because of The Town Crier spouting his news but as soon as I saw people I dived into the bivvy so I couldn't be questioned. Deep down I knew I would get sheeped up once the swim became free. The rest of the day was deadly quiet apart from the odd sheep walking past and I wondered what the night and early morning period had in store for me. Graeme was set up close by on The Main Lake, so once it was dark I went over to see him. The bats were out again, fluttering around the trees, gathering what was left before their slumber. Graeme was two swims from the corner and as we chatted he informed me that he had seen one show over his baited area. Things were looking good for him, plus he had the lake to himself. With the weather still spot on Graeme knew there was still a chance she could slip up again. The area he was fishing had form, so it was a wise move before winter took the lake in its grip. Back at my plot I watched and listened for signs but after a while I decided it was time to get my head down. Apart from a bream and the odd bleep through the night all was quiet and it seemed that the carp had done the offski. I woke up at first light just in time to see a rod go into meltdown. I pulled my boots on and connected with another carp that shot off, taking

As he turned, his scales opened up, reminding me of a leopard's coat.

some line before kiting and locking up solid. Shit this one had got stuck around the plateau. I opened the bale arm and watched the line on the surface. It started moving so I reeled into it and played him hard to keep him away from the submerged snags. Once I got him clear, I laid off the pressure, as there was no need for it now plus the line could easily be damaged. A few minutes passed before he was ready for the net and amazingly it was another fully scaled! Watching this peach go over the cord I just couldn't believe this lake held so many unknown scalys! I put the rod down because I had to have a closer look. He was long, with perfect lines of scalies, a very unique creature.

Being as it was early and I couldn't see Graeme about, I decided to leave him in the net while I sorted the rod out. Leaning it up against the bivvy, I climbed in and sat down to tie a new rig when I heard a few bleeps. Looking over, I saw the bobbin rise a few inches and stop. Thinking it was a liner, I carried on what I was doing but then there were another couple of bleeps so I walked out for a closer look. Pulling the line I realised that there was far too much slack out there so I picked the rod up and reeled the slack in until I made contact. The rod hooped over, it was definitely another carp and after a short tussle I landed another scaly one. Now I had two stunners sitting together in the net. They both looked similar in size and as I popped the hook Graeme turned up saying, "I heard that take!" "I've got two mate," I replied, "Wait 'til you see them in the flesh!" I had to get these fish sorted before my catch was rumbled so I

I reckoned that he had been trailing a tench angler's rig.

Old looking and awesome!

placed the first fish on the mat. I had a look inside its mouth and it was perfect, with no hook marks apart from mine. Suddenly, the sun came out to play so I decided to do the pictures before we weighed him. His scales lit up in the early morning sun and he looked a truly awesome specimen. To this day he's one of my favourite carp. For the record he weighed 18lb 12oz. Lowering the sling back into the lake, I whispered, "Thanks for the moment," and he swam off into the darkness; one of the special ones that I will never forget. The sun had now done a disappearing act so it was back to doom and gloom but as I lifted the net, the second carp turned in the clear water and his scales opened out, reminding me of a leopard's coat. On the mat I noticed that he had a split in his dorsal fin, which had healed and if you look in the picture there is a slight line mark on his side. I reckon he'd been trailing a rig after snapping up a tench or bream angler. There was nothing I could do to repair it because if I could, I would have stitched it back together. On the scales this old, scaly warrior weighed 19lb 6oz and after a few pictures were taken I returned him. I wished him good luck because I knew he had been through the wars but he was on his way back to his former glory.
After I returned the second fish, a carp boshed out in the corner of The Long Lake behind my bivvy. This was too good an opportunity to miss so I noted the spot and planned to put a rod on that until I packed up and headed home. All I had to do was keep an eye out for bailiffs because you aren't allowed to have rods in two lakes at the same time. Graeme legged it back to his swim and left me to it. With the rig in place

I was immediately drawn to a massive Norfolk reed bed.

The plan was to fish a tight swim that faced the reeds.

and seven free offerings around it I put the rod on the buzzer with the butt on the back of the swim. It was time to start packing down and keep an eye out for the Town Crier. Unbelievably, while I was loading the gear into the van, a buzzer screamed. Running over to the three rods, I realised that it was the snide in The Long Lake. Straight away whatever was attached stripped some line off me and headed out into the middle of the lake. Graeme appeared and grabbed the net as the fish chugged about. He was soon ready for the net though, and Graeme did the honours once again for me. I decided to reel the other rods in and lean them up against the van before we sorted the fish so I wouldn't get caught. Once I'd picked a spot and we had him on the mat, I unfolded the net to reveal an awesome, old-looking, mint-condition linear with a black back and apple-slice scales. He had no marks in his mouth either, which meant that he was another rare one… just how I like it. I popped him into Marky's weigh sling and the scales registered 21lb 12oz. What a session; fish from two lakes on my first trip on either of them in November. The Long Lake had suffered an oxygen crash after the floods and it still had problems, so any carp over 20lb were to be removed and put into The Main Lake. Several fish up to 30lb (including a Main Lake resident that had moved in the floods) had already been moved, so after the pictures were done I walked him over in the cradle and released him into The Main Lake, where he now prospers at around thirty pounds at the right time.

After packing up I baited both lakes with another 10kg for my return the following

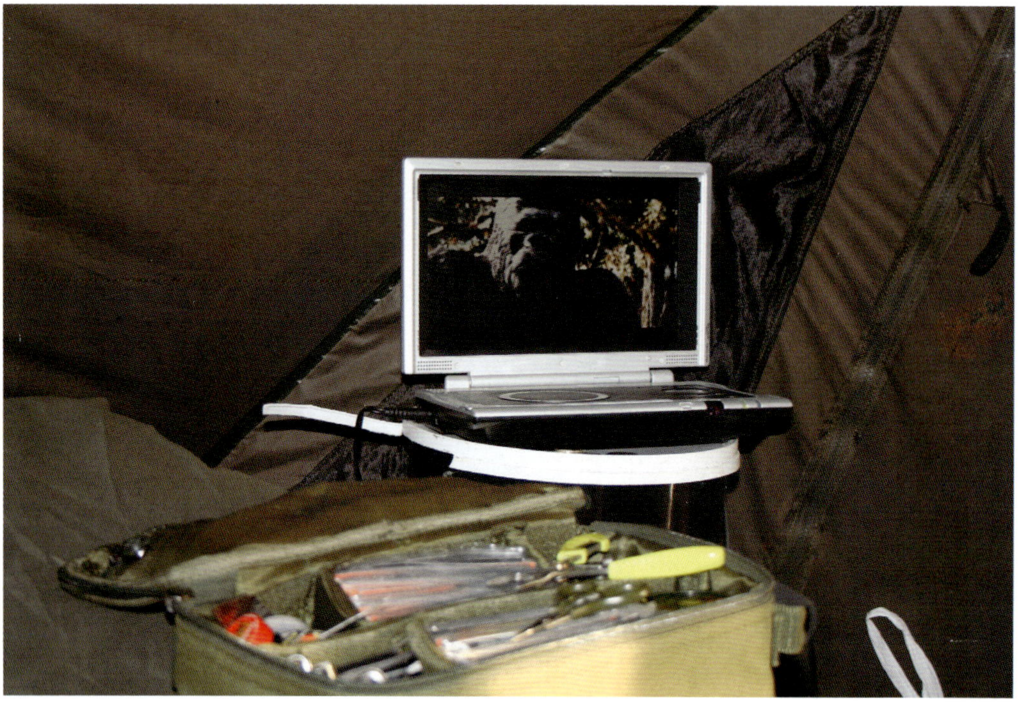

I fell asleep in front of the DVD player and when I woke, there was something quite different on the box!

week. Unfortunately, this wasn't to happen because the area I'd fished on The Tench Lake got sheeped at both ends. Also, following the capture of the big girl from The Main Lake my mobile was on meltdown with tuition bookings, so with news of the sheep shaggers in the zone, I decided to take on a lot of work, not returning to the complex that year. However, Bolton's had winter form and I fancied a go on there before my ticket ran out as I was not renewing it. Before I left the village I popped into Bolton's for a look and, as I drove through the gate, I was gobsmacked because the lake now resembled a building site. I was gutted because when I first clapped eyes on this lake it was one of the most beautiful lakes I had ever had the pleasure to see. The lake was situated in very old woodland with massive old, oak trees that must have been there since year dot. The lake looked untouched and had a magical feel to it that drew me in. Massive lily pads were dotted about for the lake's monsters to hide in; it had an unbelievable atmosphere that's hard to describe. What I was looking at now saddened me to the point that I was too upset to walk round. Just as I was turning the van round the owner, Mo, appeared and me being me, I told him what I thought about what he had done. He had raped a lot of the lake's beauty and I couldn't understand why, but I did agree with what he was doing on the other lake, which was overgrown and had silted up. What he did to the main lake was bang out of order but hey, they are his lakes. Not long after I left not knowing if I would ever return.

32lb 8oz of Bolton's finest.

Towards the end of November Babyface made another appearance at a staggering weight of 50lb plus, which was good news for Uncle Jim because the knives were out. Jealous green-eyed monsters had taken it upon themselves to knock my capture by saying that I had weighed it wrong or made up the weight. I suppose it was because of the massive weight gain this carp had put on during the season but this silenced the knockers. Just for the record, jealousy is a disease and if I ever get like this about others' captures it will be the day I give up carping. I target these fish for several reasons: the lakes they live in, their history and the people who have caught them and trust me, the weight plays no part because it is the fish I desire, FACT. Despite my misgivings, I returned to Bolton's during a mild spell in January. With the lake being mainly shallow, I thought the fish would be on the move. As I pulled up to the gate I told myself to fish the lake no matter what I thought of it now. I then parked the van, grabbed my glasses and went off for a walk around the pond. No one was about and after I had done a circuit of the lake I was immediately drawn to a massive Norfolk reed bed, which had to be a holding area. The plan was to fish a tight swim that faced the reeds, so I parked behind the swim. Before I unloaded my gear I thought it best to get a pair of wellies on because it was like a mud bath where the machinery had churned the ground up; I just hoped I would be able to get the van out when I left the venue, only time would tell.
Time was getting on I had to get the rods out. Before I tied the rig and fresh bait I wanted to make several casts around the swim with a small lead to see what the bottom felt like. It was a very mature lake so I knew the bottom would have a lot of silty areas, but after several casts and I'd found no gravel so this was sweet for my style of fishing. All I had to do was fan my three chod rigs from the reed bed, out into the lake. I spread 100 baits over the area where the rods were positioned and then got my house up before settling back and watching for anything carpy. Nothing was seen apart from small fish flipping on the surface. It had been so mild for over a week that they had to be on the mooch and I was sure I was in a good area. If I saw something else I would of course act on it and this swim gave me a great view of the lake. After dark I thought it was time to cook up some dinner and watch a film. My mate Dave had given me some new stuff to watch and I sat back and watched Dog Soldiers, drinking a nice bottle of cold white wine. I was enjoying the film in the dark with its werewolves and soldiers but I must have fallen asleep as I awoke with someone outside my bivvy asking, "Jim, what the fcuk's going on in there?" I too wondered what the fcuk was going on, as there was a girl on the DVD player screen moaning and groaning and some bloke outside the bivvy! The geezer who had taped these films for me had clearly put some porn movies on there as well! Turning it off I said, "Who's there?" The reply came, "It's Matiz, what's going on in there son?" "Some fcuking porn film…" I explained I'd fallen asleep watching Dog Soldiers and this was on the end of the film. "Yeah right Jim," was his predictable reply. "Honest mate!"

I opened the door and got out for a leak, then sat down and had a swig of wine to clear the bad taste in my mouth. As we chatted the right-hand rod bleeped twice, then the bobbin on that same rod pulled tight and the rod tip pulled down. Picking the rod up

When I arrived at the swim I could see signs that it had been fished.

I felt the satisfying weight of a carp on the other end, which took several yards of line off the clutch. Matiz grabbed the net as this fish started to kite well to the left, coming in along the margin. This wasn't good because this margin was well snaggy so I walked to the left of the swim, hopped over the rods and plunged the 13ft rod well under the surface. I hoped this ruse would keep the line away from the overhanging bushes. I felt the line pinging off the snags so I reeled down hard to steer him out and it worked. The fish came out shooting under the other rods on a short run but I kept the pressure on to slow him down. Matiz dropped the net down into the water in silence as the fish came back in close. A massive swirl appeared on the surface and suddenly he was ready for the net. Matiz lifted it and he was mine first time. I laid the rod down and grabbed my headtorch from the bivvy. Turning it on I could see a long leather with a great big head. Turning to Matt I said, "He looks like a thirty." More importantly though, it was another proper Norfolk babe to add to the collection from many of the county's best waters.

Matiz watched the fish while I shot off to get the mat and bits ready. Handing him my camera, I carefully got the fish on the mat so we could now get a better look at him. He was an old-looking warrior with a big head and his mouth was massive. He had the bottom part of his tail missing but it had healed. This was certainly from an otter attack and the sad thing is that these vermin are killing our sport. Bolton's had suffered greatly because during the period it was being sold the otters had taken many fish, which was another reason I wasn't renewing. I had pictures of many of the lake's jewels from a mate called Stewart Rackham who was lucky enough to fish it several years before as a guest. We now knew most of these special carp were gone to the teeth of the otter and many more have been lost nationwide. These vermin are protected and with no measures available to protect our fish in many cases, they are slowly but surely killing our sport and things will only get worse. I do wonder if it's the beginning of the end, perhaps we will see a sport that's only enjoyed behind fencing? Only time will tell and the clock is ticking. We placed the big leather in Marky's sling and popped him on the scales to confirm a weight of 32lb 8oz. I covered him in water then picked him up as Matiz clicked away with the camera. Laying him down I gave him the once-over, making sure he was OK. It was time to set him free and I wished him good luck but without the protection of an otter fence things weren't looking good for any fish in this area and many have been lost since to the 'cuddly' otter.

With the rod back in the zone and a few more free offerings sticked out, Matiz and I had a good chat until around midnight, when he had to go because he had work in the morning. Nothing else happened that session but before I packed up I saw a carp stick his head out over on the other side, so before I left I baited the area for my next trip. I had a proper feel around with lead too, and just found silt again. On closer inspection I also noticed that there was a dying lily bed nearby, perfect for Mr Carp to hide in, in these mild conditions. Before leaving I decided to check the back of the reed bed. The water here is shallow and you never know what you might find, as carp love reeds and at certain times in the winter carp were seen in this area. My polarising glasses helped me search through the clear water and I watched for any movements on the reed stems. I'd seen nothing when I heard the gate go; luckily I'd got my bait in without anyone seeing. It was time to leg it home so I made my way over to the van, opened the back and got my rod and baiting equipment straight in before whoever it was saw anything. It would now be bad enough that he had seen me here because the drums would be beating but I didn't want to add baiting up to the rumours too. Unbeknown to me I would need his help because my van was going nowhere in the building site's thick mud. My wheels were just spinning furiously; now I would have to ask for some help. This probably meant me getting questioned, but I was going to say nowt if asked. I was embarrassed but I had to get out of here. Luckily for me I could see that this bloke had a 4x4 and walking up to the car park I recognised the geezer as Nathan. Telling him I was stuck, he said, "Don't worry Jim, I'll soon have your van out of that shit," which he sure did and within five minutes I was free. Thanking him, I was soon on my way home to the missus before I got any therapee.

The following week I only had 24 hours because I had a lot of tuitions booked in, but I had a new zone baited ready for my return on Thursday and that day couldn't come fast enough. With several days of tuition work done you can imagine I was gagging to get back over to the pond. I was breaking all the speed limits while blowing my brains out listening to acid house and soon pulled up to the gate. I hoped there was no one about and thankfully the car park was empty… sweet as a pea. Uncle Jim knew exactly

I set the bedchair up at the front of the swim so I could watch for signs.

where he was heading for, which just happened to be over the other side, where I had primed up for my return. After six days of being left alone it should have been bang on. The conditions were the same but a cold blast was forecast to come in over the weekend, which would mean a return to winter, so this would probably be my last chance before the ticket ran out. All I could think about as I loaded my gear onto the barrow was getting round there and getting the rods out in the zone. While pushing the barrow round my confidence was sky high and as soon as I got there I looked down and noticed the swim had been fished. Oh well, this wasn't going to put me off because it was probably over the weekend and several days had passed since then. I was carrying on regardless unless I saw a sign from Mr Carp. I did notice that the mild ripple had blown quite a lot of fresh weed into the margin, which told me something had uprooted it. This could have been one of two creatures, tufted ducks or fish. There were no tufties on the pond so it had to be fish, hopefully carp. Once again, it comes back to hunting skills and the knowledge to process what is in front of you. So, with this newfound information my confidence was sky high. Thirty minutes later I had three rigs rocking in the zone, followed by around 200 baits. With the house set up at the back of the swim I thought I would lie down on the bedchair watching for any signs. With all the therapee from several tuitions I was knackered and must have fallen asleep because the next thing I knew I was woken up by a few bleeps on the middle rod. It was dark and I had crashed out for a fair few hours. "A liner," I thought, as the LED

A fitting way to sign off, but the otters soon destroyed what was a top fishery.

went out, "They must be about." It was 5pm so I must have been out for around five hours! I sat up on the edge of the bed and realised that I needed to relieve my bladder and that my stomach was rumbling. Before I cooked anything I thought I had better phone Jane up and have a chat with her before I got into trouble! With it being so mild I decided to sit out on my coat to watch and listen while I took in the surroundings and cooked. Unusually for this time of the year some bats hunted around the bushes for a bite to eat, probably knowing this would be their last chance for a while.

After a few hours I suddenly heard one roll out in the darkness, which seemed to be to the right. This was confirmed as I watched the angle the ripples came in from; somewhere near the right-hand rod. After this sighting it was time to send Jane a text message wishing her good night before turning the mobile off and climbing into the bag to chill and watch the rods for a while. Not long after I received another liner and over the next few hours I was to receive some of the most intense liners I have ever had! Some were so savage that they had me legging it down to my rods to investigate. Surely it was only a matter of time before I had a take? Eventually everything went quiet and I was drifting in and out of sleep disturbed by all those liners, coupled with the effect of all that sleep I'd had earlier. I hoped I hadn't let a chance slip by. What seemed like several hours later I had a single bleep on the middle rod. I was watching the blue LED intently when the buzzer screamed. This had to finally be a run and I ran over barefooted and picked the rod up. Line was immediately ripped from the spool at a fair old rate. The carp headed right and not long after that horrible grating sensation came back through the rod and everything went solid. He had gained sanctuary in the lily bed. Immediately I slackened off to see if there was any movement but there wasn't. Closing the bale arm, I applied some pressure to see if I could get him moving but I couldn't. Over the next couple of minutes I repeated this two or three more times but on the third attempt, something started to move. Slowly but surely I gained some line back on the reel, then he came free and darted to the left over the other rods. Fearing for the hook hold I gently played him out under the rod. Swirls appeared on the surface and I slowly pushed the net out, as a back broke the surface. Pushing the net underneath him I lifted and the water in the net exploded but he was mine. Turning on my headtorch, there laid another leathery mirror around the same size as the last one. It did cross my mind that he could be the same fish again but on closer inspection I knew it was one of the other leathers in the lake, happy days for Uncle Jim! I did some self-takes in the half-light and weighed the old brute at 33lb.

After I slipped him back I let a few close mates know what I had caught. Not long afterwards I packed up and after I closed the gate I was never to return. Mega-cold conditions hit the country and my ticket finished before the lake thawed out. It was a shame the otters had taken so many of Norfolk's finest and trust me, if they were still there I would have renewed my ticket even though its magical surroundings had been mown down.

Fen Drayton

Back Into The Wilderness

Fen is a very special place that I hold dear to my heart. It's 92-acres of semi-wilderness that is mostly left the way nature intended. Then you have the fish that live there, some of the best scaly jewels this country holds; mirrors and commons that know how to live in the real world, as they mostly eat the profusion of natural food that Fen holds. I have fished there on and off since 1999 because it's somewhere for me to hide and get away from the bullshit that surrounds certain circuit waters I fish. You cannot beat the drive down the long track; it's a buzz that sends shivers up and down my spine. Fen is like a home to me and every now and then I have to sample its magic!

After 'Marky-Mark' Shave died I hadn't fished Fen for nearly two and half years. I did go down at certain times to make sure things were OK, as it's a very special place and I am sure the carp gods have chosen me to protect and look after the venue and the fish that swim in there. Since my last book the fish have grown on and several of the uncaught fish have been banked; mind you, there are always one or two unknowns caught most years, so you always have that mystery, as you never know what you might catch. There are several fish that I haven't caught, so it's great for me when I do go and fish it. We have several forties in Fen now and they're still growing. The list includes Single, Olive, Humpy Common, Bayes Common and The Client, with loads of back-up thirties like The Angry Linear, Marcus Mirror, Pug Face Common, Black Spot and the untold amounts of scaly mirrors and those awesome Fen commons.

The anglers that fish there know the score and all get told the way of The Fen. There aren't loads of rules; just use common sense and respect the water, its surroundings and your fellow anglers. Trust me, if you don't you're told to leave. It's harder than ever to obtain a Fen ticket, as I just want the right anglers fishing there, so we have a vetting system in place now but every now and then one slips through the net. Fen has become a much-talked-about water these days. The Client is spoken about as being one of, if not the most awesome looking carp that we have in this country. So, as you can imagine, the waiting list is very long, so much so that I've put a publicity ban on the water now. Members can use the pictures but fish must be described as having

Fen is 92 acres of semi-wilderness, left the way nature intended.

been caught from a 90-acre Cambs pit. Things changed at Fen, the RSPB bought the complex and stupid rumours started to do the rounds. I heard that I wasn't running it anymore, and that there were to be no boats and no close-season fishing. Now, I can tell you all that John Turrell and I still run it together, we still have the boats and of course we can fish it all season round. We have a good relationship with the RSPB and everything runs OK, apart from someone over at Ferry Lagoon who likes to stir things up between the two syndicates and the RSPB. I have often thought about dishing the therapy out myself, but I prefer that the same old crap comes from one side of the fence and not from Fen's side, as I'm sure they wouldn't want me walking round Ferry spouting bollocks!

With Single Scale having broken the magical forty-pound barrier, Fen was now on my mind and it was time to venture back for a go. It was a hot Sunday afternoon as I drove down the lane and the familiar buzz was still there and as long I get that feeling I will continue to fish at Fen. Before the lake appeared on my right I looked up at the big clouds of insects hanging around the bushes and noticed the birds collecting them to feed their chicks. After I pulled up to the gate and opened the car door I could hear birds singing and insects buzzing around; God it was great to be back and I was buzzing at the prospect of hunting for the Fen carp again, it had been too long. It was muggy and hot and my mind was racing as to where the carp would be. They hadn't spawned yet so I knew they would be in the shallows near the spawning bay, grouping up for their yearly ritual. As I pulled into the car park I could see that I had the lake to myself. This was going to be sweet as I could now boat around to my heart's content. I drove along the road that runs along one bank until I came to the slipway, then it was time to pump the inflatable boat up and have a mooch about to see if I could find them.

I was sweating loads as I worked hard to pump the boat up in the afternoon sun, so I walked down to the water's edge, cupped my hands in the clear cool water and then covered my head in it. At the same time I noticed the margins were alive with caddis, shrimps and tiny snails. It was great to be back! I headed to my car and grabbed the bag that held my markers, a bottle of drink and of course my lifejacket. As I put my lifejacket on the memories started hitting me. I looked across at Puffer's Point where the small willow saplings that Marky and I had planted were really tall now. We had planted them years ago to give the anglers on Puffer's Point some cover from the winds that ripped through there as well as giving the fish some cover in the edge as they used the margin a lot in the warm weather.

I pushed the boat out then waded out into deeper water before jumping aboard. With one oar I started to row my boat ever so quietly as I didn't want to spook any carp if I came across them. Knowing the water so well, I headed straight to the spawning bay and as I neared the area my mind was working overtime. Which ones would I see

Memories immediately started hitting me. I looked over to Puffer's Point where the small willow saplings that Marky and I had planted were really tall now.

first? The standing position gives me a much better view of what is ahead and as I got closer the water started shallow up until I was over just three feet of water. The weed was coming up; there just had to be some in the bay. I couldn't see any as I scanned my eyes across the shallow water. There were signs that they had been about in the form of tiny clearings in the weed, with some even cleared off to the sandy bottom. I made way around the bay but no carp were seen, but I knew that it was only a matter of time before I bumped into them.

The next zone was Pet Shop Corner. This has a deep gully running into it, with snags running along the margin where they like to hide and sun themselves. It also has a massive, shallow bar running into it with a shallow plateau on the end of the bar, near some reeds close to the margin; the fish love this area. Nothing was seen here either but more carpy signs were noted and before leaving I put some salty seeds of the gods down, with a few whole and crumbed up fishmeals. When the carp came back there would be a snack waiting for them and it would serve as a good indicator for me – if the food was gone, I'd fish it. The next area I decided to check was round the island in the middle of the lake. There's a lot of shallow ground out there with four old roads running to the island in a star shape. Fen used to be four separate lakes that were joined into one and the old roadways are now used by carp when they move from area to area. At certain times, if you're lucky, these long-tow spots can do the job but as a

Before leaving I put some salty seeds of the gods down, with a few whole and crumbed up fishmeals.

There is a big plateau on the other side of the island and as I came close to it I noticed eelgrass and silkweed.

rule simple casting range is the way at Fen these days. When I didn't see anything out there either I began to worry! I was expecting to have bumped into some carp long before now… where the hell were they?

The Puffer's Point side of the island was my next staging post. There is a lot of shallow water out there and the fish can follow the bar back towards the slipway. The only other places I would check would be The Car Park area, up along The Bars Swim and then into The Pipe. Surely I had to see them soon because it was hot and muggy, perfect fish-spotting weather. There is a big plateau on the other side of the island and as I came close to it I noticed eelgrass and silkweed. Carp love this weed because when it's fresh it's normally full of snails for them to feed on. I also think they like the feel of it as they swim through, even using this weed to rid themselves of parasites, a bit like a body scrub! I noticed a rocking movement on the surface and as I stopped rowing a back subtly broke the surface, then one came up to the boat – bingo, I'd found them. The longer I watched, the more signs I saw until I gently laughed to myself, thinking how I'd boated past this area, thinking they would be in the spawning-bay area. It was great to see them again, it had been too long since I'd fished here. The buzz was back and I felt comfortable again. I found that I could now handle the inevitable memories that I shared with Marky and once again enjoy the magic at Fen.

I watched about ten fish from the boat and knew I was going to fish from Puffer's.

I had popped back at different times of year just to reminisce about the good old days Marky and I had there together.

I didn't see any of the Fen giants but they had to be close by as I was sure they were grouping up ready for their annual spawning ritual. Knowing that I had a good chance of a bite, I decided to get out of the area and leave them be until it was time to place the baits by boat, as they seemed to be mostly sitting at range in the weed. I gently picked the oar up and headed away from them, back out into deeper water before heading off to the swim. It was great to see them and I knew it was the right time to be back. I had popped back at different times of year just to reminisce about the good old days Marky and I had there together. It was just too emotional for me to fish there at that time and it was hard to put all that behind me, as Marky was more than a friend, he was more like a brother to me. It's hard for me now, as I write these words about him, seven years on with tears in my eyes; God I miss him so much and I will never forget the times we spent together. Gone but not forgotten.

As I got out of the boat I couldn't believe how high the willow saplings had grown since we planted them all those years ago, the plan had worked and had given the swim so much cover now. The car was parked on the slipway and we could drive onto Puffer's back then so this was going to be easy fishing from the road bank. I quickly unloaded the car, as I was gagging to get my rods in position because it was getting on now and I had been boating around for a few hours. The time had flown so quickly without me knowing, purely because I was enjoying being back at Fen. All four rods were to be fished on long, running chods. I checked the hooks to see if they were still

The snails and caddis can whittle hook baits in no time at all.

sharp and tied my meshed-up Scopex Squid hook baits on. The snails and caddis can whittle hook baits in no time at all, so meshing them up prolongs the life of the cork ball pop-up. Because I was to be fishing over a lot of weed, I decided to crumb some boilies up in a bucket as these would sit on the weed and be so much more visible to the carp as round baits would drop down out of sight. I planned to fish two rods on the weed and two rods on the dirty lake bed, where I could see signs that they'd been digging around.

Once the boat was kitted out with the electric outboard and battery I placed the bucket of crumb and a bag of 15mm squids in the boat before donning my life jacket and grabbing one of the rods. I pushed the boat out and climbed in just before the shelf dropped off into deeper water. I headed out to where I had seen the carpy activity and as I got close I turned the motor off and used the oar to keep the noise and disturbance down to a minimum. They were still about and I didn't want to spook them too much, so I decided to fish both my longer rods on the weed.

As I got close to the area I found some flattened weed that looked like something had spawned on it, probably bream. This flattened area looked fresh so I quickly lowered the rig down but as it was shallow water I waited for the chod pop-up to rise up the leadcore before letting the leadcore sink along the bottom. I then threw two handfuls

Once the boat was ready I placed the bucket of crumb and a bag of 15mm squids inside, donned my life jacket and headed out with a rod.

I knew that the carp passed Puffer's a lot closer in too, so I made a decision to fish two rods off the front of Puffer's and space two single rods out down the side.

of crumb around it and seven whole baits before opening the bale arm to let out line as I motored back to the swim. As I got further away I turned the motor up and when I got close to the swim I turned it off. Before getting out I took about a rod length of line off before setting foot out of the boat as I didn't want to pull the line tight and risk messing up my presentation. The other rod was fished about twenty yards away to the right of the first, on top of the weed along with a handful of crumb for visual attraction. There seemed to be two feet of water over the weed so this was an ideal spot to ambush one cruising past. Both of the rods were way out, just over hundred yards, and knowing the lake as well as I do, I knew that the carp passed Puffer's a lot closer in too, so I made a decision to fish two rods of the front of puffers and space two single rods out down the side of puffers facing the slipway, where the two roads run off the slipway and join to the island. The bank curves away to the right, forming a slight corner, lined with Norfolk reeds. There's a lot of shallow ground, around 6ft deep, but the area also has two deeper gullies running across it.

The shallow, flat areas have this soft, dark covering and when the tench, bream and carp are about you can see tiny holes in this layer where they have sifted through it. You also can see the crushed-up snail shells as they show up white through a glass-bottomed bucket. As I made my way out, I was looking for a flat, recently used area in the dark bottom, hopefully near some weed. As I got out to the area I soon found

The bank curved away to the right, forming a slight corner that is lined with Norfolk reeds.

several of these areas, five in total. One spot had a white reed leaf near it so for some reason, I placed two rods on other spots close by. However, the leaf spot played on my mind for some reason and I just couldn't get it out of my head so I jumped into the boat as the light was fading to replace one of the other rods on the reed spot. I really don't know why it attracted me so much but I was on a mission to get it placed there before I couldn't see the bottom of the lake, as the light levels were fading fast. It took around ten minutes to locate it using the bucket as I couldn't see much looking with my glasses from the boat. Once I'd found it, I quickly lowered the chod down and waited for the pop-up to rise to the top again before letting the rig settle to the bottom. I watched as the pop-up disappeared from view in six feet of water, then I threw two handfuls of crumb on top, with seven free offerings spread around.

Back on the bank, I split the rods up as I was fishing two off the front and the other two off the side of Puffer's. Everything was pukka and I felt confident of a bite as I was on the fish big time. I was halfway there so now it was time to pray to the carp gods and take in the Fen magic I had missed so much and remember the good old days with Marky for company. As the light faded I watched in awe as the sun set and those special colours that you only see at Fen painted the sky. The birds were singing heartily and the rabbits popped out from the bramble bushes to play in the grass, then the curse of the Fens emerged, in the form of many different insects; it was time to peg on

the clear view camo screen to stop them biting in the night.
I was sampling Fen at its best and I had the lake to myself. As I was chilling, I thought I noticed a light to my right and wondered if someone had turned up. I did hear a couple roll over in the area as I listened and watched long into the darkness, both sounded closer than the two long rods. Soon the biters were after me though, and as I was knackered I retreated back to the bivvy for safety. Now I was safe and protected from the insects it was time to sleep and dream about those Fen babes!
Next thing I knew, I was standing there with a rod well bent, shaking my head, wondering if I was dreaming. To this day I cannot remember the take, but this thing was stripping line off me at a mental rate. It went solid so I put the rod down after loosening the clutch as it was now going to be a boat battle; there was no way I was going to risk bullying her out when I could simply go get her from the boat. This was for real and trust me, this wasn't a wet dream. I quickly put on my life jacket and, before picking up the rod, I cupped my hands and pushed them into the cool margin, splashing my face with lake water to bring me back into the land of the living before getting in the boat.
I grabbed the rod and pushed the boat out, there was no need to worry about the net as it was already in the boat. I climbed in and reeled towards the weeded fish, I didn't need the motor until she was free. Now my thoughts turned to which one could it be, was it even still on? I hadn't felt any movement yet. I knew it couldn't be more than 60

The special colours that you only see at Fen painted the sky as the sun set.

yards out and I knew that I was getting closer as the line was getting low in the water. Next, the line was coming straight up, telling me the weeded fish was close. All of a sudden there was a massive explosion of water as I spooked the fish and the boat was dragged off by a mental surge of power from the fish, straight back towards the bank. Thank God I had the clutch set pukka, as if I hadn't this fish would have smashed me up.

The line was peeling off the spool as the boat was being dragged along at the same time, then I saw the reeds where I was fishing open and close! What the hell was going on? All movement had stopped again and I reeled myself towards the fish. I hadn't seen this animal yet and as I got to the reed bed I gently pulled it out. As the fish emerged, I saw that it was a mirror and was massive with a big, black back. "Christ Uncle, which one is it?" I wondered. I didn't want to lose this Fen jewel, as I was so close to this baby. The fish then glided out into the deep margin but without a show of power this time, which told me that it was knackered. It was time to play it gently as there was no need to add pressure after this intense battle. I just enjoyed the moment and watched the mirror in the crystal-clear water, twisting and turning beneath the boat; it looked awesome and pumped right up. The swirls on the surface indicated the carp was close to netting now and the next thing, it was on the top. I pushed the net out ready and a massive mouth was now gulping air. As I drew the net over I saw a big scale in the middle of her flank, telling me it was Single. She was out a few weeks previously at 45lb plus and looked massive as I lifted the net around her. Once she was over the cord I eased the pressure off and she slowly sunk down and I just screamed, "Yessssssssssssssss!"

I had never caught this one before and had watched her grow from 24lb when I first saw her; she was even caught by a guest of mine, Ian Pullinger, at 35lb several years back. What a welcome back, I just couldn't believe it. This place had once again given me one of its gems. I was on cloud nine as leant over and lowered my hand into the net as I was gagging to touch her. I spoke to her and whispered, "Don't worry, Uncle will look after you." I popped the hook out and lifted the rig from the net before hooking the hook onto the butt ring so it was out of harm's way. I then broke the net down and before making my way back to land, I made sure her head was pointing the same way as the boat to make sure that water passed through her gills the right way. Once I had her sorted I turned the engine on the lowest setting and made my way back to dry land. She was nice and calm and I couldn't believe how big she looked beside the boat. As I neared the swim I turned off the engine and pulled the outboard prop from the water. I gently stepped out and put the net back together so I could then leave her in it as I got everything ready. I rang Rich Stewart to make sure he was on his way, as I was booked in to do an Advanced Carp Fishing feature with him that morning. He said that he was 30 minutes away, so I sacked the fish to await his arrival. Next, I rang Jane and told her the good news before sending a load of texts out to my mates informing them that Uncle Jim had nailed one from Fen.

The phone rang and it was Matt, asking what all the commotion was. I just said, "Oi

I gently pulled the cord until it revealed this huge sack.

oi mate, I've just caught Single Scale," and Matt congratulated me, promising to be round in 45 minutes. I got all the bits ready and placed them in the margin so I could quickly weigh her and pop her straight in the sack without upsetting her too much. I manoeuvred her into Marky's weigh sling and made sure her pecs were flat. God she looked awesome and was in perfect condition. I lifted her up and she pulled the needle round to 47lb, what a welcome back.

I put her in the sack and walked her out into the water. I pushed the front of the mat under so I could gently slide her back into the water while I waited for Rich to arrive. I stayed with her until I was sure she was happy. I kept feeling her mouth and gills for movement; I love these close intimate times. Soon she was on the move so I checked the cord and knots before pushing her out into the cold, deep water to rest. As I was sorting her out my mobile was in meltdown, so I sat down reading the texts congratulating me on the capture. I had returned and Fen had given me a slice of its magic to welcome me back. I remember looking up and sticking my thumb up, whispering, "This one's for you Marky." I should have come back sooner but sometimes it's hard when you have so many special memories and you have lost such a dear friend.

Not long later I was pulled from my thoughts when I heard a car pull up and some talking. I looked over I could see Rich talking to Matt. I went to look for an area to take the pictures and laid the mat down where a bramble bush was in bloom before removing any tufts of grass that would be in the way. I collected some water and as I was walking over to the mat Rich and Matt approached and both shook my hand saying, "Well done mate." We stood looking at the sack in the margin as I told them in rough detail about the capture. I then said, "It's time," turned round to get my camera and handed it to Rich before giving Matt the video camera. I said, "Wait 'til you see this baby, boys." I walked out into the water, pulled the bank stick out and undid the knot. I then gently pulled the cord until it revealed this huge sack. Just for the record, if you must use a sack, then you should make sure that it has an extra cord with a big float attached to it. However my feeling is that sacks have no place in carp fishing and floating retainer systems should be used in their place. They cut down many dangers and are a must in your kit.

As the sack neared the margin Single thrashed the water in defiance. Once the sack was close I knelt down and rolled it up, making sure everything was OK, before placing her in the cradle for easy transport. I carried her over to the chosen spot and poured cooling lake water over her before undoing the sack. As I pulled back the sack there was one of the most awesome-looking carp I had ever caught; mind you, all Fen carp blow your mind with their beauty. This fish was no exception, with a dark back, creamy belly and tiny pearly scales towards her tail. It was time for me to have my little cuddle with Single. She was heavy as I lifted her up for the cameras so, after a few shots were taken I laid her back down and covered her body in some more water; the sun was climbing high and getting hot so I wanted to get her back quickly. I gently turned her round on the mat and lifted her once more for the final pictures to be taken of the other side. The moment was captured and it was time to get her back. Before returning

As I pulled back the sack there before me was one of the most awesome-looking carp I had ever caught.

her, we decided to get a few water shots, close to some reeds that we thought looked good.
While I looked after her in the water, Rich cleared the area where he wanted the pictures to be taken and as he was doing this I couldn't help myself and I started touching Single; I even stuck my finger in her mouth and she was sucking and blowing trying to get my finger out! When Rich was ready we got on with the shots and he reckoned that the shots were going to be a bit special and as you can see they sure are, thanks mate. I walked Single out into deeper water then it was time to say goodbye and thanks for the memories. I kissed her and as I pushed her out she blew a set of bubbles, kicked away and disappeared back into the darkness. I looked up to the sky and as the clouds raced by I whispered to myself, "Marky, this one's for you mate."
As I climbed out of the lake a fish topped out near to where I had hooked Single and over the next few minutes, as we stood talking, several more showed in this corner in front of the slipway. It looked like they were grouping up, perhaps ready to spawn in this area? This seemed odd, as I hadn't seen them do it in that area before; they normally do it in The Spawning Bay, just to the left of Clubbers (the swim on the left of Puffer's Point.)
Matt departed and Rich left me to sort myself out before we pushed on with the feature. I had a decision to make as it was clear that the fish were now to the right of Puffer's Point, so I was going to move and set my rods up off the slipway so I could spread more rods over the area they were showing. I quickly reeled the rods in, checked the hooks and tied on fresh meshed-up salty squid hook baits. All four rods were ready to go in double quick time and I grabbed two of them, a throwing stick and a bag of bait and walked the short distance to the slipway. I knew the distance I needed to cast after many years of boating; it was a shallow area and as I stood looking out from the slipway, one pushed out around eighteen to twenty yards out… sweet. I picked one of the rods up and cast the chod into the ripples marked by the carp. I slowly tightened the line so the 20lb X-Line would sink straight while I baited up with a few freebies, just enough for a bite. The other three rods were fanned out in the same area with some salty squids over the top.
Once I'd moved all the gear, I set my house up beside the reeds in the corner by the slipway, as I didn't want them seeing me if they came into the shallower water. Now I just had to move the boat. I decided to move the outboard and battery on the barrow as there was no way I was going to risk boating down the margin and spooking them, as there was a good chance of another bite before I left. Before pulling the boat along the grass verge, I decided to row round to The Spawning Bay and check it out. All I saw was a common that looked around twenty pounds, so the bulk of the fish had to be near to Puffer's and the Slipway area. As I rowed back I decided to leave the boat on the end of Puffer's as I knew I would want to keep checking the area out, so there was no need to keep pulling the boat backwards and forwards along the grass like a twat. If I hooked a carp off the slipway I could leg it round and row it over. The plan was set… all I needed was another take. Fen isn't easy but in my heart of hearts I knew I

It was time for me to have my little cuddle with Single.

I gently turned her round on the mat and lifted her once more so pictures could be taken of the other flank.

Before returning her, we decided to get a few water shots, close to some reeds.

As we stood talking, several more showed in this corner in front of the Slipway.

had a good chance of another Fen babe. I told Rich what was happening and we then got on with the mag feature. Several fish were seen but no takes materialised and we soon had the feature in the bag. Rich left wishing me good luck and I wished him all the best on the water he was fishing, chasing the last one that he hadn't caught. That's another secret story, hey mate?

It was now my time to sit back and take it all in, time to think and enjoy the Fen magic. As I sat back in the evening sun, wondering why I hadn't had another bite yet, my right-hand alarm screamed as something made the mistake of sucking in one of my chod rigs. As I bent into the fish I looked out and something exploded on the surface. Line was peeling off the spool at an alarming rate so I pushed my finger onto the spool to try and slow the fish down. The power of this carp was mental but soon it slowed and kited round to the right. I think when they pick this rig up the carp don't know what's happened and are in shock, that's why the takes can be so savage.

After the run it was now coming in fast and I threw the landing net out ready, before walking into the water. I soon got a glimpse of this angry carp; it was long and dark and as it kited in close to the left the line picked up out of the water and I could see fresh silkweed hanging off it. The carp was close and I waded out further with the net. All of a sudden, this big, black head appeared attached to a linear with big apple-slice scales. This was The Angry Linear and as he wallowed on the surface I took my chance and slid the net under him. As I lifted it Mr Angry tried to escape the net by pulling it from my grasp, and he nearly succeeded! I pulled the net back to see a very rare Fen jewel. I had caught him before in the autumn and it was mentioned in my last book, but the only other angler to catch him since was Rob Parry, who'd also caught the linear several years before me.

I unhooked him in the net and noticed that the ESP Stiff Rigger was half opened out. I know this fish fights, but there was no way I had played the fish that hard and I had my clutch set pukka. As I was wading back to the bivvy to get things ready for the pictures a van pulled up and Phil Rust got out and asked if I needed a hand as he could see I had a carp in the net. "Yes please, that would be good of you fella," I replied. I handed him the camera and went to fetch Mr Angry, who was still pumped up as when I broke the net down he once again tried to charge off! I placed him on the mat and as I pulled the mesh away I noticed that he was really rough to the touch, getting ready to shag the females no doubt, and he couldn't resist a salty squid in between doing his business!

He weighed 31lb 12oz and as I tried to pick him up, he tensed himself up and bent up like a banana, making it hard to hold him. I put him back down and poured water over him, this then relaxed him. He was now a lot easier to hold and it was perfect time to take the pictures as the light levels were dropping. We took a couple of water shots before I gently lowered him back into the lake. I love the moment when you let them free and it is funny how they instantly know. As soon as he was back in he waddled off and I watched him glide across the shallows before finally disappearing from view.

Soon I was back on my own and couldn't believe I had caught a thirty and a forty in a day from Fen, a very rare event indeed, let alone on my first trip back in two years…

This was the Angry Linear and as he wallowed on the surface I took my chance and slid the net under him.

Phil Rust turned up just in time to help me with the fish.

happy fcuking days! I sat and watched the water until dark and didn't see any more carpy signs. Knowing just how spooky the fish could be, I was now thinking that they might leg it round to The Spawning Bay area. If I hadn't seen much by the morning I planned to jump in the boat and go check the area again to see if they'd gone to their normal spawning ground. The events of the day and the effects of the heat had zapped me and I wanted to be up early and watching at first light so I settled down for some shuteye.

Before I knew it my alarm was vibrating. I leaned over and groggily turned it off; I was still shattered and suffering from sunburn so I dragged myself from the pit, and put the kettle on to make a nice, strong, milky coffee to bring me back to life. People always ask why I have such milky coffees and all I say is that I was brought up on the mother's titty… then I get called a sicko! Before the kettle boiled I went over to the water's edge and covered my head and face in several handfuls of cool lake water to soothe my sunburn and wake me up. Coffee made, I sat on the edge of the bedchair and watched the day's events start to unfold in front of me. The birds were everywhere, collecting for their families, a grass snake swam past, but there were no signs of carp as of yet. After several hours without a sighting I was itching to see if they had moved round to The Spawning Bay. I grabbed my glasses, slipped the life jacket on and pushed the boat out. Once aboard I looked down through the water as I rowed the boat slowly round to the area. Once close, I noticed a disturbance in the bay and as I neared the zone, I found myself looking at several males chasing a big 'un. As I got closer the pack of males pushed this big female right up alongside the boat; it was Single and she was being pushed about by a pack of sex-starved animals. They soon pushed her along and out of view. I now knew it was getting close to spawning so I decided to follow them into the bay, over the shallows, so I could see what else was occurring in the weedier areas. As I got further out all I saw were males, there weren't any other fat bitches about! Mind you, I didn't even see Single again.

The plan was to fish the spawning bay until the rest started spawning because I knew the sex starved pack were only going through the motions, so I rowed the boat to the swim and then legged it back and packed all the gear up. I loaded the car and drove it along the causeway, pulling up behind Spawning Bay. Once there it was time to get into machine mode and get those chods placed by boat, as an overhanging willow prevented me casting to the area. I knew the area I wanted to set the traps in and I planned to use a cane to mark the zones. Carp don't mind these more permanent markers, and you often see them shake as the fish rub up against them. Fresh salty red squid pop-ups were tied on, then it was time to crumb some baits up. With the life jacket on, I grabbed a rod and the bucket of loveliness – it was now time to get the traps set. I rowed out, looking for flat bottom with a weed covering, or a spot that had

We took a couple of water shots before I lowered him home.

been recently turned over. Bingo, I found just what I was looking for in the shape of a small clearing in the weed that had been dug out by Mr Carp.

I picked up one of the canes and pushed it into the soft bottom just away from the spot, then threw some crumb over the turned-over area before laying the chod over the top of the weed. It looked awesome sitting on the weed and it was now sinking in just how special this rig was when used in the right situations. Until I had seen it from the boat at Fen I didn't really know this, but now I had seen this for myself I knew why chodding from the bank is so deadly. The rig is well presented nearly all the time, especially when it's set up like I have it, running to the top of around nine feet of leadcore. With the rig in place, I turned the outboard on and gently made my way back to the swim, paying out braided main line as I went. Once back at the bank, I reeled in the slack and placed the rod under the water, out of harm's way, before repeating the process three more times. Each time fish were spotted but none were particularly big. I did see an odd 'un that I didn't recognise; a scaly mirror of around mid-twenty. "He would be nice," I thought but it was asking a lot as I had already nailed two Fen jewels. There were no signs of anymore spawning as of yet, so until there were I would carry on fishing, mind you, I was due to be off the following day at some point anyway.

I barrowed the rest of my gear over so I could set the bed up before laying down to

The plan was to fish the Spawning Bay until the rest started spawning because I knew the sex-starved pack were only going through the motions.

Bingo, I found just what I was looking for in the shape of a small clearing in the weed.

chill out while I waited to see if anything else would occur. This swim gives you loads of cover from the sun, unlike the Slipway, which was a suntrap. I was badly sunburnt and in all likelihood had sunstroke, so I soon fell asleep in my cooler surroundings. I was awoken by my right-hand alarm screaming as a fish made off at an alarming rate. Just as soon as it started, the run stopped and I saw a bow wave hit the surface… the fish had just done me. I reeled the rig in and found that the point was burred over. "Just one of those things," I told myself, but I was left shaking as a loss from Fen hurts because you're left wondering what you've lost. I had to carry on, get a new rig on and get a bait back on the spot ASAP. As I made my way out to the cane I didn't see much but as I got over the spot several carp came up to the boat for a look. I could see that some of the bait had been taken so it was definitely a carp that I had lost. Rather than worry about that now, it was time to get that rig back on the spot as quickly and as quietly as I could. The fish didn't seem too bothered about me and were hanging around, checking me out. Mind you, I was checking them out too, but still there were no big 'uns in residence; it seemed as though the males were hanging about waiting for the fat bitches to turn up. Back in the swim, my thoughts turned to the loss once more. It's hard not to dwell when you lose one from one of these demanding, low-stock inland seas because the next bite could be along way off!

Once back on the bedchair, I started to think about the angling pressure, or lack of it that the lake was subject to. Matt had left yesterday, leaving just me on the lake, yet

I threw some crumb over the turned-over area before laying the chod over the top of the weed.

I did spot a few carp in the area, but none were particularly big.

that season John and I had issued 45 tickets. I certainly wasn't complaining because I had 92 acres to myself and there was not a sheep in sight. It's great when the venues are quiet as it's nice to get away from the rat race of the big-fish circuit, fishing for carp that have no names. If they're big or small it doesn't matter, it's all about the hunt and preparation, not being 'sheeped-up' by the new breed of carper who has no respect for their fellow angler; they're blinded by the desire to catch at any cost. Anyway, back to Fen, where all of a sudden I had a liner on the rod that I'd just replaced. "Oi oi, Mr Carp must be about," I thought. Over the next hour the bobbin kept rising and falling and on a couple of occasions big liners had me running for the rod, only to see the bobbin fall back down just as I got close to it! There were still no signs of spawning so I knew I had the chance of another bite before I left in the morning. The light levels were dropping and the temperature with them, so the chances of the fish spawning now were diminishing. I hoped that they'd be up for a munch early the next morning, or perhaps even before. Time was getting on and I thought I had better get my bivvy up with the clear-view camo screen pegged on because I was in a bad area for the drillers of blood, as I had a tiny bay behind me where they hatched from.

While I was sorting my home out the rod that was getting all the liners pulled up tight and I stood there thinking it was a another false alarm. The bobbin just stayed tight and gave no further bleeps, Mr Carp must have kited round some weed and just sat there. I quickly put on my jacket, grabbed the rod and jumped into the boat before reeling across to where the hooked carp was sitting. As I got close I could see its tail sticking out of the weed and could see it was a carp (I had wondered if a tench might be the culprit). Before trying to free him I made sure the clutch was undone as I was expecting him to leg it once out of the weed. Sure enough, once the weed was stripped away, a black shape bolted, pushing up a bow wave. Picking the rod up, I was now in direct contact with this slightly pissed off carp. He was heading out into the deeper water and I followed him and soon I was playing him just off the boat in six feet of water. In the clear water I got a good look but didn't recognise this one as he was a long, dark common. After a little carpy therapee I had him in the net and I was sure that I hadn't seen this old character before. I was buzzing with excitement as I had a new one for me in the net, happy days. I bit the line and rolled the net up, making sure his head was pointing forwards before heading back with my prize. I could see someone standing in my swim and it turned out to be a new member who I later named Nob, as I found out that he was shit at taking pictures! The ones he took of this carp were mostly out of focus but I did get a couple of useable shots. After the pictures were taken, I had a good look at him and was sure this was a new one for the lake, as he had a couple of areas of missing scales on his belly, with a very distinctively shaped tail. I had certainly never seen him before and I later found out that he was an odd 'un. This is one of the reasons I like fishing places like Fen, as odd 'uns and the unknowns are what I crave these days. Just for the record, he weighed 26lb 8oz and as I slipped him back I wondered if we would ever see him again!

Before sorting the rod I made sure the clear-view screen was pegged on as the blood

Time was getting on and I thought I had better get my bivvy up with the clear-view camo screen pegged on because I was in a bad area for the drillers of blood.

suckers were already about; I hate it when they're in residence, hanging there waiting to vamp you. When I dropped the rig back on the zone I noticed that the spot had been opened up, as I could now see a lot more sandy bottom. I had that feeling that the carp had done the off though, and by the morning it was deadly quiet apart from the birds singing. I watched the sun rise above the trees but there were no signs of any carp by midmorning. Who was I to complain though? I had well and truly done them and they had 'done the off' to shag each other senseless. As if to prove this, a few weeks later Matiz caught Single spawned out at 35lb 12oz (by April she was back up to 44lb.) It was an awesome welcome back to Fen and it was to be my only visit of the year but just like Arnie, I'd be back!

The following year I had a couple of trips but the weather was really bad with a lot of northerly and easterly winds making the fishing in April very slow. A few came out, with Single being the biggest, but there were none for me. I did get on them several times but the fine line between a blank and a bite was not crossed. I had a tuition booked in on a Monday with a good friend of mine, Gary Puiy, and he wanted three days of Fen magic. I did tell him how hard it was and he said, "I know Jim." I promised him that we'd most likely see them showing out in open water and, given my knowledge of the place, I could perhaps show him some from the boat. When we met up early Monday morning it was blowing a mental southeasterly wind hardcore

I was sure that I hadn't seen this old character before.

straight into Pet Shop Corner. I told Gary that we needed to check this area out first as the Fen carp liked getting on a wind blowing into that corner. There's a shallow plateau in the corner, along with several deep gullies, which funnel into it, dropping to eighteen feet in places. Years ago it was near impossible to get bites below eight feet but they seem to love having it in the deeps these days, so it was just a question of finding the scaly fcukers.

Nob was in the Pet Shop and said he hadn't seen much. This bloke was sound the first year, as he was top rod, but this year he was a totally different cup of tea. Several members weren't happy with his attitude so far that spring and nor was I. His card was marked because everyone gets told the score before joining, so it was looking like a ban or no invite come June. I didn't believe that he hadn't seen anything, so after we left I decided we should stick around to see if we could see any ourselves. The wind was really cold and within fifteen minutes I was numb; maybe he was telling the truth, but knowing Nob he wouldn't be. At some point I was sure he had seen fish but maybe they had done the off? "Time to look elsewhere," I said to Gary, "Maybe they're hanging back somewhere or even in the lee of the wind," which they seem to do a lot on Fen these days. Either way, I assured him that we would find some before dark as it was well into May not March. We stood and watched from Bayes swim and then made our way further into The Jungle so we could see the sheltered back of the island, which they used a lot. I turned to Gary and said that they had to be in an area that included the Double Reedy, Stones, Bars, Car Park, Road Stones or Puffer's as that quarter of the lake was well back off the wind and had a lot of calm water in it. This quarter of Fen had to be where they were hiding, it was just a case of finding them; all we needed was a sign from the carp gods.

We left The Jungle and made our way to The Double Reedy, a swim from which you can see a lot of water. With two pairs of eyes on the job, we started to scan the water for a sign. Around thirty minutes had gone with no signs when, all off a sudden I saw one show to the left. It looked well past the Bars swim, so we set off for a closer look. I thought it was way past the Bars and as I looked out I saw another push his head out. "I told you mate," I said, "I knew that they'd be sheltering, the pussies!" Gary laughed and we legged it down to the swim under the trees. It was a lot warmer here and I thought that they'd be sunning themselves in the upper layers. I told Gary that this was the zone and that if anyone came along, we wouldn't be telling them what we'd seen. I gave Gary choice of the swims, either Under The Trees, or Car Park. Unsurprisingly, he went for Under The Trees, because that's where we'd seen the fish! Gary dropped his coat in the swim to reserve it and we headed off to the van so I could reserve the Car Park. Back at the van, Gary said that he couldn't believe that we were on 'em. "You know me mate," I said, laughing. We were now on a mission to get our gear sorted. I advised him to set up and to keep his eye out for signs of carp. I told him to make a mental note of where he saw any but not to cast out until I returned. Just as I was getting in the van Gary asked whether he should get his rods ready, "Of course mate," I replied, "See you in an hour… maximum."

Once in the swim I was in machine mode getting my house up, checking rigs and tying on fresh salty pop-ups. I couldn't really see a lot from my swim as I had set the bivvy up in between two nearby swims as I was going to split the rods up and fish two in each, as I normally did when I fishing in that area. I started to notice the wind was dropping and it was getting brighter, and by the looks of things the sun would come out. I knew it was going to calm down and clear out; perhaps there was even a chance of a frost in May? I was all set up and ready so I legged it round to Gary's plot to see what was occurring. As I walked into his swim he turned round and smiled like a Cheshire cat. "You've seen more haven't you mate?" I asked. "Yes Jim," he replied. It turned out that he'd seen five, no more than fifty to eighty yards out. I said, "Casting range then, best you get them rocking out there son!" I could tell he was gagging to get his rods out and he pointed as another one poked his head out to the right, fifty yards out.

I told him that it was OK to wade out for better casting and checked his chod rigs. I smiled as they were now tied up pukka and seeing that I approved, he winked. I must admit that he has come a long way since we first met, especially as he has caught fish up to 39lb 4oz, a mirror. It's a great feeling to see someone progress after tuitions, onwards and upwards. He put his waders on, grabbed one of his rods, then made his way out and cast out to roughly where he had seen them. "Bang on," I said and as he walked back he was smiling, which told me that he was happy with where his hook bait had landed. I grabbed another rod and handed it to him while he handed me the one he had just cast out. Soon, we had three rods sitting on the buzzers and I then passed him a throwing stick and a bag of squids. As I watched him go about his fishing it was like watching poetry in motion, and he spread around two hundred sixteen millers over the zone. As he climbed out I said, "Good angling mate, I'm off to get my rods out." I think he was stunned that I hadn't already done them! I was going to fish with two rods spread out in the bay and fish two from of the front of the Car Park swim. Twenty minutes later my traps were set in depths roughly ranging from five to twelve feet, with around fifty freebies spread around each hook bait. All the rods landed with soft drops, which would be silkweed mostly; the perfect place to have your hook baits sitting, as the natural food heads for the silkweed at that time of year, looking for food and shelter. All I had to do was present salty baits in the area they were using, the salt would pull them to my traps, and all they had to do was suck it and see! They were definitely more in front of Gary as I sat and saw a few push out near him; he was sitting pretty while I was close and had a chance, "Come on you Fen babes," I thought, "Make our day!"

Several hours passed and the wind had dropped big time. It was due to calm right off and the skies were clear. Gary and I sat in his swim and watched the sun set and

Gary said that he couldn't believe that we were on 'em. "You know me mate," I said, laughing.

noticed the temperature begin to drop as the light started to fade. We did see the odd one still in front of Gary, so things still looked sweet for a bite at some point. Gary asked me if Fen did night bites and I told him, “No mate, very few over the season.” It was very dark now and I was getting cold so I popped off to get my puffa jacket and some food from the van. Gary fired up the barbecue and we enjoyed a chinwag over a few beers and talked about all things carpy watching the odd carp showing in the moonlight. God it was so cold and frost was forming on the ground, which seemed unreal for May. I was knackered and I needed some kip because I wanted to get up early, as they were sure to show. As I walked away I said, “Be lucky and see you in the morning fella, shout me if you hook one up.”

As I put my head torch on and made my way round to my swim the grass was white with frost, it’s hard to believe how unpredictable our weather is these days! Thank God I had put the sleeping bag cover on as it had frost over it, under the brolly. Before climbing into the bag I made sure my chest waders were ready to slip on if I had a bite. It was time to dream of all things carpy and I slipped in to the land of nod. The next thing that I was aware of was being woken by someone shouting, “JIM!” I sat up and realised that it was Gary, calling to him, “You in mate?” He shouted back telling me that he was and I wondered how long he had been shouting for me! I thought I had better put my chest waders on and my puffa over the top. As I legged it round my

Traps set on a load of showing Fen carp!

feet were freezing. Once in the swim, I flicked the head torch on and asked, "What's occurring mate?" "I've been shouting you for a while," Gary explained, as I waded out with the net. He told me that this fish had stripped over 150 yards of line off him on its first run and said it had mental power. I could hear the excitement in his voice and in the moonlight I could see the oily swirls on the surface. I calmed him, reassuring him that the animal he had hooked was very close to netting. There was no way I was going to turn that torch on until the fish was in the net. I pushed the net down and as I saw something surface in the moonlight, I lifted the net, which scared the fish, as there was a massive explosion within the confines of the net.

It had crossed my mind it might be a cat, but when I flicked my head torch on and peered into the net what I saw simply took my breath away; a carp that was armour-plated and massive. I tipped the fish onto its side in the net to see if it was Marcus' Mirror, which it wasn't. Once on the mat, Gary unfolded the mesh and our head lights revealed one awesome, stunning carp that I hadn't seen before. It was massive and covered in all sorts of different scale markings. There was a jacket of scales near his head, a line of plated, apple slices along his flank and diamond-shaped, pearly scales on his belly. He was painted in an array of colours from pinks and creams to black and emerald on his back. I had never seen another carp that looked anything like this before, a true unknown gem. We slipped him into the weigh sling and felt his weight as I lifted. "Hold on Jim," Gary said, "The scales are jumping around the forty pound mark… yes, it's bang on forty." I gently lowered the carp on to the mat and shook Gary's hand, fcuking well done mate, well deserved.

We then popped him into a retaining system for a couple of hours until first light. Gary waded him out into deep water and tied the cord to a bankstick, I could hear him talking to the fish out in the darkness as he did so. My feet were like blocks of ice by now and I told Gary that I was popping back to the swim to get my boots and I'd be back for a coffee shortly. I was soon back and Gary was still in the water, making sure the fish was OK. "Come and have a coffee, he's all right," I told him, before sitting down on his bedchair and firing the stove up. By the time Gary climbed out the kettle was whistling, and he made me a milky coffee. He was very quiet, like he was in shock! I thought that I'd better break the silence and give him some Uncle Jim therapy. "Oi oi Gary! How the fcuking hell did you do that?" He grinned and started talking about the capture as we drunk the warm coffee, well, my milky one was cold – too much mother's titty! As we sat and watched the dark turn into light I realised that it was Gary's first forty, what a fish to do it with! I leant over and shook his hand again saying I think we will call this one The Client, "Oi oi, party time tonight!" "Yeah, I thought you might say that," he replied and we grinned. I heard someone enter the swim and turned to see that it was Dan 'That's My Boy'. I told him that Gary had had a result then looked round and said, "Tell him Gary." He was lost for words though, and I said, "He's caught something special; a 40lb, unknown scaly beast." Dan was clearly a bit taken aback and skeptical. "Just wait 'till you see it then," I said, "You won't believe your eyes when you see this beast."

We sat and drank some more coffee until the light was right, as it was quite misty. The time came and Gary waded out into the water to fetch his prize. As he walked back Danny saw the bulk of the fish so he knew it was a big 'un. Gary handed the beast over to me to carry to the chosen spot and as I gently lowered him on to the mat Gary was kneeling, ready to look after his prize before the pictures were taken. We had only seen him with torch light at this point and I knew he would look unbelievable in the daylight. I don't think anyone could believe what we were looking at as Gary revealed the fish. This creature was truly awesome and its scale patterns and colours were unlike anything I had ever seen before. I guess that I knew that we were witnessing a moment in carp-fishing history and I was glad I was here to see this magical carp myself. 'That's My Boy' was lost for words for once! I asked him what he thought and he just looked up, smiled and muttered the word, "Awesome." Gary was smiling like a dog with two dicks. As he lifted his prize up it was hard to take the pictures, as it wasn't the same looking at it through the camera. I was struggling to get my head around what I was seeing so I bet it was harder for Gary to take in the moment. Gary gently laid the carp down and I noticed that the fish had huge pecs, like shovels. The time had come to return the beast back to its home to fight another day. I got into the water with Gary and took a few returners for him. After that, I stood in the clear water as Gary touched this beast before he slowly glided off and disappeared from view. I shook his hand again and said, "Good angling mate, party time now me old cocker."

Later that day Gary said, "I bet you wish you had caught that?" "No mate," I replied, "It's your moment, I'm not like that mate; jealousy doesn't come into my fishing, but trust me, I'm going to have that creature sooner rather than later!" We laughed, but Gary knew I wasn't joking as I had already put the 'Eye of Uncle' on this particular target.

I left Gary drooling over the pictures on the back of my camera and headed off to get some more sleep, as I was fcuked right up. As I walked off I said, "See you later for the party!" as I wanted my place reserved but this also told him it was going to get messy later on tonight. As I walked off I shouted, "Enjoy the pictures and don't come in your pants too much son!" I went straight to sleep and when I woke up a few hours later I felt like shit. That's what you get from falling asleep in the heat. The sun had come out and the Car Park swim is a cookhouse when it's hot. I got out of the bag, pulled my boots on and went down to the water's edge to cover my head and face in cool lake water several times. Not long after I started to feel a lot better. It was 2pm, so I must have been knackered and I later found out that others had been warned to leave me be! It was time to text Gary and get that party sorted, as I was starving and the thought of food was doing my head in! Plus I needed to get some food inside me before the beers started flowing! I don't think Gary was up for drinking too much, oh well he's a pussy and the text therapy soon started. The conditions had warmed up but the wind was still blowing away from us into Pet Shop Corner. Gary told me that he had seen a couple, so they were still in residence, and there was still a chance of another. Because of that, I decided to leave my rods where they were, as I didn't want to risk spooking

Gary was already kneeling, ready to look after his prize before the pictures were taken.

I was struggling to get my head around what I was seeing so I bet it was harder for Gary to take in the moment.

them and Gary did the same.
As the evening progressed we saw several in front of me so it looked very conducive for Uncle now, would the carp gods play their part? We watched the sun set from the new boat launch and saw several more. They were all over me and as the light faded we could see the rings as they pushed their heads out and every now and again we would hear one roll over heavily. Not long after Gary disappeared to get some shuteye so I decided to sit up for a little bit longer and watch them in the moonlight. After an hour I had seen several more showing in my zone, but knowing most of the bites at Fen are in daylight hours I headed for bed and fell asleep praying for a Fen baby! Next thing I knew, one of my Fox MXs was letting out its battle cry. I jumped up and I couldn't see which rod it was but it did sound like my left pair of rods fished off the new launch. It was still dark but the birds were singing, so daylight was close as I legged it to the launch. The right-hand rod was bent over and the buzzer was still screaming its guts out, full bore. I was scared to pick the rod up, as line was ripping off the clutch. At first, I just held on as the clutch screamed and planned to let it run until it stopped. I was holding onto the rod for dear life when I heard Gary shout out as he made his way round. A weird shaking sensation transmitted up the line, as he tried to shake the hook, but at least the run had stopped and he was now kiting round to the left on a long line, heading towards the road bank. Gary arrived as the fish was kiting along the

I got into the water with Gary to record the moment.

bank and all I could say was, "This thing's an animal, it must have run over a hundred yards!" Gary laughed and said he'd heard the take. By now the fish was getting close but was way to my left, along the margin. The power of this fish had dissipated, but he was nowhere near ready for the net yet, keeping deep down on a short line. It was just a matter of time before, hopefully, I would have my first Fen carp of the season in my arms. Gary started to wade out with the net and I said, "Keep that torch off mate," as I knew if this fish saw light it would be off, and I didn't want to lose this Fen baby. Out in the half-light there was a swirl on the surface, I was close and I must admit I was shitting myself, as I wanted this carp so much. Gary waded out a little more and as its head came up he lifted the net around him and said, "He's yours son." I kicked my boots off and went straight out for a look and as I got close he turned his head torch on. As Gary pulled one side of the net to tip the fish slightly, our gaze was met by an awesome sight, a carp with a jacket of scales around his shoulders, he was unreal and I could hardly wait to get my hands on him.

Gary looked after him while I got everything ready and I decided to sack him up for an hour until we had better light levels. When we peeled back the mesh on the mat I was shocked, it was another new one. He was awesome in every way, his body had a healthy shine over it with a dark back, big apple-slice plates, mostly at the front end, which made him unique, and a light underbelly and golden chin. A truly stunning carp that I later named The Tadpole. It's so hard to put into words what it means to catch an unknown and we'd had two in two nights from a very demanding venue. Fen always throws up one or two new ones every year, that's why I will always fish there, as you never know what it might throw up. There are still known fish I haven't caught yet mind you, but I never want to catch them all so I can always go back and enjoy Fen's magic. We then weighed The Tadpole at 32lb 12oz and Gary helped me carefully pop this Fen jewel into a sack. I made sure he was in deep water and away from weed, then I called Matiz and 'That's My Boy' to come and have a look. The moment came and as I uncovered my prize they both said, "Bloody hell Jim… that's stunning." We soon had the pics done and I must say he didn't play up, I reckon he was knackered after that mental scrap. We waded out a little to take some quick water shots and as I lowered him back I whispered, "Thanks for the everlasting memory," and wished him well as he slowly swam off back from where he came. Once he was home everyone wanted a coffee but I don't do all that shit and said, "I wouldn't ask you so don't ask me!" There was loads of moaning as they headed to Gary's swim for a brew and as they walked off I could hear them taking the piss. I made myself a strong milky coffee and while I was sitting drinking it and taking in what had just happened my other rod on the slipway screamed.

As I picked the rod and pulled into another carp, one of the posse shouted over and I just shouted back, "Yes I'm in!" This fish wasn't really doing much apart from kiting down to my margin. I waded out into the cool water, as this fish was close in to my left, hugging the reed line. I could hear the posse coming as I played the fish and I still think to this day they thought I was playing a trick on them because they calmly walked into my swim and it wasn't until they saw me up to my dangly bits that they realised I was into another Fen babe! Gary came down with the net and as he waded out a bow-wave came round from the left. Luckily, Gary wasn't messing around and pushed the net out and lifted it around another one. "It's a common, looks upper-twenty," Gary told me, and I asked him to look after it while I got myself sorted. The next thing I could hear was the posse shouting "What's this Jim?" as they picked up my cup of coffee! "Leave it!" I shouted before rushing over, grabbing it and necking it! I could hear they weren't happy with that but I explained, "Oi oi boys, I have one cup only and you dirty bunch ain't sticking your lips round it, I don't know where you have been!" As you can imagine they weren't too happy with that. I then said, "Look you lot, when we have finished here I will do you all one of my special cups of coffee but you will have to get me your cups OK?" This seemed to calm the posse thank God, so I handed the camera to That's My Boy and he begrudgingly took it from me, smirking. Thank God I had calmed the situation, as I didn't want any dodgy comebacks from the posse just yet!

As I walked over to Gary, he began to tell me that the fish had a strange mouth. I instantly knew which fish he was talking about, and I hadn't had it either! I explained to Gary that this common was born with a deformed mouth like The Parrot from Horton. It was a Fen character through and through and a new one for me, which added extra gloss. I broke the net down and carried it the short distance to my unhooking mat. On the mat we could see that he didn't have any top lip at all, but apart from his deformity he was pukka. He was a very light-coloured fish with a black edging around his scales and on one side up by his shoulder he had a small patch of misshaped scales, which made ID easy. He weighed 28lb 12oz, so up in weight from his last capture, and he now weighs over 30lb, so he's slowly coming along. Mind you, any Fen carp is a right result, no matter how big or small. Later that day it was time to pack up and say our goodbyes as Gary's tuition was up and before we left Gary cooked up some bacon butties. The session had produced another piece of Fen magic; we'd had three between us including two new ones; an unreal session that will live long in the memory. When I got home I emailed the pictures over to Gary and he rang me, saying that the capture of The Client was only just sinking in. I laughed and said, "Mate, that's one of the best captures of all time, plus it's the best looking big carp in the country by far!" Already, plans were being made for next spring, as I wanted that carp myself; I had to catch The Client!

I decided that I was going to bounce two waters that next spring, Fen for The Client and the Woolpack for Paddle. I would fish one or the other depending on how busy they were and whether my targets came out. I didn't really know which one I wanted more so fcuk it, I'd go hard for both; it was going to be a tall order targeting those fish and for different reasons. Me being me though, I was up for the challenge. I started on the Woolpack first and those captures are in the Woolpack chapter, then Paddle came out, so I now knew I was going to concentrate on Fen at the right time, which was mid-April through May. I now knew I had to be hitting Fen in April as Paddle wouldn't be playing for a while, going on the evidence of past captures. I planned to stay on Lake

A truly stunning carp that I later named The Tadpole.

I instantly knew which fish Gary was talking about, and I hadn't had it either!

Seven for a few weeks and keep my eye on Fen in between looking for the signs that I needed.

Plans were made for my first visit to Fen in April but the day before I was due to go I got the text. Frenchy had caught The Client from The Bars swim… ouch. Oh well, I'd just have to carry on fishing the Wooly, hoping one of my two targets would make an appearance for me in May, as they had both been out so early in the spring. May had to offer the next big chance of nailing one of them. After three weeks I decided it was time to leg it back to Fen and try my luck. I left in the early hours so I would be there for first light and hopefully get straight on some showing fish. I drove down the track and felt excitement coursing through me as the rabbits played dare alongside van. As I opened the gate I heard the cuckoo, which is such a familiar sound in spring. There is so much to enjoy about fishing 'natural' waters like Fen, sometimes just being there is enough and I reckon that's why Fen held my attention for so long. I could see Matiz's van parked up in the car park as I drove down, sweet, only one other on 92 acres. I pulled up on the slipway, which gave me a lot of water to watch.

I got out of the van and the buzz of just being there had my mind racing, wondering where they would be. I had been in touch with some of the Fen boys and no-one had said they had seen the bream gathering in an area to spawn yet. That was one of the reasons I was around the slipway, as they have a tendency to group around this area of shallow water and the carp would home in on the spawning bream to gorge themselves on spawn; like a last hit of protein before they spawn themselves. I knew that the St Ives bream had done it already, so the Fen bream would be close. I needed a sign, either from a carp or a lot of bream in an area, but as I looked out I didn't see much apart from the odd tench mostly in the slipway area. A couple of hours had passed without event. I even had a walk round; it was unusual not to spot any carp showing at this time of the year, as they normally put on spectacular shows. It was usually easy to get on them but getting bites, now that's another question.

I was now seriously tired, so I sat down in the van and the next thing I heard was Matiz tapping on the window. "For fcuk's sake mate, I was trying to have one of my power sleeps!" I mumbled, he laughed and as I looked out, rubbing my eyes, I saw something to the right of the island. I wasn't 100% sure, so I got out and walked down to the water's edge, saying to Matiz, "Mate, I think I saw something to the right of the island". As I downed a Red Bull to get me rockin' we both saw another disturbance. As we watched we saw several movements out there, which was all the encouragement that I needed. "Right I'm going out in the boat for a look," I said, asking, "You coming mate?" Needing no second invitation, Matiz shot off to get his life jacket while I recovered my hidden Sniper boat and rowed it round to the slipway. Soon Matiz and I were heading out across to where we had seen the shows. As we got close we saw ripped-up weed floating about and then carp, so I flicked the outboard off. "Here we go mate," I said to

Gary cooked up some celebratory bacon butties before we left.

Matt, "The bream are spawning". There were hundreds of them in the mix and the Fen bream are massive. We saw odd giants, bream over 20lb, then a mirror went under the boat, then another, and Matiz said "That's Marcus." I needed no second invitation to this party, and we headed straight back to the slipway. I told Matiz that I was planning to tow my baits out from The Double Reedy, and spread my baits over the shallow areas where the bream were spawning in the weed.

As you can imagine, I was on a mission to get the boat sorted and before I headed out I got one of the rods ready so I could place it on my way over to the swim. A fresh salty squid fishmeal was tied on and of course I checked the hook was sharp. I was all set and as Matiz pushed the boat out I wished him good luck as he was on another pod of fish elsewhere. I knew I would need some crumbed-up boilies so they would sit on the weed and hopefully draw the attention of the fish, interrupting them while gorging on the spawn. As I boated across, I chewed up 15mm and 20mm baits in my mouth before spitting them into a bucket. I was a human muncher, long before Korda's Krusha. God my mouth was pouting with all this salt-covered bait… yuck! When I was finished I cupped my hand and swigged some lake water, which made my mouth a nicer place to be! When I got around fifty yards off the zone I turned the outboard down and made sure that my bait, markers and rod were close at hand. I approached the zone carefully; the plan was to find an area they were feeding over and drop a long, running chod rig over the weed, then throw some bait in and chuck a marker to the left of the rig before gently gliding away. Almost immediately, I could see bream darting around in the shallow water, then there were occasional carp on the deck, munching on the bream eggs. Most of the time they were so preoccupied that they carried on feeding as I approached. This was precisely what I was looking for and I gently lowered the hook bait in and watched the pop-up rise up the leadcore before gently letting it drop down and rest on the weed for perfect presentation. Immediately after that, I threw a couple of handfuls of crumb over the top along with a few whole baits, so as you can imagine it was a lot to do at once, but I'm a master at this type of angling! I'm in my element in a boat and boat fishing opens up a whole new world to us anglers. Trust me when I say that you can read the signs that the carp leave out and about in the lake, it's a fascinating way to fish and a big edge once mastered. I turned the outboard back onto a low speed and dropped the tip well under the water as I motored off. This helps pull the line off smoothly as you pay it off the spool. As I neared the margin I turned the outboard off and lifted the propeller clear of the bottom so I didn't damage it, before climbing out and gently tightening the main line up. I did this another three times around the same zone and I did see several more carp, with the biggest being Marcus', so I knew some of the others were creeping around. I felt that I had a really good chance of a bite at some point and hoped the carp gods would bless me once more.

The next job was to set the house up and get some much-needed sleep. Not long after doing this, the wind started blowing an absolute hoolie and the buzzers were bleeping in the gusts. Luckily, I had a trick up my sleeve to stop this and I simply clipped the bobbins onto the line on the other side of the buzzers. Gary Bayes showed me this

Matiz with Marcus' Fish.

years ago and it works, which was critical because there was no way I was going to get to sleep with them constantly bleeping and I'm a grumpy bastard if I don't get my quota of shuteye. It was bad enough as it was, what with the bivvy shaking as the wind tried its best to uproot it. I nearly jumped through the roof of the shelter as one of my alarms started screaming, wrenching me from my slumber. I quickly put my life jacket on, grabbed the offending rod and then pushed the boat out. I plunged the outboard in the water and turned it on full bore, keeping the rod well to the side of the others as I didn't want to pick them up. Heading off in hot pursuit of this carp saw me soon well over two hundred and fifty yards out!

Thankfully, this fish had shot off well to the right, away from the other lines. It was hard to keep the boat on course as the wind and waves were unreal and I just knelt down in the boat. I normally stand up but there was no way that I was going to do that today! Soon, I was close to where the fish had weeded himself and I positioned the boat just right before teasing the fish from his weedy sanctuary. He went on a short burst so I followed him and got a glimpse of a long, dark mirror. A flat spot on the surface told me that he was tiring and as I reversed the boat towards him, water was lapping over the stern, so I wanted to get this fish in the net ASAP. A back broke the surface and I reached out with the net and thankfully he went straight in. I turned the outboard off so I could drift back to my swim while I brought the net alongside the boat, quickly breaking the net down and making sure that his head was pointing the way I was headed. As I approached my swim Matiz was standing there and shouted, "Good angling mate!" before wading out to help me with the fish. I could see that I'd bagged one of the Fen linears and it looked like a fish that I hadn't had before.

As I placed him on the mat Matiz told me that he was sure that I'd just caught the scaly linear that he'd lost the previous year. One thing was for sure; I hadn't had him before, so this was another Fen babe to add to the collection. He was one of the old characters of the lake and, like all the Fen carp, in perfect nick. On the scales he weighed 29lb 12oz and I paused to admire the line of plates along his lateral line. As I picked him up for the cameras I noticed his that skin was rough, meaning that he was a male and close to spawning, letting me know that it wouldn't be long before they were at it. I waded out into the choppy water for one last cuddle before watching him swim back off into the angry-looking lake.

I somehow had to get that rod back onto the spot but it was blowing harder than ever, so it was with a little trepidation that I prepared to launch. It was hard even to get the boat out into deep enough water to set off, but I managed it and made my way out slowly but surely to the spot. I planned to roughly place the bait, as I wasn't going to mess about in these conditions but hey, I had the perfect presentation for this job. I scattered some more bait over the spot as I turned the boat and then quickly lowered the rig down. On the way back I noticed loads of weed floating on the surface, those

I clipped the bobbins on behind the buzzers to eliminate the wind bleeps.

bream must have been having it large and the carp were probably still digging around for their spawn, so everything was in the mix. As I sat back to watch for signs of carp, I noticed that I had weed blowing from the tips in the wind like tinsel.

Nothing was seen and by late evening the wind had started to drop off, so I sat back watching the sun setting in front of me. It was casting oranges and yellows over the moody surface, and I thought that I'd just caught sight of a show. Then it happened again, as a carp pushed out roughly over the zone! Over the next ten minutes I saw seven shows on the zone, happy days. All of a sudden, the right-hand rod rocked off as another Fen carp made the mistake of sampling one of my salty squids. This time the conditions were a lot safer so I could stand up in the boat, following this carp, which had shot off well to the right and weeded itself. As I got near to him a carp topped eighty yards to my left! I hoped this fish wouldn't ruck too hard as I didn't want him going back over the area where I was getting bites and spooking them, as it was clear I had several fish feasting in the zone. I needn't have worried, because as I got close to where he was weeded he rose straight to the surface and went into the net first time. I looked into the net I could see that it was that common with the deformed mouth, a repeat capture but never mind. As I made my way back to my swim I wondered if The Client was about, as I had caught the deformed one the day after Gary had bagged The Client. I have noticed over the years that certain fish seem to stick together and I couldn't help feeling that I was close. When I got back I decided to just weigh him as I had pukka pictures already so there was no need to stress him further. He was up another pound and pulled the scales round to 29lb 12oz. I saw another fish show on the zone just after putting the common back, so I made the decision not to replace the rod as I already had three others in position. There was no need to spook them any more as I had a real chance of bagging a good 'un. I saw several more show bang on where I was fishing after that, so I clearly had a good chance of another Fen babe. I decided to get my head down early as I was knackered and needed to get rid of this worn out feeling.

A bleep woke me, which wasn't unusual, but then I remembered that the bobbins were on the other side of the buzzer to stop them from bleeping. After a minute there was another bleep, so I thought that I'd better check it out, as you never know. I put my head torch on and noticed that the wind had picked up a little more. My left-hand bobbin was tight to the blank, "Flaming bream," I thought as I pulled into it. Everything was solid so I put the rod down and prepared to go afloat. I put the outboard on full bore and kept well left of the rods. Once I was in clear water, I began to reel the slack in and connected with something that felt like it was weeded solid. I turned my head torch on so I could see the angle on the line, then I heard one of my buzzers bleeping. This bream had probably kited and caught up on another one of my lines, "This could be fun now," I thought. As I neared the spot where the it was weeded, the fish, which clearly wasn't a bream, shot off with an immense surge off power, towing me along. I heard another series of bleeps, which really wasn't good. Having a powerful carp attached to another line meant that I had to play it harder than usual. Suddenly, the

He was one of the old characters of the lake and, like all the Fen carp, in perfect nick.

other line rose up in the water. I had to make a decision fast as I wanted this other line off the one with the fish on it. I dropped the rod and engaged the bait runner, then I grabbed the other line and bit through it, trying to steer the boat and control it at the same time. I had to keep the boat on the spot, which wasn't easy at all in this wind. I then hand-lined the rig that I'd bitten off in, as I couldn't leave a baited rig out there. After throwing the rig into the boat, I picked the rod up and reeled in the slack, praying that the carp was still on. Then, in the torchlight, this big, plated mirror popped up on the surface so I grabbed the net and pushed it out to the fish that was now wallowing on the surface. I then lost control of the boat so I had to slacken off while I repositioned myself and get the boat back to where the fish was sitting. It was do or die now, as I was now worrying about the hook hold. I had to get him in the net and the next time he surfaced I pushed the net out once more and this time he went in. I bit the line and turned the outboard off so I would start drifting back towards my swim while I broke the net down. I knew I had Marcus', so I didn't look again as I got him safe before turning the outboard back on and steering back to my swim. I then put the net back together so I could then get bits sorted, it was at this point that I got a shock as I peered into the net. It wasn't Marcus' as I'd thought; instead, there sat the one I wanted, The Client! "Yesss!" I shouted out across the darkness. I couldn't believe it, I was buzzing as the adrenaline rush was intense.

I caught sight of a show, out in the waves.

His colouration was breathtaking to behold.

I saw a light go on Matiz's swim then my phone rang. "What's up?" Matt asked. "Oi oi mate, I've got The Client," I replied. Matiz promised to be round in a bit so I looked at the time on my phone and it was 3am. I decided I was going to pop him into a retaining system for a couple of hours as daylight was coming fast. I waited for Matiz to come round and give me a hand sorting the fish out, and he was soon in the swim shaking my hand and congratulating me. I carefully placed him on the mat and removed the hook, then we tried to pop him into a weigh sling, but we were stunned with its beauty. "God knows what he's going to look like in daylight mate," I said; he was completely unique. We weighed him at 42lb 4oz and then I waded him out and made sure he was safe in deep water. Matiz disappeared back to his swim, promising to be back in an hour or so, to help with the pictures. Sleep wasn't going to be an option for me, so I put the kettle on, sat back and enjoyed the moment. I couldn't relax completely though, because I kept getting up to make sure he was OK. The sack cord would pull tight every now and again, which told me he was fine. I watched the water for a while before deciding that it was time to do the pictures, so I rang Matiz and he answered straight away, telling me that he was already on his way round.

As you can see in the pictures the blossom was out, which generally heralds some big-fish captures every spring and it provided a great backdrop for my shots. It was time to see his pure beauty in the light of day. His colouration was breathtaking to behold; massive pinky-coloured pecs with those awesome diamond-shaped scales on his belly that I'd noticed on our first meeting. I lifted him up and I couldn't help but smile, which is rare for me. Words cannot fully describe how special this fish is but the pictures do that perfectly as you can see. It was time to get him back into the lake and after a few returners it was time to let him go. I pumped my fist and yelled, "Yessss!" looking up to the sky and dedicating another capture to Marky. Matiz left soon after and it was time for me to pack up, head off home and plan for my next targets, The Black Mirror and Paddle.

I didn't know it as I drove back from Fen, but my life was about to change dramatically. In June 2010, my darling wife Jane found out that she had cancer. This turned my world upside down, as I had to be with her and support her through her darkest moments. I needed some time to prepare myself for what lay ahead so until the chemotherapy started I decided to fish short sessions on Fen. I needed to be around my mates, away from the twats in carp fishing because, trust me; I would have lost the plot if I had any shit from anyone. So Fen was now going to be my place to hide away. I needed somewhere special, somewhere that would see me through until March. Was I asking too much of Fen to give me another one of its jewels? Jane wanted me to carry on as normal, but I'd started fishing Ellis, and there was no way I could carry on over there now, as when I hit a water it's all or nothing. However, knowing Fen so well, I'd at least have a chance and I needed a fix of its subtle magic. Also, I had a two-day tuition with a new member called Tim 'Retro' so it was Fen for a few weeks until Jane's journey started, and thank the carp gods she is all clear now.

Over the weekend Tim and I made arrangements to meet up in the car park at 9am on

Monday. He was there before me, sitting in his old beaten-up Transit and I laughed as I drove across the gravel. The only other motor there was Dean the Roofer. I decided it would be best to take him on a guided walk around Fen, showing him some of the areas and telling the stories of past captures. While we were doing this hopefully we'd find some carp to set up on too. As we made our way along the causeway bank, I showed him The Car Park swim, The Stones, The Slipway, Clubbers and The Spawning Bay. I even took him across the little footbridge that separated the tiny spawning bay from the main lake. Clearly, I had to tell him the supposed story of me damming up the channel when I caught the Fen Linear back in 2002. As we got halfway down the bank on the way to Pet Shop Corner, I started to get a whiff of carp just past the Lifebelt swim. Tim could smell them too and I knew that we were getting close. I didn't know where Dean was but I knew we would bump into him at some point on our way round.

As it turned out, Dean was bang on them in Pet Shop but hadn't had any bites. He was packing up so I said, "OK if we go in here after you?" and he said it was fine. The wind was howling into the corner and as we watched we saw several stick their heads out. Dean said he couldn't believe that he hadn't had any action, and nor could I! After seeing the fish, we legged it to get our gear, as you would expect. By the time we had got round to the swim Dean was leaving, so Tim went in The Pet Shop, where most of the activity was, and I went next door in The Boat Graveyard.

We soon had our rods in place and the fish continued to show. A little later, the wind dropped and they pushed further out, then the lake went calm and within 10 minutes it was howling to the opposite corner, The Car Park. We stood and watched as the fish began to show well out into the pond. It was clearly time to leg it and get on that fresh wind, so within an hour we were once again casting out. Tim went in the Under The Trees swim and I went in The Car Park. Nothing was seen or smelt on the wind, as we both watched for signs but I thought that they would be about, as they'd moved well out from Pet Shop and were showing several hundred yards out when we last saw them.

Soon, the wind started really howling. They had to be about somewhere because they were right in the teeth of it in Pet Shop. I thought that they must be keeping their heads down, but we carried on scanning the water until, out of the blue, one of my rods which was in The New Slipway rattled off. This fish tore off to the right, close in and I could now feel the X-Line rubbing against the reeds so I put the rod down and opened the bale arm to let the fish run while I went and got my chest waders on. Tim commented on the amount of line leaving the spool, but there was no way I was having tension on the line, as I didn't want the reeds cutting or damaging it. Tim wasn't wrong though, it had gone a little way and I waded along the reeds retrieving line as I went. Tim ran round to the other swim where my other two rods were and I was soon standing with him, playing this fish that had run into the bay. It was a very powerful fish and an unbelievable scrap; mind you most of the Fen fish fight like their life depends on it! I started to finally gain some control, as this mad carp started to behave a little. I knew

I couldn't help but smile, which is rare for me!

I even took him across the little footbridge that separated the tiny spawning bay from the main lake.

it wasn't one of the big ones as it had no weight behind it as it fought in the upper layers. Slowly but surely he was getting closer and Tim threw me the net just as I got a glimpse of the fish. It was one of the long mirrors, probably a male, and as he came closer I could see he was a linear. I wanted this one as I hadn't had him before and not long after I lifted my net around another Fen character. I popped the hook out, then turned to Tim and said, "Wait 'till you see this one Tim!" The next thing I heard was people talking as Matiz and Cheeks walked into my swim.

Once everything was sorted, I walked over to where Matiz was looking after the fish and asked if he could bring him over to the mat for me; I was gagging to have a real good look at this one. He had a linear line of scales and big, apple-slice scales either side, along with a jacket of scales at the front end near his gill cover, like many of the Fen carp, as well as pinks and creams on his belly. As you can see these Fen carp are something special and are in perfect condition as they have the best diet going. The scales registered a new top weight for this fish called The Boss at 30lb 4oz (he now weighs nearly 34lb). Fen had given me some of its magic in my darkest hour. I was going to hit a very low point later on in my wife's illness and it was going to be a hard road for us both in the coming months. We did a few returners before I let him swim back to his world to fight another day. It was time to have a few beers with the boys before shooting home the next day. We caught nothing else, but Tim had gained vital

Tim went into Pet Shop...

... and I went next door in The Boat Graveyard.

We needed to move, so I dropped into The Car Park.

One of my rods, which was in The New Slipway, rattled off.

knowledge before challenging the mighty Fen himself. Before I left I baited the area so I had something to fall back on if I didn't find anything anywhere else. The Fen carp seemed to have been visiting that area a lot in recent years, which was ideal as I had a few more trips before I would have to look after the family and of course, my darling wife in her hour of need.

The next two trips were blanks but I did see the odd carp and kept the fishmeals going in. People were leaving the area alone for me as I had something going, that's the respect we have for each other at Fen; everyone gets their chance in the end, mind you some more so than others. I had one or two trips left and I'd seen the odd one over a deep gully near the road margin. In the end, I had all four rods fishing off the Slipway so I could cover this zone and each time I left I was spreading several kilos of salty boilies across the gully for them to have 'on me'. Jane's treatment was taking its toll so this was going to be my last trip. I couldn't leave her any more, even though she said to carry on, I just knew it was time for me to look after her.

As I made my last journey of the year to Fen it was late August, feed-up time. I had two days and a night ahead to relax and I knew where I was going to start, my little baited area off the new slipway from the car park. Matiz was the only one on the lake, so I drove down the short track off the car park that separated it from the swim. It was still dark and I wanted to be there from first light to watch for signs of carp. Once installed, I had to sort one of my strong, milky coffees to bring me into the land of the living. I grabbed one of Vision's little seat cushions so I could sit down on the damp bank in comfort and enjoyed watching the darkness turn to light. One pushed out over the zone, telling me that they were still here. Things really hotted up, and in the next hour I saw eight shows all around the pre-baited zone. Now seemed like a good time to get the three rods ready and I aimed to cast them one after each other, as I had made a mental note of where the fish had shown. By waiting a little bit I now had key information and could deploy the rods with confidence. All the fish had shown over where I had baited with my salty boilies, so they had homed in on it for sure. Carp love rock salt when used at the right time and this is another massive edge when used correctly. It was only around a thirty-yard cast so I was using 1oz square leads. I use small, square leads because they have a bigger surface area making them better for feeling the lead down, helping me to establish what I'm fishing over. As usual, I was looking for soft, weedy ground to fish my long, running curved chod rigs over. Because I was on fish I only needed enough lead to get the rig to them, there was no need to spook them with a bigger lead.

I soon had three rods rockin' on the zone with a few salty baits spread around the zone to reactivate it and get them moving around. These freebies would 're-taint' the zone with the taste of salt again and hopefully stir them up into picking the baits up. Time ticked away after casting out, I'd seen nothing else and I was getting a little worried that I had fcuked them off. Matiz had visited me and said, "Don't worry mate you've had them visiting this area on and off for a while now, be patient." I spent the day firing out seven freebies every hour or two to keep the salty taste going in and,

The Boss at 30lb 4oz.

It was time to have a few beers with the boys!

although I watched all day, there were no more signs. It was lucky that I'd got there early, as I might have moved elsewhere given how quiet it had been. I had listened and taken on board what Matiz had said and he was right, as just before dark they started again. They might well have been elsewhere in the pond and had now come back for a munch. I then texted Matiz, telling him that they were showing again and thanked him for putting my head straight. He texted me back saying, "That's what mates do, I'm on the way round for a beer." We sat and watched the display well into darkness and saw untold shows in the zone. I had a feeling that the carp gods might bless me with some good fortune as I was now very confident of a bite!

It was a cold, damp night and by 10ish Matiz was off. I climbed into the bag, watching as several ripples pushed in over the next few hours, letting me know they were still about. I did have the odd bleep that had me jumping out of bed, indicating that little things were occurring out in the lake. I had set the alarm so I was ready and watching as dawn broke. I watched, cup of coffee in hand, and that horrible feeling that they'd done the off started creeping in. I was sitting close to the rods when the left-hand rod bleeped once, making me jump. I watched the line where it entered the water and it twitched, followed by another bleep. Suddenly, the line started to pull tight, then the bobbin pulled up as my buzzer started to scream. I was on it in a flash and pulled into a slow-moving carp. My rod took on its battle curve but the fish hadn't taken any line off the clutch, instead it slowly plodded around in front of the swim, coming in close quickly. It did feel a big 'un but it just hadn't fought at all, just plodding around like it didn't know what was going on. Soon the leadcore was visible and big swirls eddied on the surface. Almost straight away his back hit the surface and I seized my chance, netting him after just three or four minutes. I waded out to see which one he was and the water was that cold I nearly pee'd myself! I could see that I'd bagged myself an awesome chunk that looked around mid-thirty. I then pulled one side of the mesh so I could get a better look, and thought, "Wowsers, look at you!" He had a cluster of scales in the middle of his body, surely another pacman, as he had that giveaway cluster of scales like Single Scale. Crazily, I didn't recognise this fish either. Matiz was by my side shortly after saying, "I told you that you'd have one Jim!" I just smiled as I was now on cloud nine! Matt got into the water for a look and as I tilted the fish he said, "Wow, I haven't seen that one before either!" I left Matt to look after the fish because my feet were freezing and I needed a leak before I pee'd myself.

I found a elderberry bush and it had little red berries hanging from it; the perfect spot to show this unknown fish off and show autumn's harvest. I asked Matt if he could bring the fish over to me because I was gagging to have a good look at this beast. We weighed him first and the scales read bang on 36lb, now I wanted to have a good look at him and give him the once over. He was perfect and I was definitely sure that he was a new one, as I know all the known Fen carp. Fen throws a new one up every

I watched a new day dawn over Fen, with a strong, milky coffee of course.

I only needed 1oz square leads to make the 30-yard cast.

The devastating long, running chod setup.

Good old Cheeks with Dropscale Linear.

year though, and that's another reason I love it there as you never know. One thing we noticed about this mirror was that he had one stumpy pec and we later named him Nemo. He had broken-linear scaling on the stumpy pec side, running up from his tail. The other side had this cluster of scales in the middle but they were more spread out compared to the other pacman in Fen. We then noticed white edging to his tail and his body had an awesome sheen over it, making him very distinctive. The whole fish is unbelievable as you can well see in the pictures. He was well behaved on the bank and just before I picked him up I covered him in lake water, now it was time to get some pictures of the Fen stunner to look back on in years to come.

As you can see, I look very sad and withdrawn in the pictures. It was a very low point in my life but hey, all's good now, thank God. After the pictures were done it was time to get a few returners before letting Nemo go. I held him in the water and watched his mouth pulsating, taking in oxygen. He kicked and as I let him go he went round in a circle; his deformed pectoral fin was playing up! Matt and I couldn't believe what we were watching. I steadied him and his next attempt was a lot better, as he slowly swam off into the darkness. I did my normal salute and pumped the sky, Fen had once again treated me to its magic with another unknown to keep me going while I looked after

Fen throws up a new one every year, which is why I love it!

A few of the Fen regulars showed up for a BBQ and a social.

Jane. Later that morning I packed up and said, “Thanks and see you soon,” to Matt. Later that week Jane wanted to see the display of shooting stars that she'd heard about. She'd never seen one before and the best place to view this with clear skies was the Cambridge area, so a few days later I took her there for the night and few of the Fen regulars turned up for a BBQ and a social.

It was late when nature laid on this spectacular display for us and Jane loved, it sitting in a chair with a sleeping bag wrapped around her to keep her warm. I would like to thank John, Lee, Cheeks, Matiz, and Ben AKA Ben Dover, for making it a great night and I would like to end this chapter with some good news, which is that Jane's now all clear from cancer. HAPPY FCUKING DAYS!

Wellington Country Park And Marlow

A Walk in the Park

The famous lake in Wellington Country Park covers 35 acres and is set deep in the oak woodland that seems to dominate that part of Berkshire. It's a pleasant, shallow pit that's got a bit of everything, with secluded bays, areas of weedy open water and several islands. Apart from the lake, the park is also home to a visitor centre, music concerts, a caravan site, kids' playground and the odd life-sized dinosaur! Of course, then there's the fishing, but I'd soon come to realise that us anglers are very much at the bottom of the list when it comes to priority. Over the years I'd heard a lot about this fishery, but it didn't interest me until circumstances conspired to push me that way. The Black Mirror was starting to dominate my thoughts and I knew that I'd need to save plenty of funds to allow me to go all-out if I got close to England's finest. That meant 20 months of hardcore tuition work, but I still needed to be on the trail of some big fish to keep my name in the headlines! I started to dig around on the internet to get all the right info and contact numbers so I could obtain this ticket discreetly. I didn't want to draw attention to myself by asking other Welly anglers, as this would probably result in me getting blocked!

So, around late April I plucked some courage to give the office at Welly a bell to ask them if there were any tickets going for the new season in June. I spoke to some bird and she said that there were still several tickets going spare. Straight away I said I was very interested and asked how much it was. She informed me that it would cost £1500 for the following year, an increase of £750 on last year's ticket fee. I knew from a few mates that a lot of the existing syndicate were very unhappy and many had already told the office they were not renewing. With this inside info I knew I had a good chance of getting in easily. She asked me if I was still interested and told me that it would help if I could get the fee to them ASAP. I gave her the name James Shelley and hoped they didn't suss me, in case they had heard bad things about Jim Shelley from the past! I

The famous Wellington Country Park.

must admit, I was worrying a lot over the next few days, as I waited in anticipation each morning for the post to arrive. In the end the missus told me to fcuk off fishing, as it was driving her mad. Typically it turned up the day after I left. Jane rang me and gave me the good news that the application had turned up; everything was sitting there ready to be sent back so by afternoon it was in the post.

I just carried on fishing, hoping that I would soon have the ticket. I had asked Jane to keep an eye on the bank account and let me know when the £1500 had been taken. She rang me and said, "Your Welly ticket has arrived," so I had the ticket before the money had been taken… happy days. Over the next few days the word was out that I had a Welly ticket, as several people contacted me asking me if it was true. I had decided to play it down until I went down to fish it, this would keep them guessing. I had a few days booked off for the start and with a tuition cancelled, I now had an extra 36 hours to play with, but my ticket didn't start till June 1st, so I decided to fish Marlow, which was about 25 miles away from Welly. This venue had a big common swimming around in it, which had reached a top weight of 47lb so far. The plan was to kill the first 36 hours on Marlow in the hope of having a little cuddle with an awesome pug-faced common, as I was still trying to catch my first 40lb common. In fact, this was one of the other reasons I wanted to fish Welly, as it had at least five in there to mid-forty.

Marlow was a tricky water to get to, as you had to park across the other side of the motorway and cross over by means of a footbridge, so as you can imagine it was going to be a mission getting over and onto the water. As I was prepared for fishing Welly I was going to have to do several trips to get all the kit across. I'd have to run the risk of it being nicked if I left it while I got the rest, as there were travellers living in the meadow beside the water. Sweat was pouring off me as I embarked on this mission from hell, but after seventeen minutes I had the barrow loaded on the far side of the motorway; it was time to have my first look at this venue. As I pushed the barrow on to a big point, I was looking for somewhere to hide it away from prying eyes so I could get on the hunt quicker and get the carp located. It soon became apparent that no-one else was about though.

After I turned right along past where the travellers were camped in the meadow, I came to an area of nooks and crannies where fish could hide. This part of the lake had pads, back channels and bays and as I followed the bank round it opened into a big expanse of water, which was in front of the point where my barrow was hidden from view. I decided that if I didn't see much then this would be the zone I would fish, as The Point swim would allow me to watch a lot of the lake. As I carried on down into a corner there was an overflow and as I crossed it, a bow-wave shot out. I had clearly scared something and as I looked into the shallow water I could see a small carp legging it out. I then saw several other movements, so I made my way quietly into this tight area to get a better look. Hidden behind a tree I strained to see through the surface, as it was covered in a film of scum. Staring intently into the dark water, I noticed several carp tucked under the bank, and by the looks of them they were low-double stockies. I had heard that the club had stocked it, so these were obviously the new guys.

You'd meet some strange creatures in the bushes around the lake!

After 20 minutes things went quiet and I stayed concealed behind the tree,

hoping that I might get a glimpse of one of the Marlow originals. Suddenly, from the right a large shape came into view. Knowing that there were only two fish of this size, I knew that I was looking at one of the lakes big 'uns, either a mirror called the Brown Fish or the jewel in the crown, The Marlow Common. The carp passed over an area where some shafts of light broke through, lighting up the gravelly bottom and as the carp's snout became visible, I could make out a very under-slung mouth with a pug face. As more of the fish came into view, I could plainly see that it was the one, The Marlow Common. There she was in all her glory. It was hard to see her fully, but what a sight, as I had only been on the lake for forty minutes. I was buzzing from seeing my main target up close and personal so quickly. After a few minutes she drifted out of sight. Christ, I'd forgotten about my gear. I felt that I'd best go and check that it was still there, so I quietly backed off from the zone and legged it back towards The Point. As I passed the nearest swim to this area I dropped my glasses in there to reserve it. There wasn't anyone about, but with the big 'un in residence I wasn't taking any chances.
As I neared the area where my gear was hidden, I could see it was still there, thank God! I was now on a mission to get round to the swim and as I turned right to go the other way I knew It was going to be a mission as the bramble bushes along this bank had not been trimmed for a while. Luckily, it was only the first part that was bad so I bashed them with a long bankstick, which saved my arms. I later found out that there was another path running along the other side of the bramble bushes so, as you can

The small overflow corner at Marlow.

The swim was tight, as a public footpath ran right past it.

imagine, I used that one to exit the venue. I was soon in the swim, which was well tight, as the path ran through the middle of it. Luckily, I had a brolly with me so I was able to squeeze it into a slot in the brambles. I decided to set up first as I didn't want my gear all over the path, as it seemed the public used both paths, which became more apparent over the next few hours. Several people walked past and a bird with big tits jogged past my bivvy! I sat back to take in the moment and thought, "This place is pukka!"

Anyway, back to the fishing. I was going to spread my rods out along the far side, which was an area that was out of bounds and the first swim along that bank couldn't interfere with me at all, plus it was clear that they were using this as the main route in and out of the snags. All three rods were set up on long, running chod rigs as usual and several fish showed to the right while I got the rods ready. They looked small by the disturbance they made, but the spots they showed were noted so I knew where I was going to cast the rigs. Two of the casts would need to be savage side-casts, as the bushes in front of the swim stuck out a fair bit. My 13ft Pursuits would make the cast a lot easier though, and the left-hand rod would be cast out to the sign that indicated there was no fishing from that bank. I soon had all three rods out, rocking on their spots, with a few squids scattered around the hook baits to get them moving over the zone. I was sitting back, watching the world go by, wondering if one of the originals

I soon had three rods out, rocking on their spots.

might visit me before I left to go to Welly, when suddenly the right-hand rod pulled round, indicating that something had made the fatal mistake of sucking and seeing. I immediately grabbed hold of the rod and as soon as I made contact, I could tell that it was a stockie, as the fight was all over the place. Not long after I netted a small mirror. I quickly unhooked him and walked him several swims up to the left, as I didn't want him scaring the others away. This seems to be a problem with stockies as they normally hang around with the proper ones.

A new rig was needed and fresh hook bait was tied on before the rod was cast back to the zone. I topped up with some more squids over all the rods, as it was now clear that they were having it, plus the noise and baits dropping through the water can get them back on the feed. I always remember from my match fishing days that feeding little and often is a big edge, as it keeps the swim active. This seems to be the way I fish these days as pre-baiting just gets the sheep shaggers jumping in on the back of all your hard work. Over the next few hours I had several more small carp and I was getting worried that the disturbance would have an adverse effect on the fishing by spooking the originals. All the action was coming to the right-hand rod and by dark I'd had eight stockies… not what the doctor ordered!

As darkness fell it seemed that most of the fish had moved out from the corner, and I watched as carp rolled and poked their heads out to the left of the swim at around 30 yards. I didn't move any rods because I didn't want to risk spooking them with a recast and anyway, my left-hand rod wasn't a million miles away. I must have fallen asleep, as the next thing I knew the birds were singing their dawn chorus and my left rod joined in, signalling a few bleeps. I was fairly sure that it was going to be another stockie, but as I got in direct contact with it, the carp it seemed to fight differently to the others I had caught. It had more power but it didn't feel like a real big 'un and after five minutes I slipped the net under a slightly bigger carp that was black, with a massive tail; an original had slipped up on its way back into the corner. I was carefully unhooking this very dark fish in the net, when there was a big bosh over the left-hand rod! Christ this was the chance, as the stockies weren't playing ball yet and it was clear that some of the originals were in residence.

I quickly checked the hook for damage, testing the point gently on my nail to see if it was burred over. It seemed fine and the hook slid into the skin on my wrist easily, so all there was left to do was re-curve the rig and get it back out on the spot with a few sweeties spread around the area. No-one else was about so I was going to do some self-takes, which was all new to me at that time, unlike now, as I'm a master at it! Most of the pictures were shit, but I did have the odd better one although there was no way I was going to do self-takes with big 'uns until I knew what I was doing.

Anyway, on the scales he weighed 19lb 12oz, not the biggest, but a right old character

Not bad for early attempts at self-takes! There was no way I was trying it with a big 'un though.

and my first proper one from the lake. As I was doing the pictures, several other fish started showing and by the looks of them they were heading back into their quiet corner to rest up for the day after their feed out in the lake. Several more stockies hung themselves over the course of the day, and I had a few quick looks in their 'layup zone', hoping to get a glimpse of that bar of gold again, but the only fish I saw were the stockies. It was clear that they were spooked from me catching so many, as I'd now had ten stockies and one original. All I could hope for was that they might pop back for a munch at some point before I left the following morning. As darkness fell on my second night, the fish moved out and started topping to my left as they had done the evening before. I watched their display and all I could hope for was a morning visit before the stockie therapee started again. I did see a couple of better fish poke their heads out, so I had a chance of one of the lake's babes.

Sometime after dark I climbed in the bag for some shuteye, and as I lay there I could hear heavy rolls and the odd crash. One of them was a massive bosh as I drifted off to dream about all things carpy. I woke standing there with a bent rod in my hand at first light. I was groggy from sleeping too hard and as I shook my head to get into the land of the living, this fish just stripped line from the spool at an alarming rate. He kited on a long line, going left, so I just kept steady pressure on and he headed for a bush up the margin to my left. I jumped in and the cool water took my breath away as it went over my gonads but at least I was now wide awake so to speak! I needed to try

The fish started topping out to my left.

Rick knew which one it was!

and take charge of the situation, as this fish knew where he wanted to go, that bloody bush! I decided to apply maximum pressure to steer him away and win the battle, as I felt that the fish I was attached to could be the one. Thankfully, my ploy worked and he seemed to give up and come along the margin. As he went past I could see that he was a mirror of around 30lb and I got a glimpse of a massive scale on his side. Now that I knew I wasn't attached to the common but one of her mates, I eased off the pressure, as I had things under control. I just played him out, watching him twisting and turning in the clear margin. When he was ready, I drew him over the net cord and lifted; he was mine. As he felt the mesh he went wild, covering me in water. I laughed as I looked in and admired my prize, noticing another massive apple-slice scale. I suddenly felt that I wasn't alone and looked round to see Rick H standing behind me. "Hello Rick, I haven't seen you for a while," I said, and he asked what I'd got. "It's a peach of a mirror around thirty with two massive scales on its side," I replied. "I think I know what one that could be Jim," Rick said.

I carefully unhooked him in the net and at this point I had a really good look at this awesome creature. You cannot beat old English carp; the weights of these proper old beasts are irrelevant. As you know, wrong 'uns have NO place in my angling. People angling for them are making a mockery of our sport and our heritage and as long as they're still about I will continue to hunt for this country's finest carp wherever that may be! I positioned the net so the carp was safe and as I climbed out I shook Rick's

James Turner with The Marlow Common, RIP.

hand and asked him if he would be so kind as to do the honours for me, handing him the camera while I got the mat and bits sorted. While I was away Rick must have had a better look at the fish and when I returned to the swim he confirmed that it was a fish called Apple Slice. We carefully transferred him into the weigh sling and Rick confirmed a weight of 31lb 12oz. This fish was awesome with those two big scales one side and random scales on the other. I lifted him for the camera and Rick captured the images for me to drool over in my album for years to come. Now it was time to slip him back to fight another day, the moment when you are as one before your quarry glides off out of your hands. I punched the sky and shouted, "Yes!" I could now go and fish Welly, so I decided to pack up and head back over the footbridge into civilization. Before I left I had one last look in the corner and once again saw the common. I decided to put five kilos of squids in and use it as a back-up water if Welly was hard or I saw her on the spot while baiting. I could keep this venue baited as I passed it on the way back and forth to Welly. This was OK for a couple of trips but later it got too busy to bait, so I didn't go back that year. Sadly, the big common died the following spring. RIP The Marlow Common.

With the van loaded I bade farewell to Marlow for the time being, punching Welly's postcode into the sat nav. I pulled into a Tesco Express for fuel and provisions for the next few days. Pulling into the country park, I drove down the long road into the wood, which eventually opened out into a car park by the visitor centre. Before I could

Several big fish up to 45lb had been caught from the little lake.

Bramble.

go fishing I had to report to the office as one of the wardens was going take me for a drive around the lake on a quad, showing me the lake and the do's and don'ts. With all the formal bollocks done it was time for me to go and enjoy a new challenge. It was going to be a tough eighteen months saving for The Mere, and I'd told myself that the hunt for The Black Mirror could take anything up to three years. When I said this to my mates they just laughed and said I'd have it straight away! Before locking the van I grabbed my water bottle just in case I found some feeding carp, as I was now in full hunt mode. Emerging from the wooded path that leads down from the car park I could see people everywhere. There were dozens of kids and dogs and everyone was shouting! This was therapee at its best but I knew by late evening the park would be quiet, as it closes to the public. I decided to walk left and this was going to be a bad move because it took me up to the buildings and there were bods everywhere, doing all sorts. People were sitting down all over this area, picnicking. With all that row going on I needed to get on my toes. I saw a bridge spanning a small channel so I quickly crossed over, away from all that bollocks. As I was crossing the bridge I had a look down, and it was clear to me that fish would use the channel in quiet times to go back and forth from the main lake into this small lake. I was to later find out that they had only just removed the netting that separated the lakes, so Mr Carp could now visit this area again, as it had been several years since they could swim from lake to lake. Later that day I was to find out that several carp to 45lb had already been caught from the little lake. On another session I was to lose a very powerful fish on a rig positioned under the bridge too!

Following the lake round, I walked my past my first occupied swim, known as Lawrie's Point, from which point the lake once again narrowed into Bramble Bay. This area was really shallow and with my polarizing glasses I could see the bottom really easily in the crystal-clear water. Most of it was covered in silkweed, so finding carp in these sorts of areas would be easy. I followed the track as it rose away from the water where the lake tapered into an even smaller bay. I recognised this area as the Korda swim and I could see that someone was bivvied up in the swim. I didn't look down into the snags out of respect for the person fishing to the far margin I was walking along. I was to see many fish in this snaggy zone on my travels, so it was definitely a hotspot. However, it was one of those swims like Lawrie's, Hole in the Bush, Goose Shit Point and The Sluices, which always seemed to be occupied. I decided that I would only play in these sorts of swims if fish were located and of course if no one was rotating them. This seemed to happen a lot over my time at Welly and was just one form of the bollocks that I was to suffer at Welly from jealous anglers. I didn't walk right down this spit to Daisy Point on the end, as there were several bivvies erected from the Korda swim, round to the Hole in the Bush swim. I just walked past and carried on into another open expanse of the water and as I paused in the corner swim called The Cold it was clear that there was going to be a lot of walking involved in fishing Welly effectively. I knew that the fish were probably always on the move as they had 30-odd acres to hide in and at times they were going to be very hard to find in such a shallow, weedy lake. However, I knew

The miniature train; it was all a bit weird!

that the hunting skills that I had learned over the years would keep me in front of the followers.

Suddenly, out of the corner of my eye, I saw a shape discreetly push out of the water. I looked for signs of anglers bivvied in the area but couldn't see anyone, so I quickly legged it as I was now on a mission to get round to the other side ASAP. As I got round to the Sluice area, I looked left and some 15 to 20 yards out, roughly where I had seen that carp show, there were tiny patches of bubbles. This was the sign I was looking for. I made my way down to the left, close to where this carpy activity was taking place and as I peered out from in between the bushes the fizzing was dead in front. It wasn't really a swim and over my time at Welly I was going to find the fish a lot in these quieter parts of the lake. After ten minutes watching I was buzzing because I knew that I was 50 percent of the way there. My water bottle secured the swim while I made a hasty retreat back to the van to get my gear. With the barrow loaded it was time to get my gear round to the Animal Farm area of the lake as quickly as my legs would carry me. I pushed my barrow alongside a finger bay that I liked the look of, no-one was fishing in there either. On my right was the miniature train that took visitors around the park; this was all a bit weird but something I did get my head round later on! You just had to switch off from it all as from late evening till 9am it was beautifully peaceful. I was on a mission to get round to the swim and get the rods rocking, and thankfully no-one was fishing anywhere near the zone I had found them in, but it wouldn't take long for

me to be noticed and visited by the sheep. They would soon know that if Uncle's got his rods out then Mr Carp's about.
The fish were still in residence as I went to work getting rods ready and the excitement was unreal as I watched, facing the area as I hurried to get these chods tied on and baited. I wanted to cast the rods one after another, so as to cause minimal disturbance. As I propped the rods up against the bushes on the left of the swim a really big mirror pushed out and slid silently back, not more than fifteen yards out to the left. I had one spot to put a bait to and I planned to fan the other rods out to the right. A few minutes later I had three rods in the zone and now it was time to get a mixture of 15mm and 20mm baits spread over the zone. I decided to spread around three kilos of baits all over the area to get them rooting about, as it was real weedy in this shallow area. This didn't take long at all with the baiting spoon, but it was something I needed to do, as I knew that these fish liked their grub and I had a plentiful supply at my disposal. My bait allowance at Nash was a tonne and half with no questions asked. Trust me, I knew I would need that at least here. With the rods out in the zone, it was time for me to put my house in order, as it was getting late. For the first time I noticed that it was now quiet. I could hear the birds singing and thought that perhaps even they were happier now that the park was empty, or was it I could just hear them now?
Once the house was up I cooked a rib-eye steak with all the trimmings, washed down with a couple of cold beers I had chilling in a bag of ice. As I cooked my dinner I kept

As I peered in I could see a brightly coloured mirror.

a watch out but all was quiet. I must have spooked them, as all the carpy activity had died off but I was sure I would get a visit by the morning at the latest. I was washing the food down with one of those ice-cold beers when I heard some people talking behind me, then someone poked his head round the bivvy. Trust me, this lad looked like a right character and it looked like he'd had a few beers. The other one stayed in the background as this lad proceeded to question the fcuk out of me, "What you seen? What you had? What you know?" He then said, "Are you Jim Shelley?" like he didn't know. "Of course," I replied, wondering what the fcuk is this bloke was on. The other bloke stayed well out of it; I think he was happy watching his mate making a right cock of himself and later encounters with this geezer confirmed he was made like this; he was wired up different to most! Suddenly, my phone rang and I told them that I had to take it. Matey turned to go and said, "I'm Paul and he's Matt," before they walked off, talking. I thought to myself, "That geezer's going to be a nightmare," and I remember describing this character to my wife Jane as we spoke on the phone... she just laughed.

As darkness fell fish started topping in front of me around forty to sixty yards out, so they were still about. I decided to put the rest of the five-kilo bag of boilies out with the throwing stick this time. Fish carried on rolling out in the moonlight as I lay on the bed chair chilling before falling asleep. Apart from a couple of single bleeps nothing occurred and I woke to the early morning chorus, as the birds sung their little hearts out. I looked out in disgust as nothing had happened and I'd just turned over and gone back to sleep when a couple of bleeps brought me back to the land of the living. As I turned over, the middle rod screamed off. I flew out of the bag and ran to the offending rod in bare feet. The fish soon weeded me up so I gave it some slack and watched the line as it entered the lake for movement. After around a minute or so the line was being taken so I pushed the bale arm over and recommenced battle. The rod took on its full battle curve as this fish tried in vain to seek safety back in the thick weed. With steady pressure I soon had it in the edge and it charged around under the rod tip. I knew this fish wasn't a giant by the way it had fought, and before long I had my first Welly carp in the net. As I peered in I could see a brightly coloured mirror that looked around 20lb. I unhooked him in the net and then went to get things ready for some self-takes, as this was my first carp from the venue. On the mat it looked like this character had some kind of inter-breeding in his blood line but least he wasn't a wrong 'un! I quickly did a couple of self-takes before letting it go free from the swim further up. I recast the rod and topped up with just a few freebies so as not to spook any fish that might be present.

As the morning progressed, it became apparent that they had done the off, so it was a case of getting back on the hunt, plus I was gagging to explore Welly further. People were passing my swim very close and this was doing my head in too so I skipped the rigs in and got ready to go looking. Before leaving the swim I decided to have a tidy up so I would be ready for the move, as I didn't want it packed up sitting on the barrow as things could go missing. I decided to head off for a look around Bramble Bay as this

Animal Farm, of course!

area was very shallow and inside info told me this was a very good day area. As I made my way round it was clear other anglers knew I was on the water and I had a feeling that I was being watched. I reckon hyper Paul had put the word out that Uncle Jim was in town! I bumped into a couple of anglers that were having their first look around, as they had just parted with the dollar. One of them said, “We had heard that you were on the lake,” and I just said, “News spreads fast.” I had a little chat with them but I just wanted to get some carp located and not long after, they left me be. I carried on and another angler approached. This big bloke was a wearing a suit and he came up and introduced himself as Rich, in a deep, northern accent. More therapee was to come, “Here we go again,” I thought as he launched into the old routine, “What you know? What you had? What you seen?” The same old mental properties of the wannabe carp angler known to us as a sheep shagger!

This bloke proceeded to tell me what had been out and where from. I wasn’t interested, as I like finding my own fish, so I tried to change the conversation by asking him if he had caught anything yet. It turned out that he hadn’t and he then informed me that he walked the lake most days, sometimes twice, as he lived on the caravan park. This was a stopgap as he was looking for a new house after moving down from Shropshire. Apparently, he’d once fished The Monument too, which didn’t impress me in the slightest; now I was talking to a wannabe wrong ’un hunter! God this bloke could jaw on, was I ever going to get left alone? Later, this bloke was to pester me on my work mobile, asking me how much one of my tuitions cost. When I answered, he said, "Fcuk that!" I asked him how much he earned in a day and he just laughed. "Cocky twat," I thought to myself. I now needed to get away from this creep as he was doing my skull in big time, plus this cock with all the info who lived on the park had caught nothing. It was now time for me to leg it, fast, as there was no way I was having any more of this therapee. Unfortunately, this was nothing compared to some of the back-stabbing bollocks that I was going to get over my time at this poorly run fishery, but this will be something featured later on in this chapter.

As I got about hundred yards away I looked out from a swim in Bramble Bay and twenty yards out I could see coloured water on a shallow plateau. As I watched from the top of the swim I could see subtle tail patterns in the cloudy water. The best thing to do was for me to make a hasty retreat back to my swim in Animal Farm and grab a few bits for a few hours' stalking. Trust me, I didn't hang around, as I could sense another chance. On the way back I hoped that no-one would stumble across my find although I need not have worried as the carp gods were on my side. I was soon standing in the swim re-curving the two chods as I watched them in the mix. The plan was to cast well past the zone and reel back and before letting the choddy drop down into the coloured zone. Once I had two rods laying on the floor with the clutches set I put out around thirty freebies and sat back to watch the line for telltale tweaks. Out of the blue the

Luckily, nobody had stumbled upon my find.

I nicknamed him Arnie.

After an uneventful fight, I had this 32lb mirror in the net.

right-hand rod pulled tight and the line ripped from the clip. I jumped down with the net and pulled into a fast-moving carp that stripped forty yards of line straight off me. I could feel a grating sensation as this fish kited behind the plateau. It was unreal that I'd had a take so soon but now I was worried about losing it.

I was hoping the blanket of silkweed would protect the line from being cut as I slowly gained on the fish with this horrible feeling transmitting up the line. Suddenly, a big bow-wave rocked the shallows; he was free and hopefully this fish would soon be mine. After a few minutes of him charging around under the rod tip I could see this pissed-off common in the clear water, trying to rid himself of the hook by shaking his head. Thankfully, I soon had this mad common in the net thrashing the water to foam. I thought it better to leave him to calm down while I got the bits ready, as I was going to do self-takes. I broke the net down and this fish continued to cover me in spray making me think that he was going to be a nightmare to get some pics of! Even in the weigh sling he kept going mental. In between the thrashing, I weighed him in at 28lb 12oz. While I tried to get some pics I named him Arnie, as he was one pee'd off carp! I soon gave up and let him go, whereupon he covered me with spray. I laughed, thinking to myself, "You mad fcuker!"

As you can imagine, things went quiet after that and I didn't see any more signs, so they clearly knew something was wrong. Knowing Bramble was a place they visited in the heat of the day I thought I'd give it a few hours and see if anything else occurred. Over the next hour I had several liners as the line pulled tighter and fell back. As I sat at the top of the swim the public drifted by but I didn't look round, as I didn't fancy any punishment. The swim was right on the path, which meant that you could only put a bivvy up once the park was closed, plus you had to leave enough room for anglers to get past with their barrows. I decided that if I ever fished in there at night I would sleep under the stars and only use a brolly if it rained, which I did on several occasions when I fished this swim.

Suddenly the left-hand rod pulled round and a big bow-wave exited the shallow spot, making me think that this was a much bigger fish. It took around forty yards off me and then kited all the way into my margin. This was another odd fighter but as I watched him in the clear water I could see this mirror doing the same thing, shaking his head violently trying to rid himself of that hook. Apart from the initial burst of power the fight was very uneventful and within a few minutes I had a nice chunky mirror in the net. It wasn't as big as I first thought but it definitely looked like a thirty and on the scales he went 32lb. Trust me, this one posed for the cameras, unlike Arnie! I was to add another common of 26lb before the water started to clear and started to wonder if any of the fish would be heading back to Animal Farm, as there were a lot of fish in there the day before.

As I barrowed my gear back I saw Paul and got more thereapee with all the normal questions. I told him what I had caught and he proceeded to rip the piss and named me the Pest Control Officer. I just laughed and asked what he'd caught, which seemed to shut him up. He told me that this bloke fishing in the entrance to the small lake

This 26lb common completed the trio.

had caught a fish called The Dark One at 45lb plus. This gave me the ammo I needed, and I asked Paul, "What are you doing bivvying up so close to him then?" He knew the shoe was now on the other foot as I rounded, "Can't you find your own carp you sheep shagger?" He just laughed, saying, "Fcuk off!" but I did notice that he went a bit red. All this time his mate Matt smirked and winked at me, letting me know he liked the therapee I had just given him. I knew this bloke would be a thorn in my side but I must say that after all the grief, we still talk and laugh about the Welly therapee to this very day. As you can probably imagine, you will be hearing more about this character. Anyway, back at the Animal Farm swim, I soon had my rods back out on the zone, as the hooks were pukka. I loaded the area up again with the baiting spoon and as I baited, I could make out someone hiding behind a tree watching what I was doing. As soon as I saw him, he disappeared. I thought, "I bet it was that geezer eyeing where I was putting my rods out," but I wasn't 100% sure that was him. However, in the morning I was going to get a visit from Paul The Sheep…

In the early hours I got up for a leak and heard one bosh close in on the zone, sweet! As I laid back down and drifted off back to dream about massive Welly carp one of the rods screamed off. I jumped out onto the cold, damp grass, grabbed my rod and pulled into another carp. Just as I did that I heard the word, "GEEZER!" behind me. I looked round and the sheep was there; he must have been watching the farm with a view to move in after I left. I focused on playing what was obviously a small carp and as I walked out to net the fish he shouted "Oi oi, Pest Control Officer!" I grinned, not wanting to give him a bite. God this one wasn't even a twenty and I unhooked him in the net. Turning to the sheep, I said, "At least it's another one!" He laughed then he hit me with the immortal words, "What time you off?" I looked round, laughing, "What? You wanna sheep me now GEEZER?" He just came straight out and said yes so I let him know that I planned to fill the swim in when I left. He simply smiled and asked whether I could leave him some baits for hook baits! I shook my head wondering if this guy was for real! He then disappeared when I looked round and a few seconds later he had his gear parked behind my bivvy. Someone else walked up and Paul The Sheep informed this bloke that he was having this swim. I couldn't believe what was going on in a swim that was hardly ever fished. I was right about this bloke, he was defo the ultimate sheep shagger and brazen with it, a fine quality if you can get away with it!

As I was packing up soon I decided not to recast the rod, because I still had two rods in the zone. As I got my head to together with a strong, milky coffee Paul was hard at work getting his rods sorted with a purpose that was scary to see, he thought this was all good angling! I just couldn't believe what I was seeing; this was definitely the carper of today. I even heard him telling other anglers that this was now his swim as they walked past. In the end I just wanted to get away from this, as it was all so unnatural in my world of angling. So, within an hour my gear was packed up and loaded on the barrow. Now it was time to do his head in by loading the swim up with 10kg. As I started to do this he seemed to revel in it as he was now fully focused on what I was doing. It seemed like he wanted me to do it, saying, "Give us a handful for hook baits Jim." I just kept it cool as I didn't want to show him he was pissing me off; I wanted to prime this area for next time so I had something to come back to. However, this time it was to be something I would regret doing. As I pushed my barrow back towards the car park a Land Rover came towards me. As it got near it pulled onto the grass and out popped this oldish bloke who then spoke to me in a Scottish accent, grinding out the words, "You must be Shelley boy?" "Oh dear," I thought, "I hope this ain't bad news." Thankfully, it wasn't as he then proceeded to tell me that he'd heard all about me. I laughed and stuck out my hand saying, "You must be Kenny?" This seemed to cement our friendship, although I had been warned about this geezer, who was an acting head bailiff when Andy P wasn't about. There were loads of rumours flying around at that time, suggesting that Andy didn't want anything to do with the running of the lake, which was a shame as I had heard he was sound.

Kenny laughed and I could see his mind working overtime as he had probably guessed that I had been warned about him. I was told he loved to dish it out and trust me, I love a bit of banter. Kenny played his trump card, or so he thought, telling me, "Shelley boy, I ain't having any stroke pulling or piss-taking here." "OK Kenny," I replied, trying to keep it cool before I played my trump card. I had heard that he liked a beer or two, so I asked him what he drank. This seemed to work as he said, "Becks" I told him to come and see me next time I was down and promised that we'd have a good chat over

All I could say was, "Good angling Paul, but not the way you did it."

As I walked across the bridge I could see that Lawrie's was vacant.

Lawrie's Point, one of the top swims.

a beer. He shook my hand and this was the start of a great relationship with someone I respected for many reasons, right to the end. Trust me, I always made sure I had some Becks for Kenny. Most didn't like him and the more they showed him that, the more he enjoyed winding them up, with several even making complaints at the office. It seems in this day and age most people cannot have a laugh; instead they just go around whining behind people's backs, just like the keyboard warriors in the cyber world.

The next morning I got the call that I was dreading. Paul The Sheep rang me on my work mobile informing me that he had caught a massive common. All I could say was, "Good angling Paul, but not the way you did it," before hanging up. This cut deep, as he had sheeped me up on this capture and it hurt even more because it was a forty-plus common. I later heard that he ran round the lake shouting at the top of his voice after catching the fish, followed by more rumours that he was off his head on something! I had to put this behind me and learn from it. I would face it again from another two-faced angler, Jamie, AKA Dangermouse, as we named him. This character would play his games by manipulating his puppet, Shaun AKA The Leg or The Shoe! As you can imagine I had to keep my cool as I was going to get untold therapee and backstabbing from them and others, including some of the old syndicate members later on in the season. I never really saw Paul much again after his first trip, thank God, but I did hear he was still up to his old tricks at weekends, which upset the weekenders! At least this kept him out of my hair, and stopped him following me about sheeping me up.

I had planned to meet up with Rich Stewart, then the editor of Advanced Carp Fishing Magazine, on my next trip, as I had a monthly column in there and have been doing features for them for around ten years. I did two days of my fishing and two days tuition, which was booked in at Farlows Lake near Heathrow. It was going to be an early start and the alarm woke me at 3am; this wasn't good but it would mean sod-all traffic on the 198-mile journey from Lowestoft to Reading. With the van loaded and two cans of Red Bull to keep me awake, I let the trance tunes, turned up full volume, sweep me along. With my foot down it was time to start eating those miles and when I got to junction 11 of the M3 I always used to shout out "Yes!" as I knew it was only a few more miles left before I pulled into the park. Rich was due midmorning, but knowing Rich he would be late, so this gave me plenty of time to find some fish.

As I pulled into the car park there were only three cars and I bet their owners were all in the going swims. I left the loaded barrow by the bridge and grabbed my water bottle; it was time to get back on the hunt for carp. The park was still closed so the barrow would be safe and I could now cover ground quicker. As I walked across the bridge heading towards Bramble Bay I noticed that Lawrie's was vacant. I decided to sit on one of the picnic benches and watch for signs as this swim was rarely vacant. After watching for a while I noticed a big, dark shape push out to the right of the island that was situated at about 10 o'clock in front of Lawrie's. Jackpot, I was now back on them. Leaving the water bottle, I quickly fetched my gear and went straight to work. I watched for further signs as I got the three rods ready. I had to shorten my leadcore leaders and step up to 4oz leads in order to reach the fish with 20lb X-Line. This meant harder fishing for me, as I would now have to spod out free offerings. I like to fish at ranges that make for easy fishing, but if that was where they were, then I would have to get out to them. Casting 20lb X-Line over 100 yards would be tricky because it isn't made for long-range casting. However, having 13ft 3.5lb test curve Pursuits should mean that I could get my rigs out to the 100 or 115-yard marks.

I had only seen one more fish show in the small cove in the side of the island, which meant I was going to fan the rods from this area to the right, with the right-hand rod pushed out to a range of around 115 yards. I soon had the rods in position, so it was time to get some bait out there. With the boilies nicely scattered across the area thanks to my spodding style, it was time to grab some sleep before Rich turned up. I was knackered from the long drive but now I was fishing and on them. Just as I was drifting off I heard, "Hello mate." I popped my head up from the bag there stood Mr Stewart. "For fcuk's sake mate, you shit the bed?" I said. "Christ I'm trying to get some much-needed sleep Rich. You're normally late and you're early for the first time! Has the missus chucked you out?" This was my time to give him some back but he just smiled as he was hardened to the Uncle Jim therapee.

Our pleasantries were interrupted by my right-hand rod, which suddenly started screaming full bore! I jumped out of the bag and pulled into this loony of a carp, which stripped untold line off the clutch. I turned round to Rich and said, "You must be a good-luck charm mate." I still needed some luck though, as this fish was heading

The scales showed 37lb.

at high speed towards this island on the right, which was around 150 plus yards from this bank. I just held on and the steady pressure took its toll as he kited back towards the margin down to my right, getting momentarily caught up in weed. This seemed to slow this mad fucker and I dropped into the shallow margin to make it easier to net him. I got a glimpse of a chunky mirror with some weed around his face as his head came out and he took a gulp of air. Rich passed me the net and I slid it straight under him and lifted. All hell then let loose as he thrashed the water to foam in the net, spraying me with cool water. I had a right angry chunk in the net vowing that he wasn't having any pictures taken of him! I gently removed the hook and handed Rich control of the net while I shot back to get things sorted. We placed him in my cradle mat and then walked the cradle to the spot I had chosen to do the pics. He looked a good thirty and the scales showed 37lb. I said to Rich, "At least they're getting bigger since the Sheep Shagger named me the Pest Control Officer."

The one thing I was beginning to notice about these Welly carp is that they hated any human contact. They fight like animals and hate having their pictures taken. I was also later to notice a lot of head shaking throughout the fights, with some of them not even fighting as they focused more on shaking their heads, trying to rid themselves of the hook. It's unreal when you witness this from a fish. With the carp returned, it was time to get some dry clothes on and get the rod back out on the spot. I had to get this feature done and hopefully bag another one before the end of the session,

The famous Hole in the Bush swim.

as I couldn't make it back to Welly for a few weeks because I was rammed out with tuitions. After the ACF feature was done it seemed to me that the fish had pushed out further into the Hole in the Bush swim's water, so later in the afternoon, with that gut feeling eating me up, I knew that it was time to act. I reeled the rods in and went off for a mooch about to see if I could get near them. Several fish were showing out in the main body of the lake around another hot area that always seemed to be occupied, so I trotted off around Bramble Bay with my water bottle to see if I could get on them. As I walked past the Korda swim I couldn't see any bivvies in residence on the spit. My mind started racing; surely that swim wasn't empty? Sure enough, there wasn't anyone about. I walked straight over to the Hole in the Bush and dropped my bottle onto the wood chip. I looked out at the great expense of water in front of this area when, all of a sudden, a big old hippo shuffled out to halfway, roughly where I had been seeing them from Lawrie's. Sweet, this was the sign I needed so I legged it straight back and packed my gear up in double-quick time.

While preparing the rods I noticed that most of the activity was to the right of the swim and with the three rods ready it was time to get them out there rocking on the spots. Getting them out there meant getting into chest waders, which would allow me the angle to get two rods up near that cove. It still necessitated a severe side-cast, even with me wading out as far as possible. I checked the angle first by wading out and taking a look before I tried this tricky cast, as it was around seventy yards up the side of an island. The first attempt was too severe and I had to pull it out of the sky, as it was heading up a tree. I stumbled a bit, letting some water into the waders, but with a 'fcuk-it' attitude I went for it this time and the cast landed bang on the money. It got a satisfyingly soft drop as I gently teased it back along the island shelf. I set the bobbin with a slight drop so I'd be aware of any drop backs. The middle rod was cast ten yards to the left of the right-hander and the left-hand rod was positioned twenty yards away to the left. I spread 5kg of 15mm and 20mm squids over the three rods to complete the trap. Just as I was contemplating cooking some dinner, I heard a motor pull up. It was Kenny and he immediately said, "What are you doing here, I thought you were on Lawrie's Point?" I laughed, "Been there, done that – there are fish out here boy!" As I leaned back into the bivvy I grabbed a Becks, handing it to him before he had a chance to play his game. This was my moment and the edge I needed to get him on my side. He muttered, "Cheers you old fcuker." I bet he thought I would forget and I think this was the turning point. We sat and chatted over a couple of cold beers about how my reputation usually preceded me on a new water. Kenny was refreshingly honest and told me that he made his own mind up about people. "Yes," I told him, "I can be controversial and once crossed, I'm out to dish the shit, but only if I'm crossed first." We sat talking about many things over the next few hours, while the carp danced in

My first night bite resulted in this 29lb 10oz mirror.

front of my swim, until Kenny said, "I've got to go now as my young lady will have my dinner ready." I later found out that she was indeed young, but hey, that's another story.

When he had left I was up for some grub and while I cooked it the carp carried on showing over the whole zone. I really felt confident of a take as I lay down on the bed; I was certainly well on them. A bleep on the middle alarm woke me and as I turned over it started screaming! It was still dark and I struggled into the chest waders before flicking the head torch on and heading down to the LED. This carp was on a mission to anywhere but here, at high speed. As I was trying to focus on playing the fish a big carp boshed out in front of me! Suddenly, there was a big shake on the rod as he tried to get rid of the hook, he then kited round to my left on a tight line. I could now tell he was a smaller one as there was no weight behind him. Not long after he was under the rod and in the dimmed torchlight I slid the net under a nice, chunky mirror. The fish responsible for my first bite at night went 29lb 10oz on the scales. I did a couple of quick self-takes before slipping him back to fight another day. I decided not to recast the rod as it was clear that there were still fish about, so instead I climbed back into the bag to get some more sleep.

I was rudely awoken by another buzzer screaming at me and as I sat up to get my chest waders on I realised that it was light. I was briefly annoyed at myself for oversleeping but I quickly forgot about that as I legged it to attend to the right-hand rod, which was bent double in the rests. The rod was nearly torn from my grasp as this carp decided that anywhere but here was its preferred destination. These fish mostly fight like demons and this one was no different, tearing off along the island. I waded out because I didn't want my line getting caught up along the island's overhanging trees, but soon realised that he had in fact snagged me. I slackened off straight away, hoping he would think he was free. This ruse worked and as the slack line picked up and I reeled down tight causing the fish to explode on the surface in front of the cove. I clamped down as he took the rod round, trying to gain the sanctuary of the snags, making him kite out. I heard someone approach and as I turned round I saw this midget thing in tow with another weird thing. "Hi," I said as I turned back and carried playing this animal of a carp, which now knew who was boss. I started to gain line at an alarming rate as this fish swam towards me at high speed and when I caught up with him he just came up and wallowed on the surface. I lifted the net around him and got the customary soaking as the water in the net erupted. I had the chesties this time so I didn't get drenched!

As I looked in the net I thought, "That's an awesome pale-looking chunk." I unhooked him in the net and turned to the two weirdos asking, "Can you take a couple of pics for me guys?" When they said that they could, I introduced myself. The one with the tooth said, "I'm Jamie" and the other one, who hopped up to me, said, "I'm Shaun." As I mentioned earlier, these two characters soon showed their hand; Dangermouse would pull the strings, getting The Leg to do his dirty work. To this day I don't think The Leg knew what Dangermouse was doing. The Leg always seemed to be at the lake

Solid as a rock and not far off forty!

I lost a powerful fish that evening, which made me up my hook size.

claiming all sorts of things and was generally there looking out who was catching from where and feeding Dangermouse the midweek info. Dangermouse would then plan his attack around this, which later got well out of hand! I've learnt to mostly rise above it all as life's too short to worry about such people. Anyway, the fish weighed in at 38lb and was as solid as a rock. Those Welly carp were in awesome condition and getting the expensive ticket for my own limited fishing time was looking like a good investment. I knew that if I continued catching at this rate the knives would be out but I wasn't going to be back for a while, which suited the situation. When I returned, I would take fifty six carp in fifty six nights, but as you can imagine I'm only going to highlight some of the best sessions and stories. Later I found out that chod rigs supposedly didn't work on Welly. Oh well, I showed them what a one-trick pony can do!

I was to lose a very powerful fish that evening after it managed to slip the hook. I decided to try and prevent any more losses by upping the hook size to a four from my next trip. I had a new plan of attack for the next trip but it would be several weeks before I could return to pursue those Welly carp because I had a diary full of tuitions. Things were to change though, as the following week I got a call from Kenny telling me that I could do tuitions on the lake. I couldn't believe my luck and asked what the day ticket price would be. He said £30, for which they would produce a receipt. This now meant that I could work and play at the same time. I certainly made sure Kenny was

I had a tuition with a young lad called Jamie.

well supplied with his Becks after that! The following week I couldn't make it as I was booked in for some floater fishing at Farlows, but the next week I was booked in for a three-day tuition with a young lad called Jamie, so when I informed him that we would be doing his trip at Welly, he was blown away! More good news was to follow, in the shape of a cancelled tuition, meaning that I could now stay at the lake for three or four days if it wasn't too busy. I always say that if I get a cancellation it's another sign from the carp gods. I got down really early and it wasn't quite light, so this would give me a good chance to find the fish before I met up with Jamie and his mum Annelise. Jamie had been on a tuition with me before, catching several fish from two different waters, so it would be a catch up to see how he had been getting on since his last trip. He told me that the knowledge he had gained had greatly improved his fishing and this time he wanted me to show him how I go about locating carp. It wasn't long before I found signs around the bridge area that connects both lakes. As Welly was close to his home and we knew each other now, we decided that Jamie's mum would stay around in the evening and leave him to his fishing in the day. That was nice because in the evenings she would bring us dinner, happy days! Before she left, I asked Annelise if she could bring some cold beers back with her so I had a thank you surprise for Kenny boy.

We both set up in the little lake to start with, which meant loads of noise as the little lake was close to the entrance of the park and surrounded by picnic tables. After dark however, things would come to life in this area as it was clear the carp used this area at night and during the early morning before the park opened its gates.

The little lake was very shallow with a lot of overhanging bushes for carp to hide up in. When they are about their presence is given away by sediment in the water. It was very cloudy that day, as I pointed out to Jamie by taking him to the other side of the bridge where the water was clear. As we stood hanging over the side, looking for signs Jamie turned and pointed, saying, "Look Jim there's a carp!" I said "Good lad, stay still," and we watched this chunky mirror in the mid thirties glide under the bridge into the little lake. "Told you," I said, "I couldn't have done that any better, now you've seen one." Now he knew what I had shown him was bang on; it's simple when you know how to process the information that's in front of you.

Later that evening Annelise turned up with a bag of ice-cold Becks, just in time too because not long after Kenny appeared and I handed him one, which he half-downed straight away. I told him that Annelise had bought them for him, and he thanked her in his deep Scottish voice. I bet he thought he had died and gone to heaven but in my book if someone looks after you it is in your best interests to look after them. Soon enough Kenny disappeared off on his rounds and later popped in to tell me that there had been a complaint about me having a tuition guest. I asked who'd complained and he said, "Don't worry, I've told them the score." I now knew the jealous backstabbers were out. After the park closed all was quiet and just before dark the first carp rolled out in the middle. Not long after this little lake came alive and out in the darkness fish showed and some sounded like cows as the ripples rocked in. It was time to get some shuteye but as I climbed into the bag a buzzer screamed into life. "That must be Jamie,"

Lawrie's was free again!

I thought as I jumped off the bedchair. I ran down the bank to see him sitting there, watching the rod. "Why haven't you pulled into that rod?" I asked. "I can't believe I've got a take at Welly!" he replied. "Come on mate, get hold of that rod!" I demanded, as the rod was just bleeping now and he finally jumped up and pulled into thin air. I didn't know what to say, as he's a young lad. Then another boshed out in front of him, which made things easier for me as I was now focused on getting that rod back out. With the rod back in position I decided not to talk about what had just happened and left him to it. We both had liners through the night but by the morning nothing had happened and looking out over the little lake, you wouldn't have believed that a few hours ago there had been carp going ape shit as it now looked dead as dodo. The water looked clearer too, so I knew we would be on the hunt again, looking for Mr Carp. After breakfast we decided to pack up before it got too hot and then Jamie's mum left us to it. With the barrows loaded we set off in the direction of the bridge and as we stood looking beneath us, one jumped clean out on the corner of the channel where it joined the main lake. Straight away I said, "Go get your gear mate," and made my way to the swim. I noticed Lawrie's was free, so that was me sorted too. Not long after Jamie appeared, I grabbed his water bottle and legged it over to claim my swim before it was too late. As I walked past Jamie to get my kit from the little lake, I said, "Get your rods ready fella I won't be long." When I got back to him, Jamie told me that he had seen several fish show in front of him. It was great hearing the excitement in his voice;

he even had his rigs re-curved and when I asked him if he had checked the hooks he replied, "They're pukka Jim!" I still double-checked them before he cast to roughly where the fish had shown. I did think he had come along way as I watched him make his three casts before baiting up; it was like poetry in motion! Of course, I told him this and it was great to see his face light up; this is the buzz I get back from tuitions along with the texts, emails, pictures and phone calls from clients, telling me how their fishing has changed for the good.

After Jamie was settled, it was time for me to get my rods out. I planned to put them roughly back where I had caught before. The day was getting hot but with a fresh breeze on our backs it made the open Lawrie's Point more comfortable. We were chatting about the day's events when one of my rods melted off and I was soon into a fast-moving carp at long range, which boiled on the surface way out, before kiting to my left. The carp was heading along the surface towards the entrance of Bramble Bay at high speed so I walked out to get a better angle on him. I started to gain line and Jamie asked "Shall I grab the net for you?" I said "Yes mate and you can do the honours for me". As he walked out, I told him to sink the net and lift it on my say-so. Soon we had a mirror in close and I could see it wasn't a big 'un but nevertheless it was another Welly carp. Not long after he surfaced and I said "Lift the net," which Jamie did and we both peered in to get a better look at our captive. We agreed that he looked

Jamie netted this 29lb 6oz mirror for me.

like an upper-twenty and the scales proved us right, registering 29lb 6oz. After a bit of therapee involving me explaining how I wanted the pictures, he did a grand job and we waded out to get a couple of water shots. At this point I noticed that the wind had changed and great big clouds were rushing overhead. The wind was now blowing into Bramble Bay as well as the little cove that was cut into the island near where I was fishing. As you can imagine, it wasn't long before I had the right-hand rod back in position and over the course of the afternoon the odd fish crashed out around the cove, indicating that several fish were in residence. Jamie still had odd fish showing in his zone too, so all-in-all it looked pukka for a bite or two.

I had heard of people sneaking over to the island to bait up and I'd even heard rumours of people swimming out. I wasn't doing that but I didn't fancy spodding 20kg of bait out either, as it had been hard enough doing the 5kg I'd put in already. As you well know, or may have heard, I'm well known for some hardcore stroke pulling so after dark I loaded the barrow up with 20kg of 15mm and 20mm squid boilies, my chesties and long-handled baiting spoon. I turned the buzzers off and told Jamie to keep an eye out just in case, and to ring me if there were any problems. Someone was in the Hole in the Bush swim and as I walked up I could hear him snoring. It was Rich, who was a so-called 'gofer' in a city bank. At least I didn't have anything to worry about now; it was time to get sorted. I made my way across the small channel in the darkness, using

The wind was blowing across me, into Bramble.

the handle to keep on the shallower gravel, as I didn't fancy getting wet! Two trips later I had 20kg of squids on the island. Now I had to climb up the high bank and make my way across the island in the dark, which wasn't easy, especially as I soon had a dangling bramble in my face! I couldn't risk turning my head torch on, as doing this would give me away. So, in the darkness, I carefully pulled it away from my face and put the hood of my sweatshirt up to try and protect face. After two trips I soon had everything in place and I opened all the bags so they were ready; I wanted to get all the bait in as quickly as possible. As I pushed the spoon into the first bag of bait I started chuckling to myself. I counted the spoons as I put the first bag out, which amounted to 10, so this lot was going to be around 40 hits. "Bloody hell," I thought, "That's a lot of noise!" Mind you, it wasn't going out any further than 15 to 20 yards from the point of the island, as my right-hand rod was 10 yards or so past the start of the island. I went to work like a mad, possessed animal getting the bait out as fast as possible. After a few minutes I could hear someone talking, "Oh dear," I thought, "All this row must have woken 'Rich the Gofer.'" I carried on as there was no point stopping now, because I had most of it in. Once it was all out, I decided to lay down and let things quieten down before making my way back along the island, as I didn't really want to draw attention to myself. After around 20 minutes I decided it was time to carefully make my way back to the gap, which was easier said than done, but least I only had to make one trip out. I gently slid down the bank and carefully waded across the channel, following the same route as before with the handle. I honestly thought I was going to get rumbled when I got across but I grabbed my boots, which were hidden, and slowly made my exit, stage left, before changing back into my boots. I cut across the point, towards the Korda swim and followed the tree line but before disappearing into the bushes I stood and listened, as it seemed two people were definitely talking. I smiled, as it seemed that I had got away with it and the mission was successful, leaving people wondering what the hell all that noise was about! Now I needed to leg it and get round Bramble Bay without bumping into anyone, as I didn't want people putting two and two together.

As I walked into the swim Jamie was laughing, "That was unreal Jim, listening to all that bait going in!" I just laughed, "That's proper baiting, Uncle Jim style." (Several comments were made in the morning, but I just said that I hadn't heard a thing and must have been asleep!)

Not long after my adventure, I decided to hit the sack and told Jamie that I'd see him in the morning. I must admit that with all that bait out there I thought it would be 24 hours at least before I had a chance of a take, but it was clear the fish were there as I had caught one. The cove seemed to be a meeting area for the fish and as such, there always seemed to be a few about. It was a really hot swim and I felt lucky to have got in there, as it's normally one out and one in. It was a cloudy, muggy night and as I climbed on to the bedchair the moon popped out and lit up the lake. After all the excitement I fell asleep happy in the knowledge that my mission had worked.

Sometime in the night I had a single bleep and turned over to see the blue LED on my right-hand rod lit up. I was half expecting something to materialize but it didn't. It was damp so I decided it was time to climb into the bag. As I lay in bed I saw a big fish jump by the light of the moon and its re-entry sounded like someone had dropped a breeze block in. When that same rod bleeped again I thought that I must have a very good chance of a bite before I had to leave. A series of bleeps on the right-hander had me running out to the rod and as I turned my head torch on I could see the line twitching where it entered the water. I thought that there must have been a fish on, shaking his head, trying to rid itself of the rig. I grabbed the rod and pulled into a brick wall of resistance, which suddenly came to life as the rod took on its full battle curve, silhouetted against the eastern sky. It was now just before first light, as I could see the subtle colour changes in the sky. The stage was set and somewhere out there in the dark a very powerful fish made a slow run and took line off the spool like it was in control and I was hanging on for the ride! Was this the big 'un I had been waiting for? The fish stopped and the rod bounced fiercely. I thought that I had lost it but I got a couple of turns of the reel and I was back in contact. I turned my head torch on to see the line angle, which was way to the right so I slowly followed it with the net in the darkness. My mind was racing, wondering what was on the end as I was sure it was a big 'un. I saw a swirl closer in than I expected so I stepped into the shallow margin and started to wade out to where I had seen him. A big back broke the surface and momentarily I struggled to get hold of the net. I managed to locate it and slid the net out to where he was wallowing on the top and lifted. All hell broke loose in the confines of the mesh, as this unhappy carp shot off, nearly ripping the net from my grasp. I turned the torch on to reveal a massive golden carp. I pulled the mesh away and there lay a massive common. It looked huge, but I couldn't allow myself to be disappointed if it wasn't over the magical forty-pound barrier. I unhooked him and over the next few minutes I stood in awe of this creature. I touched him, feeling down his side; fcuk he was big. I was blown away by it all, this carp was perfect in every way and now it was time to see if my dream of a forty-pound common was fulfilled. Deep down I knew it was. Jamie appeared out of the gloom asking, "Jim have you got one?" "Oi oi mate I've got a massive common! Come and have a look." "Jim that's a chunk," Jamie said, peering into the net.

By now it was pretty much daylight, so with everything ready for the magical moment I made my way back over to Jamie, handed him the camera and showed him how it use it before calming him down, as I think he was shitting himself with this responsibility! When I lifted the net from the water I knew for sure that it was a forty, in fact it was much bigger! I took him to the spot by a small silver birch, and carefully unfolded the net to reveal an awesome sight. He was covered in hundreds of gold sovereign scales and I was totally blown away. We placed him in Marky Mark's weigh sling (a ritual I performed in his memory with every fish I caught until it disappeared one night without trace) and Jamie read off "Forty three… forty four… bloody hell, 44lb 12oz!" I did believe him but I had to have a look for myself and found that he was spot on. As you can see from the pictures, Jamie did me proud, so cheers mate; I owe you one! After a few shots it was time for a couple of returners and that intimate moment when

"Bloody hell... 44lb 12oz!"

What I'd come to Welly for. Jamie did me proud with the pictures.

That intimate moment before you release them.

you release them and watch them glide off back into their home. As you can imagine, I was on cloud nine and phoned Jane with the good news. I didn't stop smiling for hours! Nothing else happened that trip and while I was packing up two characters popped over to have a chat and asked what I had caught. They both shook my hand and told me that they had been fishing the swim a bit lately. Before they left, they asked me about my tuitions as they said they were both interested at some point. Over time Carl and Colin became good mates and we shared many a beer and banter, and still do to this very day. A few hours later I packed up, as it was time to get back home and this capture made the long journey all the sweeter. Over the weekend I found out that the common I'd caught was the one Paul had poached off me a while back too!

I couldn't get back over the next few weeks, but mates kept me informed. It became clear that a posse of haters had formed on the lake. The dreaded sheep shaggers were up to no good again, bad-mouthing me about the amount of bait I was using, the fish I was catching, the time I was doing, tuitions and everything else to do with Jim Shelley fishing at the kids' park. Heading the posse at that time was Rich AKA 'Ten Dollar' as we named him. One evening he even rang me trying to make me see that I shouldn't be doing tuitions, as they had paid £1500 to fish there and guests were fishing it for £30 per 24 hours. I told him that every member could guest people and I argued my case until I lost the plot, calling him and his posse a bunch of backstabbing twats! I

Before setting up I decided to have a look in the channel to my right.

informed him that I was well aware of what they were up to and before I hung up, I shouted "Fcuk off!" down the phone. At least by doing this they now knew the score! Towards the end of the second week away, I fitted in a two-day session. It was around the harvest moon period in September and a key time in the carper's calendar. I know I should really have been on the bank for longer around this special time but saving extra dollar for my Mere assault meant more at the time. After finishing a tuition at Farlows I headed off towards Welly in the mid-morning rush.

I had another stroke up my sleeve to save the long walk round the lake. This time, I'd be unloading my gear further down past the angler's car park, near the Animal Farm, where the public pitch up tents and park caravans for the night. I fancied heading around the other side of the lake in the Hole in the Bush or Bramble Bay areas, as I knew the carp were using these zones a lot. Calls to a couple of anglers I swapped info with confirmed this, so I quickly got the barrow loaded and stashed it in the bushes to await my return once I had located some carp. I bumped into an angler on his way out who told me that he had just vacated the Hole in the Bush, so with this news I was now on a mission to get round there ASAP, unless I found them elsewhere, as this swim was never empty for long. I decided to head off in the direction of Bramble Bay, which meant I could check that area first. Deep down, I knew where the fish were and as I neared the Korda swim I was looking through the bushes to try and see if Hole in the Bush was free but it was tricky and I was getting frustrated worrying about a swim, which is rare these days! I took a short cut through the bushes and ran out over the grass behind the swim, which I could see was free. Just as I put two bags of bait down to claim my prize, Ten Dollar Rich came into view with his gear. His face was a picture as he was out of breath and Uncle Jim was in the swim he wanted. I just nodded and he walked over sweating and moaning about me swearing at him on the phone. I just laughed, as I knew I had just fcuked him over. He walked off muttering some old bollocks in his strange lingo. He pushed his barrow into the Korda swim behind me and I thought, "I bet he's going try and therapee me up!" I looked round as I walked off and I could see in his face that he wasn't happy with the situation! "Oh well," I thought, "You reap what you sow son."

Around fifteen minutes later I arrived back with my gear. It was time to get the rods out and back on the spots I fished last session, so I got straight to work and three rods were soon ready. I couldn't risk four with the town crier so close by. I slipped the waders on and not long after I had the rods back on the spots, rocking with a few kilos of squids spread over the zone. Before putting the house up, I decided to have a look in the channel to my right, God knows why as I had never seen any fish there, but it was a place I always checked on my walks. As I approached the area I kept to the left so the bushes hid me from view. I peered through the foliage and straight away saw eight carp following each other like sheep do, coming from the main lake through this tiny

I quickly had rods in the area, on the routes that the fish were using.

We weighed him at a massive 48lb 12oz.

channel that linked into Bramble Bay. These gut feelings of mine are spooky, as more often than not they pay off for me.

As I watched, several other fish appeared on the same route, coming into view from the left and going along the far margin in mega-shallow water. I love all this up-close-and-personal shit, as you can learn so much from them. It was now clear that there was a stalking chance so I decided to calmly walk back the 30 yards and get a bucket before I lost this chance. Ten Dollar was none the wiser to the pot of gold I had just found, so I prepared a couple of rods for stalking. I was going to stick with the chod rigs as the silkweed was really bad in this shallow water. I approached the area very quietly with two rods, a net and a pocket full of squids. I looked to see if the coast was clear before stepping out to make the casts. One was under-armed out towards the overhang on the island and the lead landed on the clean, gravely bottom but I watched the hook bait drop back, resting on the silkweed. I cast the other one down to the right, along side a bush that hung off the island. This was all going well until knob-head Rich clocked that I was up to something. I then turned to him and went "Shhhhhhhh!" and gestured to him to move away, which he did, thank God. I chewed seven baits in half and was throwing them in half a bait at a time, when suddenly I saw a massive black back glide over the first hook bait. I slowly retreated back into the cover of the bushes and the phone started to ring. I looked down and saw John Knight flashing in

I got one useable water shot!

By morning I'd caught a low-twenty common.

the display so I answered and straight away he shouted "FAT LADY!" "Bloody hell mate, good angling!" I replied, and while I listened to him recount the tale, I watched a mid-twenty common come into view and stop near the hook bait. It then proceeded to follow the X-Line right into my margin and to this day I don't know why I did this but as he turned I walked out, pinning the phone to my ear with my shoulder then picked the rod up and reeled it in. The fish swam off down the centre of the channel and I backed off to get back behind cover again. All this time I was listening with excitement to John as he relived his capture and suddenly I heard the rasp of my other clutch! "John… got to go I'm in!" I shouted, dropping the phone onto the floor and grabbing the rod.

I pulled into a snagged carp but I could feel him still on so I kept steady pressure on him. I saw the branches on the bush move, then suddenly there was a kick and he was free so I clamped down to keep him from getting back in there. He then ran towards me and I reeled fast, trying to keep in touch with him. He surfaced and I got a really good look at him; he was a very long fish with a black back. I threw the net into the water and kicked my trainers off as I was going to need to get in to land this one, as it was mega shallow close in. I tripped as I made my way out and the fish came to life shooting off. Luckily I had the clutch set and I steadied myself as he ploughed across the top, heading for the open water of the main lake. There was no way I could let this happen as I still had a rod cast out and the line ran in front of the gap, so I slowly applied more pressure to try to stop him. All off a sudden this fish rose up like a dolphin, tail walking, with me hanging on in vain trying to stop him! As he slid back down he kited and swam back towards me, so I laid off the pressure fearing for the hook hold after this awesome show of power. As I waded out further I heard the familiar sound of the Ten Dollar; "Fcuking hell Jim, that's massive!" "Shhh!" I said as I steered him towards the waiting net. Once captured, the fish went mental, as I was now coming to expect! There was no way I was letting this creature free until I was finished though! I turned off to the bollocks behind me because this was my time. I looked in to reveal the awesome sight of a massive carp with a humped back like The Dustbin from Yateley. I spoke to him as I touched his side and removed the hook as he was nailed perfectly. Rich waded in and asked if he could get a better look. I said "OK, can you watch him while I get the things sorted." As I walked out he said, "That's The Turtle, Jim." I already had a good idea which one he was, I just carried on with a big smile on my face, as I knew that capture would hurt him; nothing like letting your angling do the talking! It was getting dark so we had to hurry to get some half-decent pictures with the light that was left. We weighed him at a massive 48lb 12oz and he was looking awesome and definitely well on his way to fifty pounds in the near future. On the mat he was so long and there wasn't an ounce of fat on him. He was clearly a male, as I noticed him milting, so I'd caught the king of the lake. I was buzzing my head off as this capture had happened purely because I'd acted on a gut feeling. I do like it when I silence my critics and this capture was no different. As I held him up for a quick water shot I knew this was hurting Ten Dollar. I checked the camera after we got out of the lake and guess what? All the water shots had bits of tail or head and cut off but I did get one useable one. Bitter and twisted eh? I would never do that and that's if I lowered myself to take the shots. After the shots were done, I never saw Ten Dollar again and this told me he was bitter. I saw nothing else in the gap but by the morning I'd caught a low twenty common fishing along the island in front of the cove. It had been an unreal couple of sessions around key moon phases during that special month of September and I always make sure I'm fishing around the harvest moon and equinox every year. As normal, I couldn't make it back for a few weeks as I had mega amounts of tuitions booked in. I must admit I didn't like it in reality, being so limited in time when I was ripping it up! I couldn't complain though, plus I mistakenly assumed that the posse of backstabbers would lay off me a bit. Kenny later belled me saying there had been several complaints about me using loads of bait and doing too much time. Kenny told me not to worry as he had told them the score. It makes my blood boil because I went out of my way to be helpful and talk to the syndicate members (apart from the twats, as you can imagine) and I thought the backstabbing would die down, but it didn't! I had started to notice the colder, damp mornings begin so autumn was just around the corner and with 24-hour tuition booked in at Welly with my old mate Gary Puiy on Wednesday, I would be able to do a three-day session. I knew roughly what area I wanted be in, plus I had been kept up to speed with what was what while I was away. However, I would still have a good look about first. I made the long journey through

the early hours as I didn't want to get caught in any of the rush-hour antics on the M25. When I arrived at the lake there were only two cars in the car park so I made my way over to Goose Shit Point to see if I could spot where they were plotted up. As I looked out over the lake I could see they were in Lawrie's and the Hole in the Bush swim. I decided to go straight over to Bramble Bay for a look and straight away I noticed the water was coloured and there was a lot of weed floating about, which indicated to me that they had been in here somewhere and ripped the bottom up. All I had to do was to locate where the carp were now, which didn't take too long. I hit the jackpot as I looked down onto the Korda spot, clocking several black shapes sitting tight on the bottom in feeding mode, I then tucked myself behind a tree as I didn't want to risk spooking them, I wanted to watch them for a while. Up to that point I was catching consistently because I was fishing in the weedy, silty areas of the lake, yet these fish were feeding over gravel, which made things tricky. Catching one necessitated a change over to 'dark side' bottom-bait setups because fishing a chod on the gravel was too blatant. Over the next fifteen minutes I saw several more and a couple looked massive! It was time to claim the swim before I lost it, so I legged it round there and laid my coat down.
On the way back I was thinking about what bits I needed to make up these dark side rigs, as I must confess I didn't carry much else other than stuff I needed for chodding! After about five or so minutes I found all the bits I needed and before they were packed I laid it all out on the driver's seat to check I had everything. I knew once I texted my

Rods out in the Korda swim.

With the house up, it was time to make some spare rigs and bags.

mates I would get a load of abuse for dark-side fishing! As I neared the zone I parked the barrow up and looked down; they were still in residence. I reached underneath the barrow for a jar of salty seeds as I thought that I might as well put some bait in while I was there. The funny thing was, though the fish did spook, as I watched they moved slowly back over the bait and started feeding. I was now gagging to get my rods out so I legged it round to the Korda swim and went straight to work, but I must admit that it didn't feel right cutting my chod leaders off! I was going to keep the dark-side rigs simple, using a Diffusion Camo leader, a 3oz lead, ten inches of coated braid, with the coating stripped back by an inch. The bait was presented blow-back style on a size-10 Longshank X, with the lead running on the leader. This would make it much harder for the fish to use the lead to throw the hook, plus as they righted themselves, the lead would run down the leader, away from them, making it hard for Mr Carp to get away with it. My hook baits were going to be 20mm barrel-shaped boilies, fished hard on the bottom with a tiny mesh bag of boilies and rock salt, which would help stop tangles when casting. I would be casting towards the far margin.

Now for the cast and this was going to be tricky until I had it marked, so I prayed to the carp gods to help me get the rig in first cast, then I could mark the line and later mark it out on the bank. I had all three rods ready so if I fcuked up I could quickly grab another. Anyway, it took two casts to get it bang on, whereupon I marked it up so I could get the recasts back there straight away. I was only going to fish two rods

Kenny pulled up screaming, "Shelley boy, you got one?"

and the other rod was cast ten yards to the right, where I noticed that a tiny bit of the black detritus had been cleared. This cast was really tight and took several goes to get it on the money. Once I had the rods in position I couldn't help myself and grabbed the bait bucket and went for a look. I honestly thought there wouldn't be anything there but as I slowly approached the zone and peered down my eyes nearly popped out of my head, as beneath me were four fish munching. I quickly threw some more seeds in along with some crumbed boilies up and as I watched them flutter down I saw one of the carp with a lump on its side slowly move over and start munching. I had to go, as I was expecting a bite any minute! I backed off and then went to have a look at the other spot. It didn't take long to find the hook bait as it had laid right on the black and the mesh bag had done its job so I threw several handfuls of the mixture over it and then beat a hasty retreat back to my plot.

Next thing was to get the house set up and get some spare rigs and bags tied up ready. Rich Stewart the ACF editor rang me up checking where I was, as I had a mag feature to do in the morning. I told him everything was bang on and I was on them in the Korda swim and it looked promising for a bite or two. He said, "Look Jim, I'm after a cover for the mag so you better get your finger out!" I laughed and said, "That's going to cost you!" He told me to ring him if I got a big 'un and if he didn't hear from me, then he'd be there at 8am. After lying on the bed for a bit, willing a rod to go, I couldn't help myself and grabbed the bucket for some more baiting. As I neared the spot I could see that they were still there and it looked like they had cleared the food, so this time I put several handfuls in. I thought it might spook them but it didn't. It started to dawn on me that these fish were in the groove, doing what they do and baiting didn't bother them, as they knew they were getting fed. Nothing had changed on the other spot, so I put a small handful of the seeds of the gods onto it to prime it with fresh oily hemp liquid. On the way back to the swim I got a single bleep and ran round to the rods in time to see that the left-hand LED was on, but nothing else happened. The light levels were falling fast now and I heard someone walking behind the bivvy. I stood up to see Shaun The Leg come hobbling along and the same old bollocks came out, "What you seen? What you know? What you had?" Thankfully, just at the right time Jane rang me, so he fcuked off. The timing could not have been more fortuitous as the left-hand rod suddenly pulled tight. The clutch was locked up so the carp couldn't seek sanctuary in the snags, so it just kited left on a tight line. On making contact, all I could feel was a shaking sensation coming back through the rod. It was quite clear that this carp was another one of the head-shakers, trying to rid itself of the hook. This didn't work and as he got closer I watched him doing his dirty act. Just as I slipped the net under him Kenny pulled up screaming, "Shelley boy you got one?" "Yes mate, come here and give me a hand you old fcuker!" I replied. We weighed him at 35lb, an old-looking mirror

The first wake-up call resulted in this 26lb 12oz mirror.

On the scales we confirmed a weight of 38lb.

I turned to Rich and remarked, "Do I get a bonus for this one then?"

and after a few tries with my camera Kenny did the honours. Light levels were falling fast and Kenny wouldn't shut up so I handed him a Becks so I could get the rod sorted and back out on the spot. After I re-baited one showed out in the dark towards the spot I had just baited, amazing really when you think about it. Suddenly after dark carp feel safe to show, but this just confirmed to me that they were still about. We sat and talked, sharing a couple more beers while listening to the bay come alive. Random shows all over the place indicated that there were a lot of carp in the general area. As long as I hadn't scared them I should be in for another chance or two. Kenny soon left but later that night he rang, informing me that he'd popped into the office and there had been another complaint about me hogging swims and baiting heavily. I asked, "Who was it?" and this time he told me, Shaun the Leg. "You what?" I retorted, "He was just round here before you turned up the two-faced twat." I knew he was the main culprit in this conspiracy and I wasn't having any more of it. I told Kenny that I would have it out with Shaun and he agreed in principle. As you can imagine I was now fuming. Five or so beers later, I had calmed down a little.

Through the night I had two wake-up calls, one from a 26lb 12oz mirror and the other resulting in the loss of a very heavy, powerful fish that snagged me on the right-hand rod. After I slackened off he broke free of the snag and as he kited way to my left he started that head-shaking treatment and dropped the rig close in. This left me gutted, as I was so close to netting that one and it didn't make things any easier that it felt really heavy. After that I didn't recast that rod, as there was no way I could get it back in position; it was tricky enough in daylight! I couldn't wait to see if the spot had changed in any way overnight. I went back to sleep even more pissed off and if that Leg showed his face he was going to get both barrels. I was woken by a single bleep, which was followed by three more. As I turned over I could see the line pulling tight in the half-light of the morning. I jumped out of bed, ran over to the rod and commenced battle with this slow-moving weight, which certainly didn't feel small. I knew what was in store for me soon, it seemed that if they didn't fight in Welly, then they were head shakers and not long after he was doing the Welly dance all the way in to the net. Next thing, the phone rang and Rich had arrived. "Christ that's a second time you are on time!" I said, "Look mate don't mess about I just caught you that front cover you wanted." "Really?" he asked. "Yes mate, get your arse round here." His voice changed, knowing I wasn't therapeeing him up. Before I knew it, he was there and was out of breath. Rich picked the shot he wanted and got the camera sorted; it was now time to see what he weighed. I lifted the net after checking his pecs and knew that he was an upper-thirty. On the scales we confirmed a weight of 38lb. I turned to Rich and remarked, "Do I get a bonus for this one then?" Rich laughed and I lifted another beast for the camera.

After I had returned him I decided to leg it round to see if I could see any on the spot. No-one was home so I baited it and put one rod out. It was time to get on with the feature, which Rich wanted to do on my new dark-side approach. In between doing the shots, I kept popping round to see if any were about but each time the spot was

I had loads that winter, topped by this 32lb 12oz linear from G Lake.

empty. After the feature was done Rich departed and I decided to stay put, as I thought they might come back. In the afternoon I got the other rod back on the spot I'd lost one from and re-baited both spots with crumb and the salty seeds. Later that evening, as I was sitting there looking out over the water I noticed a head bouncing up and down and I could see that The Shoe was on his info-gathering mission again. I felt myself starting to flush with heat. This was my time to set the story straight and as he walked into my swim I unleashed. "I fcuking know it was you, you twat! Grassing, spreading bollocks up at the office, trying to get me kicked out, you two-faced, lying, backstabbing cunt. I know your game; sneaking round here, gathering the info for the posse… you can fcuk off!" I was shouting at the top of my voice and I reckon the public walking round the park could hear all this going on, but I was on a mission to sort it, as this had gone on far too long. The next thing I said was a bit out of order, as I threatened to cut The Shoe's leg off and then told him to fcuk off. I must admit I felt a hell of a lot better after doing this, as he would no doubt report back to the posse. In fact, before he even left the park he went straight to the office and told them what I had just said.

Before I knew it, I had Andy Pye, the head bailiff on the phone, asking me what had happened. I told him my version of events and he came round to the swim. He seemed to know the score and just said, "Next time don't take things into your own hands." I wasn't a grass though, and I certainly wasn't going to keep going over to the office

I also enjoyed a couple of trips up to Burgh Castle.

Oli Bastian popped round for a look.

moaning. He then said, “I don’t think you’ll get any more trouble anyway, as Shaun has handed his ticket in.” I was happy with this news, as the posse’s puppet wouldn’t be gathering their info anymore, now let’s see how they get on. I think Andy knew what was going on but kept out of it as he had his own problems with the powers that run the park and had taken a step back. After that I felt a lot better as it was now out in the open and I hoped that would be the end of it. The following day Gary turned up for his 24-hour tuition and I lost one to a hook pull in the area where I’d caught The Turtle, after it got snagged up. I also lost another one through a hook pull as another head shaker got away with it. That evening Dangermouse walked round as Gary and I sat watching the water. “Here we go,” I thought and I told Gary to leg it, as I didn’t want a client to see this if it kicked off. The mouse even came into my swim and asked how I was getting on. I was gobsmacked that he didn’t say anything about the leg incident, but then nor did I and five minutes later he left. I thought this was very sneaky and I wondered if he was going to do his own dirty work now? Of course, you know the score and yes he did! Anyway, we blanked and Gary had the only bite, which he lost, so we packed up, said our goodbyes and I headed back home. I had a lot of tuitions booked now, so apart from the odd trip catching a couple to 26lb, and the lake shutting up shop, I stayed local and worked my arse off saving as much as possible for my Mere adventure. I knew I would be back to Welly in the new year. I had plenty of tuitions at Waveney Valley lakes and I had loads of fish that winter, topped by a nice 32lb 12oz linear from G Lake. I also enjoyed a couple of trips to Burgh Castle Fishery catching several up to 25lb 12oz but I always had Welly and its inhabitants at the back of my mind.

Watching the weather closely, I noticed a long mild period was forecast for February so I rang Kenny after a few days to see if the lake had thawed. He said, “No, you can walk on it but it’s creaking in the windy conditions and with rain coming it won’t be long.” I asked Kenny to let me know when it was liquid and that Sunday I got the call… “Shelley boy, it’s fishable now.” I thanked him for the info and made plans for my first visit of the New Year. I knew the fish would be on the lookout for some grub, and I was going to use my white amber strawberry bait and knew roughly where I wanted to start my session. I got there really early and there were no cars in the car park so I thought “Fcuk it” and drove all the way round the lake with the headlights turned off to the Hole in the Bush swim, dumped everything in a pile and headed straight back. It’s funny when you think about it; when I pulled the odd stroke I wasn’t getting caught but I was getting grief from rumours! Like many have said to me, it’s all down to the green-eyed monster… oh to be successful in life!

I had a two-day session in front of me, but had to be back at Waveney for Thursday, so I was going home Wednesday evening so that I was fresh for the tuition, unless I caught. Anyway, nothing much happened apart from a few liners in the early hours of Wednesday morning, so something was about and just after first light Oli Bastian popped round for a look. We exchanged pleasantries and I asked him if he was fishing, which he was. “I’m off in a bit mate, I’ve had a few liners so it’d be a good bet to go in

The next thing I knew, the birds were singing and I couldn't believe that I hadn't had a take!

behind me," I told him. After I packed up he dropped in and had a 27lb common so they were about, like I'd thought! I asked him to tell no-one because hopefully I could get back in there next time. Kenny informed me that there were a few on over the weekend so it was going to get busy, plus he later informed me that two forties had been caught from the Hole swim! Shit, now it was going to be hard, but when I arrived for my next session the angler occupying the Hole was just packing up, sweet. He had caught a forty and was getting loads of liners; as you can imagine I was gagging to get in there. Ian turned up for a chat and later Ten Dollar walked round and brought his bird with him. I had just got my rods in position and spodded out around nine kilos of whole and crumbed 20mm and 15mm boilies to a spot to the left at around 90 yards. Ten Dollar walked over and got his fancy white trainers dirty, which amused us. We talked under our breath so he couldn't hear us but he looked like he was on a mission. His bird stayed back so this indicated something sinister might be happening, as he marched over, trying to show some authority. This time his anger was aimed straight at Ian, pointing his finger, which was somewhat funny; so it wasn't just me then. Ian wasn't having any of this bollocks and roared into him. As Ian stepped forward Ten Dollar backed off, then walked off and nearly slipped over! He was mumbling some old crap and then had a go at his bird. I turned to Ian and said, "What the hell is his problem?" We both felt sorry for his bird, as he was downright right rude to her. I said

He clearly wasn't going to fit into the mat!

to Ian, "God knows what she sees in him." Ian suggested that, "Maybe he'd a bad day running his errands for the big-boy bankers?" We both remembered Kenny saying that he was no banker; instead he was a runner in the city, commonly known as a gofer. All I knew was that he was a backstabber of the highest order and there seemed to be too many on this lake. The people who ran the lake seemed to do nothing but clearly thought that ten green-eyed monsters equalled £15,000 and I was just one angler at £1,500, which is a sad state of affairs in my book. Anyway, back to the fishing. Ian decided to fish the Korda swim, as he had caught a few from there and knew the area well. Before dark Marcus popped round for a chat as he had just set up on Lawrie's and informed us that Ten Dollar had been round spouting some old bollocks. Ian brought The Turtle into the conversation saying, "I bet he's 50lb." Straight away I said, "Don't mention him, I have a tendency to catch the same fish again!" All I got was, "Yeah right Jim!" but it's true. Later that evening Carl the Butcher turned up for a chat, as he was having a look around before fishing in the morning. As he left Carl turned and said, "I bet you get one Jim." "OK," I replied, "See you in the morning mate." It was getting late and as darkness fell, Ian and I were stood talking about all things carpy when out there in the dark, a fish rolled over heavily. Now I knew they were still about and not long after I started getting liners on all four rods. Yes I'd been a naughty boy and sneaked the snide rod in just before dark. Kenny had said he didn't have a problem with it after

Ian broke the silence, "Jim, he looks fifty."

A recapture, but at 51lb I wasn't complaining!

dark, so at certain times Uncle Jim increased his chances by being a naughty boy! The next thing I heard was the dawn chorus and upon rolling over to have a look out into the half-light, I just couldn't believe I hadn't had a take. The alarms had been bleeping all through the night and some of the liners even had me legging it towards the rods, as I thought they were takes! Just as I started to feel dejected about the lack of action, the left-hand rod pulled tight. I stayed put thinking it was a liner but it steadfastly held up tight. "Shit, I'm in!" I thought, as I jumped up and pulled my chesties on before legging it over to the rod and pulling into something that immediately stripped thirty yards of line off me at high speed! This fish then kited well left but I managed to gain some back as it headed towards my left-hand margin. Suddenly, I realised what he was up to as I had this bush to the left of my swim, which I knew I couldn't walk round. Thankfully, no one was fishing in the next swim, as this would have caused me a lot of problems! I needed to wade out as far as I could so the line wouldn't get caught up in this bush, so with my rod out as far as I could, I just kept the pressure on hoping he would kite out before hitting the bush. He didn't and now I was getting worried about what this carp was going to do me in this snag, but as he got closer I stepped out, which gave me a wet surprise! Christ the water was cold and it took my breath away as it ran down inside of my waders. It had to be done though and as I increased the pressure he finally came round the bush and in the clear water I got a glimpse of a massive carp, which was long

I popped him into a sack while I got things sorted.

Marcus and Ian were ready with the cameras.

I gave him a kiss on the head and thanked him for the moment.

with a dark back. I was shitting myself because I now knew I was definitely attached to a chunk, which was now so close. He swam past then suddenly popped up on top revealing a massive head that took a mouthful of air. My next problem was that the net was still resting up against the bush, so I slackened the line off and grabbed it. Luckily, as I turned back he was just sitting there so I marched out and slid it straight under him. I then lifted the handle to secure him and as the mesh touched him he came back to life, covering me with ice-cold spray, which made me gasp; a fitting end to a most memorable battle! I screamed, "Yesssss!" before looking in on my prize.

Before me lay The Turtle, looking awesome in his winter colours and pumped right up. Suddenly, Ian appeared asking, "You had one Jim?" "Yes mate, and it looks like The Turtle! I told you not to talk about him in my swim! Can you hold onto the net while I get everything sorted?" I unhooked him in the net and couldn't keep my eyes off him as I broke the arms down and rolled the mesh up around them. I double-checked that his pecs were folded flat along his body and tried to lift… 'kin hell he was heavy! We tried to lay him down on the mat but it was now clear that he was not going to fit in, so Ian quickly undid both Velcro flaps at either end so we could place him onto the mat. Ian broke the silence, "Jim, he looks fifty." I was lost in the moment as we transferred

Carl AKA Woody popped his head around the door and handed me a bottle of Champagne.

Kenny turned up to congratulate me.

him into Marky Mark's weigh sling. With the scales zeroed, the dial swung past the magical fifty-pound mark and we confirmed a weight of 51lb, happy days! I popped my prize into a sack while I got things sorted and made a few calls, including to Jane relaying the good news that I had just caught my fourth fifty. She replied, "Well done darling!" Next, I sent a text to Carl and he later rang me to offer his congratulations. Ian must have texted Marcus and Chris, because they appeared, along with Oli Bastian. Oli had a bag of donuts, which he handed out; this would build up my energy levels before I lifted my prize up. I dropped into the water to retrieve my prize, which was a winter fifty, a rare achievement indeed. The lads gasped when I lifted the sack clear of the water, as they could clearly see how big he was by the size of the bulging sack. We laid him down on the mat and I slowly revealed my prize to the posse and they gasped in awe of the beast. The colours were awesome with a dark back and a polished, grey body. I then looked up with the biggest smile, and said, "Look at it boys, what an awesome creature, Welly's first fifty." Marcus and Ian were ready with both cameras and the only other person I allowed to take some pictures was Chris, with his mega camera! He was well behaved for a Welly carp, probably because he had only just woken from his winter slumber. The hunger must have got the better of him and he made the mistake of visiting my baited zone. All of those liners indicated to me that he wasn't alone. Now it was time to have my cuddle with the king of the lake once more; a moment I will never forget. I held him up for a few water shots before giving him

Was this really happening to me?

The Dark One at 46lb 4oz.

a kiss on the head and thanking him for this moment. I wished him good luck as I lowered him back into the clear margin and he kicked off into deeper water. I shouted after him, "Fcuking yessss!" As I stood out in the lake it began to dawn on me what had just happened.

After a while the lads drifted away, which left me with my thoughts, when suddenly Carl popped his head round the door and handed me a bottle of Champagne! He said, "Don't waste it drinking it here mate, save it for a special moment when you're at home with Jane." I was gobsmacked at Carl's kind gesture and I shook his hand, thanking him. When he left the news had spread far and wide and my phone was on meltdown as I tried to answer all the texts in between the calls! Later that morning I reeled in as a party was booked in, so I popped out for some wine for the night ahead.

When I returned to my swim it was time to get the rods back out and rocking, but this time I decided to stick to the rules and put three out, as I didn't fancy getting up too early! Plus, there was no need to take any chances, as I was sure the knives would be out at some point. Once the rods were out I topped the swim up with another hit of bait and by the time all this was done it was party time and the light was starting to fade. Kenny turned up saying, "Well done Shelley boy!" I walked down to the water's edge and pulled a bottle of Fiano out that was chilling in the cool margin along with a couple of Becks for the old git. I told him we were having a few beers and he said, "Keep

I started trickling bait into Animal Farm again, well to the right of The Sluices.

Fresh weed floating in the edge could only mean one thing!

Darkness was falling fast over the park.

it low key." I nodded, as I knew exactly what he was on about. After he had drunk his beers he departed saying, "Have a few for me." Just after dark the boys turned up for a few drinks and not long after I started to receive some liners, telling me that Mr Carp was out and about on the munch again. Over the next few hours several carp danced out in the zone, in between the liners and carpy chat. With all this activity going on I knew I was going to get another chance. One by one the posse left, leaving me alone with my thoughts. Not long after I climbed into the bag I had another series of bleeps on the left-hand rod positioned where I'd caught The Turtle. As I lay down on the bedchair, I looked out into the darkness, confident of another bite. I soon fell asleep and was only woken by the odd liner until the magical bite time. At first light I woke to a steady take on that left-hand rod again. I flew out and pulled into a solid resistance, which then moved off, kiting to the right at a slow pace. As I looked up I could see that the rod was bent well over, telling me that there was another chunk on. This fish just used his weight to stay deep and came back in front of me and just plodded about now under the rod tip. I reckon that this fish wasn't quite sure what was going on, as he had probably only just woken up. Ian appeared by my side and I asked him to do the honours for me as he had boots on. He waded out into the edge, as this fish was close now, sending up big, oily swirls to the surface. A big, wide back popped up and Ian inched closer, lifting the net around him at the first attempt. I shouted out, "Is he big?" Ian peered in and turned to me saying, "Oh yes mate, well over forty!" I looked

The Banana Fish put up a spirited scrap.

up thinking, "Is this really happening to me?" Yes it was, big time! We recorded a weight of 46lb 4oz and we later found out that the fish was The Dark One, looking very light in colour. We popped him into a sack and I notified the posse of the good news, asking if they wanted to come and have a look and give a hand, which of course they did. After the boys had gone I was left to ponder this special session, which I'll probably never equal. What a brace of carp to catch at any time, let alone in the winter! The carp gods had once again looked after Uncle Jim. I did another night but nothing else materialised, not even a liner. This told me that they had done the off. I knew this swim would be at the top of the campers' list and would now be rotated by the mobile-phone sheep shaggers. Luckily, Uncle Jim had other plans in place and I had been baiting other zones at night, so I had several areas prepped. Now that's what I call good angling!

The next session was a blank even though I did manage to get back in the Hole in the Bush once more. When I arrived early in the morning I went round for a chat to ask the angler that was fishing in the Hole when was he going. Naming no names, he informed me that he might be going in an hour but the way he spoke gave me the feeling that something was weird, so I asked if he minded if I left my barrow behind him, just in case he decided to pack up within the hour. I had a quick look and returned thirty minutes later to find that he was nearly packed up. "OK, you're off then?" I said. "Look Jim, I was holding the swim for someone else but you're here first and that's it," he replied. I had a feeling that this was happening and the angler did come round and wasn't too chuffed to find me set up in the swim! Was I bothered? No! This made me realise one thing and another lesson had been learned; I had to do my own thing. I blanked this trip and the next session but I did see some show in a zone that I had been baiting for weeks, so I loaded it up really heavy the night before I left on the next trip. I also trickled some into the other back-up areas in Animal Farm. I had never seen anyone fish this quiet corner since I joined in June. It was well to the right of The Sluices swim, which was a mostly shallow area. The swim I wanted to fish this area from was just to the right of the corner. The problem was, it was only big enough for the rods, so I bivvied up on the other side of the path in the wood; at least I would be nicely tucked away when I fished it.

When I arrived for the next session I just had a feeling that I had to get straight round to Animal Farm, so I drove past the car park and went straight up to where I dropped my gear off. Kenny had warned me that others had moaned about this, but I just didn't give a fcuk any more; all I wanted to do was get on with my angling without all this bollocks. As you can imagine, I had nearly made my mind up that I was not renewing for the coming season, as there was no way I was paying £1500 for this kind of treatment, so I had decided to fish there until I got bored or went elsewhere to get away from the grief. Once the barrow was loaded I made my way round to the swim that had no name, which I later named Shelley's! As I walked into the swim I could see that there was fresh weed floating in the edge with a gentle warm wind blowing into the zone. I also noticed that the water was coloured; it looked and felt right, like I had hit

On the mat he was revealed as an awesome specimen, with a darkish back and a pale, creamy complexion to him.

The other flank of the forty-two.

By morning I'd had mirrors of 27lb and this one at 29lb 12oz.

I knew I wouldn't be up too early.

Oli looked out from my swim and asked, "What's that blue thing?"

For the record he weighed in at 36lb.

I knew it wasn't a big one. It turned out to be a mid-twenty common.

the jackpot. I positioned myself behind a tree to the right because I had a feeling they were in close. I put my polarising glasses on and looked into the water, which I could now see had clear water mixed in. This told me the fish were close in. I had spread the bait out from close in to around thirty yards out and as I looked further out over a shallow bar the water was clearer, indicating that whatever species was doing this was extremely close. The stage was now set and I was well excited. All I needed now was positive proof as to who was in the mix, when suddenly a carp showed himself right in close. Now I was buzzing, as I had the proof I needed. I slowly retreated to the back of the swim where the barrow was parked up and quickly got to work getting three rods sorted. With the fish being so close I decided to cast further out, reel it back over the zone and then gently let it drop down. Once I had the rods in position I used the throwing stick to get fifty baits out, one by one, so it was quieter and cut down the risk of spooking the fish too much. I then gently pushed the sticks in and placed the rods on the buzzers. I was buzzing because this undercover baiting I had been doing had worked once again. An angler approached and asked the normal stuff and I just said that I had seen nothing and decided to set up here so I could watch a lot of water and then act on any sightings. I was praying nothing showed and gave the game away while he was there. I needn't have worried though, as he was soon on his way. Kenny then pulled up and I just whispered, "Shhh!" before he slammed the door. "Shelley boy what the fcuk are you doing here?" he asked. Handing him a beer, I made him swear to

The Dog Run.

secrecy, as I told him the score. He replied with, "I will not say nowt," so I handed him another beer, as he'd downed the first one already, greedy so and so.

Kenny left me to set my house up and get sorted, as darkness was falling fast. I sat by the edge of my swim swigging a beer when fish started showing behind the bar. This was a problem, as all my rods were well inside of that feature and over the next fifteen minutes leading into darkness, I saw several more, which got me thinking that I should be repositioning the rods ASAP. I was only going to do two of them at first but out there in the gloom the carp were going mental. All three rods were now reeled in; the rigs were checked and re-curved, then cast back out roughly to where they were showing. As the 1oz leads hit the water I made sure I felt them go down so I knew they were on soft or weedy areas and not on that shallow, clean bar. With it being dark it was now prime feeding time so I decided to bait up with around a hundred baits per rod. This time I loaded the throwing stick up with around fifteen at a time so this didn't take too long but getting a decent spread would get them moving and grubbing about in the activated zone. This was a massive risk but nothing was showing this side of the bar and I felt it was the right thing to do. I was cooking my dinner when the middle rod bleeped, "Oi oi!" I thought. As I watched the LED go out the left-hand bobbin pulled up tight and the buzzer screamed! I commenced battle with a carp that went on a mental run, stripping line off the clutch. He stopped and kited, but didn't

I was up for going undercover!

Just as I was packing up I had a take.

The last act of an acrimonious period!

feel heavy and after a spirited fight I netted a long mirror of around thirty pounds. To be exact, he went 32lb 12oz on the scales and one of the syndicate members came round after hearing the take and did the honours for me, at which point he informed me that it was a fish called The Banana Fish.

With the rod roughly back in the zone after getting a bite so quickly I re-baited all the rods, as it was now clear they were having it and it was time to finish my dinner, which was cold by now. Not long after one rolled indicating that they were still in residence. Then the liners started and when you get this happening at Welly, this is normally a good pointer for a bite. I sat back listening and watching out for the carpy signs, praying for another visit. It was unreal as carp rolled and pushed out in front of me. All this undercover prep work in a shit swim over several weeks was now paying off big time. Suddenly, the middle rod bleeped again and then roared off! For a split second I watched in disbelief as it melted off, as something out in the darkness realised that it had made a mistake. As I picked the rod up it was nearly wrenched from my grasp, as this unseen beast pulled untold line off me. This one felt like one of the bigger inhabitants and I held on for dear life as the clutch went into meltdown. I heard footsteps as a syndicate member entered the swim saying, "Christ Jim, that was a mental run!" I replied saying, "I know, I'm still hanging on," when all of a sudden I felt the line go slack. I started to reel in with that sickening feeling when suddenly the rod hooped over again and took on its full battle curve. "Mate, I'm still in!" I shouted; he had run back towards me. Thank God I had the clutch set correctly, because if I hadn't I would have probably pulled out as I made contact again. Now this one knew what he was up to, so I would have to have my wits about me. I asked matey if he would do me the honours, and he grabbed the net and made his way down to the water's edge. A few minutes later we could see boils in the light of the moon, and suddenly we saw this big carp break the surface. Matey took his chance and netted the as-yet-unseen beast. I flicked my head torch on, dimming the light so we could get a better look. There in the net was a chunk of a carp, which we agreed had to be over forty. While matey watched my prize I walked over to the bivvy to make sure everything was ready from the previous capture. I handed the camera to matey, asking him once again if he would be so kind as to do the honours for me. He then passed me the net and I couldn't help myself, as I peered in for another look. He now looked even wider and I couldn't wait to admire my prize more closely. On the mat he was revealed as an awesome specimen, with a darkish back and a pale, creamy complexion to him. We carefully weighed him in at 42lb. I poured some water over him and gently slid my hands under him, as it was time to have my little cuddle with the beast. He was well behaved on the bank, unlike most of his mates I'd had the pleasure of meeting!

The rod was recast back to the area and once again I re-baited the whole zone. I sat on the bedchair and opened a Becks as I listened and took in the moment. All was quiet apart from a single bleep so it was a good time to get my head down. Sometime in the early hours I added mirrors of 27lb and 29lb 12oz, so as you can imagine it was a busy night and I was knackered! I was just thinking that I wouldn't be up too early after all this disturbed sleep when all of a sudden the right-hand rod was off again! For a split second I watched it in disbelief, as another one made the mistake. My head was spinning from the lack of sleep. Shortly after a spirited battle I landed a plump, chunky mirror of around 35lb. Knowing that someone would be here any minute, I sacked him up and texted Oli to see if he could pop round and do me a favour by taking a few pictures. He soon text back saying that he was on his way. The kettle was fired up as I hoped one of my super-charged coffees would sort my head out. When he turned up, Oli said that he'd never seen anyone fish the swim before! He looked out from my swim and he then turned and asked me, "What's that blue thing?" I said, "Mate, that's my float, which is attached to the sack by a separate cord, so we could find the sack if it ever got lost." Not long after tackle companies started bringing out sacks with tiny, poxy floats attached to them. I pulled my waders on and handed the camera to Oli as it was time to sort this fish out. For the record he weighed 36lb and was returned to fight another day, what a session in March; Welly was really rockin' for me big time!

During the day I watched the zone closely for any signs but nothing occurred. It looked dead but with all this carpy action I had to cover the swim for another night and around midday I thought it was safe to recast the rods and top the swim up again. Later that evening Kenny called in for his usual chat over a couple of beers. He said to me, "You have the best time to come yet; the spring normally produces mental action."

That night was quiet, with no shows, so I was surprised when one of the rods rattled off at first light. Straight away I could tell he was a small one and within a few minutes a common was landed, which weighed 25lb. That seemed like a good time to pack up and head off home for some family time.

The next trip was an undercover affair, as I had a tuition booked in with Carl and Colin who were on the syndicate. We decided to do it as a social and as we walked round I knew roughly where we were heading, as I had loaded up the Animal Farm area. The boys doubled up in The Sluices while I fished another area round to their left, in a swim (if you can call it at a swim) that I named The Dog Run, where the walkers let their dogs in for a paddle. The swim was right next to the forbidden drop-off area that I was using so I bivvied up on the grass a short walk from the van. Anyway, later that evening we were sitting, chilling and having a few beers when Ten Dollar walked up with his chest puffed out. He immediately went into a tirade of the same old bollocks. One minute it's Ian and now it's me; the twat wasn't even fishing much. It was all a bit bizarre and I thought all this grief was out of order. In reality, most of it was centred around me catching again, probably with Dangermouse in the background pulling the strings. That was it, I stood up and he backed off. I said, "Oi oi Rich, where is that £12 you owe me for that bait?" As the creep backed off next to his bird this killed him bang in his tracks. The tight northern git handed me a tenner saying, "I owe you £2," and I said, "Bring it tomorrow." I turned around, gave the tenner to Carl saying, "Put that in a charity box for me." Rich wasn't happy about this, as I just looked out over the lake and turned off from it all. In the end Carl told him to pee off. He walked off muttering something until he was no more. Carl was well up for a laugh, and he had been wearing an Afro wig up until this point, somewhat bizarrely. I said, "Mate, let me wear that now as I'm up for going undercover!" It was all getting too much and I had made my mind up. I told the boys that this wasn't my sort of fishing and I was going to leave in the early hours and head off to pastures new, namely The Woolpack, as my ticket started in the morning.

I texted a few of the boys and of course Kenny, and he came to see me and tried to change my mind. After our conversation he knew I wasn't having any more of this and before he left, he handed me a bottle of his home-brewed sloe whisky. It was all a bit sad but there was no way I was fishing there with all that bullshit going on; it seemed one-sided and to cap it off, later that night Andy came down to ask me what had happened as the petty grass had been up to the office saying I had threatened him. I told Andy what had happened and that I had witnesses to this so-called 'threatening'. He went up and had a word, then came back and was OK with what he had been told by Carl and Colin. We sat up chatting for a while hearing the odd fish show. That night Carl had one and lost one and just as I was packing up I had a take and landed a 34lb mirror. The take must have woken up Mr Fairbrass and, even though it was only a short push with the barrow to the van, I thought "Fcuk it," and drove the van to the swim, loaded it and drove out with the tunes going full bore. "Fcuk this place," I thought, "I'm not having my memories spoilt any more." If only it had ended there. Later that morning

I was banned for something I knew nothing about. Rich had made an accusation that I had scratched his car and he wasn't even fishing the lake that night! This was all a bit over the top now and several calls from mates on the syndicate revealed that I was now banned. I phoned Kenny and he told me that I wasn't banned, very strange. However, he rang me later to confirm that it was now true and I was indeed banned, and so was Rich Ten Dollar!

After I got back from The Woolpack there was a letter waiting for me, informing me that I was banned but giving no reason why. There was no way I was having this bollocks, so one of my mates, who is a solicitor, kindly drafted me a letter basically asking why I was banned. The answer was they didn't need a reason, so a second letter was sent explaining that they owed me some money, and I received a cheque, which paid for my Woolpack ticket… happy days!

Snake Pit

In Pursuit of the Snake Pit Common

Once I'd returned Dippy The Wandering Mirror to Snake Pit's clear waters, I never thought I would ever be going back, apart from for the odd social with Jay and Wayne, as I was still a member of the club. Several years had passed when I started hearing that one of the commons in Snake was piling the weight on, with a bloke called Joe catching it at 36lb plus. This particular fish weighed around 22lb when I was fishing for Dippy, so things were looking good for the future! It wasn't long before, one February night on the full moon, Ash caught her at 43lb. When I got the call this interested me greatly because this fish was now the queen of the pond, which meant I had another water to play with if I was lost, and I knew at some point I would be on the hunt for her.

And so it was, on a mild morning in April that I pulled up to the gate and unlocked it. I was surprised to find that the lake was totally empty, as it can get really busy at times, being on a club ticket. In busy times the fish would normally would be found hiding in one of the various snaggy areas that littered the pond, but I knew at certain times of the day or night they would move out for a mooch about. After finding nothing in the main snags down the bank to the left of the gate, I thought that The Point would be the best place to start my campaign, partly because I'd caught Dippy from there and also, I could see most of the lake from there, so if I saw anything I could move straight onto it, if it stayed quiet that is.

It was weird to be back, but there was no way I could pass up the opportunity to catch a mid-forty common. Dippy had died several years before so there was no chance of a recapture, plus I hadn't caught the other big mirrors that lived in the pond, which were Lettuce Leaf, Stomper's Linear and both of the Lumpys. I had already decided not to get into this 'camping-in-the-snags' crap unless it was needed, as I knew that the common fought like a demon from hell and was often lost because people fished so close to certain snags. Plus, these swims in question, Big and Small Snags, were rotated permanently. The one good thing that the club had done in my absence was to close the Small Snags swim. Most of the anglers that fished this swim would wade out and cast up in to this channel that entered the snags. This was the main swim that anglers wanted back in the day, and it was the source of many arguments because certain 'campers' fished in this swim for weeks and weeks, baiting the snags. This did fcuk the rest of the lake, as they kept the fish in the snags for far too much time. The carp didn't need to leave the main snags until the weed came up, when they would take up residence out in the pond. The closure was good for the fishery and the fish, as some of them were showing signs of mouth damage. Those areas were no good for me and my style of angling anyway, so my plan was to bait up out in the lake, as I knew these fish loved their grub and I had untold amounts to give them, which hopefully would be an edge for me. However, with it being so busy at times, I knew I would have to have backup plans and Uncle Jim would have to play his games! I had been warned about the head bailiff, Greg, aka Pickled Egg; he was a punishing twat who fished days only and used to sit in his green twat-mobile getting wasted.

Suddenly, I heard the gate go and a green car appeared. I decided to quickly put my house up and hide as this idiot loved punishing so called 'named' anglers. The rods would have to wait until he had gone and with the house up and everything inside, I zipped the door down so I couldn't get pestered and laid on the bed listening. The temperature quickly rose in the bivvy as there was no shade on The Point! Sweat was pissing off me when suddenly I heard someone approach, then a voice asked, "Can I see your ticket?" "Who is that?" I asked, and he answered, "I'm Greg the bailiff." I posted my ticket under the door, and after a moment's silence, during which I could tell his mind was ticking over, "Ah, you're Jim Shelley!" I answered saying, "Yes I'm not well, can you leave me be? This virus I've contracted is no good for man nor beast!" Suddenly, he pushed my ticket back under the door, and I quipped, "Cheers fella, if I were you I would disinfect my hands!" while trying not to laugh. Greg muttered something, but by now I had buried my head into my pillow to stifle my mirth. All was silent, but I knew he was standing there. I was running out of air, shacked up in there, cooking in the confines of my bivvy, but finally he let out a grunt as he walked off. I gave it around a minute, before diving for the door, zipping it down and gasping in the fresh air. After a couple minutes I had a look to see if it was safe, as there was no way I wanted him anywhere near me. It seemed OK, as I spotted him opposite and to the left of me in Al's Bar.

Now that I knew I was safe, I undid the door so I could cool down. I thought it was best to get the rods ready now, undercover, so he didn't think it was a bit weird me suddenly appearing not long after he had left. While tucked away, I could keep an eye on the lake and around an hour later it was finally time to get the rods out. I showed myself and as I looked across it appeared that Greg was asleep. This was my chance as the boys had told me that he often went off to sleep over there. I fanned all three rods out roughly over the zone I caught Dippy from all those years ago, feeling for soft drops on the silkweed, as it was clear from looking in the margins that like many lakes at this time of the year, Snake was full of this fresh 'jelly-type' weed. I call it spring's first harvest, and silkweed normally contains untold natural food, such as shrimps and snails, and the various animals further up the food chain now harvested these areas,

I fanned all three rods out across the zone that I'd caught Dippy from all those years back.

building up energy levels prior to spawning or hatching. I had worked this out over many years, but it was down to me to watch, look and learn, trying to find the area that held the pot of gold that the carp were visiting. Once I had the sign I had to act on it.
After I had spread several kilos of White Amber Strawberry boilies over the area it was time to try and keep an eye on Greg, as I knew he would be back; I just hoped I saw him and made it back into hiding so avoiding the punishment. I had already made my mind up to tell him to bog off if he did catch me out, as I don't like visitors trying to pump me for info. I got so engrossed in watching, looking for a sign, that I had taken my eye off the ball and suddenly I heard some someone approaching. Quickly, I zipped the door up and laid on the bed chair. He was soon standing in my swim but there were now two of them – he must have brought one of his sheep with him. "Jim, you in there?" he asked. I didn't say anything, there was a short silence then, again, "Jim you OK?" I had to try hard not to laugh as I shouted, "Leave me alone, I'm ill!" They just stood there talking and after a few more minutes I shouted, "Go away, I'm trying to sleep this shit off!" This seemed to work as they drifted off. Thankfully, the heat had decreased somewhat inside the green cell and I stayed up well into dark, but apart from tench showing no carpy signs were seen. Before going to sleep I set the alarm for first light, as I was sure I would get a sign then.

It felt like I'd just drifted off when the alarm woke me. All was sweet with the rods, and I'd had no tench therapy, which was good. I fired up the stove as I needed my

caffeine to get me back into the land of the living. I just laid in bed, drinking my coffee, watching the tench showing, when suddenly, out of the corner of my eye, I saw the phone light up. It wasn't the missus, it was Lee Yeatman, aka Mollusc, giving me 'cut/cut' treatment; trust me, that's another story! "Boy, what you had?" he asked. I answered, "Shut the fcuk up, you rang just as I saw something!" It could only be a grebe or cormorant as it been down too long, unless it's Mr Carp. Nothing showed, and not long after there was another sign. "Look Mol, you're going to have to pee off as I'm missing all this," I told my mate. Ten minutes later, with my eyes fixed on the zone in the Car Park Snags, a carp poked his head out. The phone went again and this time it was Jane. I told her what I was seeing and over the next five minutes, while we chatted, I saw two more fish. It was time to act on this sign so I reeled the rods in, grabbed the landing net and a few bits, plus a bag of bait and the throwing stick and then legged it round to the zone. Nothing else was seen as I made my way round to the swim. Thankfully, there was nobody about so this was a real chance of a bite, but more importantly I was now getting on the fish, which is the main priority in my angling. Once I have locked onto their location it's game on and Uncle Jim goes to work.
Once in the swim, I propped the rods up against the bush so I could check the rigs and re-curve them, plus, I could keep watching the zone for my signs. I only saw one carp show just after getting the rods ready and he got a hook bait straight on his head

My first fish of the new Snake campaign was the Little Linear at 17lb 12oz. Not the biggest, but one of the prettiest.

As I watched I noticed a few little plucks on the semi-tight lines – there were clearly carp about.

with a few freebies following close behind. Not long after, I had three rods in the mix. I laid them on the ground with the clutches done up tight as I was fishing near snags, so this meant I would have to be on them straight away if I got a bite and it wouldn't take a lot for them to be pulled in. As I watched, I got a few little plucks on the semi-tight line, indicating to me that there were several carp about. Not long after, the left-hand rod, which had been cast to the showing fish pulled tight. I grabbed the rod and commenced battle with my first Snake Pit carp of the new campaign. Straight away this fish felt small, but I was sure that it was a carp and not long after I was able to pull him over the net cord. He was an awesome, apple-slice-scale linear called the Little Linear. While he wasn't one of the biggest at 17lb 12oz, he was one of the prettiest. It's always nice to get the first one from a water, plus I had now located them so I had an area to concentrate on. It did worry me that I was fishing near the second-biggest area of snags and I knew that I'd have to play fish hard to keep them up in the water. That meant that everything, tackle-wise, had to be spot on.

With the fish returned, I decided to reel the rods in, pack the rest of the gear up and get moved into this zone. I felt that it'd be stupid to stay camped on the point. After an hour I had all of my kit round in the Car Park Snags but before repositioning the rods back on the spots, I grabbed my glasses and went for a little look in the snags to see if I could see any carp at close quarters. After inching down the steep drop

The Little Linear meanders back down the weedy marginal slope.

into the bottom of the snags I hid behind a small tree to break up my silhouette. I was very close to the water and if they were about I didn't want to scare them. I just wanted to see which ones were about and of course spot the main target. As I poked my head round to have a look I noticed a small clearing up the marginal slope, in shallow water. A tiny spot was being cleared, which told me that they were using the area and over time this spot got completely cleaned off. I never fed them in there, as there was no point, I just watched and learned. The main objective was to find her; I love watching them up-close-and-personal, because to me this is part of the hunt. I made myself comfortable so I could just watch for signs of carp. The water was really clear, which meant I could watch for signs out into deeper water near the overhangs. The anticipation and excitement while waiting to see one is an awesome buzz for me! Suddenly, from the left I saw a dark shadow appear from the overhangs and swim towards me, getting bigger and bigger as he came up the shelf where I got a good look at him. He was a dark mirror that looked around 25lb and he was closely followed by five more, the biggest of which looked around 30lb. I guessed that it was Lettuce Leaf, which is a real scaly gem and one I wanted to catch while I waited for the common. Although I saw several more, there were no sightings of her. I knew she had to be in one of the two sets of snags. It was time to get out of there, as I wanted to get a better look from the high bank above where I had just caught the linear. I turned, quietly climbed out and then made my way further round so I was now above the zone.

As I looked over into the crystal-clear water I could see several snags poking up from the bottom, with about an inch sticking out of the water. This would be my marker to cast towards, while keeping to the right of them. The area was covered in silkweed, so my long, running chod rig suited this bottom. However, the club had banned leadcore, so this meant I would have to use the naked chod on 20lb X-Line, as this was the best sinking line on the market and would act a bit like leadcore. I can understand why it was banned, but it certainly wasn't my favourite way to fish the chod. Back in the swim, I got the rods all sorted with fresh baits on and checked that the hooks were sharp before re-curving the filament into its aggressive shape, a bit like a Withy Pool rig. Deciding that it was a bit too tight for three rods, I cast two rigs down to where I had caught the linear and dropped the left-hand rod straight out, into a deep gully around ten yards out. All rods were baited with my trusty old catapult with around a kilo of White Ambers. It was time to get the house set up. It was a bit tight in there, but I had to make sure I was as close as possible to the rods, especially the two cast up to the right. As you can imagine, I fished the lines tighter than normal because I needed instant indication. The setup was rock solid as I had the clutches done right up; I didn't wanted to be wasting time doing the clutch up, giving them the chance to power off into the many snags that littered the lake, many of which you couldn't even see.

With the house set up so I was right on the rods it was time to sit back in camping

I inched down into the car park snags with my glasses on to see if I could spot my target.

All the rods were within catapult range so I used my trusty old 'pult to introduce a kilo of White Ambers over each spot.

mode, unless I saw something elsewhere. I saw nothing until just before dark, down in the corner, which told me that they were still about. I hadn't long seen the show when the left-hand rod pulled tight. It made me jump, as I was not expecting much to happen on that rod. As I pulled into it I felt the telltale knocking on the tip of the rod that told me I was attached to a tench. This thing went mental, like it was possessed, but the gear I was using was too strong for this redeye, which was quickly unhooked and returned. This rod was to give me loads of tench therapee over coming sessions, but never a carp. The snag rods in the corner only ever produced two tench bites, I thought this was mad, but I think the carp kept them out. The tench in Snake must have hated snags or perhaps they were where the catfish lurked in waiting, so this kept them away?

Several carp were spotted after dark, all in the corner area, so as I climbed in the bag I was confident that I was going to get my string pulled at some point by morning. I woke to the dawn chorus with that sickening feeling, as nothing had happened in the zone. I had two more tench and decided I'd had enough of that therapee. I leaned over to put the stove on for one of my coffees when, suddenly, the right-hand rod bleeped. As I looked up I could see that the rod was being pulled round. I dropped the kettle and pulled into the fish. The rod was bent well over as I held on for dear life, trying not to let this fish reach the sanctuary of the bush in the corner. Suddenly, there was an explosion in the front of it, I just held on as there was no way I could let it make it in there. Thankfully, the pressure on the rod began to lessen as the fish kited out. I pumped it back towards me and, once he was close, I eased off the pressure and loosened the clutch as there was no need for it to be locked up now. This had all taken place in less than a minute and he was now close in, chugging up and down the bottom of the shelf. Without warning, he made a dash some ten yards in his last bid for freedom, after which he surfaced and wallowed, allowing me to lead him in whereupon I scooped up carp number two. This one was a common that looked around 20lb. On the scales he went 23lb 12oz and looked a bit of a warrior but was another one chalked up nevertheless. I did catch this one again a few weeks later at 24lb 12oz, so it was clearly tuned into the bait! For now though, I had to get the rod back onto the zone because the common would not be on his own and it was clear that mornings were bite time. With the rod back out and rocking it was time to get the self-takes done, as I needed to keep as many of the captures secret as possible, to keep the sheep off my back.

As I slid him back to his watery home I heard the gate go behind me. "Shit," I thought, as all the gear was still up on top. I legged it back up to the top of the bank and grabbed all the bits before I was spotted and the word got out. Thankfully I got away with hiding all the bits! I stayed hidden in my house, watching Pickled Egg's green car head down to his favoured camping spot to the right of Al's Bar. Mistakenly, I thought that I was safe for a while, but he turned around and drove back up, pulling up behind my

The Car Park corner produced this 23lb 12oz common. I went on to catch him again a few weeks later!

swim and slamming the door. I heard footsteps, then the fatal words, "Jim, it's Greg, what you seen? What you had?" I kept quiet. "Jim… you there?" I had to answer, "For Christ's sake, I'm trying to sleep after loads of early-hours tench therapee." There was then silence before he walked off, thank fcuk.

I heard the gate go and I crept up to the top of my swim just in time to spot his car exiting the venue. The gate was closed and as I was climbing back onto my bedchair, I had a bleep. I looked round as another bleep rang out. I jumped back out, grabbing the rod and lifting into another carp. Luckily, this fish didn't pull as hard as the last one, he just kited on a tight line on the top, sending a big bow-wave up as he darted out. I couldn't help but think how lucky I had been, as Greg the town crier had missed out on seeing the action by seconds and my cover would have been blown and the sheep would be out in force, raping my spots. The fish was soon netted and another of the Snake carp was mine. This time, I decided to get the fish sorted before getting the rod back out. He was one of the lake's bigger mirrors and weighed 27lb 12oz. With the self-takes done and everything tidied up and out of view I got the rod back out on the spot and rebaited. I couldn't help but think how lucky I was to have caught three from this tricky venue so quickly. However, I knew that if you can get on the right water at the right time mega results can be had, plus, nobody knew about my captures and Jay had told me that nothing had been out. It was like they were waiting for news and there was no way I was going to tell anyone, not just yet, as I needed the edge, not the

One of the lake's bigger mirrors at 27lb 12oz; Greg missed the action by seconds!

I became aware of dark clouds gathering in the distance. Not long after, a huge storm hit.

sheep shaggers. Frankly, I couldn't believe I was the only one fishing it, given how mild it was. Being as Snake was a club water, I knew that things would change, although hopefully not just yet.

As the morning progressed nothing was seen apart from the odd tench. A couple of quick looks in the bush confirmed my gut feeling that they might have done the off and later that afternoon I was to see one show over in Al's Bar, so I laid on the bed chair with my eyes fixed on the area to see if anything else showed. I became aware of dark clouds gathering in the distance and things began to look stormy with a fresh wind picking up and blowing straight at me. Not long after an awesome storm hit; it went dark and moody and then some of the worst rain I have fished in thundered down along with hailstones and the odd rumble of thunder. As I looked out from under the dripping canvas I saw something show again over in Al's Bar, but with these adverse conditions it was really hard to see out over the other side of the pond. As the storm started to ease off a back came up and slid over, now I had the sighting and I was gagging to move, so as I waited for the storm to pass I began packing the gear away in the bivvy. Soon, lighter colours appeared over the horizon meaning I could be on the move soon.

Packing up and moving swims was easy here as you could drive around 70 per cent of the pond. With all the gear in the van I was soon in the swim and as I pulled up a fish rolled off the bush to the right of the swim, a maximum of eight yards out! I had fished this swim several times in the Dippy era, so I knew it quite well but as of yet I hadn't caught from there. The swim itself was tight, but once you were in it was pukka and stopped the sheep coming in, which suited me, plus you didn't want visitors in such a tight swim making any noise, especially as the fishing was mainly at close quarters. Before setting up I decided to walk down to the right and have a closer look, to see if they were in the bush. I crept in and got myself into a comfortable position so I could watch, hidden, to see what was about. Straight away I noticed, right where I was standing, say three feet out in four to five feet of water, the bottom was more cleaned off than the other spot in the Car Park Snag corner, this told me they had been in here a lot and, not long after, I watched several fish move over this spot, grazing as they went along. At least I now knew that they were in feeding mode. A short while later, I saw a movement to the right but further out, in deeper water. The fish looked big but I couldn't get a good look so I wasn't sure which one it was. I watched and waited, hoping he would move out in front of me when, suddenly, a dark shaped brushed alongside the big 'un and this is when I realised that it was probably the common. The other fish, a dark mirror, ghosted up the shelf and I was able to ID it as Lettuce Leaf. Knowing that this fish was around 30lb told me that the other one was massive and as I peered round for a look, there beneath me was the jewel in the crown, the Snake Pit Common in all her glory. Being so close, I was in awe. My hunting instinct had once again tuned me into the habits of my main target. She came in even closer and mooched over the clear sandy spot, before suddenly kicking her tail, flanking along the bottom and gliding up gently, rolling in front of me, not three feet out. This memory is still so vivid and will remain one of those special moments I will always treasure. She looked flawless with her light, creamy belly and bronze jacket of gold sovereigns. After the little display, she disappeared into the darkest water to the left of the swim. I remembered seeing Lettuce Leaf in the Car Park Snags the day before and I was now sure she had been somewhere close by then, as I was to see these two fish together a lot.

This was my time to get out and get myself into position as quickly and quietly as possible. I fanned the rods out, positioning the right-hand rod just off the bush, with the middle fished fifteen yards out over a silkweed-covered area of silt and the left-hander was placed at the foot of a bar that ran from in front of the swim in a sort of horseshoe shape, ending behind the bush. This was a natural roadway for them to follow in and out of the zone.

With everything sorted it was time for me to chill out and play the camping game. After an hour I could stand it no longer; I needed to know that they were still in residence. As soon as I entered the snags I clocked one straight away so I decided to leg it back and chill on the bedchair, watching the water for any carpy signs. Around ten minutes later one head-and-shouldered quietly over the right-hand rod and sank down, bubbling right over the baited area. After a few minutes I saw some pinhead bubbles over the zone, so things were now looking good for a bite. The rod on that area soon pulled tight and I flew off the bedchair and grabbed the rod. Straight away I could

I settled down to watch the sun set hoping that the common would come out to play.

feel a horrible grating sensation coming back up the line; he had made the sanctuary of the bush. I slackened off and, as I looked over, I could see the bush moving, this wasn't good. Nothing was moving and I was sure that he was caught up in the upper parts of the branches. I decided to put the rod down on the clutch to go and have a look to see if I could locate where this psycho carp was snagged up. When I got round there I could see swirls on the top and as I neared the area I could see a mirror laying on top of the branches. As I edged closer there was an eruption and then nothing. I then legged it back and picked the rod up but I knew that all was gone. On closer inspection the chod hook length had been cut through, probably on the zebra mussels that coated the snags. I was gutted after getting a bite so quickly. Thankfully, I knew that the lost fish was safe and I hadn't lost the big girl.

I got the rod back out near the snag again but not as close this time, then re-baited all the rods. I was concerned about the levels of bait left in the swim after having a bite so quickly, plus the noise of the bait hitting the water often draws fish in to investigate. I sat back and the phone went, it was Rich Stewart checking where I was as I was booked in for an ACF feature. I told him where I was and he said, "I'll see you at first light." I laughed, then said "More like 10am!" as our Mr Stewart has a tendency for being a tad late most of the time!

I couldn't resist taking another look into the bush before dark. Once my eyes were

I thought, "I know you!" It was Lettuce Leaf in all its glory.

accustomed to the lower light levels, I could just make out the paler parts of a mouth moving in the same place that I'd seen the common. After a few minutes there was movement and, sure enough, it was her. At least I hadn't scared her from the zone when I lost the fish. It seemed that I was still in with a chance, I then returned back to the bivvy, sat down and watched the sunset, hoping after my observation of her in the bush she might come out to play.

After dark I had a lot of bleeps and, not wanting to bore you with loads of tench-catching therapee, I'll summarise by saying that I caught twelve of the bastards that night. As you can imagine, I was knackered. Not only that, but I was sure that every carp would have legged it from the zone. Shortly after first light I received what I thought was a tenchy bite on the middle rod. It was bizarre; I just pumped this dead weight in, thinking it was a redeye all the way, until up popped a scaly carp, which momentarily wallowed on the surface. I just grabbed the net and scooped it straight up, then all hell let loose and the water in the net exploded, covering me in a cool spray that properly brought me into the land of the living! Looking into the net I thought, "I know you." It was Lettuce Leaf in all his glory; one that I dearly wanted to catch.

I unhooked him as there was no point in getting him out until Rich turned up, so I gave him a call to see where he was. He told me that he was twenty minutes away and I told him what I had waiting for him. Not long after he arrived I dished out the therapee, ripping the pee out of him because he was basically on time for once! I must have been in a good mood, God knows why given how knackered I was, because I offered him one of my coffees; yep, I'm a tight git when it comes to handouts.

I had noticed bluebells flowering on the bank behind me and thought that if I was luckily enough to catch one, that would make the perfect backdrop. So, I placed the mat while Rich got his camera ready. The scale pattern on this fish is spectacular, with random apple slices scattered over him. We noticed that he had a disfigured pectoral fin, making him a very unique character and the first target I could tick off my list. For the record, he weighed 30lb 12oz. I lifted my prize up in the early morning sun and the little blue flowers of spring added a splash of colour. Now all that was left was for Rich to do his magic. It was now time for that special moment when you release your prize back to fight another day. As I lowered the mat in, I knelt down, scooping up cool lake water and splashing it over him. I bid him farewell as he slid away and we watched him disappear from view.

I filled Rich in on what had happened over the last two days but asked him if it was OK to leave shooting the feature for a few more hours, until I was happy with where I was fishing. My gut feeling was telling me that I needed to move and this was confirmed after I looked in the snags, nothing seemed to be about. I reeled the other rods in and it was time to get back on the hunt for Mr Carp. I wondered where they were now, I honestly thought they would be in the Car Park Snags but there were no signs. This left two places really, the Main Snags or out in the middle, but I knew they were running

I felt that I had to move, but to where? Perhaps the Main Snags?

We counted five carp. It looked like they were expecting to be fed.

scared from Uncle Jim! I still had the lake to myself and I thought that it was weird that Pickled Egg wasn't about yet; maybe the therapee was taking its toll on 'Growler', as he was also known? Surely it was only a matter of time before the camping sheep shaggers would turn up?

We made our way over to the Main Snags. This area is dotted with bushes sticking out of the water, with untold snags that you couldn't see. We made our way to what they call the Viewing Area, which was right in the middle of the snags in the corner, a spot where the carp were fed a lot. Some guys insisted on piling the bait in, which was no good because this would keep them in the Little Snags swim for far too long, until the weed came up. Luckily though, things had changed for the better, as I mentioned earlier. As I entered the viewing area, with Rich behind me, I put my glasses on and straight away noticed a massive cleaned-off area that had been polished off by endless carp feeding on it. All of a sudden, several carp moved across the area and I nudged Rich. We counted five carp, it was like they knew we were here and they expected to be fed. I would never bait up places like that, but a few baits to help you gauge their reaction helps you to gain confidence in your bait choice. I got some baits out of my pocket and was about to throw them in when suddenly, from the right, a massive shape made its way towards us, the Snake Pit Common. She came into full view, not eight feet out, giving us a good look at what was probably a 45lb plus frame. All of a sudden, there was a white cloud in the water behind her and it dawned on me that she had just done a big, white shit, which meant one thing; the bitch had done me over last night in Al's Bar! To rub salt into the wound, she now flaunted the fact. Even though

She came into view, not eight feet out.

A few baits helped me gauge their reaction to the bait, which gave me enormous confidence.

I'd had all that tench therapee, at some point she was there, in the mix. At least I knew she liked the bait. Disgusted, I tossed a handful of 15mm and 20mm whites over her. I thought this would scare her, but it had the opposite effect as she took several on the drop! We watched her gills pulsating as she crunched them up. I then started throwing one in at a time and she just sucked them up. Neither Rich nor I could believe what we were watching unfold in front of our very eyes. Her mouth was full and her gills flared as she tried to crunch them up. When some bits started to fall out she tried to suck them back up. This was awesome and was so funny as she was now getting in a right tizz. Other carp approached and she charged them, staking her claim to the free food; this fat bitch wanted the lot, but in the end it was every carp for himself as the spot filled up. They went on a mass rampage, upending and ripping the bottom up as loads of tiny bubbles popped on the surface. All this info told me one thing, they liked this white bait, which gave me even more confidence and by the way she was having it, there was a very good chance of nailing her on it. That said, I already knew she liked the squids and it wouldn't be too long before I would be using them again. Within the next trip or two I would be mixing the two baits to wean them onto the squids.

I decided not to put any more boilies in as I didn't want to fill them up in the snags and I needed them back out in the lake, where I could fish for them. As we talked about what we'd just seen, she carried on circling the area just under the surface, waiting for more, but there was no way I was playing her game. I did want to see her reaction to floaters though, so I left Rich watching while I went to fetch some mixers from the van. When I got back she was still there and straight away I threw a handful at her. As they settled on the surface, her behaviour changed and it was clear to see that she was fixed on them now. She circled underneath them before rising, trying to take one. She missed, then went for another go; this was mind-blowing and we watched as, after three attempts, she took one. After that she cleared all the mixers up and none of the other carp came near as the queen feasted. At least I now knew that she loved floaters. We hung around but after about an hour the snags had emptied. With all this intelligence I decided to leg it back to Al's Bar and pack up. I knew that it was going to be a sunny day and it would be silly of me not to put some floaters out from the Main Snags for a while to see if I could get a chance. As it happened, the odd fish did take a mixer as they drifted into the snags. I was able to occasionally tease them out of the snags, but we needed to get on with the ACF feature as the time was marching on so I reeled in and went for a look back in the Main Snags.

There was nothing at home, which was strange after what we had witnessed just a few hours earlier. We walked up to the Car Park Snags and I decided to have a look from the high bank first to see if any were on the top. Jackpot, there were several sitting, basking in the sun more or less over the top of the area I had caught from two days earlier. I had baited the area twice since leaving and by the colour of the water, they had been in the mix again. I didn't waste any more time and got the rods back out, rocking in the zone. It was time to get on with the feature as magazine work is part of how I earn my bread and butter, while keeping the sponsors happy. With the rods

Caught in the act!

placed on the buzzers we commenced work on the feature, holding items up. Posing for the camera like some so-called superstar isn't really for me. I like promoting the things that I'm genuinely using, and being as informative as I can, because there are far too many 'superstars' out there, misleading their followers.

I was saved from posing for the camera in fine style, when my right-hand rod whacked round as another Snake carp made the mistake of sucking and seeing. This one tried his hardest to gain the sanctuary of the bush but I held on not giving any line. This pressure worked, as he then kited left on a tight line, along the edge of the bushes. I knew that, as long as I kept the pressure on until he was in front of me, everything would be OK. While I was playing this carp I could hear Rich clicking away with his camera, taking action shots. I was buzzing off the action that I was getting and I just prayed no-one saw anything as I lifted the net around another one. He looked awesome, a clean, chunky mirror with big apple-slice scales randomly placed over his body. Simply stunning.

Rich watched the fish while I got things sorted and we then weighed him at 25lb 12oz. As I lifted him up for the camera, I heard the gate open, but it was too late and I was left with the sickening feeling that comes with being rumbled. The green mobile came into view, now I knew I was fcuked! Greg got out and looked straight at me as I held my prize up, while Rich took the pictures. This meant only one thing to me, this twat would spread the news. He shut the gate and came over to investigate so he could be

Before dark I managed another one, The Root Fish at 21lb 8oz.

the town crier from the pit. As I put the fish down he blurted out, "God, how many you had?" I looked up, straight-faced, and grunted out, "Only the one." You could see envy smouldering as he walked off and as I watched, his hand went into his pocket."Look Rich, now he's telling everyone," I muttered. As I picked up the mat to carry the fish back, I couldn't help myself and shouted after Greg, "YOU!" He looked round with his phone against his ear, and I said "Cheers," and he knew I'd rumbled him as he scurried off back to the mobile and drove off towards Al's Bar. As I returned the fish I looked over and, even at that range, I could see him spreading the news. It had been quiet but, as you can imagine, before dark several people walked round. I just hid underneath my bivvy! Not long after the capture of the twenty five our work was done and Rich departed, leaving me to it. Before dark I caught another one, a mirror called The Root Fish at 21lb 8oz. Wayne did the pictures for me and Pickled Egg watched on and I thought that I could hear a faint, "Oyez! Oyez!" from the direction of Al's Bar. Fortunately, Colchester's Town Crier left on dark, scurrying back from where he came. I knew it was going to get busy now and I knew that I was going to fill the corner in! Hopefully someone would be around to witness it; this is where the games would be played now, and I'd be using every trick in the book to get ahead.

That night Jay rang me as he'd heard the news. This told me all I wanted to know; it was out. Because Jay was a good mate who I'd known for many years, I told him what I had caught, making him swear to secrecy as I wanted to try and keep these other captures quiet for as long as possible.

After another quiet night I had another bite as I was packing up and landed a common called Elvis, which weighed 20lb 12oz. As you can imagine, I was well chuffed catching that lot on my first trip. Pickled Egg witnessed that one as well as he was back at the lake at bang on first light. I was about to use his town crying skills for my own gain though, to keep the sheep out of the swim until I returned to claim it back. I reversed the van back round to the high bank above the spot, whereupon I got 30kg of White Amber out, grabbed the baiting spoon and got to work. I was laughing uncontrollably as I ladled the bait in, knowing that the news would get out before the dust had settled on the track! The hit of bait would give the fish a feast and ensure that they stayed in the zone. Over the weekend, Jay informed me that someone did go into the swim but had caught nothing thus far, and he was packing up early on Monday to go to work. After getting this news I planned to be there just before first light to claim the swim back.

As you could imagine, I was gagging to get back into the swim. During the journey over all I could think about was getting back in that zone, as something inside me was telling me that she would be about. The excitement and anticipation was unreal as I drove like a loony through the early morning mist. It's an unreal feeling, when you know that you're close. If you could bottle it, you'd be minted!

I pulled up to the gate and was so focused on getting that swim that I hopped over the

A common called Elvis – what a first trip this was turning out to be!

stile before opening the gate to see if anyone else was there. Luckily, there was just one motor, belonging to the matey who was in the swim and it was open, which told me he was packing down. I was now buzzing as I had secured the swim. As I drove up to the swim, matey was putting his gear in the motor. I pulled up and got out, saying, "I hope you don't mind me parking my car in here?" He said that he didn't, and told me that Jay had informed him that I wanted to get back in there. He had played the game, telling the others that he was in there until Monday evening, playing straight into my hands! I shook his hand thanking him. He also mentioned that people had repeatedly visited him, asking when he was going. These sort of anglers make my blood boil, they're just fishing off the back of others. Matey had simply seen loads of fish rolling and fizzing in the corner, but only later found out why. Now, anglers that find their own fish, regardless of whether the area has been primed, that's good angling in my book. He didn't know that I'd baited the zone until he spoke to Jay later that evening.
After that I left him to it, wandering up to the Main Snags to find that someone was in there. I carried on up to the viewing area to see if I could see any fish waiting to be fed. There was no way that I would put any bait in with someone fishing the Main Snags; even though it was seventy to eighty yards away it would have been disrespectful, so I was just going for a look. Many dickheads did though, coming down in the night and filling the area in. I couldn't understand this because they couldn't even get a bait anywhere near it. As I approached the area I popped my glasses on, but the mist rolling

I was focused on getting back into the Car Park Corner after priming it.

The mist rolling across the surface put paid to me seeing anything.

over the surface put paid to me seeing anything, which was probably a good thing in hindsight, as I was fully focused on the Car Park Corner that I had primed up ready. Looking along the bank, I could see that matey had gone, but then there was a clank as the gate opened and Pickled Egg emerged, immediately looking down the track towards me. His face was a picture as I smiled and, in a raised voice, said, "Morning Greg!" He grunted and looked away; I could tell that he was gutted, as I bet he had plans to get in the swim. The carp gods were on my side and not on the side of the sheep shaggers. I do find this sort of approach to fishing amusing, as many think that jumping on the back of other's hard work is good angling when it's clearly not.

Pickled Egg scurried off into his swim and probably informed his followers that Uncle Jim was back in his zone. I turned off from this and turned my attentions towards getting those rods out and rocking on the spots. As I stood out on the front of the swim, about to make the first cast, I noticed that the zone was covered with loads of bubbles. I paused and suddenly a carp pushed out over the main zone. This was all textbook fishing, as the rig landed in the ripples where Mr Carp had just re-entered, pukka. The other rod was cast just to the left of the spot. I decided not to put any freebies out because I didn't know if they had cleared it all yet. I left the tench therapee rod out as I wanted to concentrate on the rods in the zone. Over the next thirty minutes several more fish showed over the rigs but I had no action. Something inside me was telling me to put some bait out, so I acted on this gut feeling and put out several hundred baits. Not long after, a rod shook in the rests. I watched but nothing developed. I was starting to understand that this was the sort of sign you sometimes got before getting a take on Snake. I knew that they were feeding again and the greedy bastards had only just cleared away 30kg! Matey was unlucky as he'd had to pack up and go to work. Out of the corner of my eye I saw the rod tip pull round and the alarm let out a bleep and I was in. I grabbed the rod and straight away I felt this fish was a lot heavier than the others. I held on for dear life as he surged off for that bush. The rod was bent double as something had to give. An explosion rocked the surface right up against the branches that hung well down into the water and the bush moved. I was starting to feel that this wasn't looking good when, suddenly, the pressure on the rod eased and I was able to pump this brute back towards me. I started to wonder which one it was, and not long after a big shape appeared down at the bottom of the shelf in the crystal-clear water. It was big, but I couldn't quite see which one he was. As he was now close in and relatively safe, I slackened off the clutch so I could play him properly. There was no need to bully him and risk pulling out so I played him carefully under the rod tip until he tired himself out. After several minutes, the leadcore started to rise from the water and I knew that the battle was coming to an end. I was fixed on him, trying to identify which one he was, when a mirror with a lump on its side rolled on the surface. It wasn't her, but by the size of him, I could see that I was attached to a fish of well over 30lb. It had to be one of the two lumpy mirrors, which both weighed around mid-thirty at the right time. Finally, he wallowed on the surface and took a gulp of air; surely he was now beaten? I slid the net out while drawing this mirror ever closer to the cord. I took my chance and he went in first time. I peered in for a better look at my prize, while he just sat there motionless on the surface. He looked big, with a massive set of shoulders and a lump on his right side. I heard someone approach behind me and assumed that it was going to be Pickled Egg, but I turned round to see Joe Morgan standing there. "Alright mate how's it going?" I asked. Joe replied in his Essex way, "Pukka Jim, what you got? Looks like Right Lumpy; he hasn't been out for a while." All I knew was that I had another target in my net. It was a bit surreal as I hadn't been on the lake long and I was racking them up. I was buzzing and my confidence was sky high, surely I was close to her? Joe kindly helped me out with the pictures of Right Lumpy, which weighed in at 34lb 4oz and was in awesome condition. When I released him I wondered how long it would be before he was banked again. Later on I rang Jay up to tell him the good news and he told me that Right Lumpy hadn't been out for over two years. I love catching the hard ones; it's something that I have the knack of doing a lot. With 48 hours of this session left, things were looking good for another bite or two. There were still carpy signs in the zone and it was time to get the rod back on the spot. It seemed as though they knew the score as all the bites were now coming to the right-hand rod, which was the nearest to the bush where they were hiding. However, I had found a nice smooth spot close to the far margin, under the high bank some six to eight feet away from the overhanging branches of the bush. This was to become the only spot where I could get bites from Mr Carp in this swim; I did try a couple of other spots around the bush but nothing came of it.

Jay was a great ally on Snake.

Joe said, "It looks like Right Lumpy, he hasn't been out for a while."

When I released him I wondered how long it'd be before he was banked again.

My first bite for thirty-odd hours was this 19lb 14oz common.

Joe and I chatted for a while as we hadn't seen each other for ages and before he left he said, "If you need anyone to take any pictures let me know, because I'm only down the road." After he left, I set my house up and then sat back, watching for signs. Things were a little quiet for the next few hours, then the liners started up on the right-hand rod, so I sat up ready, knowing that something was going to happen. I watched tiny, telltale twitches on the line where it entered the water and several times they were so savage that I went for the rod. I knew that I was close to a bite, so when the alarm signalled a take, I quickly grabbed the rod and heaved into another one that kited out on the surface. By the way it was kicking this fish did not feel anything like the last one and not long after I netted an awesome, heavily scaled mirror that weighed 20lb 12oz; another one of the lake's scaly gems. I did self-takes of this one and as I returned him, I looked out to see Pickled Egg on the phone again. Seeing that he was doing his town crier impersonation again, I knew that this swim was going to be harder to get back into every trip and, over the weekend, things were going to get nasty, as you will find out.

Over the next 24 hours the swim went dead but I saw nothing else and several other people had turned up, filling all the top swims, so it wouldn't be easy to move anyway. I was now camping but it still felt good here and I kept the bait going in, hoping that they would visit the spot again as they'd eaten so much bait off this area. I had caught a few off it so they were probably spooked and a little full. On the last morning, at first light, I received my first bite for thirty-odd hours, which had me scrambling towards the rod, which was bent well round by the time I had got hold of it. Straight away, I could tell that it was a smaller one, which didn't cause me any problems and, not long after, another mirror was landed. For the record he weighed 19lb 14oz and as I returned him, I could feel eyes burning into me from over in Al's Bar. Before I left, I filled the swim with 20kg of White Amber and a 10kg taster of the salty squids. Several of Pickled Egg's posse turned up and stood with him, probably giving it large about me, but I was doing nothing wrong apart from getting on with my own angling. Little did I know what they were planning until, on Saturday morning I received an alarming call from one of the boys informing me that Pickled Egg and his posse were going to fcuk me over by rotating the swim to keep me out. As you can imagine, this news well and truly pissed me off, because this was a concerted effort to fcuk up what I was doing. I knew that it wasn't my swim but this was well out of order, knowingly occupying the swim to stop me doing my own thing. I couldn't leave it with them thinking that they had won and nicking the ultimate prize, especially as I felt so close to her, even though I hadn't seen her in the zone yet. This was savage news for me and I was now on the warpath. I got Greg's number and rang it but he wouldn't answer, so, in the end, I left a long voice message so he would know that he had been rumbled. The boys kept me posted as they (including the head bailiff) occupied the swim with loads of rods. I sat at home stewing over this all weekend as it was bang out of order and I was definitely going to have it out with him.

By the Monday morning I was on a mission, flying down the A12 because I needed to ask him what his problem was and why he was doing this to me. Deep down I knew, there was clearly jealousy over the results that I was having, as apart from my captures there hadn't been anything out yet. So, some of the green-eyed dope smokers had come out to play and I wasn't having any of this bollocks. I tried to keep calm, but as I opened the gate and looked to the left and saw the green mobile parked up, I began to feel myself losing it, especially after being so pumped up over the weekend. Jane had tried to calm me but I knew I was going to lose it. As I climbed out of the van I saw a head pop round, so now they knew I was here. It was time to go straight in for the kill. Three of them were sitting together and I tore into Greg, "What the fcuk's all this about? Rotating a swim to stop me getting in again?" All he said was, "Jim, we're just keeping the swim for you." I retorted, "Is that the best you can do?" before ripping into him, hard core, telling them the score and asking, why he hadn't returned my call, after I'd left a message. Greg said, "I didn't have a call from you Jim" so I got my phone out, and rang the number I was given. I could see the discomfort in his face as he was about to get rumbled. A split second later, his phone burst into life, "There you go!" I shouted, "You're a fcuking joke and you call yourself a bailiff!" "Jim, you can have the swim back," he squirmed. I told him to stick it and pointed at him, telling him to get on with his own fishing and to stop fcuking with mine. Fearing that I might do something I'd regret, I walked off, because I really didn't want to lose my ticket. I carried on down to the Main Snags to calm down. I did feel good but I started

One of the fish that cost me my ticket, albeit briefly. She weighed 30lb 4oz.

to think that I had just played into his hands and, knowing that he was a weasel, I had a feeling that he would try to turn this into something more by grassing me up to the club. I decided that it was better to leave there and then, so I decided to go and chill at Layer. I'd just obtained my Layer ticket after people gave me four work party tickets, yes, without me doing any work parties! This is the norm but Uncle was going to get more therapee that day.

I pulled into the car park, grabbed the unhooking mat with my floater gear in it, along with three rods and set off along the right-hand side of the lake, where the path dropped down and ran along the water's edge. I was noticed straight away, and I said "Hello" and carried on as it was very busy along that bank. Round a corner, the lake narrowed down into a bottleneck and then ran into a bay. As soon as I strolled into this bay it was clear that there were carp everywhere and, what's more, no-one was fishing in there, which I thought was a bit strange. I walked further along and stopped about halfway along. Looking out, I was staggered to see backs bobbing around all over the zone; there must have been several hundred carp in residence, I'd never witnessed anything like this before! I put my gear down, grabbed the spod rod and proceeded to put out several loads of mixers. As soon as I did this, the fish moved left, like they were starting a mass exodus. I quickly chucked a few spods of mixers, snatching the spod back as it hit the water to spray the mixers more widely. I watched, waiting for the first one to take some bait, because once one starts the rest normally follow suit. Suddenly, two fish took at the same time! I was so excited, and I did have to wonder how the hell was I going to keep a shoal like this fed adequately to stop them moving on. All too soon it was a frenzy out there, which spurred me on to act on it straight away. I grabbed one of the floater rods, which thankfully was ready to go, but while I was putting the rod together I really didn't know whether to spod some more floaters out or cast a hook bait out! I opted to cast out and fuzzed the rod beyond the main body of fish, before easing the hook bait into position. As soon as I had done that, I grabbed the spod rod again and proceeded to get some more floaters in the mix before they all legged it, as loads had bow-waved out into the main body of the lake. Suddenly, the rod on the floor pulled tight and I was straight into my first Layer Pits carp. Unbelievably, as I was playing the fish in, this bloke appeared and started giving me a load of bollocks, saying that I shouldn't be fishing, as I didn't have a ticket! I calmly said, "Look mate, let me land this fish and I'll show you my ticket." I later found out that this twat was called Chris (the head bailiff, now you can see what I was alluding to earlier!) and, as soon as I slipped the fish, a common, into the net, I handed him my ticket… which clearly said 'Layer upgrade' on it. He looked indignant and barked, "You haven't done any work parties!" I had to agree and said, "I was given these by three members and a committee member, and the ticket was sent back to me." This rude, gobby, jobsworth was bang out of order in the way he was speaking to me, and my ordeal wasn't over yet, because he then said, "I want your ticket." I handed it to him, and he told me that he would be handing it in and reporting me for obtaining the upgrades incorrectly. Finally, he told that I had five minutes to get off the water. I still don't know how I kept my cool after two lots of crap from two head bailiffs! I returned the common and made another quick cast and I quickly hooked another one! After a spirited battle I landed another common that was bigger than the last! I quickly photographed him, on the scales he weighed 30lb 4oz, I slipped him back and legged it out. I made a call to the club, but they didn't want to know at that point telling me that I couldn't fish without my ticket.

Before I headed for home I popped back to have a look at Snake. The swim was empty and Pickled Egg had gone, but before leaving I stood above the zone and, just to rub salt into the wound, there beneath me sat my main target. I was gutted like you don't want to know; it was like she was waiting to be fed. I nearly cried because I knew I was so close. After a few days I received a letter saying that I couldn't fish CAPS waters at all until my case had been heard at a committee meeting at the end of the month. To cut a long story short, I received a call telling me that my ticket was on its way back to me with the Layer Upgrade! So, in the end nothing had happened but I had missed five to six weeks fishing on the Snake. To make things worse, I had moved onto another water during that time, so all that hard work was wasted too. I bet Pickled Egg thought he had won but, in hindsight, it was probably for the best; I knew I would be back at some point.

I returned in August of the following year, while I was fishing for The Black Mirror

I decided to fish just the one rod on the special spot.

over at The Mere. I had twisted my knee badly and there was no way I could fish The Mere until it was better. The doctor had given me painkillers so until they kicked in and the knee felt better, there was no hardcore fishing for me. That's when Snake Pit popped back into my head, because I could fish a lot of the swims from the van. This meant that I could chill while fishing with my leg up, with a chance of a big 'un. More importantly, I had unfinished business there; I needed to catch The Snake Pit Common and catch The Black Mirror too before I could commence work on my second book. This was a tall order because they were two tricky fish to catch for different reasons. I remember a conversation with Jay one night about the next book and my dilemma. I didn't know whether to carry on chasing after the common, she hadn't been out yet and she was definitely on the cards, but I had been fishing The Mere with such 'tunnel vision' that not being there was hard and very frustrating. The quest for this country's finest had well and truly got under my skin, plus we were coming up on that special of month of September when she seemed to put in an appearance around the harvest moon and autumn equinox. All Jay said was, "If anyone could do it, Uncle Jim could." This mission was a tall order for many reasons, even for Uncle Jim, but in my world you never say never, because you never know what the carp gods have in store when they roll their dice of fate.

I was plotted up in the Corner Snags swim again because a quick recce in the snags saw me eye-to-eye with THE massive common, along with a few bodyguards dotted around. She was so close that I could almost touch her. I watched her for a while until, for some reason, she dropped down in the water, maybe the others had alerted her that someone was about, or perhaps she had heard me on the phone talking to Steve Allcott about my find? Knowing the swim so well, I decided to just fish the one rod on that special spot that I'd caught so many from last year. It was a tricky side cast and because my knee was so painful there was no way I was going to risk it while perched on the end of the swim, leaning slightly out, which meant chest waders and standing in the edge. Suddenly, Jay and Wayne arrived to dole out more therapee as I struggled to put the waders on. I grabbed my rod, made my way down to the water's edge and carefully dropped into the clear water. I could see every stone and weed frond on the bottom and watched as the bugs went around their business. I carefully made my way to the right of the swim but, suddenly, I tripped and in trying to protect my knee, I fell forward, dropped the rod and went headfirst into the reeds. I put my arms out to try and save myself from going completely under the water and, as I got up, I could see that Jay was pissing himself while Wayne was trying to keep straight-faced. Now, as you can imagine, I felt like a right plonker but I just looked up, smiling at them, and said, "At least I saved my knee." Pulling silkweed off my face, I got down to business and after two casts I got the rig bang on. Jay piped up, saying, "I didn't think you meant that close?" because I had tried to describe the spot to him over the phone. "Mate," I said, "That cast I've just made is a bite, because the lead went down exactly the same as last year."

As I climbed out I started to feel cool water running down the inside of the waders. As it reached something that made me gasp in shock, Jay said, "What's up mate?" and we fell about laughing. I placed the rod on the rest, gently tightened the line and placed the bobbin on. After screwing the clutch down tight and turning the buzzer on, I walked off to the back of the van to change my clothes while the lads watched the rod for me.

After I returned we sat on my bedchair chatting about all things carpy. Top of the list for me was Pickled Egg, or rather, his absence. Apparently, he'd had some grief on his estate which led to his tyres being slashed, so he had no wheels to get down to the lake, which was great news for us, because I didn't fancy all that therapee again. Also, they informed me that the common hadn't been out yet, but had probably been lost once or twice, so she was well and truly on the cards. However, my mind was elsewhere. Most of all, I wanted to be at The Mere, and that's what Jay and Wayne wanted to hear about most. They were fascinated by my stories of the realities of fishing over at The Mere, and as you can imagine, they listened hard as I told them about some of my adventures over there. While I was in full flow, the rod bleeped and, I gingerly flew over to it, trying to protect my knee. The unseen carp tried to seek sanctuary in the bush, surging into it. Everything went solid and I eased off slightly. Jay and Wayne were by my side and we could see the branches moving. I tightened up because it looked like the fish was trying to get out of the bush and, luckily, he popped free. After that the fight was plain sailing, as he kited back and went straight into the net first time. Initially, we

An awesome little character with a red tinge to him.

He was passing the bait over the mat so I had to give him a wash before we could photograph him!

didn't recognize this chunky mirror with a red tinge to him, he was an awesome little character and was milting and shitting the bait out all over the mat. Before I could hold him up for some pictures we had to give him a wash! At 21lb 12oz he was a nice welcome back and my first fish off the bottom since June, as I had been over The Mere. I'd banked a few off the top during floater-fishing day tuitions but I just didn't want to get into going for bites when I was Mere-fishing, so this was a welcome confidence boost that everything I was doing was working. Bites were few and far between at The Mere and I was yet to receive any action. To be fair though, I spent most of my time up there fishing for The Black Mirror in the swim with the strongest history of captures, regardless of whether fish were there or not.

After I slipped him back it was time to get the rod back on the spot, but this time without falling in. Jay and Wayne tried their hardest to put me off, but I was full of bravado, telling them to "Watch this boys," as I swept the rod back. They watched on as the rig went in pukka, they hadn't seen that I'd clipped the line on the spool clip, and as the rig went down I unclipped it! I turned, saying "Oi oi, have that boys!" After a bit of banter (during which I kept the stroke pulling a secret, of course!) they left me to it. It was great to be back, plus there was only one other person on, fishing up to my right in the Main Snags swim. Nothing else happened that evening and nothing showed, but I knew they were about because I'd quickly checked the snags when I popped round

One of the advantages of fishing Snake – parking behind the swims!

to put some bait in over the zone. It did look good, plus I was certain I was going to get a visit in the morning.

The night was quiet, not even a bleep disturbed me, but at first light I received a single bleep and though I flew out to the rod, nothing else happened. Just like before, the liner had told me that they were on the move, and I had to be ready. I decided to get sorted and get the kettle on while I listened to the birds singing. The kettle boiled and as I lifted it off the stove, I heard a series of bleeps as the rod suddenly pulled round. I threw the kettle of boiling water away as I didn't want to risk scalding myself and pulled into the well-bent rod. Thankfully this one kited away from the bush, bow-waving across the surface at high speed. I held on until he was well away from the snags, before easing off and setting the clutch. As I played him under the tip, I thought that I recognised him as a common with a fat rear end. Were it to be that fish, this would be my third capture of him. As he came towards the waiting net, I got a better look and it sure was him again. I did a couple of self-takes for reference and slipped him straight back without weighing him.

The rod was repositioned back on the money and baited lightly. I had to go as my knee was killing me and that morning Jane booked me in to see the doc again that very evening. After breakfast I had a slow pack-up, just leaving the bedchair out to sit on for a few hours before I had to leave. The liners started again and before leaving I landed a mirror of 17lb 12oz, which was photographed for me by one of the dog walkers. I didn't want to pack up and go, but I had to put things into perspective, which meant getting the knee sorted so I could get back into my quest over at The Mere. The doctor had another look at my knee, telling me that it could be a torn ligament. He prescribed me stronger painkillers and told me to rest it this time! Two days into my course I had no pain whatsoever, so I headed back to The Mere, as you do.

After a couple of sessions over at The Mere in early September, for reasons that will be highlighted in The Mere chapter, I was to return to the Snake Pit for a couple of weeks. I got there just before first light so I could hopefully find the fish, but I had inside info from Jay, as he was fishing the Car Park swim and catching from where I had left off.

The night before he'd told me that they were holed up in this quarter of the lake and were venturing out in front of The Double and showing at first light, before going back in the Car Park Snags for the day. When I arrived I went straight to the swim, it was still empty so I parked the van to the side of the double and, before popping round to see Jay, I put a bag of bait in the swim just to make sure it was mine. If this inside info was right, I was expecting them to be bouncing out in front of the swim soon. I legged it round to see Jay and dish him out some therapee, as you do. He was up and ready for it and we both stood, listening in the semi-darkness, when suddenly there was a crash as one went over. We talked as we waited for the ripples to come rolling in. I said, "Oi oi Jay, they're out there mate," as several rolled over, making that telltale noise when they're showing on the quiet. I could stand it no longer and headed off to get the rods ready so that I could cast at them as soon as I could see exactly where they were.

As each rod was set up ready, with new rigs and fresh baits tied on, I simply leant them up against the van until all three were ready, then I took them down to the swim. It was time to get them out to where the fish were showing. I had been watching them pushing out in the half light, at around eighty five yards and all I needed now was another to show and I'd spread the rods over the active zone. When this was done, I laid the rods on the ground with the clutches set. For some reason, I decided not to put any free offerings out, which is unlike me. Something inside told me just to fish singles to start with. There were so many showing out there that this was probably the right thing to do, because I didn't want to risk spooking them back into the snags. All this was happening right now in front of me and I must admit, I was slightly surprised that Jay wasn't in here already, fishing the early morning in here and legging back to his base camp when they started to move back into his day-take zone. Maybe he wanted his rigs sitting untouched for their return? He did have another spot rocking, straight out from his swim that he was getting mid-morning bites from, so I did understand his logic.

I decided to sit on the bottom step and watch the rods, while drinking a Red Bull. The carp danced out in front of me and I was so confident of a take, surely it was a matter of time before one pulled tight? It was no surprise when one of the rods roared off, bouncing on the ground as something made off with one of my super, salted-up specials! As soon as I pulled into this carp I knew that it was one of the smaller residents. Before long, I was slipping the net under my old mate Elvis; the third time I'd caught him now. Even with his misshaped mouth he sure liked his chod rigs, or perhaps found them hard to deal with. I unhooked him in the net and, as he was only lightly hooked, the rig was still pukka so I quickly re-curved it and got it back out, rocking on the spot. Jay arrived to do the pictures for me saying, "That didn't take you long Uncle." I wanted to keep the capture on the quiet to stop the sheep following me into the area to the right, because news spreads fast on these busy waters. Fishing on the 'Slippery Snake' was no different; there were only two other anglers fishing the pond, one in the Main Snags and someone opposite me in the Hole In The Wall swim. The geezer in the Hole In The Wall swim was asleep with his bivvy door closed so I got all the bits ready at the top of the swim, behind the bushes, so hopefully this capture could be photographed out of sight and out of mind. Luckily, no-one saw and Elvis was returned on the quiet. I told Jay not to tell anyone before he legged it back to get his rods back out.

I sat back down but nothing was showing here or anywhere else for that matter. They most definitely knew they were now being angled for and were now keeping a low profile from Uncle Jim. I watched the zone, keeping an eye on the lines for liners and over the next hour I received several of these, which told me that Mr Carp was still in residence. Because I was watching this zone like a hawk, I noticed immediately when one of the lines twitched and then pulled tight. I jumped up and commenced battle with another Snake carp that took some line off me as he made a short run for freedom. This made me think he was one of the bigger ones, but not long after he came in like a dog on a lead. Jay appeared, grabbed the net and did the honours, netting a chunky, high-backed common that looked like a scraper twenty. I knelt down and discreetly unhooked him in the net, while Jay quickly got the mat, sling and scales sorted, which were hidden up the side of the van so no-one could suss my captures. This unusually shaped common was weighed away from prying eyes, behind the hedge, at 19lb 12oz. Jay once again did the shots for me and the fish was returned like it was a military exercise. Still no-one was any wiser to Uncle's captures… sweet!

With the rod back out in the mix, it was time for me to put the rods on the buzzers,

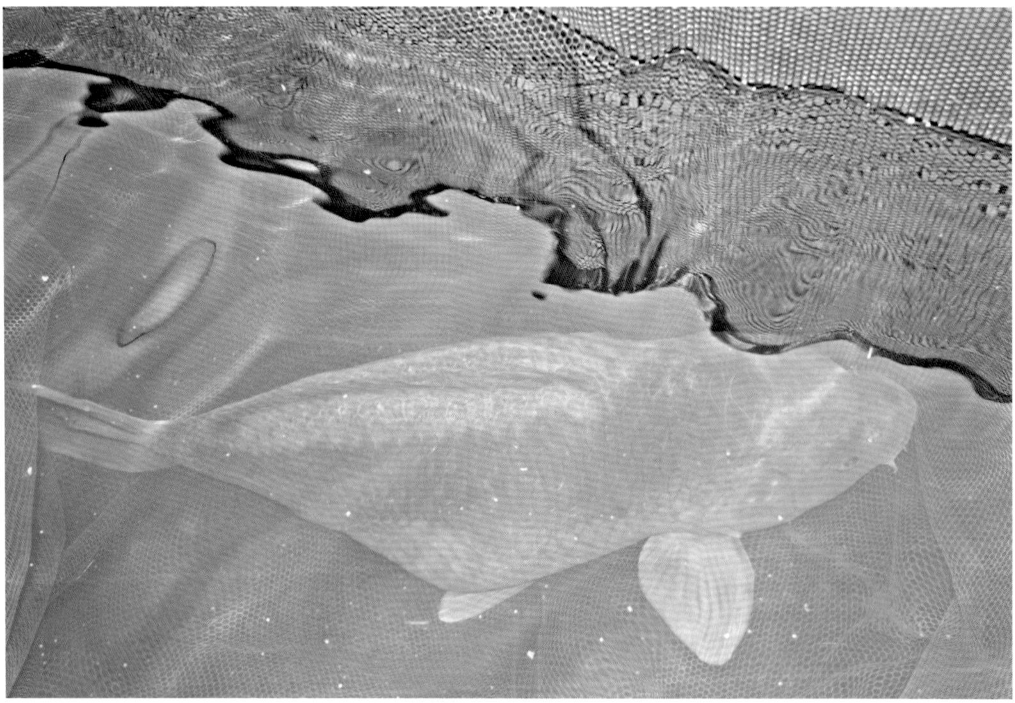

I knelt down and discreetly unhooked him in the net so no-one could suss my captures.

We did the pictures away from prying eyes, behind the hedge.

with the volume turned down of course, wink wink! Plus, I needed to get the house set up as I was definitely going to be camping in here for 24 hours after catching those two so quickly on the quiet.

I saw nothing throughout the day and that evening I decided to load up the zone with a mixture of 12mm and 15mm salty red squids. I spread them all along the gully I was fishing, between two bars. The 12mms were spodded out and to get the spread-baiting effect, I was using my favourite snatching-back method on impact. I thought that 5kg over the zone would really stir them up, but two hours after first light I hadn't spotted anything, which was a bit weird to say the least. This had not been the norm over the previous few mornings. I got a text from Jay asking if I had seen anything because he had laid in and thought that he'd missed the morning show. He was gobsmacked when I rang him to say that I'd only seen tench so far. Something was wrong; was it the captures or the bait? There were no signs whatsoever… where the hell were they? By 10:15am still nothing had shown and I was getting itchy feet. The problem was, I had nothing to go on so until something appeared I was in observation mode, looking out from the bank at the top of my swim. Suddenly, out of the corner of my eye, I saw something roll to the right, at perhaps half the distance I was fishing. I wasn't sure that it was definitely a carp until a plume of big bubbles popped on the surface. I was just thinking about how I'd never seen one there before when another showed, not 45 yards out in front of the next swim along. I walked down to the rods and reeled one of

There were no signs at all... where the hell were they?

them in, re-curved the chod and fuzzed it out into the area that the fish had shown. After placing the rod on the buzzer I legged it up to the top of the swim to get a Red Bull as I was feeling tired. I opened the back of the van and started looking for a can when someone spoke. I turned round to see one of my old mates, Daryl Stile, aka Darius. Daryl asked me if I had caught anything else and I told him that I'd just cast one of the rods to a showing fish. We then walked over to the top of the swim and straightaway we noticed that the right-hand rod was bent right round, I had forgotten to turn the buzzer back on! I handed the Red Bull to Daryl, shot down the steps and lifted into the fish, which by now was solid in weed. I applied steady pressure but nothing budged so I tried walking up to the top of the bank and bending hard into the solid mass. Suddenly, there was a slight movement, which released a dead weight that I inched back under maximum pressure. At no point could I feel a carp, I literally just kept this huge weight on the move, inching it slowly towards me. Daryl went down with the net as a massive weed bed surfaced and we saw movement right at the back of the weed. I walked down into the swim, while keeping the pressure on and we saw a kick... "Oi oi mate, that's a carp!" I panicked because this was some weed bed that Daryl had to net, along with a fish. The mass got closer and Daryl sunk the net and lifted, engulfing the lot in one go. I dropped the rod and started ripping the weed out and the carp, a mirror, just got bigger and bigger until we could make out an old-looking fish with crinkly skin and a massively wide set of shoulders. It was a short fish with a lump on his left-hand side, which I thought I recognised. Jay appeared just in time to ID it. "Oi oi Uncle, what you got?" he asked. "I think it's Left Lumpy," I said, "Have a look mate." Jay looked in and confirmed that it was indeed Left Lumpy, telling me that he hadn't been out for nearly three years! This was just unreal in such a pressured water, yet there he lay, in the folds of my net; another one of the lake's main targets ticked off the list!

I carefully removed the hook while Jay once again brought the mat out from its hiding place up the side of the van. We then commenced the military exercise to get that fish up the top and photographed. It was unreal how high this chunk sat off the mat

We commenced the military operation to get the fish photographed and returned unseen.

Jay confirmed that it was indeed Left Lumpy, weighing in at 35lb 6oz.

and as I removed him from the net he looked awesome, a very old carp indeed, pale in complexion with a walnut-textured, wrinkly skin covered in a thick film of slime; a proper old English carp, just how I like 'em. He weighed in at 35lb 6oz, which was enough to make any session.

Jay did the honours as we all kept low-key. Trying not to bring attention to this gathering, we all knelt, hidden behind the bushes and, just as I lifted my prize, the gate clanked. Darius looked round saying "Someone's just driven in." What could I do? It was all in the lap of the carp gods and as I carried on posing with my prize, I could hear the car coming closer. "Oh well boys, we've been rumbled now," I thought, and as the car pulled up I had a look and then carried on. This was not good news because all I could think about was anglers coming down tonight as I was sure the drums would be beating very soon. My main concern was people turning up and going in the nearest swims to my right, so I was now in a dilemma; should I stay or move? The decision was made when another fish poked his head two swims down now, in the Apple Tree swim, which I later renamed to Jim's Tree! The carp gods were pointing me in the right direction, so I reeled the other rods in, checked that everything was pukka and re-curved them so they were ready and hung the leads through the 50mm butt rings, with the rods resting up against the van. Before leaving I asked Darius if he could guide the casts in from where we were. I pointed out a certain bush, right where I needed the leads to land. Darius shouted up to tell me that my first cast was 15 yards too far. I didn't need a third go as he shouted up, "Bang on Uncle," as the rig dropped through the water. Laying the rod down, which was straight out, I cast one to the left and the other to the right. I now had three singles out, all on the same zone, 15 yards apart. I noticed someone watching me from over on The Point, in one of the little side swims, so I shouted "Oi oi!" and waved. The head disappeared from view and Darius walked up asking, "You what mate?" I told him that we were being watched and pointed over, when suddenly the sheep shagger appeared again. I jumped up and started waving. We were pissing ourselves as he hadn't heard this new carpy word of mine before and as I explained the meaning we both laughed uncontrollably.

Time was getting on, plus it looked moody as clouds were gathering in the distance and the odd spit of rain could be felt in the air. Darius watched the rods for me so I could go and get packed up without worrying about being off my rods and my camp was set up within twenty minutes. I barely had enough room to walk out and round the bivvy in this tight swim. It soon started to rain and over the next couple of hours it got steadily worse as the clouds built up, dropping the light to late-evening levels. Darius and I talked about the good old days at Toll Pits, about Nanny and my old mate The Tollminator while peering out into the gloom from under my brolly. No carp had been seen since that earlier sighting but suddenly the middle rod bleeped, then it screamed and I dived out from the bivvy, grabbing the rod, which pulled down savagely and was nearly ripped from my grasp. This unseen monster stripped untold line off me even though I tried to apply pressure with my finger on the spool. I was beginning to think that it was one of the big catfish that inhabit the lake's snags, because whatever it was on

Darius lifted the net around the queen of the lake.

the other end I was just hanging on for dear life! Eventually, everything came to an abrupt halt and wouldn't budge. I bent into the fish but nothing moved. Thinking quickly, I handed the rod to Darius and skirted round the back of the bivvy, then took the rod back and went up to the top of the bank again, to try and pry him from his sanctuary. All sorts of things were running through my head as I bent well into this fish. I wondered if it was still on because I couldn't feel anything on the other end. The rod was bent way beyond its normal curve and, just at the point I thought about slackening off and getting the boat from the van, there was movement on the other end. Something moved off, sullen like a dead weight. I was now convinced that this was a catfish as the power of the beast was immense. I made my way down into the swim and Darius once again manned the net. He asked "Do you want me to net it for you mate?" I then replied, "Too right, anyway it's a catfish and I'll need some help with this thing." Fearing for the hook hold, I played him out cautiously because I wanted to see what this beast was, even if I lost him, because I had never played anything like this before. Ominously, a huge weed bed popped up on the surface very close in. I undid the bale arm and let the beast run off while Darius ripped the weed off the line. When it was clear, he shouted "It's off!" and I recommenced battle. Straight away, the fish came in close, moving along the bottom of the shelf. I just prayed it would stay on and Darius was quiet as a mouse. Deep down, we caught a flash of gold, making me stutter, "Darius that is no catfish." After a few calming words from Darius a massive common surfaced. I shouted "Have it mate," as he lifted the net around the queen of the lake. I was emotionally drained from that awesome battle, one that I will never forget. I shouted out, "Yesssssssssssssss!" across the lake and Daryl stood up to shake my hand, saying, "Awesome, well done mate". I leant down, unhooked her and, touching her face, I whispered, "Thanks for this special moment." It was still peeing down and the light levels were disappearing fast so it was time to leg it and get all the bits I needed

I was emotionally drained from the battle and let out a cry across the lake.

I gathered a posse and we carefully transported her up the bank.

Her welfare was paramount, especially after I saw that she was carrying an injury.

We kept pictures to a minimum so I could treat and return her.

Given her injury, we decided to photo her good side only.

from the van. I bumped into Jay and Wayne en route, they knew what I had caught because they'd heard the shout and they helped me to carry the gear down to the swim. The spot was chosen and I went down into the swim whereupon Daryl informed me that she had an area of damage on the side of her belly. I had a look at the wound as I turned her in the net. It looked bad, like a perfect slice of ham that had been cut off by a very sharp object. Thankfully, Gary Bayes had just sorted me out with some Medicarp. The wound looked several weeks old, because it had started to heal, so I covered the damaged area with Medicarp after the pictures were done. To be honest, it took the edge off the capture because I was more worried about the common's welfare. It's a real shame when they get damaged, but I always look after them.

Because I wanted to keep pictures to a minimum, to get her back, I allowed my good friend Jay to do some on his camera as a backup and Darius used mine. A posse gathered as we carefully transported her up the bank. She was very quiet and I promised her that I would give her all the love and care she now deserved. I decided to only take

I was emotionally drained from the battle and let out a cry across the lake.

47lb 8oz of English common carp.

pictures of her good side and get straight on with applying this Medicarp treatment to the wounded area. It looked bigger on the bank, and I applied this stuff with my hand, which was then dyed blue. We weighed her and she banged the scales round to 47lb 8oz.

It was time to get her back to her home and as I lowered her back into the water, I wished her good luck. As I watched her glide off into the darkness, I knew where she would go. While Darius watched my rods, I went to a special spot in the lake that she visits a lot for some peace and quiet and threw in 10kg of salty squids for her to feast on and give her a real good chance of getting over this. When I got back Jay got a call from Pickled Egg. I demanded the phone and shouted, "Yes, I've caught her and you can fcuk off, twat!" Yes, I did feel better after that and as I hung up, I told the lads that it was party time and Uncle Jim was paying. The rods were reeled in and we shot off down to Tesco to get some beers; I even bought myself a bottle of Lanson Champagne along with a pukka bottle of red, some cider and the boys chipped in as well. As you can imagine this was going to get messy. Ash turned up as we started drinking and made the fatal mistake of setting up in the double we were partying in. The beers were flowing nicely and sometime after 10pm we started to get hungry and ordered a massive Chinese. When it arrived we were like a pack of wolves, whacking this Chinese down. A pissed-up Wayne managed to drop some food on the floor and then ate it off the floor! It was gross watching this savage eating food that was covered in

My head was pounding, but as I looked out I knew that the chapter was closed.

My good friend Ben Dowers with the common at 49lb. Totally healed and looking awesome.

grit… yuck! Ash went to bed after the Chinese, but we carried on partying, throwing the bottles and cans into his swim. He was warned though, and when he packed up in the morning to go to work he left the mess for us to clear up… I did think this was a bit out of order somewhat!

It was a great night and in the morning I was hanging. My head was pounding as I looked out, knowing this chapter was now closed. Before I left, I looked out over the water, wishing the common good luck. I popped over with Jay to see if she was in the special area, and sure enough she was there and feasting on the salty squids. I topped her larder up with another 5kg and I dropped by several times over the next few weeks to feed her and keep her in the snags to stop her from being caught. I knew that she'd be on a feeding mission to get her wound healed and it would do her no favours getting caught again. When she came out the following spring she was totally healed. What's more, she now weighed 49lb, caught by my good friend Ben Dowers looking awesome.

The Mere

Jungle Warfare in Search of the Ultimate Prize

The Black Mirror was rightly regarded as the finest carp in the land and the atmospheric venue it lived in, Colnemere, simply accentuated the aura around the fish. The Mere is set right in the heart of bandit country, near Heathrow, and it's protected from view by two other overgrown lakes. Fishing this lake required the right mental attitude. There was no room for luxuries and the punishing walk onto the venue meant that kit had to be kept to an absolute minimum. I remember talking to Steve Allcott about his adventures on there and he told me that when you are ready to fish it you only need to take the things you really need and leave other things hidden back at base camp in the van, parked in the lay by. You couldn't leave things on view either, so this also meant the van had to be cleared out but I still had odd tuitions to do. This was a problem I had to solve, where I could stash my extra kit for work? At that time I was using Farlows, which was just down the road, for my tuitions. I decided to ask Charles, the fishery manger, if I could leave my gear with him and he very kindly let me put it in his office, which was a big weight off my mind. Come September and October there was no way I was working because I had worked so hard over the last eighteen months, saving mega amounts of dollar so I could stay no matter what, without worrying about paying bills. I had set aside three years for this quest, but when I told my good friend Gary Puiy I remember him saying, "Three fcuking years Jim? You'll have him within a year!" I told Gary that this was so different to other targets but he laughed, repeating his prediction; at least he had faith! I was looking at this target rationally because there would be a lot of blood and guts, along with many highs and more lows as I tried to catch the last one I really wanted. Once upon a time, there were three main targets on my hit list: Mary, Two-Tone and The Black Mirror, and when the desire to catch The Black Mirror started to take hold of me, I spoke to Jane, my darling wife, telling her that I really needed to catch this one last target before it was too late. She understood and told me to go for it; I just hoped it wouldn't take over my life. I had to do it or it would eat me up and I would regret not going for the final carp on my hit list, fishing The Mere and if the carp gods allowed it, taking my moment with The Black Mirror.

Colnemere. Enough said.

Dave Mallin told me straight, "Go to the Mere."

After I caught Two-Tone several years back Dave Mallin told me straight, "Jim, go to The Mere," but I didn't listen because my personal life was a mess but that's another story. Things are a lot better now, even though I can be a moody bastard, eh Jane? She has got me on the straight and narrow somehow and I must admit I am a lot happier these days with a balance in my life. Come on Uncle, let's get back on with this chapter.
Over the years I had been lucky enough to see and touch The Black Mirror on two occasions. The first was Dave Mallin's capture when Marky Mark and I popped over to do the pictures for Dave and the second time was when Bill Dawson had his moment, I hoped that our third meeting would be my moment with him, only time would tell but I was fully focused on what I had to do. Steve was fuelling the fire with his stories and giving me tips on how to plan out this mission. My fishing had to change, there was to be no wavering or legging it somewhere for a bite, because this had to be tunnel vision for The Mere only. It was clearly going to be one of the hardest projects I had attempted but at least my journey in search of The Black Mirror was underway.
Just into the New Year of 2009 I drew up a list of essential 'Mere kit'. The first thing was an army Bergen rucksack, which was borrowed off my good friend Jay from Snake Pit, who had left the army. Next was a bivvy, but it needed to be small and lightweight, so I searched on the net and found a pop-up tent, which was unreal. The next thing was a blow-up bed; Steve reckoned this would be better than lugging a bedchair around The

My 'kettle' and stove!

Mere, plus I got a small battery-operated pump too – Christ, I had to have the odd luxury! I ordered a small sleeping bag from Nashy, plus a lightweight mountaineering cooker from Millets with a metal cup that was going to be a kettle, a plastic plate, knives and forks and a couple of containers for coffee and sugar. I also ordered a water purifier from America because Steve had told me it gets very hot and humid at times, so water would be a priority plus Steve had told me that if I ever popped out, not to return empty handed. I planned to take spare water, gas and even food to stash around the lake. My tackle box was very small and I only carried what I needed; a few leads would be hidden around the lake and when it came to packing the rucksack Jay had advised me to have the heavy things at the bottom, which would generally be up to 10kg of bait.

I soon had everything ready so now all I needed to do was get these tuitions I had booked up in March and April done. The magical date was written in my diary, "NO TUITIONS… MERE TIME." I had six weeks ahead of myself fishing four days per week and if things were looking good I would go on a Sunday afternoon. If I had The Black Mirror in the zone then I'd be there for as long as it took. Doing the tuitions was a bit taxing because my mind was always over at The Mere. It didn't help that my good friend Darrell Stile, AKA Darius, was already fishing there and his stories and the excitement in his voice were fuelling the fire within me. God I wanted to be there so much, he was in there midweek and basically had the lake to himself, but to be fair it was still cold. By the third week of April he had started to see them and over the following two mornings he kept moving onto them until he had to leave. Before he left he baited the zone off the Upside Down Tree swim with several squids that he had. This was to be a mistake though, because a bloke walking round on his first session moved in after seeing them show later that morning. Darius had left but matey realised his dream because by the following morning he'd nailed The Black

Mirror, good angling in my book. This was to be a low point because the following week was supposed to be my first trip to The Mere and the start of my adventure. I didn't go, which is something I now regret but hey, you can't always get it right. There were around thirty other fish, give or take one or two, in The Mere; most were commons with a couple that went 40lb plus. I would have gained more knowledge by fishing for these carp but with hindsight I was so focused on The Black Mirror that I thought it would be better to book some more tuitions in and return in June.

Darius had kept on with his mission and soon we arranged to meet in the lay by for my first trip. I knew where it was but hadn't walked it for several years, since I fished The Road Lake and popped over for a walk one mild night in January. I'd sat in The Rathole for an hour or so while the birds sang, which was unusual in itself. I was the only one there but it is a moment I will never forget, simply magical. We met up on June 3rd and, as you can imagine, I was gagging to get on there, 'doing it', as Mad Martyn would say. Before parking up in the lay by I noticed an Environment Agency van outside one of the houses. Me being me, I thought I'd park my car right outside, which meant the Environment Agency could look after Uncle Jim's motor! I'd stripped the van bare, so there was nothing on view apart from a painter's tray and brushes, plus a dustsheet over the floor of the van. This was another ploy that Steve had told me about, and with several tins of paint dotted around the interior of the van I hoped

The tackle box was very small and I only carried what I needed.

I arranged to meet Darius in the lay by.

I'd sat in The Rathole one cold dawn.

We were now in full view of motorists as they drove past.

it would get ignored. I didn't wish to flaunt the fact that this was a carper's van for the bandits to target. Inside the van I had a safe where I hid things, so the only thing I had in the back was my bedchair, which was laid flat with the dustsheet covering it and a few bags of squids underneath.

Darius soon turned up and parked behind my van. I opened the back up and grabbed my Mere gear, which was a rucksack, a three-rod sleeve with buzzers on single bank sticks, a landing net and a small, square Nash cool bag with my food for a couple of days. As you can imagine, I was now on a mission and gagging to start my new adventure. It was starting to get hot and I wasn't dressed for the day, wearing thicker clothing and a Free Spirit coat with a hat and glasses on to protect me from the brambles and thorns. I picked up my rucksack and swung it over my back, Christ it was heavy, but once the straps were done up it felt a lot better. We walked off across the green and were now in full view of motorists as they drove past. We crossed the road and proceeded up the side of Hythe Lagoon, walking along the road like we were on an army exercise. We came to the entrance that took you to the water ski club on the Ski Lake but after around 100 yards on the left we nipped through a hole in the fence and headed along the Lagoon, across grassland until we got to a path that disappeared into old woodland. I was getting excited because I had been here several times with Marky Mark, I was close, I could smell it; that odour given off by weed on the wind is unmistakable. I was now gagging to see the lake as my eyes searched through the

The path disappeared into old woodland.

darkened, enclosed wood, looking for light at the end of the tunnel. Suddenly, I saw that light and as I walked closer I became aware of the birds singing, which gave me a feeling that I was being welcomed. The glow of light got bigger and bigger and took on a bluey haze as I started to see more and more of The Mere.

I was greeted by more than I could ever imagine, as we both walked out onto a grassy area before heading off up the lake. Nothing was said and Darius left me to take in the moment, which I had waited so long for. This had been eighteen months in the planning and I was finally there. The feeling I got from just being there was unreal. I walked down to the water's edge and there was the depth gauge in front of me. I was struck dumb by the place and as I turned to Darius, all I could manage was, "Awesome."

The water was clear, which by all accounts was unusual for that time of the year because The Mere suffers from algae blooms once the water temperatures rise. Long ago Darius and I had decided to fish The Mere together. As we now chatted I told him of my regret about putting off my start after The Black Mirror came out. I had missed so much information and insight. Somewhere out in the lake, surrounded by a vast, overgrown wilderness, were some truly awesome carp and The Black Mirror himself; the excitement was unbelievable and I felt like a racehorse waiting in the stalls.

Suddenly, some hundred and eighty yards or so to my right a movement caught my eye. Darius had seen it too and we agreed that it was a carp show. My head was spinning because I hadn't been there more than ten minutes and the carp gods had given us a sign. We stood there, in silence, watching and hoping that it wasn't a one-off. Several minutes had passed when all of a sudden a dark shape pushed out up to the wrist of its tail. We looked at each other, "That had to be him, it was massive!" Darius uttered. "Let's go," I replied picking up my rods and doubling back some thirty yards to a boggy area, where a narrow path entered the Norfolk reeds. I headed off like a man possessed following the track through this bog, walking on this black, spongy surface. The path forked and Darius said, "Go left," as we then came up onto dry land. Sweat was pissing out of me already and the humidity was intense. A bramble hit me and grabbed hold of the side of my face and I pulled it off, muttering. Darius laughed as I pulled the hood of my coat over my head; I then turned and smiled as I had learnt my first lesson, when on the move keep covered up. As soon as he saw my face Darius said, "I like your war wound Jim!" I touched my face and found my hand covered in blood, that was one nil to The Mere! We carried on and once again it turned dark, as we entered the jungle. Sweat was running down my back and now I realised what Steve meant about water being a priority in here.

The lake was on our left but it was very hard to see any water through the bushes. A track split off to the left and I stopped Darius to ask where it went. He said that it led to Tom's Beach, but there was no way I was stopping to have a look as I wanted to get down to where we had seen the two shows. There were loads of fallen trees in the

There was the depth gauge, just in front of us.

Massive trees blocked the path.

water but no swims and then, a massive, fallen-down willow blocked the path. Passing it meant getting onto your hands and knees and crawling. Just as I was getting up a pain hit me in the hand. I looked down at the palm of my hand to see that a big, black thorn had buried itself deep into me; two nil. There was no way I was stopping to dig that out yet, "Mate, where's the first swim?" I asked, "Not far," he replied. There was more of a defined path now, plus the surroundings had opened up somewhat and I could see the lake. I carried on but kept an eye on the lake, looking for any signs. We had to be near where we had seen them now and Darius said, "Here's the swim, Jim." "What swim?" I replied, because all I could see was a small gap dug into the path, so no hiding for us. The only place we could camp was on the path, so this would have to be done late evening and we'd be packed away early morning. We stood at the front of this tight swim, hoping that those two shows weren't too far to the left. I was just thinking that chest waders would be needed for casting, when another one came up. It was massive, a big, long, black job. We looked at each other and I grabbed my rod. As I made the rod up Darius said, "There's another Jim!" I couldn't believe that I was going to be casting a rig at fish within thirty minutes of arriving! I had already tied the baits on at home so all I had to do was shape the chod, but I was shaking with excitement. Darius then said, "Look mate, another!" "Shhh!" I hissed; I was getting myself into a panic. I pulled my chesties from my rucksack, sat down and pulled them on, looking up just in time to see that long, black job jump right beside a swan! I shouted, "Look at that mate!" The poor swan must have shit itself because he legged it after that. Taking the rod, I waded out into the pond; this was going to be a bastard of a side-cast. I had a willow branch running straight from the margin, so wading further out it would make the cast easier. Suddenly, I felt water run down the inside of my waders. Stepping back, I heard Darius laughing in the background. Blocking it all out, I gave it the big 'un because I needed to punch the lead out a good eighty yards or so. I let rip and watched the chod rig in flight, making sure it had flown back to the top bead. Just before the lead hit the water I feathered it down so it plopped in so I could feel the 3oz lead down onto soft ground, perfect. Five minutes later I had two rigs into position, followed by around 150 salty squids. As soon as Darius saw the wet patch he had his moment of glory and he proceeded to rip the piss. Well, I wasn't biting because I had two rods out on the money, so I was well and truly happy as I sat in the warm, drying out. Now it was his turn and not long after we had four rods rockin' in the zone, surely it was only a matter of time?

The swim seemed to go quiet, which wasn't surprising really. We had set our traps with minimal disturbance so hopefully they would return, unless we had spooked them. About an hour later we were sitting at the front of the swim, looking for a sign, when one stuck its head out in between our rigs. It was looking bang on for a bite and by the evening we had seen several more so the fish were still in residence. The weather started to change and things looked moody; the temperature had dropped dramatically and it didn't feel like June at all. Darius agreed that it looked like rain so we decided to set up camp. Removing the pop-up bivvy from its bag, I dropped it on the floor and bang, my little baby was erect within seconds. Darius liked the look of it, but I was more worried about what he was up to because by the look of things, he was going to be sleeping on the floor on a roll mat. Given that he was unwell at times I thought it wasn't a good idea and I told him, shaking my head as I carried on getting my blow-up bed sorted. Once it was laid out I turned the pump on; Steve had told me that it was an awesome night's sleep. "What the hell's that?" Darius quizzed, all I said was, "This is the edge mate!" The pump whizzed away, inflating my new pride and joy and I got my blow-up pillow out so I had some home comforts. With everything sorted I laid down to try this bed out but as soon as I lay down I knew that I didn't like it at all. When you're a hunter of carp and always on the move you need a good night's kip and there was no way I was suffering on this thing. I told Darius that I was bringing a bedchair next time, which made him think along the same lines. I was constantly planning things for the next session, especially as we had to get a boat in and stashed before we left, just in case one got weeded or for looking about. I thought it was best to fish it from the bank until we knew the score about safe times to boat about though.

Once everything was sorted we took up position watching for more signs until dark. It was a lot colder and there was a fine rain in the air. Moody clouds raced overhead, the scene was set, all we needed now was for the carp to play ball. It was getting dark when suddenly up to our right we heard twigs breaking in the distance. There was

"Mate, where's the first swim?" I asked, "Not far," he replied.

Moody clouds raced overhead, the scene was set.

nowhere to hide because our gear was on the path so we just sat still until a big, ghostly shape appeared from the darkness. This bloke just got bigger and bigger until he was in front of us; it was an old mate from the Yateley days, none other than Mad Martyn in all his glory. Straight away he dished the therapee out, "What the hell are you doing here? This is a man's water!" Knowing Mad very well from the Yateley days I knew it was best to agree with him and I had luck on my side for now, because the light was fading fast and he needed to get set up. I bid him good luck and shook his hand before he marched off into the darkness. I knew he had been fishing The Mere since leaving Yateley and he was sound, unlike a lot of the old Yateley clique, but that's another story, eh boys? We saw the odd fish as the wind got up but now it felt like winter, which meant it was time to cook up some cheeseburgers with sweet chilli sauce to warm me up. The smell of the food was too much for Darius and the next thing I knew, he was hanging around outside. Knowing him of old this meant only one thing; he was now on the ponce and he was well and truly focused, eyeing up one of my burgers. Being the kind-hearted person I am, I offered him one and he nearly bit my hand off as I passed him some of my dinner, followed by a beer. The conditions deteriorated so I decided to head to the airbed. I wished Darius good luck and as soon as I lay down I could tell that I was in for an uncomfortable night. Steve Allcott had told me that sleeping on one was the bollocks; yeah-right mate, it sure was bollocks! There was no way I was sleeping on that next trip but it was heaven compared to what Darius was

A big, ghostly shape appeared in front of us.

sleeping on! I knew it would take several trips before I was happy with my approach to angling on The Mere; at least I had a real good buzz about it all though, which was all that mattered. I was on fish and as I fell asleep my thoughts turned into dreams. Somewhere out there in this special place was some of the best fishing this country could offer, coupled with an awesome stock of carp. All I had to do was enjoy the hunt for The Black Mirror and his mates.

I'd been twisting and turning all night when I was finally woken up by the birds singing their little hearts out. I jumped up and my back was killing me. I could see Darius curled up on the floor and I asked him if he was OK, thankfully there was movement so I asked him if he wanted a coffee. He did, so I popped the metal cup onto the cooker while I walked over to the back of the swim for a leak. I couldn't believe how cold it was for the time of the year and that northerly was blowing even harder now. I climbed back into the tent putting my hands above the stove to warm them up. Darius was on the move so I handed him his cup. After he'd finished my super-charged coffee it was my turn so I popped the cup back on the stove to boil. Until I get that big caffeine hit in the morning I'm a grumpy bastard. With the wind blowing slightly into us we huddled behind the tree for shelter while watching for signs. As we watched we soon got onto the subject of sleeping arrangements for next time. I told him that I couldn't believe that he had carried on sleeping rough like that, because you need a good night's kip to recharge the batteries for the next morning when you're a mobile angler. The luxury of a bedchair was a must for next time and once the bed was in I was going to stash it in the bushes for the next trip instead of lugging it in and out every session. After all those shows the previous day, we were restricted to one 'maybe' out in the waves; that's fishing I guess but at least I had seen some on the first trip. We decided to stay put unless we saw a sign elsewhere, so the first thing to do was to get the house packed up and everything stashed at the back of the swim. With it being unusually cold for June it was time to fire up the stove for some egg, bacon and cheese rolls and yes, as soon as the smell of bacon filled the air our Darius made it quite clear that he was on the prowl again, after Uncle Jim's brekkie. I told him that he was hitting my food allowance for the trip and he just smiled, keeping an eye on the sizzling bacon. At least he was getting better grub than the shit muesli he had brought with him, which was no good for man or beast in these cold conditions. Handing him the bacon roll I said, "Oi oi, next time breakfast is on you son, and not that rabbit food stuff you feed yourself!"

After brekkie we watched for signs and over the next hour we saw two fish but they were now more to the right of the swim, in Darius' water with their heads pointing right. We both thought they were on the move in the cold conditions and we now had fine rain in the wind, blowing slightly at us from right to left. Over in the distance, dark clouds were gathering; it looked like we were going to get wet at some point. We heard a noise coming from the right, along the path, which got louder and louder until Mad Martyn appeared with a big grin on his face. "Got one, a 30lb mirror, have you got a camera with you?" he said. I replied, "Yes," and he asked, "Could you do me some pictures then?" I agreed and after he disappeared I turned to Darius and said, "That's the nicest thing he has ever said to me without him dishing out any sort of therapee!"

We both laughed, I grabbed my camera and we set off in hot pursuit. As we walked along the path, crunching twigs underfoot, I kept looking out through the holes in the brambles to get a look at the water, because it had been a while since I had been there. It was strange really because Marky Mark and I had walked round several times in the past. I got a sense that he was watching over me. Without the tragic events of that cold Wraysbury day he would have been there with us, which was one of the reasons I wanted to fish The Mere. Marky Mark is a big force in my fishing and every carp I catch is for him. Carrying on along the path it was mental how much darker it was up there, but I could see it was getting lighter in front and I could now see Martyn in the distance sorting things out. This was going to be awesome to see one of The Mere's jewels. Martyn got into the water in his chesties and carried his prize up to his sleeping bag whereupon he revealed an awesome, chestnut mirror. As before, when I came over to do the pictures of The Black Mirror, I just had to touch it. It's not every day you get to see one of these special fish that inhabit this wild, windswept pit. This fish was no different and I looked at Darius and whispered, "This is what this place is all about."

After the pictures were done we melted away, leaving Martyn to revel in the moment, because it's not every day you catch a Mere carp. On the way back we knew they'd gone and not long afterwards, the heavens opened up and my Free Spirit coat leaked like a sieve. It rained hard all day as we huddled under a tree and I was soaked through.

I got the sense that Marky Mark was watching over me.

The Mere was teaching me a lesson but this place wasn't going to break me, because I was staying here until the job was done. We decided to plot up early and get the cookers rocking in my tent to try to get dried off. While we were warming up we made firm plans for the next trip. Before we left in the morning we would go and get the boat from the van and get that stashed for when it was needed. By the morning we'd seen nothing more and I wanted to get off early. After the boat was hidden I was on a mission to Colchester to Dragon Supplies for some army-issue waterproof clothing and a rucksack cover, camo of course. I also got an army basher and luggage straps so I could set up this tent in the bushes in better conditions. I knew that it would be a few trips before I was in the groove and I remember Steve telling me the place would make me a better angler.

The second trip was to be a three-day affair and thankfully we were back to summer conditions. The van was parked outside the EA geezer's house. I quickly loaded my rucksack and then set off on the long walk in. Darius couldn't make it that week, as he was feeling under the weather. The sleeping rough had taken its toll on his health and he couldn't afford to get ill with his chronic heart condition. Not a lot happened on that trip, apart from finding them holed up in acres of weed, mostly in the middle of the lake in between The Rathole swim on the far side and The Southwesterly swim. I fished chod rigs in the eelgrass, which isn't the best stuff to fish in and quickly realised that you really needed a boat when fishing these areas. For some reason I didn't get the boat out but this was something I was to change on my next session. The nearest clear swim worth fishing was a swim called The Upside-Down Tree, where matey had caught The Black Mirror from earlier in the year. Knowing they had been using this bank a lot I decided to load this swim up with 10kg for next time, so I had somewhere baited to keep dropping in on if I couldn't find any to fish for. I didn't see any other anglers during that trip and it was great to have the lake to myself; things seemed friendlier at the lake, unlike last time. Over the final two afternoons I noticed somebody using a boat, but he wasn't fishing because he would appear and disappear after a few hours. I rang Martyn about this on the second occasion and he couldn't believe that someone was boating at that time of the day because if he was spotted and reported that meant one thing, a raid, as the authorities have to act on this within 24 hours. The problem was that this twat wasn't fishing, just boating about over the other side, placing markers and lightly baiting on the second day. This meant that if he got spotted I was the only one on, so on the second occasion that he appeared I shouted across to him but he just carried on regardless, the selfish idiot. This made my last night a bit uneasy and after baiting that swim up I left earlier than normal. As I walked out I felt like I was at home though; I had really enjoyed the trip and was gagging to get back because The Mere had really grabbed hold of me.

Over the weekend I filled Darius in on what I had seen and as he was feeling a lot better

Martyn placed it onto his sleeping bag for protection.

It was awesome to see one of The Mere's jewels.

I found them holed up in the weed.

we arranged to meet on the following Tuesday morning. In the end he couldn't make it until Wednesday, so I would have a 24-hour head start. As I got to the depth gauge I looked down the lake for a few minutes and could clearly see the weed at the far end, so I decided to head off to the same area that I had fished the previous week. Around fifteen minutes later I was standing in the same area but I couldn't see anything in the weed, probably due to the cooler conditions. After an hour I headed for the pre-baited swim to make a start, but once the rods were cast out to their silty, smooth spots, I planned to keep an eye further up the bank to my right, especially if that sun came out because I knew they would be back in that weed sunning themselves. Nothing much was seen carp-wise but several tench showed just before dark. I slept like a baby but was up at the crack of dawn when the birds started singing. It was nice and warm in the bag but I had a problem in that I was desperate for a leak, so I dragged myself out. After washing my hands in the lake I covered my face and head in cool water. "Now that should help wake Uncle up," I thought, but to do the job properly I need one of my super-charged coffees. Five minutes later I was pacing the bank, searching for signs of carp. Apart from several red-eyes, nothing showed. It was a clear morning and looked like it was going to be a hot day; surely I would see some? After about an hour watching from my swim I decided it was time to have a trot about. I had one of those feelings and even though it was cold in the bushes it looked red hot outside. I neared

The nearest clear swim was The Upside-Down Tree.

I spotted someone using the boat, in the middle of the day!

the swim Dave Mallin caught The Black Mirror from the second time and carefully walked towards the little cut in the bushes where there was just enough room to poke your rods through. I glanced up and straight away I saw one cruising past to my right. This was my second sighting in three trips, so as you can imagine I was buzzing my head off. Quietly, I hid behind the bush so I would be concealed, knowing the chances were that he wouldn't be on his own. Over the next thirty minutes I saw five more cruise past on the same route from left to right. This area had more weed but nowhere near as much as the next swim down, plus the distance they cruised past was about the same as I was fishing, so they had come past me and I did wonder if they had eaten any of that bait I had put in the previous week.
Not long after I backed off because I hadn't seen anything for a while and headed off up to the high bank for a better look. As I looked out across the water I could see several Mere carp sitting out in the weed, not too far away from where I saw them cruise past. Knowing Darius would be down later in the morning I decided to move up one swim and fish the distance they'd cruised past. Around forty minutes later I had my gear in the swim and with chesties on I could spread my rods out a lot more. I checked the hooks for supreme sharpness and then re-curved the chods before walking out into the crystal-clear water, where I could see myriad bugs swimming around. This place was rammed full of naturals of all types. It wasn't an easy cast because I couldn't walk out too far but I wasn't fishing more than thirty yards out. As the lead plopped in I felt

it down on a tight line and got a lovely, smooth touchdown. The other two went down nice as well. The third spot, which was at about two o'clock, was especially sweet and later on this spot was to be named Two Tits. Why, you may ask yourself? Well, with all the time you have on your own at The Mere, sometimes things can play on your mind! Little did I know that this spot of beauty would become very special for me.

With the traps set in this silty gully, and Mere carp in residence in the weed behind it, I did feel a little confident of a bite, especially in the morning if they followed the same route back in after feeding elsewhere in the pond. Only they knew where to get the best pickings from and this is one of the many reasons why catching a Mere carp is so difficult. As you can imagine I was gagging to see The Black Mirror with my own eyes, surely it would only be a matter of time before I clocked him in his home? All I had to do was locate feeding areas and prime them once they were found. Knowing that this area of the lake had mega form for captures, especially of The Black Mirror, meant that this was going to be the zone I would mainly concentrate on. I had to find the feeding zones though, and with the sea of weed covering a lot of this zone it would only be a matter of time before I used the boat to locate spots in the green stuff. I knew that, thanks to the safety and warmth offered by the weed, they would stay in there a lot. I broke off from watching the lake when I heard something approaching in the distance. I hid as best I could, but this area had been largely cleared by the EA so I thought,

After an hour I headed for the pre-baited swim to make a start.

The distance that they were cruising past was similar to that which I was fishing.

The High Bank was a great vantage point.

I moved one 'swim' up, nearer to the fish I'd seen.

"Fcuk it!" and prepared for the worst. Thankfully, Darius crept into view and put his gear down to catch his breath. I started to fill him in on all I had seen since I had been there and we carried on chatting as the sun rose. Things started to get really humid and after about fifty minutes Darius picked his gear up and said, "I'm going into the swim you just left." I agreed that it would be a good move with the fish coming through that area, plus I told him I had primed it up. With him close we could have a social, mind you he probably had my grub on his mind, bless him; I hoped he had brought enough to share with me this time! As the day went on more carp turned up in front of me, sunning themselves. I could see backs bobbing about and as the hours ticked by, I began to wonder if The Black Mirror was one of those out there in the weed, I bet he was. As the sun dropped low in the sky we had a few beers and watched as the backs disappeared. They were on the move now they were warmed up thoroughly. It was dinnertime and all we had to do was leave the rods in place and be quiet. I was up for an early night after my dawn start but, before I knew it, I was opening my eyes to the dawn chorus again!

I lay there wanting to shut my eyes but I had to get up and be on it, looking for signs of carp. After a nice strong coffee I headed up to see if Darius was about. Sure enough, he was perched on the tree looking out. Neither of us had seen anything, but we both knew that these fish could show at any time in the morning. As we watched, several tench began to roll around Darius' swim, which is better than nowt. I legged it back to my plot to watch my water, plus I was gagging for another super-charged milky coffee. Next thing, I heard a load of twigs breaking as Darius burst into my swim, saying that he had one on and it was weeded up bad. Thankfully, we had the boat stashed further down the bank so we both legged it at high speed to get it and the pump, lifejackets and oar. I had to calm him down a little as he was panicking a bit but I said, "If you're meant to catch it mate, you will. Sorting this boat out is part of it, trust me mate, he'll still be there…" We took it in turns pumping the boat up, then we put our life jackets on and I pushed the boat out. Darius picked the rod up and climbed into the boat while I held onto it, then I placed the landing net in and climbed aboard. I said, "As I row us out there you can reel the slack in and when we get close I'll tell you to stop. If you can't get it moving then slacken off." Once we were over the fish he reeled down with the rod well bent. Nothing moved so he slackened off and it was up to me to get things moving by applying more pressure through hand lining. I decided to change the angle of the boat and pull it the other way. Thankfully, it wasn't windy so I could focus on the job in hand and inch-by-inch I gained some line until I could feel movement on the other end. I told him the good news and suddenly all hell broke loose as a carp bolted from his weedy sanctuary at high speed. I held on for a second, telling Darius to get ready and when I let go as he commenced battle with his first Mere carp. I bet he was shitting himself big time because we didn't know what he was attached to. We were now being towed along and he kept the fish on a short lead, with me watching from the front of the boat with my glasses on. I stared hard into the water but it was out of sight. Darius kept asking me which one it was and all I said was "Don't worry." He kept it out of the weed even though he must have been crapping himself playing a Mere carp, because I tell you what, I would have been! Suddenly there was a flash of gold and I saw a common twisting and turning in the clear water. I told him it was a common and he gained more line, bringing the leadcore leader clear of the surface. This carp was nearly beaten and massive, oily swirls appeared on the surface. I lowered the net ready and watched as the fish made his last bid for freedom. Darius moved in the boat to try to see the fish but there was no way he could unless he stood up. In front of me a head broke the surface, gulping air, and Darius led the fish towards the net. He went in first time and I lifted the net as he slackened off and shouted, "Yesss!" Carefully, he moved towards me at the front of the boat, looking over my shoulders to get a better glimpse of his prize. He was so excited; I could hear it in his voice. This was one of those moments we were waiting for while fishing this very demanding lake. It isn't every day you bag a Mere carp! We chatted excitedly as we drifted in the boat, I was so happy for him. I slid my hands down the fish's side and gently removed the hook. It was mad touching him because this carp had been with all of the lake's jewels. That moment when I touched him will stay with me forever, as it sent shivers down my spine. After that I handed Darius the net handle so I could row back to the swim.

All I could think about was they had eaten all that bait I had put in, which is a good thing because this told me they were on the bait. Once we were back on land Darius shot off while I looked after the common. The fish just laid in the net all quiet, this was

Sure enough, Darius was up, watching.

unreal. Darius returned and I left him with the net and legged it off to my swim for the camera. Back at the swim it was time for him to have his little cuddle. He laid the common down on his sleeping bag and it was an incredible moment as he revealed his prize. The fish tensed up and I could hear Darius whispering to him. I was so excited to be sharing that moment with him. He looked up and said, "What do you think he weighs?" With no scales at the lake, I said, "22lb to 24lb", which Darius agreed with. He picked the fish up for a few quick trophy shots as I clicked away, then he walked over to the lake with the net to return him. I stood back and watched so Darius could have his moment then the common was gone and I heard him whisper, "See ya mate." I shook his hand and said, "Well done mate, well deserved." After a few minutes I thought I would leave him to it to revel in the capture and as I walked off I turned and said, "I'll be back soon for brekkie!" He laughed, saying, "Cheers mate."

When I got back to my swim I could clearly see movement out in the weed, which told me they were back to sun themselves and digest what they had feasted on. I had other things on my mind; I needed to have a look out in the weed. I planned to use the boat for a reconnaissance mission before we left because I knew there had to be clear spots out there in the sea of weed. After hiding the boat we decided that the following evening would be the time to venture out into their world and investigate things more closely. Trust me, I was gagging to get out there, but I would do it at the right times instead of blatantly drawing attention while others were angling. As you

With no scales at the lake, I said, "22lb to 24lb."

could imagine we had a few beers after dinner to toast Daruis' capture, plus the Mere jewels were in attendance, bobbing around in the weed in the last rays of the evening sun. It was awesome just being there, let alone fishing for the Holy Grail. The thought of doing battle with one of these carp excited me, but the main target was of course The Black Mirror and I was yet to even see him. However, I was sure I had seen him show at least once and with the extreme clarity of the water at the time, I was gagging to get out there in the boat and try and find him because I'm a master of finding areas and sneaking up on carp in the boat. You just can't beat watching them from the boat and tomorrow evening we were going out there into their world to gain more knowledge and to see if they were up to no good out in the sea of weed.

After dark we saw several fish show out in front of me but well out in the weed, this told me one thing; they were now on the move in search for food. I had left my baits untouched because the meshed hook baits would still be intact and if I brought them in it would only be to cast them back to the same spots. I am a great believer of leaving rigs in position as long as the carp are still about. If it feels right and I see fizzing or showing fish in the zone, I may sometimes top the swim up with some more bait. This seems to work more on tough, demanding venues because the carp I fish for mostly aren't stupid. This little ruse has paid off big time over the years, but it takes a lot of confidence to leave rigs out there without touching them for several days. Walking

back to my plot through the jungle in this darkness was a nightmare but there was no way I was turning my headtorch on. I made sure my hoodie was over my head so I wouldn't get caught by the brambles that were ready to cut you up to hell. I made it back in one piece and before I jumped in the bag for some much-needed sleep, I looked out over the lake and wondered what was in store for us when we ventured out in the boat the following evening; there was no way I was going out in the morning, bang on bite time when Darius had nailed one. Once I was in the bag it didn't take long before I was pushing out the zeds; being up at the crack of dawn and permanently on the go, coupled with continued sleep deprivation leaves you feeling like shit. When you're a mobile, hunting angler this is one of the things you have to put up with but thankfully this only happens a few times a year. You have to fight through it sometimes in the hunt for success and these sacrifices put some anglers in a different league.
All too soon the birds were singing but I was destroyed and I knew that Darius would be up and looking, so I turned over and sneaked some more zeds in, which was a bit naughty but fishing together meant that we could take it in turns to get up when needed. A little while later I jolted awake and my head was buzzing from having too much sleep. I sat up on the edge of the bedchair and turned the stove on for a cuppa. While I waited for that to boil I looked through the brambles thinking, "That's bright." Turning the mobile on I now realised why I felt so rough, it was 9am! I wasn't happy

He whispered, "See ya mate."

with the fact I had slept in that long but my body must have needed it. With the cup boiling it was time to get myself back into the land of the living. I stood up and carefully made way to the front of the swim to get a better look and sure enough several backs were clearly visible out in the weed already; the evening recce couldn't come quick enough for me. I legged it down the bank to find out what I had missed and Darius dished out the therapee! Sleeping in was very unusual for me and he took advantage, saying I came up to see you and you were snoring like a stuck pig. Being the therapee master I had to take it like a man and I let him have his moment of glory! After that the conversation turned to, "What you seen? What you know? What you had?" He laughed, "Naff all Jim, just a few tench." I told him that they were in the weed in front of me and he informed me that they had been there since first light, so that meant the fcukers had stayed in the weed all night for a change. We were like two kids that day, speculating, hoping we might find something out there in the vastness of the green stuff that festooned this shallower area of the lake. We planned to go out around 7pm, which would be a much better time to avoid being seen. The lake is a European SSSI and it carried a £2000 price tag if you were caught out in the boat. Matey had been back out in the boat since our encounter and Mad Martyn AKA 'The Mere Guardian' had shouted at him several times before marching round there and giving him what for. At least after that he knew there was a code of practice to abide by and trust me we were sticking to it because if you crossed the Mad One, anything could happen!
When the time came we got the boat from its stash place and put it in the swim, ready for the adventure out into the unknown. At 6:45pm it was getting too much for us so we thought, "Fcuk it, let's get out there and see if our hunch was right," and they had indeed cleared little zones in this football pitch of weed. Darius sat in the back of the boat and would only stand up once things were spotted because having two people standing up in a small boat was a bit dodgy. I pushed the boat out and gently rowed out into the lake; visibility still being so good, which was very unusual for this time of the year because this lake suffers really bad algae blooms. It seemed that this was indeed a rare opportunity to see into this lake. Straight away I headed to the right of my swim to have a look along this vast network of snags, because with the sun starting to set to the left of us there could be a chance we could spot one in there. Darius was looking off the side of the boat and this area looked awesome and interested me greatly because of the gully that ran along this bank. The lake bed then rose up slightly towards the weed and we could see the odd gravel hump. The other thing that took my interest was the black, silty bottom, which was covered in this sort of cress-like weed, which interested both of us, because Darius would stand up and have a look when we passed over it. This was an awesome learning curve but I had already told myself there was no way I would be getting into placing my baits if I could cast them from the bank. We then ventured out further into the pond to have a look in the green stuff. Surely they must have some little areas out there they favoured because the weed held everything, from natural food items to sanctuary. In hindsight this is something we should have done the week before but never mind, we were out there looking now. No carp were seen

The site was a SSSI and carried a £2000 fine if you were caught out in a boat.

from the boat but suddenly, twenty yards in front of me something took my attention and I pointed it out to Darius. It was a tiny area in the weed but from the bank there was no way you would see it. Was this the jackpot we were looking for? Sure enough, as we got closer it was looking good and when I got over the spot I looked in. It was totally clear right to the bottom but looking more closely in the clearer water I could see a cleaned-off glowing spot. Telling Darius the good news, I reversed the boat so he could have a look. While doing this I noticed another two of these areas nearer to The Rathole. I steered us over to have a look and even before I got to them, I knew these were also going to be cleared-off feeding spots, but these two were a lot bigger. I was buzzing because I had something to work on now and I could fish for them in the sea of weed they were holed up in. The trouble was that these spots needed loading up but the bait was in the van. Funnily enough, we continued to look for more spots but none were to be found.

With the light starting to fade, I marked the areas with lumps of surface weed so we could find them in the dark. We then paddled Hawaii Five-0 style down the lake to the depth gauge, stashed the boat to the right in the bushes and legged it to the van for a 20kg hit of 15mm and 20mm squids. While I was there I grabbed a couple of beers because this was a right mission and I think we deserved it for our efforts. We did make it back to the zone before dark and I decided to break some of the baits up but it was taking too long by hand so I chucked several at a time into my mouth and

When the time came, we got the boat from its stash place.

Had they cleared little zones in the weed?

crunched them up. Darius was taking the piss because I ended up spitting them over the spot, trying not to laugh as he dished me the therapee. Despite nearly choking at one point I carried on relentlessly chewing and splitting more out like a machine. After about ten minutes of forcing squids into my gob I got jaw ache, which got so painful that I stopped chewing, fearing I was going to get lock-jaw. Darius was rolling about in the back of the boat having totally lost the plot. With the whole twenty kilos in I had a look; the spot was totally covered and I did wonder if I had overdone it. Time would tell and plans were made to get back late Sunday evening. Knowing that all this disturbance had probably ruined our chances, we made plans for an early morning exit and by the time we got back to the swims it was dark. I dropped Darius off and boated back across to the Rathole swim, where I deflated the boat and stashed it in the bushes for Sunday's mission. Forty minutes later I was back at the swim. We chatted over a beer about what we had found and it turned out that Darius probably couldn't make next week, as he had a few things on, so it looked like I was going to be hitting this zone myself. I was up really early and, once my head was sorted, I packed up because I wanted to get home and get everything sorted for the next trip as I had promised to take Jane out for a meal. Before I legged it out I said goodbye to Darius and this time I was going out at the other end, along Hythe Lagoon, because I wanted to stash the bedchair near to The Rathole ready for Sunday. Walking out this end was

I ventured further out into the green stuff.

With time running out, we needed to get bait out before dark.

a lot longer but it was a lot easier because I didn't have to climb over and under fallen trees or fight through the jungle that wanted to rip you to shreds. All I thought about on the long journey home was those spots and I wondered if I had fcuked it by over-baiting, only time would tell. Roll on Sunday! In the meantime I had booked us into a very expensive seafood restaurant in Great Yarmouth and, as you can imagine we hit the place hard and lived it up like lords, spending a fortune. It makes me laugh when I get stick for supposedly 'only having fishing in my life'!

Late Sunday afternoon saw me fighting to get through the traffic. Lowestoft is the most easterly point in the country, which makes getting anywhere a nightmare, because the nearest motorway is 40 to 50 miles, whichever way I want to go. Therefore, patience is needed when you want to get anywhere, which is why I much prefer going in the early hours. Once on the motorway you can normally put the foot down but I knew I was in for some therapee time on the M25 that day. I was stuck in savage traffic crawling along at a snail's pace, which peed me off because I was gagging to get back to the pond and check those baited areas. Time was getting on and when I finally arrived at the lay by and parked the van outside the EA bloke's house, it had taken me an extra hour to get there. This meant I would have to be on a mission to get in and sorted before dark. It had been a very hot day and as soon as I got outside the van the humidity hit me hard because I'd had the air con on full blast all the way there. The walk in was going to be a sweaty affair, especially given that I had been partying the night before! Once

I was loaded up I marched off down the path towards the river. I crossed the road, climbed over the stile and trudged down the path with the river on my left and Hythe Lagoon on my right. As you would expect, I kept my eyes on the lake for any signs. I had walked this way several years back but not since I had been fishing The Mere and it sure was a much longer walk in. It was a good 15 minutes before I got to the end but this time there was no grief fighting my way in and I only had a short distance to fight my way up to The Rathole. Sweat was pouring off me and as soon as I got into the swim I crawled under a bush, just dumped everything on the ground, stripped off into shorts and a T-shirt and took on some much-needed water.

Next thing was to get the boat from its hiding place and get the thing pumped up ASAP. I had fun pumping the thing up and I was soon gasping for air in this hot, dry heat; it was like doing a workout in poxy Thailand! Several minutes later the job was done and it was time to get the rods ready as light levels were dropping fast. All this time I was wondering if the bait was still out there; I thought it would be. Looking out I could see the piles of weed that marked the three spots and while I was tying on the first bait curiosity got the better of me and I decided to go and have a little look. I put the life jacket on and pushed the boat down the bank. Grabbing the oar I made my way down through the foliage, stinging my legs to hell on the nettles. Before jumping into the boat I bashed them down with the oar. Looking down on the first spot I could see that all the bait was gone; "No fcuking way," I thought to myself. I checked the others and all three spots were gone; the greedy fcukers had cleared 20kg of squids in two days. With a good chance of a visit from the fish I knew I had to act fast to get rigs out on the three spots especially as they had to be boated and placed by hand. Back on dry land I went straight to work. The rigs were baited, so all that was left for me to do was put the aggressive curve in the filament. The rods were placed on the buzzers with the clutch slackened so all I had to do was put the lead in my mouth and tow it out to the spot. With three ready to go I quickly chewed some squids up and it wasn't long until my jaw was aching. Thankfully, I only needed about a kilo of crumb because I was after a bite and the chances they would return seemed high. It was getting dark and with three rigs to drop things were going to be tight and it didn't help that I couldn't see twelve feet down over the first clear spot. I positioned the boat to the back edge of the spot, then lowered the rig down and watched the pop-up disappear from view. The lead touched down and I let the leadcore go so the rig would fall away from me and set itself on the bottom. Before leaving I dropped a handful of crumb over the spot, along with 50 free offerings. Before I left the area I put the oar alongside the line that was running across the weed and pushed down hard, this put a deep V in the weed, giving the line a channel to drop into. I was on a mission and by dark I had three rigs on the money and as I rowed back I was buzzing, full of anticipation for the night ahead. Once I was back on dry land I pulled the boat out and dragged it to the back of the swim. All I had to do now was fuzz the fourth rod out twenty yards to the left, just off the edge of the weed in a silty gully. I got a lovely soft drop on that one too and while gently sinking the line I looked out over the zone. The scene was set, there was nothing

else I could do now apart from sit back and pray to the carp gods.
The humidity was unreal, it was like being in a jungle in the tropics but I'd saved the best 'til last; I had several beers in my rucksack chilling in between two 5kg bags of frozen bait! My mouth was dry and I'd been fighting the urge to open one until I was sorted but when I grabbed the first can it was still ice cold. My mouth was dry and trust me, it didn't even touch the sides as I downed a Kroney in one.
While I was enjoying the other ice cold beer I received several bleeps on the right-hand rod, which made me jump. "Oi oi," I thought, "I bet Mr Carp's about." Over the next hour or so the liners got more intense, making me run for the rod a couple of times. I didn't know what to make of these occurrences on all the three rods that were towed out and at one point I was standing by the rods, watching to see if the bats were giving me therapee or whether too much beer was making me hear things. It got so intense that in the end it dawned on me what was happening; they were spawning. I decided to reel them in and let them get on with it and after I reeled in and climbed into the bag, all I could think about was how close I had been to them. If I had stayed over the weekend I would have probably caught but in hindsight, I did what I thought was right; at least I knew they had feasted on the bait, which was a big confidence boost because I knew they had eaten it. As you can imagine, I was up at first light sitting on the edge of the bed, trying to get my eyes to focus. I could see several backs sitting out

I looked over the zone; the scene was set.

in the weed not thirty yards out and there was ripped-up weed in the margin, so they had indeed spawned in the night. Putting the kettle on, I was unsure what to do next but deep down I knew I had to go and leave them to chill out. I quickly realised that this was the ideal opportunity to go out and have a look at them, up close and personal. While I sat there drinking my coffee I noticed a big fish with a black back and suddenly he rose slightly higher helping me to ID him thanks to the famous cropped top tail lobe. There, out in front of me, was my main target The Black Mirror. He was sitting no more than thirty yards in front of my swim and I watched him intently while I finished my coffee. There was no way I was going to miss the chance to get a good look at what was probably the best carp in the land. This was going to be a moment I would never forget.

I was shaking with excitement as I lowered the boat into the water; I knew this would almost feel like catching. My mind was racing at the thought of seeing him in his natural environment and before I pushed out I made sure I was standing up in a comfortable position because any sudden movements could ruin a special moment in time. I edged out over the water and slowly made my way to my target, watching his every move. Apart from the odd flick of his tail and slight bobbing in the water, he stayed in exactly the same spot. A dragonfly landed on my nose, which nearly gave the game away, as it made me jump but I was too focused to mess this opportunity up. I quietly brushed him off me, thinking to myself that I must try harder and I was now talking to myself as I edged ever closer to this carp that was growing in size. Suddenly, he dipped and I immediately stopped, he'd sensed something and I was no more than fifteen feet from him! Luckily, there was no wind and I gently slid the oar into the weed to stop the boat making any movement. It was an unbelievable atmosphere as I waited and hoping that he hadn't done the off. After about two minutes his back broke the surface again; I whispered "Sweet" to myself and smiled. I decided to stay still for a while and let him settle down before I tried to get closer. He turned round and I got the feeling that I was being looked at; it was mental, like a standoff at the OK Corral. I watched his gills flare and I could see his lips moving. He then did something that I wasn't expecting; he edged towards me! This was unreal, all I could think about was keeping still as he dropped down a couple of feet and then swam alongside the boat not four feet away. This moment blew my mind and he swam round the whole boat without a care in the world, checking me out. I could see every mark on him and I got eye contact. He looked awesome in the water; words can't describe this special moment. I whispered "See you soon mate," as he swam off into the weed, pretty much returning to the same spot to bask in the sun. I decided to back off out of respect and left him in peace to chill out. This fish had given me an everlasting memory that I will treasure to my dying day. What else could I do now but go and sit down, drink a coffee and relive the encounter?

After several hours spent watching him and his mates with their backs out I decided it was best to leave them to it. Before I left I baited the three spots for next time and while I was packing up Mad Martyn popped in on one of his regular walk-rounds. While I was packing up the Vango tent I told him what I had seen and things soon turned into therapee, as I had forgotten to fold the tent up. He started filming me on his phone, saying, "Here we are on The Mere with Jim Shelley trying to pack away a Vango tent!" This wasn't good because now he had video footage of me struggling to pack this fcuking thing away. I looked up totally shell-shocked because he had got me bang to rights and I said, "Fcuk off!" What else could I say? One of the bramble hangers then stuck to the side off my face and I ripped it off, which wasn't good as the blood started to run down my face, leaving Mad peeing himself laughing. With the tent packed I walked down to the water's edge and cleaned the blood off my face. Suddenly, we heard someone approaching and a geezer popped out of the bushes wearing a white T-shirt, which is a bit bizarre at The Mere. Mad and I looked at each other in disbelief, our faces must have been a picture! I noticed that he was holding something and I don't think we were quite sure what to expect next when he said, "Hi, do you know where The Mere is?" Mad walked towards him and I followed closely behind. This geezer was holding a map and we pointed off along the bank that just happened to be the worst bank to walk along because it was so overgrown! We thought it fitting that he found out what walking the banks of The Mere without the proper clobber was like! He disappeared into this savage undergrowth and several times we heard him shout. We were rolling around on the bank pissing ourselves and we later heard that he was spotted at the far end of the pond with blood running down his arms and his nice white top stained red. I think we taught him a lesson and we never saw him again… I wonder why?

After Mad departed I went out to bait up and noticed that the water was murky. On closer inspection the dreaded algae bloom was starting so I knew things were going to get worse because every year, usually before that point, the lake suffers badly from it. With mega-hot temperatures forecast for a while I knew the bloom would only thicken. Once this happens the lake shuts up big time and I'm not going to dwell on the next few long weeks because things got extremely tough. I carried on relentlessly in my pursuit in sweltering conditions but it proved hard to keep myself hydrated and motivated. They were truly testing times and, to cap it all off, no matter how hard and long I looked, no carp were seen, which was mentally hard tough for a hunter like me! Because of this, I decided to bait and fish The Rathole because this swim had mega form for The Black Mirror. Plus, I had also seen him there now, so a plan was hatched to fish this swim on the baited zones unless I saw something carpy to move onto. After several weeks of nothingness, my relentless pursuit had me questioning my own sanity but I carried on in the hope of one day realising my dream. It wasn't all bad during this time though, because I got a call from the Angler's Mail confirming that I had won Carp Angler of the Year for a second time. More importantly, Uncle Jim had won £5000 from Nashy who sponsored the competition at the time. I was straight on the phone to Jane, telling her to book somewhere up hot for August. Ten days in Mexico were booked up and more brownie points came my way; we both needed a break away from it all and we partied it to the max on tequila slammers, laying in the

The Vango tent that Martyn took the piss out of!

sun recharging the batteries and getting a nice suntan (until I got burnt and had to spend a few days covered up!). I decided to leave my phones in the car because there was no way I wanted to know if he came out while I was away because that would have pee'd me off. So, when we landed back in the UK I turned my mobiles on and was fully expecting a text saying that he had been out. I didn't have any Mere-related texts apart from two from Mad saying, "You fcuk off when it's shit and now you arrive back and the vis has improved, you timed that break just right," and one from Steve Allcott confirming that The Black Mirror hadn't been out. It looked like I had got away with it and, as you can imagine, I was gagging to get back. It seemed like ages since I had been there and, by the sound of Mad's text, things were going to get better in September. I had to be fully focused in this prime month because The Black Mirror was known to slip up around the harvest moon and equinox.

The clarity had gone again on my return, so it was back to fishing blind on the baited zone out from The Rathole. Mad later told me that the area had been left alone, which I expected because, apart from me, no-one had been fishing it. Now there were several anglers having a go because it was common knowledge that September was the month. I did see one show but it was down at the other end, near the safe zone that they liked to lay up in. They were generally left alone apart from people casting or towing up to the area from Tom's Beach. I didn't do this because it was savage, hit-and-hold snag

The Rathole certainly had form for the Black Mirror.

Ten days in Mexico were booked. I just hoped that it wouldn't come out.

fishing and the chance of a loss or worse, a fish getting snagged up, was too much for me. An angler who shall remain nameless had several fish from there after I left though and something was to happen in this bush the following year, culminating in The Black Mirror's last capture before the kill. A fish-at-any-cost merchant fished in their safe area, in the Rainbow-Lake style that he is known for. The Black Mirror was dragged out on savage tackle and the pictures were later doctored to make it look better because the great fish was pale and washed out from the stress of being dragged out of its safe area. Sometimes a line has to be drawn and respect has to be shown. Every other Mere angler had respected this area until then but hey, I suppose five years on there had taken its toll.

Things were to go from bad to worse for me because I tore a ligament getting out of the boat and on the next session the lake was to get even busier. Pecky had started over there a few weeks earlier and we'd had several socials but on arriving on this next session, which was around the harvest moon, Pecky and I were met with an incredible nineteen anglers on! We both stood there in disbelief and while I was talking to Mad on the phone, I saw a bait boat going out, which did me in big time. This was The Mere, not a circuit water. People had heard about the captures at this end of the lake and every nook and cranny was taken. I turned to Pecky and said, "Fcuk this for a game of soldiers." Because of my damaged knee, I had boated across Hythe Lagoon and parked the boat behind the Canopy swim. Suddenly, someone appeared and I realised it was The Schoolteacher. As soon as he saw me he questioned me about the boat and I played dumb, but this character thought he owned the lake because he had fished there years ago. He backed off from where he came and I took this as a sign from the carp gods. I explained to Pecky who Schoolteacher was and told him that the twat would probably report the angling, making The Mere a target for a possible EA raid. As I boated off I saw him watching me through the bushes like a dirty old man and I shouted, "YOU! YOU! YOU!" which echoed across the lake.

As you now know, I ended up over at the Snake Pit and I was praying that he didn't come out while I was away and that the angling pressure would die down. We had since worked out why it was so busy over there; it was all down to a reference in a book about the 7th of September. The author had caught The Black Mirror but it had also been out on that date several times over the years. After two trips over the Snake and catching my target, I shot straight back to The Mere for the double. I felt that I needed to catch two more target fish for this book before the line-up was complete. Things were a hell of a lot quieter on my next trip, but more importantly The Black Mirror hadn't succumbed either, so everything was to play for. All I needed to do was catch him, so I decided to get my arse back into The Rathole, on the big baited area. After all the pressure down at the other end I thought that they'd be running scared now and The Rathole had to be the logical place they would turn up next. With the area free of eel grass I could now chod fish, casting from the bank and spread baiting.

After getting the rods out, it was time for sleep.

Given the continued baiting and the swim's form for The Black Mirror, surely it was only a matter of time?

After I got the rods out it was time to catch up on some sleep, but in the hot and sunny conditions I woke up feeling awful. I went down to the edge to splash my head with water and noticed that the visibility was slightly better; I could now see several feet into it. This was a good sign and I knew deep down that it would only be a matter of time before he would make an appearance. These developments fired me up and I knew I was on borrowed time. I had to work hard and be on it 100%, standing there scanning the water for any signs. I had an awesome view watching the lake while drinking a cold beer. For a change, I decided to sit up for a while to see if I could hear anything show. I had surface doubts about their location, but deep down I knew I couldn't be in a better position, with nothing to go on. Suddenly, I heard one bosh out, well over towards the other side somewhere. Knowing The Rathole was a good swim to be in for a night time or early morning bite, I decided to stay put for the minute. Moving swims was easy with the boat and things were looking promising for a change. Over the next two hours I heard several more show in the same area. I watched the angle of the ripples, as they rolled in by the moonlight; this was the moment I had been waiting for so long. I was buzzing with excitement because I had a really good chance of a bite but in the end I dived into the bag for some sleep, dreaming of a Mere carp. Upon waking, I looked at my rods with that sickening feeling that comes with a blank night. With the cup on the stove for a coffee, I scanned the water for any signs and by midmorning nothing had shown. Nothing gave its presence away for the rest of the day and once again I decided to stay put and leave the rods untouched. I did put some more bait out over the zone just in case I'd been tucked up by the carp.

After dinner I sat up again and not long after dark the ripples started to roll in again. This time I hadn't heard anything though, which meant they were showing more subtly. After another set of ripples rolled in I decided to go and investigate to try to pinpoint exactly where they were. I grabbed my life jacket and set off quietly along the edge, well away from my swim, before crossing the lake towards the Upside down Tree swim. Once I was there, I climbed out and gently pulled the boat into the swim. I made my way through the undergrowth trying not to make too much noise while looking for the swim in which Mallin had caught him for the second time, round near the Southwesterly swim. As I neared the edge ripples were lapping the bank and not long after I saw one stick his head out and go over in the moonlight. This was awesome and several more were seen until something massive jumped clear, making me jump! By the sound of it, it was probably The Black Mirror. Knowing that when he showed he was very catchable, I decided to stay put for the remainder of my session. Hopefully I had a chance of a visit in the night, or early morning. As I rowed back I thought it better to keep this info to myself, only telling Steve Allcott anything from now on and he agreed I was in prime position in The Rathole. Normally I would have moved straight away and while I was packing up the next day I knew I had probably made a bad decision, given the info in front of me. This was now eating me up and I regretted

I knew that I couldn't miss a thing now.

not acting on it but you can't get it right all of the time. To rub salt into the wound I now had Beadle texting me therapee saying, "How many have you caught then?" I saw red but tried not to bite and instead texted Mad Martyn and said, "Let's do a combined double hit text assault." He was well up for it, so two hardcore therapists started upon a massive texting hit, which was XXX rated and ran into hundreds of abusive texts. In the end Beadle rang me to complain and, seizing my chance, I told him I was here for one bite only. All I had to do now was catch him, easier said than done but if anyone could Uncle could. On the long journey home my mind was racing, I knew I was close and I was kicking myself for not acting on it. I made the decision to fish The Mere how I would usually fish. The trouble was, it was my last trip because we had a two-week holiday booked up in Egypt. This meant I only had six days fishing the following week, but thankfully I could fish around the equinox, so it was going to be do or die the next week.

All weekend I was shitting myself because every time the phone rang I was worried it was going to be bad news. However, Sunday came and no news was good news, so I loaded the van and headed off full of confidence with the knowledge I had gained last trip. This time I was going to wait until as late as possible before setting up. After loading the boat and hiding it under the overhangs in the corner of Hythe Lagoon, I quickly drove the van down to the lay by and with the rods on my shoulder, I quickly legged it back to my gear, which was only a couple of minutes' walk from the van. Now it was time to get on with it and I jumped into the boat and headed off to an area behind the Canopy swim where the boat could be stashed, leaving me free to set off and look for Mere carp. I had a feeling that they would be sunning themselves in the snags to the right where I had been watching them show because the sun hits this area in the afternoon. There was someone asleep in the Canopy but by the time I'd got round to the swim I'd seen no one else, a bit different from a couple of weeks back. I was sweating buckets because we were having an Indian summer and I knew the carp would be somewhere lapping this up before winter arrived. Walking into the swim I noticed it was even clearer now and the wind was blowing a northerly right to left. I was getting a good vibe in there but that was probably because of the sightings the previous week. I still had to try and find them though, and I looked among the twisted sets of snags that lined that bank, but nothing was seen. I did get a whiff of carp as I got towards the end of the snags, close to a little sandy spot that I knew was right in the edge. I looked down the path and decided not to bother checking it because I had checked this spot many a time without seeing anything. Something told me to look though, and as I neared the edge the water over this very shallow spot was cloudy. As I peered in a ghostly shape appeared. I froze on the spot and watched this mid-thirty common hang mid-water. I watched his mouth moving, sifting out the

About to set sail on Hythe.

bits he wanted. This taught me another lesson; not to take things for granted because this could have cost me big time. Thankfully it hadn't though, and suddenly, another common appeared from the left. That was it, I had seen enough; it was now clear that my hunch had paid off, all I needed to do now was to get my gear over, which is easier said than done!

I didn't hang about getting back to the boat; I was now on a mission and boated up to the back of The Rathole. Pulling in behind the swim, I went straight to work unloading the boat and walking it to the front of The Rathole. I dragged the boat across the narrow causeway and slid it down the bank and into The Mere before reloading it. This seemed to take no time at all and I climbed in the boat and set off to the right, shooting up the margin several hundred yards before I started to cross the lake to get the other side. I didn't want to boat anywhere near them and risk spooking them off. Once I got down there I slowly rowed the boat to the margin, near to where I wanted to fish. All I had to do now was quietly walk my gear down to the swim. Things seemed to be coming together and I must admit I felt very close for a change. With the rods ready to rock all I had to do now was re-curve the rigs and get everything 100% on the money before dark. With three rods ready, I slipped into my chesties because there was no way I was casting two of the rigs down to the right from the bank. I grabbed a rod and quietly slid into the margin; it was deeper close in here so the cast was still

I looked down the path and decided not to check the spot.

I was on a mission and boated up to the back of The Rathole.

going to be tricky in the tight swim. After a couple of attempts the rig touched down soft, ten yards off the side of the snag to the right of the Two Tits spot. I put the second rig on the Two Tits, with the third going straight out in front no more than thirty yards out. All were fishing in the silty gully that ran close in along this margin, shallowing slightly near the snags. After the rods were sorted and the bobbins clipped on I spread around a 150 salty squids around each rod. Things were going bang on and with the traps set I turned the alarms on before getting out of the water. Now it was time to get the house set up and chill out. Jane had made me smoked salmon, thinly sliced red onion and chillies with olive oil and vinaigrette so I sat back and ate, feeling well happy with myself and mega confident of a take because these fish had been here for at least a week and that meant they were here for a reason. While I was tucking into dinner I remembered that I had a bottle of white wine chilling between two bags of frozen squids in my rucksack. Unscrewing the bottle top I took a swig of this ice-cold wine and, as I swallowed it, I raised the bottle to the lake and carried on eating dinner, taking in the moment. There was nothing more I could do; it was up to the Mere carp to make my day. With the light levels fading fast, I sat up watching from the bedchair, wondering if I was going to see any shows after dark like before.

All I saw were bats, fluttering around the bushes, collecting the blood suckers for supper. Hopefully that would stop a few drilling the hell out of me. Over time you got used to these vampires of the night but I slapped the back of my neck, as I felt that

I shot up the margin and then crossed the Mere.

Once I got close, I unloaded the boat and walked the gear to the swim.

horrible sensation of something being thrust into my body. I wasn't having any more of this, so I beat a hasty retreat to the tent. Because the fish were so close I didn't want to risk making any noise, so I climbed into the bag for some sleep. The next thing I knew, it was daylight and the birds were singing, which just happened to be my alarm call but this time I turned my back on the water, deciding sleep was more important for a change. Sometime later something woke me and I jumped up thinking wondering what time it was. Turning the phone on I found that it was 8am. "I must have needed that," I thought. With the cup nearly boiling I heard someone approaching and Pecky appeared. While I drunk my coffee he told me that he had seen several shows over the other side in front of Snag Point. I told him that I thought it was all show and no go over there, as Darius and I had chased them over there several times after they'd showed over the deep water. Darrell soon legged it back to his swim and with this info he'd given me I did start to wonder if they'd done the off. I told myself to stay put until the afternoon, because they'd been visiting this area on and off for a while.

By 10am my head was telling me to go and have a look down the margin where I had seen them yesterday. All was quiet but, as I was walking back to my plot, I heard a bleep, which then turned into a screamer! As I started to run back to the swim it stopped but as I approached the swim there was another bleep. Everything was tight on the right-hand-middle rod. I pulled into something that was solid, probably in weed I thought. Pecky appeared on the horizon and shouted, "Are you in Jim?" I shouted back that

I thought so and with the rod bent right over on maximum pressure I felt it quiver. At this point I knew there was a carp on the other end! Shitting myself, I tried to get things moving but couldn't. All I could hear was Pecky shouting and legging it round; by the look of it he was motoring through the undergrowth. I decided to put the rod down on the rest and get the boat from its hiding place. All sorts of things were going through my head; I needed this carp in my net! I frantically tried to get my waders on, which seemed to take ages and all the time I was doing this I watched the rod tip for any signs of movement. Nothing had moved by the time I grabbed my life jacket, so I ran off in search of my hidden boat. Climbing in, I needed to calm down but this wasn't easy and as I rowed down the margin all I could think about was whether this carp was still on. As I docked at my swim I jumped out and placed the net in the boat. Grabbing the rod, I hopped in and pushed off in the boat. I reeled myself out until I was clear of the other lines, then turned the outboard on and headed off, reeling and following the line to where this fish was hopefully still weeded. After about a minute I knew from the angle of the line that I was getting closer and I cut the outboard. Once I was above it I leant into it and things started to move, but there were no signs of life on the other end. I thought there was nothing on the other end as the leadcore started to rise from the depths. I looked into the cloudy water for signs and was checking my clutch when I suddenly caught a glimpse of something black. Suddenly, this carp rose to the surface, it was still on and as it turned I clocked its tail and shit myself, knowing I was attached to him… The Black Mirror. He shot off on a mental run, which stripped line off the spool so fast it was a joke. Dragging me behind him, he must have taken at least forty yards of line and was still taking line when I started to realise that he was dragging us towards the snags. This wasn't good. I put the boat into reverse and applied finger pressure to the spool and the rod took on its full battle curve. I was now starting to panic, thinking, "He cannot get in there!" I clamped down, which worked and seemed to stop him in his tracks, thank God. He kited left, away from the savage snags and back out into open water. At this point I slackened off slightly and things seemed to settle down a bit. I could now enjoy the fight, which is easier said than done when you're attached to one of, if not the most, desirable carp in the country. I was still shitting myself big time because I was so close now to realising my dream. In the distance I could still hear Pecky shouting, but I had turned off from that and was fully focused on the job in hand. Not long after there was a swirl on the surface, the end was now getting very close and I picked up the net. He was around fifteen feet off the boat, looking immense, long and black as I inched him closer and closer. I prayed to the carp gods to make my day. At this point he was so close and I reached out with the net and watched him just squeeze over the cord. Feelings and emotions that I can't describe flowed through my body. I looked into the net just to make sure I wasn't dreaming! I was in awe of this creature; the ultimate goal was now mine. All this hard work had paid off and with tears in my eyes I looked up and screamed to Marky Mark, "Black fcukin' Mirror!" I wanted to take this moment in to the maximum and, as I drifted on the wind back towards my swim, I rang Jane and Steve Allcott with the good news.

The rods were ready to go, I just had to re-curve the chods.

About to cast towards the Two Tits!

I asked Pecky if he could look after him while I legged it back to the van.

By this time Pecky was standing at the front of my swim and as I got closer I said, "Mate he's mine." He said, "Well done Jim," and as I got out of the water he shook my hand. At this point I touched the great fish for the first time and gently removed the hook saying, "Don't worry mate, I will look after you." With the net safely strapped to the boat, I asked Pecky if he could look after him while I legged it back to the van for the mat and scales. I bet he touched him while I was away, who wouldn't? On the long journey to the van I phoned several people, including Darius, telling them the good news. It was a pity he couldn't be there but he was very ill. After that my mobile went into meltdown and Mad said he would be down within half an hour with his video camera. Back at the swim, I tried to find the right place to do the pictures, which was tough as it was so dark in there. Eventually I found somewhere, but I had to clear the area of stingers first. With the scene set it was time to fetch my prize. Pecky got out of the water and gave me my chesties back. This was the moment I had waited so long for. I looked into the net just to make sure I wasn't dreaming, but in the bottom lay England's finest carp. I watched his mouth moving then I put my hand in and stuck my finger into his mouth, which made his gills flare. It was an amazing feeling touching him, knowing my moment had finally come. On the downside this also meant one thing, my time fishing The Mere had come to an end.

I unfolded the mesh to reveal this most awesome creature. He was so long, jet-black like carbon with a chestnut-coloured side and a creamy underside. We were all blown away and it was time to hold my prize up. As you can see, Darrell did me proud. With the pics done I held him in the water while he regained his strength and I whispered, "Thanks for the moment." He kicked and it was time to set him free to fight another day. I watched him slowly disappear from view, a moment in my carping life that I will never forget. I felt my pocket vibrating; it was Beadle calling me. "Oi oi Uncle, I hear you've caught him?" "No," I replied, laughing. It was payback time now and I said, "Not five years or eight to ten fish; one bite, one fish. Forty-odd nights… job done, 51lb 8oz!" He laughed saying, "Fair play Uncle!" Most of my mates know that I'm definitely up for some therapee… After an hour or so I was packed up and, as I boated out down the centre of the lake at full speed, I looked back and punched the sky, shouting, "Yessss!"

I met Mad Martyn in the lay by, as we had agreed to go to Pat's café and I had promised to buy him dinner. While we were sitting in Pat's he said, "I bet you mag it." I replied "No, never. It will only be published in my next book." Some six months later he rang me out of the blue saying, "You went from doin' it to done it. Fair play on not magging it." I think at that point I gained some respect for not whoring it about, unlike others. All I said to the Mere guardian was, "Cheers Mad and thanks". After leaving Pat's Café I decided to try my luck for the 50lb common that lives in the Woolpack, but en route I stopped off to get myself a bottle of Lanson Champagne and a very expensive bottle of red to celebrate The Black Mirror capture. I did indeed find Paddle all clayed up in a swim called The Last In Five but I got nothing, apart from a sore head. In reality, I think I was pushing my luck trying to catch a 50lb common in the same session as The

I'd looked up and screamed, "Black feukin' Mirror!" to Marky.

51lb 8oz of one of the finest UK carp ever.

Time to set him free.

Could I catch Paddle as well?

Black Mirror!

The following year bad news was to rip into the heart of proper English carp fishing when The Mere suffered a massive fish kill. I received a call from Jon Mac informing me that Sean Leverett had found the carp dead and was standing in the water with the body of The Black Mirror. This news sickened me, but knowing full well that the glory hunters would be about for trophy shots I phoned Mad the Mere guardian so he could help Sean. I called Sean back and told him to bury The Black Mirror and keep its location to himself. We all agreed that the fish should stay in the lake.

Sean has very kindly written down the facts for this book, which gives some fitting closure for The Mere…

Putting The Story Straight

Sean Leverett

It was on Saturday the 14th of August 2010, a few days after catching Pingewood's Brute, that I made the biggest decision of my angling to date. The decision I made was to go and fish the Mere and target the magnificent Black Mirror. On the following Monday morning I made the journey round the M25 and at a little after 2pm I passed the entrance to The Mere. After parking in the nearby lay-by, I crossed over the road, hopped the fence and after a short walk I was soon standing at the south end of the lake. I remember getting that feeling of excitement in my stomach, as somewhere out there was the fish I had longed to fish for. The feeling was something else to say the least. Within minutes the Mere had grabbed me, I was standing, looking at such a special place. I ended up spending the next six hours walking round, fighting my way through the dense bramble bushes, taking in the atmosphere. Every now and then I would find a clearing in the undergrowth, which exposed a small section of water together with a small swim that had been so perfectly hidden. You could so easily miss these areas if you weren't looking hard enough.

I had to ring someone as I was on a natural high and what better a person to call than my old mate Jon Mac. Jon knew that I was going up for a look and I knew he would understand how I was feeling, as he had been there. He answered the phone with "You there?" to which I replied, "Yep, I'm here pal." He came back with, "You're on the fucking Mere my son, how do you feel knowing that out there somewhere is The Black Mirror? What a place ain't it?" He was right, somewhere out there The Black Mirror was swimming about and what a place! I knew straight away that this was just what I needed; this was a bit of me, that's for sure. This wasn't going to be your everyday fishing trip though. As I'm sure many of you will know, especially after reading Jim's chapter, this was to be a stealthy mission where you really needed your wits about you. As I drove back home that night my head was all over the place and thoughts of The Black Mirror were spinning round in my mind. Throughout the rest of the week I walked the lake every day, trickling a little bait in and just looking for signs of activity. I remember thinking that the water was pretty coloured but understood that this was normal for the time of year so thought no more of it. When I wasn't over there, I was at home sorting all my kit out ready for my start.

On the Thursday I walked the lake and managed to find a small group of commons up the north end in some shallow water, acting as if they were searching the area for food. I couldn't wait for the Sunday afternoon when I would be making the journey with all

Who dares wins.

my kit with the intention of doing a five-day session. The big day arrived and at a little after twelve I pulled off my drive and excitedly started my journey. When I reached my destination, some one and a half hours later, I was full of nervous energy. I stopped off at The George Pub and had a roast lunch before parking the van up in the nearby side road. With just a rucksack on my back, a bucket and a small rod bag I started the walk by taking the path along the side of Hythe Lagoon and up to the lake. Twenty minutes later, around two thirty, I was standing at the narrow, north end of the Mere looking down its full length and admiring the 40 acres. I was buzzing with excitement just as I was the first time I set eyes on the place and, after a few moments of taking everything in, I made my way to a swim to stash my kit and have a proper look around. When I say swim, it was a small area known as The Rathole, a place where you were tucked away from everyone. There was a strange smell about the place that day but I just put it down to the algae smelling more than usual, as it was a relatively hot day.

I stashed my bag and rods in the little cubbyhole and sat at the top of the bank to catch my breath and have a quick drink. While I sat looking out across the lake I noticed a large object floating on the surface opposite, just to the left of the swim known as the Southwesterly. I searched through my rucksack until I found my binoculars then looked out across the lake, hoping to get a better view of what I thought I had seen. The sight I saw through the binoculars will stay with me forever. My blood ran cold and I got a cold shiver right through my entire body. It was a bloody great mirror and if I'm honest, I knew which fish it was straight away.

I made my way round to the other bank, which was no easy task due to all the undergrowth. The whole time I was battling my way round I was hoping and praying that I was wrong and that it was just a large piece of wood floating on the surface. On arriving at the Southwesterly, I climbed one of the trees in an attempt to get a better look at the fish. My fears were immediately confirmed when I instantly saw the flat lobe of the tail, it was The Black Mirror! Not only was that fish there, dead on the surface, but it was accompanied by another fish, I think it was the Twisty Mouth Common, several large tench and some small fish. I didn't know what the hell to do. My phone was in my rucksack, as were my chest waders, so I had to head back round to The Rathole to get them. All the way back I felt sick and I couldn't believe what was happening. This was not what I was expecting for my first session on The Mere, that's for sure!.

On returning to the swim the first person I rang was Jon and as soon as he answered the phone I blurted down the phone to him, "The Black Mirror's dead mate and so are loads of other fish!" I started to tell him what I had found and as I did I started to notice lots of other dead fish in the margins. At first I'm sure he didn't believe me but as I told him more I could hear the tone in his voice change. He knew I wasn't bullshitting, he could hear it in my voice. I left him to make a couple of calls and see if he could get someone else down to the lake, as I didn't know what the fuck to do. Within a couple of minutes he rang me back to let me know that help was on the way. I started to have a look about along the bank and that's when the severity of the situation

In the Southwesterly, where Sean's worst fears were realised.

One target that Sean was able to get to grips with. The Fat Lady from St Ives Lagoon.

became clear. There were dead fish everywhere, not just carp but pike, tench, bream, eels, perch and thousands of small silver fish. This wasn't just a couple of dead fish, but a major fish kill. I relayed this back to Jon and told him just how bad it was. I counted about a dozen carp up to mid to upper thirty, as well as The Black Mirror. The trouble was that where the fish were made them difficult to reach and as a result we couldn't get close enough to them to see exactly just how big they actually were.

After about ten minutes my phone started ringing and the first call I received was actually from Jim. I told him of the situation and during our conversation I remember him saying to me, "Just make sure no one takes The Black Mirror away from the lake and make sure it's buried on site". I assured him I would make sure nothing happened to it and it would stay here. Soon after, my phone went into meltdown with people calling me to see if it was true. I ended up ignoring the calls as I really couldn't deal with one hundred and one questions from people. Some forty minutes later help turned up in the shape of Mad Martyn and a couple of the lads from the Car Park. I had met Martyn before when I did the winter with Jon on Dinton. With help at hand I waded out into the lake and with the aid of a large branch, managed to move The Black Mirror from out in the lake to the margins of the Southwesterly swim. Both The Black Mirror and the common that was floating beside it had large amounts of blood seeping from under their scales as well as blood coming out from the gill areas. The back of the common had split open along the side of its dorsal fin and there was a sort

of gas bubbling forming on its bare flesh. What the hell had caused this?
By this time a few more people were turning up as word had got out about the situation. I was truly concerned that someone was going to try to take The Black Mirror away from the lake. One person that did turn up was Simon Hartop and it turned out that he had a dinghy stashed in the swim he'd been fishing. We had seen what we thought was a big common at the base of the high bank and were keen to see which fish it was so with that Simon went off to retrieve the dinghy. While he was gone, Martyn stayed in the swim to make sure The Black Mirror wasn't taken (you don't mess with Martin) and I went to see if I could reach the common. I tried to wade down the margin in my waders but it was impossible to reach it, as it was too deep. I also wrecked my waders on a snag, rendering them useless, whilst trying to negotiate the margin snags. All the time I was wading I was surrounded by a sea of dead silver fish and stinking algae; it was heart breaking to see such devastation. Imagine the smell that you had to deal with when you're wading through a sea of dead fish. It's pretty bloody grim and no matter where you went it went with you.
Simon eventually returned with his dinghy and I set about inflating it. Unfortunately, something had decided to bury itself inside the main chamber and as fast as I was blowing it up it was going down and it really wasn't safe enough to risk going out in. All I kept thinking about was the conversation I'd had with Jim and the fact that The Black Mirror had to be buried on site. The last thing I wanted was the fish being taken by someone in order to get it mounted and cased and a fortune made from it. We considered burying the fish at the back of the swim but the ground was solid and almost impossible to dig. Also, we didn't want anything or anyone digging it up after we had left so, after chatting to Jon, Jim, Martin, Simon and a few of the guys that fished there, the decision was made that The Black Mirror would be laid to rest in a similar way that the late, great Mary was and that was by placing it in a sack, weighting the sack with rocks and bricks and then taking the fish out into the lake and sinking it. That would be its final resting place, back in the lake that it was king of and the place where it was always known to reside. As I lifted The Black Mirror from the water and into the sack I remember thinking to myself that this wasn't the way I wanted to be holding such a beautiful creature and that it was such a cruel act of nature that had shattered so many dreams, mine included. I felt sick and there was an awkward silence while this all went on.
Once the great fish was laid to rest in the deep water of the lake, people started trying to identify some of the other stunning carp that were dead on the surface. Everyone was talking of a massive, fifty or sixty-pound common that was also dead and at one point I too thought that the large common along the bottom of the high bank was that fish, but in all honesty no massive common had been found. We did find a fish around the mid to upper thirty bracket but nothing bigger had surfaced. With The Black Mirror back in its home I made a call to the Environment Agency emergency hotline, informed them of the situation and after giving them all the information, they assured me someone would be down before dark. You have to remember that

at this point we were all standing on a SSSI water and I'm trying to explain to the EA why we are there and how I came across this. They were asking a lot of questions but eventually accepted what I was telling them. While we waited for them to arrive a few of us went walking round to see what else was washed up. During this time more and more people turned up, a lot of whom had never even set foot on the place before but just wanted to be there. There were a few faces milling about, one of which was Steve Briggs and just seeing the look on his face said it all. Steve was the last person to catch The Black Mirror and I felt angry with him for going public with his capture to the point that I couldn't even talk to him, as I wanted to let rip into him. I have always felt that The Black Mirror was a fish that didn't need putting in the press anymore than it already had been but I guess people have their own reasons for doing such things. I remembered something Jon so rightly said to me once, "It's the no-pain, no-gain, no-fame mirror," and I felt that was such a true saying. I have since apologised to Steve for my behaviour that day though, as although I don't agree with what he did, I shouldn't have taken it so personally and it was clear that he was as upset as everyone else that day.

The EA arrived later that evening and carried out their tests but we all knew that The Mere was no more. There were a lot of people talking of foul play and I too thought the same due to all the blood, but really it was more the fact that everyone just wanted someone to blame for this disaster. On talking to the EA it became pretty clear that there had been a massive oxygen crash after a storm the previous evening and this is what had most likely caused the fate of the Mere.

As darkness fell we all left the lake but it was heartbreaking to see such devastation, not just the carp but also all species, some of which were of record sizes. I walked back to my van with Simon and a few of the other lads but there was very little talk on that journey. After our goodbyes I drove over to Pingewood and stayed the night with friends because, as mad as it sounds, I didn't want to go back to an empty house. We all had a good drink that night and I eventually got into the back of my van a little the worse for wear. I didn't sleep a wink that night though, as all I could think about was the sight that had greeted me when I climbed that tree in the Southwesterly, as well as the smell of death.

I returned to the Mere the following morning as I couldn't get the place out of my head and wanted to have a proper look just to see the devastation that had been caused. I walked round trying to take in just what had actually happened, but in the end it was all too much and I had to get away from the place. As I was driving off I bumped into a well-respected angler that had actually been one of the few blessed enough to have landed the great fish. He said that he felt the need have one last look at the place and pay his respects to it, as he had fond memories of both the fish and the lake. It was during this conversation that the subject of how the fish had been laid to rest in the lake came up. It was mentioned that, as much as he respected what had been done, from what I picked up from him I think he felt that it would have been nice to have had the fish mounted and cased, so that there was some sort of lasting reminder. I couldn't agree less. It would have been an awful thing to have had The Black Mirror cased as it clearly belonged in that lake and I'm just glad we did what we did, as if we hadn't then who knows where that fish would have ended up and how much dirty money would have changed hands for someone to have got hold of it. I was quite surprised and a little disappointed by his comments at first but after thinking about it I suppose we are all entitled to our views and, as much as I didn't agree with him, I admired his open honesty and my respect for him, as an angler, didn't change.

He had been talking to the lady from the EA and when they took samples late the previous evening the oxygen levels were so low that it would have been almost impossible for anything to survive. Although levels had risen that day, they were still critical. I can't actually remember the exact levels but my God were they low! I had decided earlier that day to take my own water samples and get them tested just for my own peace of mind, but when I received the results they came back inconclusive due to germs that were in the bottle before it was filled with the lake water. I was told that it was more than likely that no foul play had taken place though and that Mother Nature had in fact been behind this cruel act. It seems that the storm on the Saturday night, coupled with an algae bloom, had sealed the demise of the lake. Whether anything had survived I don't know but I very much doubt it judging by the severity of what we witnessed.

The sad loss of The Black Mirror and all the other fish in the lake for that matter will, I'm sure, have affected many anglers around this land but I can tell you this, the sight of The Black Mirror, as I held it dead in my arms will be etched in my memory for many a year…

The Woolpack

The Quest for the Queen

The Woolpack fishery is around 35 years old and was dug to provide hardcore for the construction of the A14. Like most venues along our main transport arteries, it consists of a number of lakes now split across two different syndicates, lakes One, Two and Three at the top and lakes Four, Five, Six, Seven and Eight on the other syndicate.

I actually fished the Woolpack as far back as eighteen or twenty years ago, when a bloke who worked in a Huntingdon tackle shop ran the fishing. I didn't like this chap as he let all sorts on back then, including time bandits who left their bivvies in swims for weeks, whilst at work. The bailiffs didn't lift a finger, as it seemed that they were in on the act as well. This bull mostly happened on lakes Four, Five and Six (which are actually one lake) and Lake Seven where the bigger fish lived back then. These swim-hogs ensured that the best swims were out of commission for ages, so I concentrated on lakes One, Two, Three and Eight, hoping that I could get onto the busy lakes when it cooled off.

I did in fact get chances later on, during the autumn, but it was really hard back then and I didn't have the knowledge and watercraft that I have now. Although I was lacking in those key areas, the drive to succeed was cemented into my brain. Although I didn't account for any of the big 'uns, that drive helped me to catch 40 fish from the complex during that first year. The fish weren't massive by today's standards, but I loved the peaceful surroundings, with its myriad wildlife like birds, badgers, foxes and deer. I often thought that one day I would have to return and fish the lakes again.

Around ten years ago I started to hear whispers that the fish in Lake Five and Six had grown somewhat. I contacted the tackle shop several times to try to get a ticket, but I was always fed cock-and-bull stories so after a while I stopped. Mind you, I was fishing Fen Drayton back then and that mysterious pit was consuming all of my fishing time. When my good friend Steve Allcott got a ticket I was able to put some solid facts together about the stock in the Woolpack. It seemed that there were even more big 'uns in Lake Five and Six than I had imagined, plus the stock had been boosted when several fish had moved into the lake during the floods from lakes Four and Seven.

Steve told me that an A-Team of incredible commons were the main players in the lake, including Paddle, The Woodcarving, Willy, Slopehead and The Long Common. There were only two big mirrors, called Cluster and The Big Fully. I was gagging to get a ticket but when I finally made contact I was told, "No way Mr Shelley." I could only look on from the outside, listening intently as Steve brought me news from the complex. It turned out that Paddle had fallen to an angler fishing the Tea Bag swim at a new high of 49lb. Knowing all this was doing my head in, but my philosophy has always been, "Never say never."

Two or three years passed, then one evening Steve rang me while I was on Welly, telling me to ring my old mate Pikey Mick, as a bloke called Andy Stafford had just bought the Woolpack and Mick was to be the head bailiff. I told Steve that I thought I was blocked, but he replied saying, "Jim, you know Pikey though." His words fell on deaf ears as I had just got it into my head that there was no chance. Several weeks later, I was driving back from Welly and I decided to ring Pikey up. "Oi oi mate, how's it going?" Pikey's voice sounded deep, like he knew exactly what I was after! "Pikey, I hear that you're the new head bailiff on the Wooly now…" he cut me off, guessing my intentions; "Jim… you want a ticket?" "Yes mate," I replied and he started laughing. "Look, I will be good and if I play up you can keep the ticket money," I implored him. He told me that Andy, the new owner, had been told by the tackle shop owner not to let me in. I pleaded with Pikey to speak to Andy for me and to wipe the metaphorical slate clean, which he promised to do, assuring me that whatever the answer, he'd get back to me with a few hours. Those hours seemed like days.

Two hours later Pikey rang me back, telling me that Andy had said no, but that he'd had words with him and turned Andy's decision around. "As I'm vouching for you, if you left me down I'm gonna arse-fuck you," was his sober warning. I told him that I wouldn't let him down and, before hanging up, admitted that I owed him one, big time. "Christ," I thought, "One second it's no-go and the next I'm in… happy days." Mind you, I'm sure that the carp gods played their part for me. When I got home there was an email from Andy. I phoned him the next day and we had a good chat about all things carp fishing.

After the call, I received another email from Andy detailing all the do's and don'ts and he attached a picture of a common, titled "The best common in the country." It was The Carving from Lake Five and Six… Christ I had to have this gem. Trust me, that dollar was in the post straight away, recorded delivery! The next week, Jane rang me and said, "Your Woolpack ticket is at home," sweeeeet.

I couldn't fish there until April 1st so I carried on at Welly, but the last week of March was to be my last trip there as I'd had enough of it all. So, armed with my Wooly ticket, I fished my last night at the Park and said goodbye to the place, as I wasn't going back there, even though my ticket was valid up until June. My last night at Welly was a social with mates that are still friends to this very day. In the early hours I had a 34lb mirror from a swim that no one fishes in a quiet bay. I bet my buzzers screaming at full bore made Mr Fairbrass jump in his sleep as he was fishing on the end of a point in front of me. I set the alarm for 4am, as I wanted to get on the road well before the traffic built up. Now, as I knew I wasn't going back to Welly again, I decided to drive my van round to the swim and load my gear there. With the van loaded, it was time to leave Reading and head to the Woolpack. As I drove along the lake, I turned the trance tunes on full whack… have it suckers!

I wanted to be there for first light to see any shows and get straight on them. When I arrived, the car park was busy, telling me that there were a lot of anglers fishing the complex. "Right," I thought, "Let's go have a look on Lake Five and Six first," as that's the lake where the giants lived. As I walked out of the car park and made my way along the path towards Five and Six, I kept an eye on Lake Seven next door. As I walked, I was struck by how similar the surroundings were to Fen Drayton, with reed beds and massive, drooping willows. The swims looked pukka, not big, manicured constructions like most places, but how it should be, with just enough space to set up and get the rods out.

I couldn't see many anglers on Seven, in fact there were none. This told me that the bulk of them were on Five and Six and as I neared the lake the number of bivvies that I could see bore this out. Unless I could find the fish, I wasn't going to camp on the lake, so I set about having a good look around. The lake is around seven acres with an island running along the middle, separating the two 'lakes'. There are four channels cutting through the island, so the fish could get around the lake with ease.

I knew the lake quite well from when I fished there before, so I knew where to go and where the swims were. As I carried on up the path along Lake Six, I could see that most swims had a bivvy in them! This was not looking good but my mantra has always been find them/cast to them/bait them and hopefully catch them.

I kept my hoodie up because I didn't want to draw attention to the fact that I was a member just yet. I walked past a very popular swim called Lumpy's, which was one of the best back when I first fished the complex because it had a shallow area in front that the fish used a lot when going from lake to lake. It seemed like a daytime zone but with deep water all around and a set of lilies to the left in a small bay, I knew at the right time fish would be there, day or night.

As I got to the end of Lake Six I turned right with Lake Six now to my right and Lake Four on my left. Lake Four was no-fishing as Andy was turning this little reed-fringed water into his stock pond! Further along on the right you could look in the channel and see if any fish were about but only if there was no one in Lumpy's or the opposite swim on Lake Five. Effectively this meant that there was no fishing along this whole bank and the two swims facing the channel were the only spots you could angle to this area from. These two swims turned out to be very kind to me later on in my campaign!

All the main swims on Lake Five were taken, which told me that the bulk of the fish were currently resident in this side. With all the pressure being brought to bear on Lake Five, I decided to hightail it to Lake Seven in search of some peace. One look up the long, tapering lake told me that no one was fishing. I knew the lakes could get

Lake Seven holds a good head of scaly carp, with 15 over the 30lb mark at the right time.

very weedy later on in the year, so I went to the car and grabbed one of my rods with a very small lead on it. As I didn't have any sightings to go on, I decided to locate the weed beds as they hold lots natural food like snails, shrimps and mussels and provide some cover for the carp. As no weed beds were visible on the surface, the plan was to locate the weed by casting a small lead three or four times in every swim until I found the weed on the bottom.

I decided to walk along the causeway that separates lakes Seven and Eight and put my plan into action. The first swim near the car park held no weed but did have a soft bottom. Two swims up, there was an awesome looking reed bed that stuck out into the lake, definitely a safe zone for the fish and a place for them to lay up out of the way and sun themselves. Now, the next swim was really sexy, with loads of cover and that enticing reed bed to my right. I cast right up to the stems and felt the lead down through six feet of water, before it landed on a soft but firm bottom. I then chucked the lead around, hoping to find weed as I got a good vibe standing in this swim. No weed was found so I carried on to the next swim and straight away found what I was looking for.

Several casts in the area revealed a long, thin band of weed lying over a hard area as occasionally the lead would donk down hard. I wouldn't normally fish these areas, as I like the silty, weedy areas of the lake to fish my long running chods on. However, this hard area had weed covering it, so the long running chod rig would sit pukka on the weed. Now, this seemed to be the place but I had to check out the other swims as well

before making my decision. The rest of swims were all devoid of weed, apart from the one opposite. Because the weed bed happened to be in the centre of the lake, I could see 80% of the lake, so if I saw anything show I could react and move onto them.
I knew that Lake Seven held a good head of scaly carp, with around fifty or sixty fish present. Fifteen could be over 30lb at the right time, plus several around the mid to upper thirty mark. Among these were a linear, plus two big 'uns, a mirror and common, that hadn't been out for around three to four years. The common was called Fred and the mirror was called The Grey One. The lake was around seven acres in size and shaped a bit like a long, thin triangle surrounded by Norfolk reeds and willow trees. All the lakes were like this, like small versions of Fen, which is probably why I feel so at home there and still fish on the Woolpack to this very day.
As I got back to my car Steve Allcott turned up. He was on a mission and after a few minutes chatting he was off to Lake Five and Six, telling me that he would pop by to see me on his way out the next day. I wished him luck and started loading my barrow as I was gagging to get the rods out on that weedy area. As I neared the swim a fish jumped somewhere to my right. As I looked right to where it had jumped, I said to myself, "Oi oi Mr Carp," because I now knew that I was close. I logged the area as the disturbance it made was in the swim to the right of where I was going to fish, and roughly the same distance as the weedy area, so I could cast to it from my chosen swim.
As you can imagine, all I wanted to do was get those rods out double quick so now I was in robot mode. Like a machine, I began checking hooks to see if they were sharp and if they weren't, they got sharpened or the rig was changed. My lovingly rolled cork ball hook baits were already meshed and soaking in my salty dip. Now, at certain times of the year carp crave salt, so I had my hook baits soaking in it and Gary Bayes had rolled salt into my Amber Strawberry boilies.
Fresh, white hook baits were tied on and the chod was curved aggressively as I like it. I clipped on a stealthy, 1oz lead, as the chuck was 40 yards at the most.
I like to get all the rods sorted before I cast, so that I can chuck them out one after another to keep the disturbance down. Three rods can be cast and baiting completed in five minutes. I always prepare the rods while facing the water too, just so I don't miss any signs while getting sorted. I leant the three rods that were ready against the reeds and placed the bag of Ambers and throwing stick at the front of the swim, ready to go.
Out went the first rod and as the small lead finished its descent through nine or ten feet of water, I felt it drop onto weed. The other two rods were cast to the left of the first one and all went down pukka. I then spread sixty 16mm Ambers with the throwing stick, seven at a time, achieving a nice spread that gets the carp moving around, increasing the chances of one making a mistake when picking the hook bait up.
As the weather was nice, I decided to ring Jane and have a chat. As we were talking, the right-hand rod pulled up tight, "Gotta go babe," I stuttered. On picking the rod up something kicked and then was off, "What the…?" I thought, as all sorts of things went through my head. Ten minutes for a bite? My mind was working overtime and I

told myself that it was a pike… it made me feel better anyway. I reeled in and checked that the rig was sweet, which it was so I just cast it back out to the spot.

I sunk the line slowly, placed the rod on the buzzer, clipped the bobbin on and made sure that everything was hanging slack. As I turned my back to get my phone that same rod roared off again, taking line off the reel mega-quick.

I spun round and grabbed the rod as what was clearly a carp powered off… this was no pike. It went from right to left and off up the lake for some forty to fifty yards, shaking its head; this creature sure was pissed off with me! As he kited into the bank on a tight line I heard someone behind me say, "Hi Jim, you're making the 'Pack look easy." It was Martin and he could clearly see that I had just cast out because my house wasn't even set up.

I carried on playing this animal and Martin stood beside me and offered his netting services. I told him to grab the net for me, so he kindly placed it in the water ready. In the meantime, the fight continued to be unreal, with big surges of power and several times huge swirls unravelled on the glassy surface, something I love to see.

All of a sudden, the middle rod pulled up tight and as the hooked fish was nowhere near the other lines, I reasoned that I had another carp on! I told Martin that I'd have him when I got this fish in and turned the buzzer off. The middle rod suddenly stopped taking line so I was happy that he was just sulking down the margin. As all this was going on I was trying to get the first one closer, but the more pressure I put on him, the

It was 2-1 to the Wooly carp, but I had a 33lb 12oz common in the net!

Peering into the net, I could see a two-tone common that looked around the mid-twenty mark.

more he pulled back, stripping line off me. I had to calm myself before I messed it up, because I was more worried about getting it landed and grabbing the other rod.

I had been playing this fish for nearly ten minutes and trust me, I don't mess about, but the power this fish had was unreal. However, soon I got a glimpse of a massive tail and knew that the fight was coming to an end. Not long after, a massive, long common lay on the surface and I leant down, grabbed the net, drew him that little bit closer and got him. I laid the net down safely in the margin and grabbed the other rod. I was expecting to feel some resistance on the other end as I began to reel, but all I felt was the lead coming back with nothing on the end…

It was one to Uncle Jim and two to the Wooly carp, but never mind, as I had a real peach of a common in my net. I phoned Andy up to see if he would like to come and see this beast and he signed off, promising to be there in ten minutes.

I unhooked him in the net, which I always do as it gives the carp and the angler a chance to chill out. A crowd had gathered as I gently lowered the carp on to the cradle and unfolded the mesh. Others were commenting on this awesome creature, which Andy later informed me was called The Long Common.

I put him into Marky Mark's old weigh sling and the scales were already zeroed, so I hooked the sling on to the scales, lifted it up and we settled on a weight of 33lb 12oz. All this time the carp was tensing up and all his fins were sticking out, what's more, he kept making a strange barking noise! It was well weird and as you can see in the

pictures, he sure was a proud old carp in perfect condition. Andy did some shots on his mega camera… thanks mate. As I lowered the mat into the lake and water passed over his body he knew it was time and in a flash he was gone, covering me in spray!
Once the crowd had dispersed, I tied on a new rig and bait and cast it back out to the zone, followed by a few more freebies, as it was clear there were carp about and having it. Once I'd tidied the bombsite, I sat back trying to take in the fact that I'd had three bites in less than an hour! Just as I was relaxing, the right-hand rod pulled up and I was onto it in a flash. This fish didn't fight anything like the other one, just kiting to my right before wallowing up the margin with weed on its head and dropping into the net.
Peering into the net, I could see a two-tone common of around mid-twenty. All I could think was, "This can't be happening," but it was; it was now 2-2 and Uncle was out for revenge. After weighing the stunning bar of gold at 24lb 12oz, Andy did the honours and we returned the common to its watery home. It seemed mad that I was getting all this action on three rods on a tight zone. I kept baiting the zone on a little and often basis but by nightfall no more bites had materialised. This wasn't a great surprise, because the area had had a battering. The night was quiet, making me think that they'd legged it for cover, but carp being carp, they'd be back… hopefully.
I had to go home later that morning, but at least the journey was shorter and didn't involve any M25 therapy. As I was sitting watching the water, Steve popped in for

The scales showed 24lb 4oz and he looked awesome in the early morning sun.

Gently lowering my prize back into Lake Seven – I was now 3-2 up!

a chat as he was off elsewhere. As we were chatting, my middle rod was off again! I legged it to the rods and pulled into a carp that darted all over the place, telling me that it wasn't a big 'un.

After a spirited, five-minute battle, I was admiring another common in the net. I got all the bits ready and asked Steve if he would do the honours, handing him my camera. The scales showed 24lb 4oz and as I held him up in the early morning sun he looked awesome. It was now 3-2 to Uncle Jim! Steve was off and bade me good luck for the last few hours. I still had the lake to myself, so it was time to bait up Jim Shelley style… wink.

I had 40kg in the back of the van, so I decided that half was going into several zones, as it was clear these fish liked the white bait. There was no need to change to Scopex Squids yet, but next session I was definitely going to put some in so they got a taste for it. As I reeled the rods in I knew there was more to come from Lake Seven and at least I knew I had a backup plan if Lake Five and Six was busy.

The lake had a three-on and then three-off rule, which suited my fishing time down to a tee, as I do one or two days tuition per week. Before leaving, the wind blew up a northerly and as I baited from a swim from which you can see the whole lake, I saw them showing off the reed bed that had received most of that 20kg. Thinking that this looked superb, I went back to the van for another 4kg!

While I was away, Paddle came out of Lake Six at a massive 49lb 6oz to a bloke that

Steve had named Spare Rib, as he had the misfortune of falling out of a tree and breaking his ribs!

When I arrived on my next session, I had a look on Lake Five and Six, which was quieter, but I still fancied Lake Seven. Despite this, I decided to go back to the van and grab two bags of 10mm Scopex Squids and bait the little corner of Lake Six where a pipe trickled in from Lake Seven. I could do this unnoticed because all the anglers seemed to be fishing in a line on Lake Five and this little bit of prepping would mean that I'd have something to go at next time. It seemed that some had Cluster, The Carving, The Long, Willy and Slope on their minds because they hadn't been out yet. These guys were fishing Five and Six all spring, no matter what.

While getting the bait, I kept an eye on seven and I could see fish showing near to the reed bed that I had baited up on the last trip, so I was going to fish in the swim just to the left of it. From leading about, I knew that there was a shallow area in front of the reed bed, with a smooth bottom in about 5ft to 6ft of water, so the right-hand rod was going to be fished near the reed bed.

The left-hand rod was fished at twenty yards in slightly deeper water and the middle rod was cast to a lovely soft gully. A few showed before dark so I was happy being in the swim especially after I'd baited it. With the rods out I sat back and poured a nice glass of chilled white wine from the freezer bag.

I turned in under a clear sky but it wasn't long before a heavy mist came down. I was

Pikey leapt forwards, grabbed the net and said, "That's THE Linear mate!"

Not long after, this low-twenty common joined the Linear in the net.

up just before first light and turned my phone on, which told me that Pikey had bagged one. I phoned him up and he told me that he'd got Cluster in the sack at 45lb. I asked him to text me when he was doing the pics because this stunner was high on my list of targets from Lake Five and Six. Out of the blue, my left-hand rod screamed into life. I ran down to the rod and pulled into this fast-moving beast. The carp raced along the reed line, putting my line in danger so I told to myself to put the rod down and get the chesties on. Struggling into the waders, I grabbed the rod and made my way into the margin. I worked my way out onto the shallower area, which gave me a better angle to gain some line back and this worked, thank God, as this angry carp kited out in front of me, away from the reed bed. All of a sudden, the middle rod roared off too. Scarcely able to take in what was happening, I stepped back and turned the buzzer off.

The power of the carp was unreal, big surges of power told me that it was a good 'un, but he was tiring and the surges were getting less and less ferocious. I knew that I was close when the end of the leadcore broke surface. I was admiring the impressive swirls that broke on the glassy surface when I got a glimpse of a big mirror twisting and turning in the clear water. As the fish surrendered, I got a good look at his linear scaling. I slid the net into position as he coughed water and a split second later he was mine. I made sure that he was safe before whirling round and picking up the other rod. As I turned, I could see Pikey standing behind, clearly wondering what the hell was going on! I told him that I had an awesome linear in the net, at which point, he leapt forwards, grabbed the net and said, “That’s THE Linear mate!” He looked after the fish in the net and not long after a low-twenty common joined the Linear in the mesh.

I quickly unhooked them both in the net so they wouldn’t get damaged; two rigs attached to carp in the net at the same time isn’t good! While I was thinking about how to give the fish the best care we could, Pikey decided to give me some therapy about my buzzers being too loud and catching two at once. I told him that I liked everyone to know when Uncle’s about and catching!

I took the net off Pikey and stuck the butt of the net handle into the soft clay so I could leave the carp in the net while I got all the bits ready for the pictures.

I then handed Pikey my camera so he could do the honours for me. I slid the common into Marky’s old weigh sling and he turned the needle to 22lb. We snapped off a couple of quick pics before he was returned home.

With the Linear left in the net, I pulled the handle out of the clay, broke the net up and rolled the mesh around the two arms, making it easy to transport him to the mat. On the mat I was struck by the fact that he didn’t look as big as he normally does, and the scales soon confirmed this, registering a slimline 35lb 8oz (he had been 38lb in the past). I wasn’t worried because, as you can see, he was a stunner!

Pikey Mick and I went back years, he helped to secure my Wooly ticket.

Pikey left me to sort out the chaos in my swim, telling me that he’d be photographing Cluster in ten minutes. Now, from what I had heard Cluster was supposed to be a real awesome beast so I was gagging to see this baby in the flesh. When I got round to Pikey’s swim I had to shuffle in among a load of anglers eager to see the fish. When he pulled the sack out, the bulk of the carp was unreal to behold, and when he laid him down on the mat, we could all see that this was one hell of a chunk of mirror carp.

There were gasps all around when Pikey unzipped the sack, revealing 43lb 6oz of prime Cambridgeshire mirror. When Pikey had put it back he was going on about the fish not counting because it was still the close season! I just said, “Why the hell are you here then?” This bloke seriously puts a downer on everything in fishing; I wonder if he’s like that at home!

On my way back to the swim, I knew on my next session I was definitely going to hit Lake Five and Six especially after Pikey had caught the big mirror from the little corner that I’d been trickling bait into. This told me that they liked the bait and that my baiting was bang on, and it gave me the confidence to get on with it straight away.

I returned to my swim and fuzzed the rods out, roughly back to the spots. Knowing it was going to be a hot day, I knew I only had a few hours fishing on the bottom, as I would be hunting them on the top soon. Two hours later I detected the first signs of carpy activity on the top.

I had already started a slow pack-up, as I wanted my gear packed away on the barrow because a move was looking on the cards later on that evening. The rods were reeled in and packed away in their sleeves. As I left the car park, I walked to the right as I had seen fish well to the right of the swim I was fishing that morning. I had the lake to myself still so I was loving the peace and quiet and not getting 'sheeped up' by other anglers. In time I was going see this desperate side of angling, over on Lake Five and Six, where respect for others meant nothing. Anyway, as I made my way round the lake, I came to a reed-fringed corner where I had seen the subtle carpy movements, which in this case were lines of bubbles as they came up from the deeper water, and slight blemishes as the carp sat just under the water's surface.

Lake Seven turned out to be a brilliant floater water and my oily freebies quickly attracted the carp's attention.

There was a tiny tree that gave a good view over this area; a part of the lake that I was to find that the fish visited a lot on hot days. As I climbed the small tree and looked out over the area, I could clearly see several carp in residence… sweet. I spent several minutes watching them and counted twelve different ones.

I grabbed the catapult and a handful of mixers, shinned back up the tree and fired a few biscuits out near to the bulk of fish. Shuffling my weight to make myself comfortable, I waited to see what their reaction would be. I could see the oil from the mixers dispersing across the water, and noticed the fish become a little more active, their slumber in the sun digesting the night's grub now interrupted.

One starting taking and it wasn't long before others joined in. Now, there was a swim further up the bank to my right that offered access to the zone, with a decent side cast left up the bank. The first thing I did was to get the rod set up with a light Bolt Machine controller and a 6ft of 10lb Double Strength hook link, tied to a size-10 Wide Gape. They were having it big time while I was setting the rod up, so I fired some more mixers out to keep them busy. I noticed that they had started to drift out of the corner, so they were now nearly in front of the swim I was going to fish. The fish were a fair way out but right in front of the swim, so I fired the mixers as far as I could and as I watched the fish seemed to home in on them.

It was time to make a cast and I chose to flick the rig to the left, just away from the main bulk of carpy activity. The rig landed some 15ft behind the activity and I slowly inched it back in towards the fish, leaving it just behind them. Suddenly, there were several carp having it large closer in, so I carefully reeled the rig a bit closer. Straight away there was a swirl as a carp tucked me up, then all of a sudden the hook bait went black, meaning the white pop-up was in the carp's mouth. I call this technique twitcher hitting, as you have to have lightning reactions to strike. So, I struck as the hook bait went black and the line tightened up. There was an explosion, as, for a split second, the carp didn't know what had happened, before the clutch started singing. As he took line I gently applied pressure to the rim of the spool, slowing the fish before I tweaked the clutch tighter.

He then kited on a long line to the left and as the pressure eased, I pressed home my advantage, gaining valuable yards. Soon, he was close in, in front of me, and I shipped the net out ready. After a couple of minutes I could see what looked like a mirror twisting and turning in the gin-clear water. Suddenly, I got a glimpse of some scales and he looked like a linear as he rose up in the water. Christ, he looked awesome and as he lay on his side, nearly ready for the net, his scales lit up in the late-morning sun. I grabbed the net and he went straight in… happy days.

Mark was about and asked if I needed some help. I asked him to take some pictures for me. Up on the scales, he went 24lb 4oz; not the biggest, but he sure was one of the prettiest! Mark was soon on his way home so I thanked him and told him that I'd see him next week. Catching one that quick was a right result and I thought that there just had to be a big window for more action. After all the commotion, the fish had moved out to about 80 yards, in the middle of the lake. It was clearly time to get the freebies out with the spod. Now, this is one big edge, even in floater fishing, as most carp know what the noise of a spod means… food.

I know that this sounds crazy, but I normally like to land the spod right among the fish because this gets their attention! When I've shown people on my tuitions I don't think

A stunning floater-caught mirror that weighed in at 24lb 4oz.

that they can get their heads around it, because it goes against all the laws of floater fishing! When you're kitted up properly for long-range floater fishing, it's devastating. I use 12ft Nash Pursuits with Emblem Pro reels, loaded with 10lb or 12lb line and rigged up with the Bolt Machine controllers, which allows you to bang hook baits, tangle free, to 100 yards with no problems.

It was time to get some mixers out there. I made the cast to the area and just before the spod touched down, I snatched it across the surface creating a nice spread. There were soon feeding boils all around the zone; I'd clearly stirred them up and they were taking floaters before the spod was back in my hand. I grabbed the rod and tied on a bigger Bolt Machine so I could get out there easily. I also threaded on new hook bait, which was a cut-down pale pop-up soaked in fish oil.

I made the cast and, as before, it landed well behind the feeding fish. I left it in position while I grabbed the spod rod and put some more mixers out where they were feeding. As I swung the spod in, I leant it up against the bush to my right, now it was time to pick up the slack line and tweak the hook bait into place.

Before I knew what was happening, I was in again. This one had hooked itself against the heavy controller and straight away it went deep before the line fell slack. I reeled in, trying to keep in contact, but I knew deep down that I'd just been cut off. It felt like a good fish too and I wasn't amused.

I worked the swim for another hour but it seemed that I had spooked the main hit squad away and the ones that were left were being very cagey. I don't give up easily though, and if its takes me all day to hook one, then so be it. I started to notice that they were snatching from a cluster of mixers, before disappearing. So, I formulated a new plan. I'd spod fifteen or so mixers out, then get the spod halfway back and make the cast to the back of the cluster. Once I'd tweaked it back to them, I finished reeling the spod in.

The controller was right at the back of the cluster of mixers when the first sign appeared right in the middle of them. Next, a mouth came up and started pac-manning the mixers one by one, so I tweaked the hook bait a bit closer. A mouth came up and the pale hook bait went black. I struck and made contact with a fish that went on a mental 60-yard run, before steady pressure on the spool slowed him down. His next move was to kite left on a long line, towards the reedy bay. As he made the bay I dropped the rod down so the line was mostly under the water. I needn't have worried though, as he stayed deep and soon moved out again.

He was now in front of me on a short line, plodding around deep down. This went on for some four to five minutes before I got a glimpse of what looked like a mirror. The net was in the water ready and after a while he was forced into the upper layers and I could see he was a mirror and under my control.

He came up on the top and just as I was going to net him he surged off showing me he wasn't ready yet, but I knew it was only a matter of time. I coaxed him back and this time I made no mistakes and he was in my net. Ten minutes later Andy was in my swim all smiles and congratulating me on the capture. The fish went 30lb 10oz and Andy later named the fish Billy, although God knows why! He was a deep-bellied mirror in perfect condition and as I held him up for the camera in the evening sun I couldn't be any happier. Welly seemed a distant memory – for all the big fish it held, I was happy to have left. As I slid him back I wondered what other gems this complex of lakes had in store for me.

Before long, it was time to think where I was going to position the rods for the night. After an hour or so, I decided to drop back into the same swim. Dinner was sorted as Pikey was ordering pizza and I shouted his for helping me get my Wooly ticket. The cheeky git even came round for the dollar; he definitely didn't trust me! As I lay back, chilling on the bedchair after that pizza, it was time to ring Jane and see how she was. She told me that a low pressure with big southwesterly winds was coming in by the morning. After a chat I wished her good night and then it was time for me to get some sleep and recharge the batteries.

In the early hours I was woken by the wind tugging at my brolly. Half asleep, I knew that this fresh wind would have the carp moving on it, and I knew that I'd be following them. I always wake up when the birds start to sing just before first light, so as soon as I swung my feet out of the bed it was time for a blast of strong coffee. As the kettle was boiling, "Bosh," a carp jumped out to my left within casting range. I thought, "Sod it, he's getting a chod on him." I reeled in the right-hand rod from near the reeds, checked the hook, tweaked the chod back into its aggressive curve then recast the rod into the

For some reason, Andy later named this deep-bodied thirty Billy! Fish like this made Welly seem a distant memory.

area where Mr Carp had showed himself. I laid the rod down with a semi-tight line so the 20lb X-Line would sink by itself, grabbed the throwing stick and spread twenty freebies in the general area.

Rod on the buzzer and bobbin hanging slack, it was time to finish that coffee and watch for carpy signs. The wind was still pushing down towards the other end, and I was expecting the carp to be on it. I had the feeling that the carp that had showed was on his way down there, but all of a sudden the left-hand rod burst into life as a carp made a powerful surge off down the lake, ripping 40 to 50 yards of line off me. I applied steady pressure to slow him down and not long after, the carp kited out to the right on a long line, well over towards the other side of the lake. There was no weed so really as long as it was well hooked it would be mine. As I was playing this one, a fish showed itself even further down, and then another and another in short succession well down towards the other end. I now knew that as soon as I got this carp sorted I would be on the move two swims down, to a hidden swim in the brambles.

As I played this carp I kept an eye on the area and I did see two more stick their heads out. The carp was close by now and it was time to get the net ready. As I watched, I saw a nice common in the clear margin and not long after there was an old-looking, upper-twenty common in the folds of my net. It does seem unreal, thinking back to all that action, but there was nobody else on during the midweek on Lake Seven, so it was easy to get on them. I unhooked him and made sure he was safe before grabbing a bag of bait and legging it to the new swim. I just had to make sure that I didn't lose the swim. "Christ Jim," I thought, "What are you doing; there's no one about!" I just had to get in there though and, as I looked out from the swim a right chunk pushed out, not 15 yards out in front of me. My mind was racing at the thought of all these fish showing in the area and I was now gagging to get on them.

On the way back to the swim I called Andy and asked if he could do some pictures of the fish for me. When I put this fish on the mat and unrolled the mesh we were both struck by how the scales were almost lost in the body of the carp; you couldn't even feel them. He weighed 28lb 12oz and was a nice start to the day. I had to wonder to myself what else might happen once I moved into the new zone! As I returned the fish, Andy said, "There's one," pointing down to the other end. I said, "I know mate, I've already got something in the swim!" Andy smiled and left me to it, as he knew I was on a mission to get packed up and move onto those fish. Andy texted me later to say the common was called Houdini, that explains it!.

As you can imagine, my gear was packed up in double-quick time and it seemed that every time I looked up I saw a carp. Christ, there must have been untold numbers down there on that new wind. As I made my way down the path towards the new swim I noticed that the wind was blowing even harder; it was the first real wind I had fished

Andy and I were both struck by how the common's scales were almost 'lost' in the body of the fish – you couldn't even feel them!

The Linear for the second time, he's the king of the lake to this day.

in on here. First the rigs and hooks were checked and fresh pop-ups were tied on. I got all the three rods ready first, before casting them out to the spots. Fish were still showing while I was doing this, revealing three different areas of activity, so all I had to do was cast them out. The swim was a bit tight; as to the left I had a bed of Norfolk reeds to cast over and brambles behind me. Nevertheless, the rods went out OK apart from the first when the wind blew the line into the reeds.

Once I was happy with the rods it was time to spread some white boilies about over the zone. As the swim was tight I had to make sure the rods were set up well to the right, so I had plenty of room to erect my house. As I was sorting this out, I heard a noise as the left-hand butt had smashed into the other rods on the take; I'd forgotten to turn the alarms on! I jumped up and grabbed the rod as the fish came straight up, swirling violently on the surface. After that the fight was pretty much over and I was able to lead him in on a long line. As he got close I noticed a white cloud projecting out behind him; this carp was shitting out loads of pre-digested boilies! I'd never seen anything quite like that before and he continued to pass the bait in the net and on the mat. I actually couldn't believe that this twenty pounder had so much bait inside him! He was one greedy fish that seemed to like the white stuff, as you can see in the pictures.

After passing all that bait, he weighed 21lb 12oz and was a weird looking fellow with a small mouth, massive pecs and tail; even as I slipped him back he did another big white shit as he legged it, probably to feast on the white again. With him back, it was high time to fuzz the rod back out to the spot where the phantom shitter had made his mistake.

With the rods in position, it was time to chill out on the bedchair for some sleep as I was on the fish again. I was woken by the middle buzzer screaming at me and I scrambled to put my boots on and grab the rod. As the fish surged away, taking plenty of line off the clutch, I remember thinking to myself, "This action I'm having is unreal." The fish darted all over the lake on mental runs and for a while I thought I might lose him and had to lay off with the pressure. I reckon some of these carp hadn't been caught for a while or so, which might have explained the fights that I was having.

As he came in close I got a glimpse of what looked like a chunky mirror and not long after I netted a real stunner covered in pearly scales. With some help from Shaun, another member, we got the mirror on the mat; it was a tight swim so the more help the better. I peeled the mesh back to reveal an awesome, scaly beast that had pearly scales and broken-linear scaling, with a creamy yellow belly; you don't get much better than this, whatever the size. It's still one of my favourite carp that I've ever caught and trust me I've caught a few stunners along the way! For the record he weighed 26lb 12oz.

I found it strange that the right-hand rod hadn't had a bite yet, as I had seen several shows near it. Around fifty more baits were put around all rods just to keep the zone baited, as they sure were on the munch. Things had definitely gone quiet now, plus, the wind had dropped and as I was cooking dinner I had a bleep on that middle rod again. As I looked up, it went "Bleeeeeeeeeep." As I got up I turned the stove off and after trying not to knock my dinner over I finally grabbed the rod. The fish swirled on top straight away and kited on a short line before going deep and hugging the bottom. Big plumes of bubbles kept coming up as he tried to rid himself of the hook against the lakebed.

He came in close but stayed deep, shaking his head, but soon I was able to land another old-looking common. As Shaun had disappeared I texted Andy to see if he was still about to do the pictures for me. He was soon at my side and I explained that I had caught another awesome common with a pug face, tiny pecs and a very pale belly. As I opened the net there lay this fat and very wide carp with a little pug face; a right old character, which went 28lb on the scales.

You just can't beat the old Cambridgeshire strains of carp for looks; in fact, we owe Bill Chillingsworth a lot for stocking those scaly mirrors and golden commons all those years ago. The floods of April 1998 saw an injection of those special carp into the Great Ouse, and many of them found new homes in pits along its banks, in waters like Fen Drayton, Swavesey, Ferry Lagoon, various nature reserves, and the Scout and Cub pits.

Anyway, nothing else happened nor was much seen until I was packing up when there was a show down at the other end. My time was finished though, as I had promised

This weird-looking fellow with a small mouth, massive pecs and a huge tail passed loads of bait on the mat.

I peeled the mesh back to reveal an awesome, scaly beast that had pearly scales and broken-linear scaling; it's still one of my favourite carp that I've ever caught.

to take Jane out for lunch. When I get home carp fishing is mostly forgotten until I get ready to go again. The only things I allow myself to do is roll cork-ball pop-ups, change my line and answer tuition enquiries as my family time is vital and even my mates know not to bug me at weekends!

It just happened I needed to get a batch of 200 x 16mm Scopex Squid cork-ball pop-ups rolled, dried and put in pots to glug, a process that takes me about two hours.

On my next trip, I arrived in the car park to find the complex practically empty. Christ, it was really getting quiet on the Wooly. Now, I already had a plan set in my head; I was going to load the barrow and leave it parked by the corner of Lake Six before grabbing a bottle of water to mark my swim. As I made my way up Lake Six and got to the top I'd yet to encounter anyone, so it seemed that several of the 'Paddle Hunters' had gone elsewhere for a while! That was sweet for me as I wanted as many of the stock as possible, plus the big 'un could come out again at any time.

I climbed the tree that overlooked a shallow area in a gap in the island to see what was about. Nothing was immediately visible, but I could see a clearing that they had made on this shallower area. Knowing that this would be a day zone, and given that I was there early, it was time to wait and watch. By mid-morning I had started to notice slight movements thirty to fifty yards away, coming up Lake Five, and as I watched, a 30lb mirror came into view. Not long after, I had a group of seven fish present and some were swimming through the gap. Now, it's nice to watch them, but I needed to secure the swim fast, so I climbed down the tree and legged it round to Lumpy's swim, put the bottle in there and then made my way down to fetch my barrow.

I parked it in the swim and was gagging to get back up the tree and watch. I wanted to see if they were coming into Lake Six, or favouring Lake Five. Watching from up the tree would show me the routes they were using, so I could plan where to put my hook baits. They were going through the gap more and more into Lake Six, so Lumpy's was going to be the swim. I'd noticed that they seemed to hug the near margin before heading into a small bay with several lily beds that were sending their leaves up to the surface to the left of the swim.

Some would go right and some would go left, along the deeper shelf and disappear from view. The plan was to have a hook bait to the right and left of the gap and to fish the other rod in the bay in the day. If I stayed for the night I planned to move that rod well right into open water.

As I sorted the three rods out with long, running chod rigs and discreet, 1oz leads, I kept an eye on the gap. I wasn't seeing many carpy signs, but occasionally I would notice something that gave them away, the

This awesome common with a pug face, tiny pecs and a very pale belly fell to the ever-faithful Scopex Squids.

cheeky buggers were creeping about on the rob!

Once the rods were out, I scattered fifty baits around the area; I didn't see any signs of them spooking either, so hopefully I had got away with it. I chilled out for a bit, but couldn't resist and eventually had to get back up the tree for another look. As I crept round and peered through the reeds, I could see several fish in residence, milling around in the gap. There were two bigger ones that I wanted to get a closer look at, so I climbed the tree to get above them. One was Cluster and the other was a common that wasn't as big and had a growth sticking out of his tail. I was later to find out from Steve Webb that he was called Willy. The others seemed to be big twenties to low thirties.

I was buzzing because I had 35 per cent of the stock in front of me, with two of the big 'uns in residence; happy days, Uncle was back on them big time! Later that evening I saw The Carving for the first time, which was an eye opener I can tell you. I was later to find out that Webby had caught him a few days earlier at 39lb 6oz but hadn't told anyone, secret squirrel that he is. God knows why he told me though!

I decided to stay put as they were hanging around the gap. Even though I thought that they would drift into Lake Five I had my traps laid nice and quiet, so I was ready for them should they mooch back. If they didn't reappear, I would be 'offski', on the hunt again for them.

As darkness approached they seemed to drift off back into Lake Five as expected. The birds started to sing just before first light waking me in time to get the kettle on for my caffeine hit. As I looked out, 'JC' was setting up opposite. I chuckled, thinking that as soon as he started his 'oxygenation' with the marker rod, it'd cut the fish off. I knew that I had to pack up straight away. The weather conditions had changed for the better; it was cloudy, colder with a northerly wind. I reckoned that those conditions would get them on the munch somewhere. One quick look in my side of the gap revealed that there were no fish about.

It was time to get back to the swim and get the barrow loaded. Unbeknown to me, JC forcing me to relocate was to pay off spectacularly. Lake Five was to be the first port of call because that was the last known destination of the fish that had drifted off me the day before. No one else was about and I needed to find them quick, so I left my barrow in a swim in the middle of Lake Five and went for a mooch round.

I found nothing, but the wind was blowing through The Point swim into a little bay. After several laps of the lake I was none the wiser but as I watched from the gap, hidden from JC, I saw a movement out of the corner of my eye. It was a small roll ten yards out in front of The Point; I didn't know if it was a carp or tench. As I fixated on the area Mr Carp subtly rolled in the same spot. Straight away I said to myself, "Jim, go now." I was now praying that no one else had seen it and as I got to the barrow I manhandled it around the hedges to The Point; sweet, no one was there and JC was caught catnapping after his long drive and late night playing 'I'm a DJ' to all the boys and girls!

I carefully parked my barrow and quietly walked to the edge. As I reached the water, a carp rolled subtly in front of me! Uncle was up them again! The long, running chod rig rules out any worries about presentation, plus there's no need for a marker rod to find clear areas for your rig, because my setup is at home when fished over the dirty areas of the lake.

The only blot on the horizon was that Andy had dropped the water table for lake maintenance, so waders were necessary to make sure that fish could be landed safely. As I was going to be fishing close, less than twenty yards out, I could employ a little edge of mine. I cast out a long way past where I wanted to fish and then reeled the rig back in over the spot before letting it drop bang on target. When feeling the lead down you have to keep the rod tip up high and maintain a tight line to the lead to make sure that the chod rests against the top bead on descent.

With all three rods positioned in this fashion it was time for some bait. I wanted to keep disturbance down to a minimum, so I catapulted seven baits around each hook bait, one at a time. I was confident of a bite again because I was sure that this was the area that they had been feeding in. If the conditions were hot they drifted up to the other end of the lake to sun themselves in the warmer, shallow water of the gap and along the island that separated the two lakes.

As time drifted I laid back on the bed chair watching the sunset and taking in the natural beauty of the lake and its surroundings. I saw one more carp and that was further out but I didn't want to move any rods unless a lot started showing further out.

The night was clear and cold but the wind kept up, and I soon drifted off. Knowing that takes were coming in the day meant that I had to be up at first light to watch for signs. I opened my eyes sometime in the night. The wind had brought in new cloud cover that had lifted the temperature, but it was still raw and I felt this when I got out for a leak in the bushes.

As I turned round and headed back to the bivvy I heard a carp push out 35 yards into the lake, where the other fish had shown the evening before. That was it, it was time to crank a rod in and get it out there. I checked the hook to make sure it was still sharp and re-curved the chod. I didn't need to put a fresh bait on as I'd meshed the hook baits with ladies' tights to prolong their life. So, within five minutes I had the rig on the new zone with seven free offerings around it – just enough to get their attention without arousing their suspicion.

Before I knew it, I was firing up the stove for the routine caffeine hit. For a change, I had turned the alarm volume down, as I didn't want the sheep knowing if I had liners or action. As I sat back drinking my mug of warm, milky coffee another one rolled to the left, around the same distance. This one looked a lot bigger and over the next twenty minutes I saw a further five carp all around the zone; time to get the other two rods out to where all this carpy activity was going on. I reeled them in, checked and re-curved them, before fuzzing them out as far past the showing fish as I could with a 1.5oz lead and reeling them back over the new spots. Each rod got its customary seven baits.

Before sitting down I made sure the lines were hanging completely slack. As I watched what was going on in front of me, the middle rod bleeped then screamed! The

The birds started to sing just before first light, waking me in time to get the kettle on for my caffeine hit.

excitement of the first run from a new water is unreal and I immediately wondered which fish I was about to be attached to. As I legged it to the rods, I turned the buzzer off and tried to wriggle into my chesties… the things we have to do for a carp! The fish had stopped taking line and when I got into full contact with him he was kiting on a tight line, well left into the bay. "At least he's well away from the zone," I thought, as I slipped into the lake taking the net with me.

As well as playing the fish, I had to force my way through the thick silt to reach water that was deep enough to let me safely land him, not easy, I can tell you! I was soon in the right spot though, and after a short tussle I slid the net under an old-looking mirror. I peered into the net and touched my prize before popping the hook out gently while he just lay there in the net, gills slowly pulsing.

As I was pushing the landing net handle into the silt, I heard some noise and looked up to see JC standing there. He asked if I wanted help, but I replied with a stern, "No!" Now, JC and I don't get on, but that's another story, and he was warned not to talk to me! I rang Andy to see if he could do the honours and five minutes later he was there. I was delighted to get my first from the lake and, to cap it all off, it was a thirty too, weighing in at 30lb 10oz. A nice, cold bottle of white wine was called for to celebrate in style.

Nothing else had shown while all this was happening, but I was well confident of another take if the carp gods would bless me again.

I sat back to watch the lake but, no sooner had my mind turned to what other carp could be in front, than I was away on the recast rod! The rod was bent right over in the rests as this carp decided to head elsewhere. With the chest waders on, out I went to fetch another prize.

This carp had done a mental run, going over fifty yards straight out, heading towards one of the other gaps. Thankfully, he eventually stopped and started to kite left on what was now a long line! Once again, he was well away from the zone, so hopefully the chance of further action wouldn't be ruined by a hooked carp charging all over the place.

He was now well in the corner to my left and heading for a lily bed. I wasn't unduly worried as the lilies were only just growing back. I eased him round on a long line and he soon ended up in front of me, but stayed deep down at the bottom of the shelf. I couldn't see much as I had stirred the bottom up wading out, so there was no way I was going to see which one he was until he was ready for the net. After a couple of minutes big, oily swirls started to hit the top and the leadcore leader was visible above the surface. The next thing I knew, the carp's head hit the top and he took a gulp of air, before turning and surging away again. In that fleeting moment, I'd noticed that he was a common, and a good one too.

The only blot on the horizon was that Andy had dropped the water table for lake maintenance, so waders were necessary to make sure that fish could be landed safely.

My first from Five & Six was this awesome old character. I celebrated with a chilled bottle of white wine!

He was tiring and didn't get far and it wasn't long before he hit the surface and I scooped him up. A glance at my prize revealed a short, stocky common that looked to be a low thirty. Once I had the hook out in the net, I pushed the handle into the silt to secure him while I sorted out the necessaries. I called Andy, and before I could say anything, he was asking, "Have you got another?" I replied in the affirmative and Andy laughed, saying, "Jim, this is going to start costing you soon!"

All the bits were still there from the last one, so all I had to do was get some more water to keep him moist when on the mat. I sat down to wait and sent out some texts out letting my mates know what I'd just caught. Andy then popped his head round the bivvy and said, "Well done mate," and I just smiled as I was on cloud nine! As I got up, Pikey popped in asking, "What have you had Uncle?" "Oi oi mate, just a couple of scraper thirties that don't count in the spring," I replied. He just grunted; I knew he was worried. There's nothing like a bit of therapy to keep everyone in check, oh the games we play!

I gave my camera to Pikey as Andy had his this time. As I slipped into the waders to go and fetch the common, I could hear Pikey moaning about something; God, he's a boy! As I laid the fish down on the mat and unrolled the mesh, Pikey piped up, saying, "That's Clover." We weighed the fish at 32lb 8oz; sweet, another one bites the dust. Not long after they both left and there was no sign of JC thankfully, but I bet Pikey told him.

After changing the rig, I made the recast and felt it down onto the soft bottom that I had caught over and flicked out seven more free offerings. Rod recast, it was time to tidy my swim up as it looked like a bomb had hit it. Just as I had nearly finished, my mobile rang. It was Steve Allcott ringing for a chat and to congratulate me on my captures.

I was standing on the end of the point watching the lake and talking to Steve when, just to the right, but well behind my right-hand rod, a massive fish rose vertically from the water and slid back in with hardly a sound and almost no disturbance whatsoever. "Steve, I've just seen a right chunk come out over me," I said, trapping the phone against my ear with my shoulder, before grabbing a rod and reeling it in. I checked the rig, tweaked the curve a bit and then fired the bait out to where the fish had shown. It touched down on soft bottom and I decided to fish this rod as a single as they were clearly on the munch! Steve then went and I clipped the bobbin on, set the clutch and made sure the line was hanging slack before deciding that I needed something to eat now, as I hadn't had breakfast. I plumped for a bacon sarnie and as I was getting the cooking bits ready the right-hand alarm emitted a series of bleeps, before just tearing off! Three runs in less than two hours! Judging from the ferocity with which line was being stripped from the clutch, this fish was not happy at having made a mistake! As I was trying to put my waders on I heard that noise again and looked round to see JC standing there, watching me. I just carried on struggling with the waders before grabbing the rod, chucking the net into the lake and making my way out into the lake to fight this carp. It had immense power and zigzagged right and left.

Another of those thirties that 'Didn't count in the spring!' This one is Clover – a fish that I was to catch a few times!

I noticed that the rod was well bent, so it was definitely a big 'un! One minute I thought I had him under control, and then the next he was showing me who was the boss with awesome surges of power. I loved the moment, just him and me fighting each other.

I heard talking behind me, but I didn't look and carried on with the job in hand. He was now well right in the bay. I did wonder why they headed there, and I later found out that this was one of Paddle's hiding places. Were they warning her? It's funny what runs through your mind at times! The surges had stopped, but the power was there as the beast hugged the bottom. Clearly not wanting to come up and see Uncle Jim, he just stayed about fifteen yards out, not coming any closer for a good while. Just when it looked like he wouldn't surrender his position in the corner, there was a swirl out in the lake as he gave ground. I could see the leadcore, I was close, I was in awe of this beast and I was desperate to see which one he was.

I saw a shape and just as I thought I was winning, his tail kicked and he was down deep again but he was now very close to me. The clouded water cut the visibility, but then suddenly, up came the leadcore and there in front of me laid a bar of gold. It was clear to me now it was one of the big commons. I looked at him and then I started to talk him to the net on a short line, "Come on baby, come and see Uncle." He slid in, finally conceding defeat and I shouted, "Yesssss!" I brought the net closer to me and in the folds of my net there lay one special carp, the one Andy had emailed me a picture of…

The Carving! Oh my God… the one I wanted!

As I put my hand into the net to gently touch him, I whispered, "Don't worry mate, I will look after you." I was in my own little world, with one of the best-looking commons in the country in my net. All through the fight I had switched off from the crowd but now I heard a voice, "Jim what fish is it?" I looked round it to see Andy talking to me, "Mate, it's The Carving," I replied.

I turned round and unhooked him in the net and all this time he was quiet. I pushed the landing net handle into the clay and made my way back to the bank. Andy put his hand out to help me back on to dry land and then shook my hand and said, "Well done!" Pikey was next; I kept away from JC like he wasn't even there.

As I was getting everything sorted for the pictures I heard a noise and I looked round to see The Carving thrashing the water to a foam in my net; he wasn't a happy chap now. I went out to get him and I spent time talking and telling him I would look after him as I'd promised.

With the fish safely rolled up in the net, I made my way back to dry land where Andy took the fish off me and placed it in the mat. We carried him to the chosen spot, in front of a bush that was in full bloom. He was well behaved on the mat and as I placed him into Marky Mark's weigh sling, I whispered to myself, "There you go mate; there's another carp for you." Ever since he left us, I have weighed my carp in his sling and scales as a tribute to my best mate. He lives on in me and I will never forget him. Anyway, The Carving weighed in at 39lb 10oz, what a beast.

As I went to pick up my kettle of water, JC grabbed it first. I said "No thanks," and I took it back, glaring at him. Later that day I gave my trusty old kettle a ceremonial burial in the depths of the Woolpack as I didn't want his bad angling pheromones infecting my own fishing! As I held the fish up for the camera, I knew that I was cradling one of the best-looking commons in the country and it was another target sorted. After a few minutes it was time to release him back to his home to fight another day. These are the moments I love; touching them in the net and then the release; holding them in the water, watching them swim off – precious moments to remember.

After twenty minutes everyone had gone, leaving me to my own thoughts. Texts were sent out and my phone was buzzing for ages. The rod was cast back to the spot but the swim now looked dead. I'd had three takes really quickly, so they were likely to have done the off, but you never know and I had until 8am the following morning. I sat back with a nice glass of wine and watched the sun set on cloud nine, as you'd expect. Nothing happened overnight and before long I had to start packing away. Before leaving, I spread 4kg over the area for the sheep. I later found out that one went in after me; I bet he didn't know what I had put in though! I loaded the van and grabbed another 4kg bag of squids and baited Lake Seven too before heading off for a boat-fishing tuition at Fen.

Nothing had happened by my return on Monday but, as you would expect, I was gagging to get back on Five and Six. I had a night before another tuition, so it was a case of finding them, hopefully on Five and Six. The lake was busy though, and I

The Carving comes ashore.

was forced to drop onto the backup, Lake Seven. As I scanned the water, I saw a fish show on the wind that was blowing into the car park. I decided to watch for a while and see what else showed on the northerly wind. Not long afterwards, I saw another and in the next ten or so minutes I saw another eight fish. Some seemed to be holding back at the mouth of the bay.

I came up with a plan… I decided to fish in the platform swim as it gave me a lot more scope. The swim was tight and the rods would have to be in the water; thankfully, I use long storm sticks anyway, although I'd have to get in the water to cast out. The light was fading fast now and as

I was overwhelmed to be holding the fish that Andy had email me a picture of – what a creature.

Stunning... what more can be said?

After a short tussle, I landed a truly stunning carp that weighed in at 26lb.

I laid my rods against the reeds I saw more shows. I was gagging to get the rods out. With chest waders on, I made my way to the water's edge and grabbed my throwing stick, a bag of squids and my buzzers on the way.

I carefully picked my way along the side of the platform, leaving my bait and stick on the end of the structure so I had them to hand. Gas bubbled to the surface as I pushed the sticks into the soft bottom, ready to prop the rods on after casting. I had taken a mental note of where the fish had been showing, so I could flick the rigs out on the money first time. I cast all three rods out and then baited them up, spreading around two hundred squid boilies over a big area. I wanted to get the carp grazing over a large area, making them more prone to making a mistake. This is completely at odds with the way that most anglers fish these days, trying to bait tight over small, clear areas. It was time to set up the bedchair and lay out my sleeping bag and bedchair cover to keep the damp off me. The swim was tidied up and the bits put away for a quick move.

I grabbed a smoked-salmon sandwich that Jane had made me for a snack. I watched after dark and they carried on showing all over the zone, happy days, they were still there. Not long after, it was time to get some sleep and recharge the batteries for the tuition in the morning. I was woken up by one of my buzzers screaming at me as an angry carp made off with one on my hook baits. "Christ Uncle, get yourself sorted," I thought. It was on with the head torch and into the waders, while the buzzer carried on screaming a total one-toner.

The blue LED was glowing as I made my way along the wooden platform, indicating the right-hand rod in deep water. I just couldn't believe this take; the rod was practically bent in half round to the right. I then turned the buzzer off and made contact. He was still pulling line, but I knew that with steady pressure I would get him to slow down. Not long after he did before starting to kite left, back out into the middle of the lake. I think the way that he had screamed off had zapped his energy and I soon found myself gaining loads of line. Soon he was chugging around to the left, close in, so I then grabbed the net and made my way to him. When I was in position I switched the torch off, as I didn't want to scare him with the light.

Soon, I could see the swirls in the moonlight and I got a glimpse of solid flank, he was close now. I grabbed the net and pushed it out to the shape in the darkness. I lifted the net and he was mine. I turned on the torch and the water exploded, as he wasn't happy with that! I peered in once he had calmed down and could make out the substantial frame of a nice mirror. I tipped him onto his side… "Bloody hell Uncle, that's the linear you had two weeks ago." I already had good pictures, so I decided to slip him back without stressing him any further. I touched him and whispered, "Sorry mate." I do have a tendency to catch them again, possibly due to the way that I fish. As I bent down and gently pushed him out, I said farewell and watched him swim off into the darkness. Gathering my senses, I noticed that the wind had dropped and I decided not to recast as I think there had been enough disturbance already. I turned the mobile on to see what the time was and the screen glowed, showing 11:30pm. Time to get back into the bag for some more sleep before the birds started their morning chorus.

Davyd, who is a regular client, arrived for his tuition and had located carp straight away up the other end of the lake. We set up in the nearest two swims to the fish and I went straight into fishing mode to get the rods out ASAP. It wasn't long before Davyd received a savage take on his left-hand rod, which amazingly resulted in landing the same big linear again at 36lb, some twelve hours after I'd put him back! Not to be outdone, I got in on the action and after a short tussle I landed an absolute gem of a carp, which weighed in at 26lb.

Later, while on my tea break, I decided to pop round to see my old mate Gary Puiy, who was booked in for a five-day tuition in a few weeks. As I walked down the side of Lake Five, fish were topping in front of the swim called the Last in Five. Straight away, I ran back to quickly reel in one of my rods and grab some squids, throwing stick and landing net; this was an opportunity I couldn't miss! As I was trying to re-curve the rig, fish were rolling and fizzing all over the zone in front of the gap. I cast past where they were showing and reeled the rig back over, close to the surface, so it made minimal disturbance over the zone, before gently sinking the line and laying the rod down with the clutch set. Gary then appeared asking, "What are you up to Uncle?" I told him that I was en route to him when I'd seen fish. As we talked another pushed out! Gary couldn't believe it as he was only fishing next door in the swim called The Stench and had seen nothing. "How do you do it?" he sighed. "God knows," I replied, adding, "That's what you get for being asleep and camping!"

Suddenly, Gary pointed, spluttering, "Look, the line has pulled tight." Something had grabbed the chod before I'd even managed to get any bait out. The water was really low in this swim, which made netting the fish hard, so Gary grabbed his thigh waders and I kicked off my boots as he guided my feet into them. This fish kited down to the right, along the reeds, before eventually chugging around under the rod tip where I could see a long, dark mirror. After a couple of minutes I slipped the net under the carp. At that moment, my mate, Matt 'Matiz' Gosling walked into the swim and I could hear Gary going on about how I'd only been in the swim for five minutes! I was smiling cheekily as I walked back to the bank with my prize. Pikey then came round the corner shouting, "You should be with your client, plus you aren't allowed to fish here when you're on another lake!" I replied, "Oh well, are you going to fcuking ban me then?" He just muttered, "I've just helped your client with a fish as he was having problems." "Oh, good angling Pikey, I'll just get this photographed and I'll go back". Pikey walked off grunting some old bollocks. I quickly got the fish weighed and photographed. It was a fish called Little Lumpy, weighing in at 24lb 4oz. I legged it back to Davyd, where he informed me that he'd just had a stunning broken linear of 29lb 12oz. I laughed, telling him that I'd poached one out of Lake Five on my tea break and got some therapy from Pikey for being a naughty boy! After Davyd's tuition drew to a close, I knew that it was time to have a break and spend some quality time with the wife and trust me, we do.

Little Lumpy at 24lb 4oz, Pikey wasn't happy!

Davyd's cracking broken linear of 29lb 12oz – one happy customer!

The next trip yielded a blank. The weather was a lot hotter and the fish seemed to be hanging around Lumpy's on Lake Six and a swim called Last on Five and guess what? I couldn't get near them. I needed to make a change to get on fish. I decided to start my sessions on a Sunday evening, rather than the usual Tuesday. The following week I was gagging to get back; the trouble was, I was booked in for a five-day tuition with Bob, a syndicate member, and he wanted to fish Lake Seven really. He bagged a few, topped by Houdini the common, at 29lb 12oz. It was time for some watercraft tuition, so we reeled the rods in and set off. It wasn't long before we found them towards the top end of Lake Six, milling around in front of the swims that are named the Middle channel and the Back Door. We decided to have a go for them, so we put a pair of Bob's glasses in the Back Door and I put mine in Lumpy's, hoping that they would visit us at some point.

I couldn't believe how quiet Lake Five and Six was and we had hit the jackpot; the carp gods seemed to be pointing us in the right direction. We quickly headed back to our swims and packed up in double-quick time and we were soon barrowing round to our chosen swims. Bob had picked the Back Door, which meant he could fan his rods out and cover the water down to the right, in front of the Middle Gap. Most of the fish were in this area, showing long towards the far margin. They were ripping it up and pushing out over the area; he had a really good chance of a chunk!

Before casting out I changed his lead to a 1oz, as it was no more than a 35-yard cast to the zone. The rig was checked and a fresh salty squid cork-ball pop-up was tied on. He got the rig on the spot perfectly and put several freebies out one at a time to reduce the chance of spooking them. It seemed to have worked, as not long after, one pushed out and the fizzing carried on.

Once he had put the rod on the rest and slackened off, clipped the bobbin on and set the clutch I told him to leave the rod alone unless he got a take.

I went back to my swim and got my rods out. The left-hand rod was in the corner by some lilies and the other two rods were cast into the gap, in the shallow water. I was hoping some might drift up to me at some point, as they seemed to visit the gap on a regular basis. Once the rods were out, I baited up, spreading around a hundred boilies over my traps. After a few hours it seemed dead, especially after Bob had touched his rod which I had asked him not to, all because he had problems with drifting silkweed, when will people listen and leave well alone. After he had repositioned the rod it seemed to spook the fish away… up in front of me in Lumpy's where I had my traps set.

It was getting late, the sun was setting and the carp had now gone on the missing list. After dark there were ripples coming from my left in the corner. I still had a rod in there; at least I had done as I was told and left them be!

I was confident of a bite but they seemed to all be day bites at the time, apart from Pikey's capture of Cluster in the early hours. Several times in the night I was woken by chunks jumping in that area to the left, surely a bite would come? By first light nothing had occurred and by the time the sun was climbing into the sky I'd only seen a couple move through the gap. The answer was clear, they'd done the off into Lake Five at some point.

It was starting to get really hot and I said to Bob, "Let's go to Fen for the last 24 hours." He said, "What's the chance of a bite from there?" "Oi oi, what's one of the main things I taught you?" I asked, "Find them, catch them. So let's go and find them. Plus, you couldn't be with a better person in terms of knowledge of the ways of Fen carp." So, we decided to have a slow pack up and reel in by 11am. Me being me, I just packed straight up so I was ready for the off. I sent Bob a text saying "Fifteen minutes and we're off," I then decided to reel the left-hand rod in. Next was the right-hand rod and as I swung the lead to hand I noticed the other line pick up. I dropped the other rod and pulled in to it before it had taken line off the clutch, how lucky was that?

The fish surged off powerfully, pulling the rod down, and as I looked up, a huge bow-wave went up the gap. What the hell was I attached to? This brute forced its way into Lake Five, leaving me wondering what the hell I was going to do next. I shouted for Bob, but couldn't raise him. Although I was able to gain a little line back, the fact remained that the fish had taken me through the gap into Lake Five and, with the water level being so low, I couldn't force him back through.

A plan was needed, quickly I climbed into the chesties, slackened the clutch and set off to find Bob. He was in a world of his own and hadn't heard my calls for help. As we got into my swim I told him, "Right you hold the rod and when I shout to you, flick

Old English all the way. Cluster at a colossal 45lb 4oz.

I'd never had a carp run me around with such power.

A quick kiss for the biggest mirror in the lake before he goes back.

We pulled into the car park at Fen and I got a whiff of carp on the wind.

I was able to show Bob fish like Bayes' Common and The Pug-Faced Common feeding in shallow water. Needless to say, we set up on them!

the free spool lever to give line." As I was explaining all this to him Matiz turned up. I explained the situation to Matty and told him to grab the net and I took one of my rods off the rest. Matiz and I legged it round the side of Lake Six and soon we were standing in the gap. I planned to cast the rod that I was holding over the other line and reel it in (with Bob playing off slack to allow me to do this). I soon had the rig and the other line in my hand. "Right mate," I told Matiz, "You hold the end with the fish on as I'm going to bite it off and tie it to this rod." Although Matty wasn't keen, I told him that it would only take me seconds to tie the two lines together. Matiz wrapped the line round his hand and gave me tag end, then I quickly tied it back onto the rod I was holding, Matiz let it go and I quickly reeled the knot back on to the spool!

Now, was the carp still on and if so, where the hell was it? I dropped down into the gap and made my way along, reeling the line in. With each turn gained the knot was further back and safer. I was soon standing in the gap at the side of Lake Five and the line was going well right of the gap and up the island. Matiz couldn't get his head round where the fish had taken me! I said, "Mate, I've never had a carp run me around this much, with such power." As the line tightened, I made contact with something but it seemed snagged. Luckily, I soon had something moving but I wasn't getting the telltale signs that a fish was still on. As I was reeling in a dead weight, like a huge lump of weed, I felt something and said to Matt, "I think it's still on." I coaxed it back to me

Within three hours of setting foot on Fen, Bob had banked a 27lb common!

Later that evening, I banked a 28lb 12oz common too!

and there was indeed a carp on the other end. As he got close some of the weed came off and he livened up. There was no way I was letting him go again though, so I bullied him in and then Matiz slid the net under a mirror that looked about 30lb.

I turned to Matiz and said, "That looks like a low-thirty mate," and he said, "It's bigger than that Jim." I turned to have a look in the net and as I started to pull away some of the weed that was covering it I got a shock, as there in the net lay that mirror I wanted… Cluster! I shouted, now I was buzzing! I just couldn't believe it but really I should have known it was him as he's known as an animal of a fighter!

Bob came round with the mat and Matiz and I walked him back to the swim. As we entered the swim I dropped down into the clear water in the margin, then carefully lowered him into the water in the net. Matiz passed me the handle and I put the arms in the spreader block and pushed the handle into the soft bottom while I sorted things out and got my head together. Everything was soon ready and the moment had come for my little cuddle with this awesome beast.

On the scales he weighed 45lb 4oz, mind you the weight means nothing to me, it's all about the fish and their history, old English all the way and this one sure was one of these.

As I got into the water I looked up to the sky and said, "This one's for you Marky." I even wore his favourite hat for the pics. I broke the net down and Matiz readied the cradle for me to put him in. Once he was safely in, Matiz took the fish to the spot and

I knew that locating the larders of natural food was key to tracking Paddle down.

I had a new baiting plan for the spring, it involved groundbait!

I slowly climbed out of the water gagging to hold my prize. As you can see from the pictures, he sure is a stunner and I must admit that, as I touched him, I was in awe of that creature. He was well behaved on the bank, nothing like he was out in the lake!
As I lowered him back into his home, I gave him a kiss and whispered to him, "Thanks for an everlasting memory," and as he disappeared back into the darkness I punched the sky and shouted "Yessss!"
We were running a bit late by now but not too long after we were on the banks of Fen. We pulled into the car park and I got a whiff of carp on the wind. I said to Bob that I had just smelled carp. He chuckled, but I wasn't laughing. I took him round to a tree that overlooked the car park bay and, sure enough, there was a load of carp beneath, feeding in the shallow water. I think seeing those fish did Bob in a little. Five minutes on Fen and he was looking at Bayes' Common and The Pug-Faced Common feeding, at least, they were the ones I could name. I guided him to a known pick-up spot a rod length out and, to cut a long story short, Bob landed a 27lb common within three hours of setting foot on Fen. Later that evening I had a 28lb 12oz common too. As you can imagine, we were both very happy and I think Bob had his money's worth and went away a happy chappy. Over the weekend Andy rang me and said that the lake was now closed to let them get on with spawning and would stay closed for a week or two afterwards for them to get over it.
Now, this was the time for me to leg it elsewhere for the summer, as I wanted to catch

Paddle at the best weight possible. This meant I would only be hunting her in the spring and autumn. Spring was the best time to get her really big so when the following spring arrived, I would be putting as much time in as possible. I had a few trips in the autumn and did have her and others pushing out in front of me in Lake Five, near the point. I had no action, but at least it gave me more pieces to add to the jigsaw. I couldn't get Paddle off my mind over the winter. I was thinking about her all the time; where she could be and how big, because she had done 49lb plus on several occasions. Surely she'd be 50lb this year.

After winter loosened its grip, my first trip was in March, when I had a 24-hour tuition booked. No one was fishing on the entire complex, which seemed crazy, as it was so mild. I couldn't help but think that the sheep were waiting for the first one to come out, constantly ringing Andy for the info; a bloody joke if you ask me. I got there early and spent time watching on Five and Six before the tuition started, looking for a sign to start on, however all I could see were tench. I even made myself get up in the night and take a stroll to see if I could hear any. However, the fish were clearly lying low, as it was all quiet. First light couldn't have been more different; I watched for 30 minutes and, bingo, they were sticking their heads out – definite carp. I legged it back to Lake Seven to grab an item of tackle to reserve the swim as quickly as I could. With the

I was even wrapping my pop-ups in a layer of groundbait, before securing it in place with a section of ladies' tights.

Willy at 40lb 3oz; I knew that I had to do self-takes to keep things on the QT!

I knew that it wouldn't be long before the sheep arrived.

I went for a walk around Swavesey on my way home; it was years since I'd last fished there with Marky.

swim reserved, I could relax and it was soon time for us to go our separate ways.
Even though I was knackered from getting up in the night, I decided to watch for any shows before getting my rods out and having one of my power-sleeps to recharge my batteries. I saw three more shows so all I had to do was to check the hooks, re-curve the rigs and cast roughly where Mr Carp had shown. All the leads landed on relatively firm bottom, not the soft drops I'd had in the autumn. It was like the bottom had been fed on and cleaned off. As I was knackered it was time to grab that power-sleep; at least I had chance as I was on them now. However, I did notice the last one that showed was 80 yards away from me, like it was on the move elsewhere. I woke up sweating as the sun had been on me while I was asleep. I felt like shit, but I had a plan. I downed a tin of Red Bull, now it was time to act on the plan that had come to me in my sleep; I'm sure the carp gods had given me the vision!
All I had on my mind when I woke up was to go and find the silt and new weed growth that would hold the natural food that the carp were after. I had an idea where this would be; near the shallow water up at the other end close to the gap that connects both lakes. I grabbed the spod rod, cut the spod off and tied on a two-ounce lead on. I made my way from swim to swim, flicking the lead out in search of those softer drops. As I got to the swim called The Stench, the lead started to drag more, telling me I was getting close. It was close to that prime area near the gap where the carp sunned

After finding the fish I struck gold with this 31lb 12oz common.

themselves in the warmer water after munching. I made another cast, slightly to the right, near the gap. It was harder to pull back clean. When I reeled it in I had loads of new weed growth and silkweed and, when I opened it, there were bloodworm and shrimps, bingo; this had to be the zone. I decided to fish it from The Stench, which is not what I'd normally do if others were about because the swim called the Last in Five controlled that water, plus it had a good track record and was popular with the members. I took the chance and fished it from a different angle; it would be interesting to see what effect it had.

The rigs were unchanged from the previous season, but I'd tweaked the hook baits slightly. I'd meshed some of my spod mix around the chocolate malt cork-ball, just to add some attraction and match the mix that I'd decided to introduce on that trip. I was to fish over a hemp groundbait mixed with crushed hemp and crumbed-up chocolate boilies, with a few 10mm mixed in. Once the rods were out, I spodded out seven spodfuls of the mixture over the rigs. To get a nice spread, I snatched the spod back just as it landed, making it cartwheel, spraying bait over a wider area. I hoped to get them rooting about over a greater area and increase my chance of a bite by getting them moving around, searching out the bits and pieces. After I'd finished, there was a nice slick spreading over the area and this, combined with the natural food, just had to get them interested. To finish the baiting, I spread a hundred 15mm choccy malt boilies over the area.

With the house set up I watched until late but saw nothing, however I did feel close simply because I knew that it was an area that they used a lot and the fresh weed growth was a definite draw. That night I didn't hear anything and as soon as the birds started singing before first light I starting stirring. A bleep from the right-hand alarm grabbed my attention and as I watched the blue LED go out, I wondered if something was mooching over the zone, as it must have been a liner. It was calm and very mild, prime time for a bite. I sat on the edge of my bedchair, drinking my coffee, watching for carpy signs. It wasn't long before I decided to have a walk up the bank to my left, to have a look where the fish were showing the morning before. As I got towards The Point swim I heard another bleep and ran back to see which rod was responsible. When I entered the swim I noticed the line from the right-hand rod twitching as it entered the water. With no more bleeps from the buzzer, I decided to put my chesties on and gently pull the line to see if it was a drop back. As I started to pull it, the line was pulled through my fingers, fish on!

I picked the rod up and started to reel up the slack, trying to catch up with whatever was on the other end. I noticed the line was well left of the left-hand rod so whatever I had on was on a mission elsewhere up the lake! All of a sudden, I caught up with something big! Oi oi Mr Carp! I'm sure it was tired after running well left because it allowed itself to be led easily into the margin, fifteen or so yards up the bank just out from the shelf. I positioned the net to the left, against the old Norfolk reeds and walked into the clear water, just up from the net. I think at this point he knew I was approaching as he shot out into the lake on a mental power surge, telling me that this

Paddle hunting at the top end of Lake Five.

Colin told me that he'd bagged a fish called Twiglet at 29lb 12oz and lost a powerful fish that morning.

could be a big 'un, but which one? Soon I had this as-yet unseen beast under the rod tip and deep, angry boils were coming to the surface. Suddenly, I saw a golden flash of scales telling me it was a common. Was it one of the A-Team? The leadcore broke surface, telling me he was close and I saw a big head deep down. "Christ, it's one of the big 'uns for sure," I thought. I turned round, grabbed the net and placed it in readiness.

In slow motion, a huge back broke the surface; it was wide and looked a right chunk. I bent down and grabbed the handle of my net and as I pushed it out, I lifted the net and this beast of a common went in first time. "Yesssssss," I shouted across the lake and then immediately regretted it. I was kicking myself for potentially alerting the sheep that it was time to descend on the Woolpack. It was best to keep things quiet, so I quickly sacked the carp up and hid him along the margins until I had checked to see if anyone was about. I had a look about and after five minutes I knew it was safe to do some self-takes. In all the rush of concealing my prize I hadn't looked to see which one it was. What I did know, however, was that it was a big kipper.

I got everything ready for the weighing and self-takes, and then looked across the lake to see if I could see anyone coming along the bank. All was clear so it was time to go get my prize and have a look at him. I gently brought him ashore and placed him on the mat. As I peeled back the sack I noticed his tail had this growth on it that looked like a willy! "Christ, it's Willy," I thought, remembering my conversation with Steve Webb after I had described it swimming through the gap the previous year. Now I knew I had another one of the A-Team for sure.

On the scales he went 40lb 3oz, and it's always nice to get the first chunk of the year under your belt! As far I knew this was the first one of the year from this demanding venue… happy days. People still question me about doing self-takes of such a big fish, but I'm a master of self-takes as you can see from the picture! Plus, it allowed me to keep everything on the QT, which can be worth a few extra fish at times. I knew that I had at least another trip without the crowds descending on such a small water but I also knew that it wouldn't be long before another one was caught and the sheep arrived. All the wet equipment was hidden and I left the wet net in the edge so that it wasn't spotted and questioned. I also noticed that my sweatshirt had slime on it and I smelt of carp, so I put my coat on to conceal it if I bumped into anyone and legged it to the van to get a clean one. You have got to be on the ball these days to keep one step ahead!

After a blank night Pikey turned up just before bite time and asked me if I had seen or caught anything. I told him that I hadn't and he said "Put the kettle on Fester" (that's what he was calling me at that time). I said, "No, I don't do that and nor would I ask you for one," he wasn't too happy and told me that he was going in next door, in Last in Five. I consoled myself that at least I'd caught one, but I knew that I couldn't bait up as I would normally have done after a capture, or if I was fishing a swim a lot. At least there was likely to be some bait out there after I'd re-baited following the capture.

Andy rang me when I got home to see if I had caught. He's such a nice fellow that I laughed and swore him to secrecy. He didn't like it, but he said "You have two weeks, then I want it in the book." I just laughed and said "If you're lucky I might show you the pictures when I'm down next." Apart from Steve Allcott, Matiz and Andy, I kept this capture to myself. It was busy over the following weekend; I bet the sheep had heard I'd been down! Nothing came out and the next two trips were blanks. I did manage to get on them in a swim called the First in Five. It seemed that they were using the gap at the other end of the lake to travel between lakes for a change. The next two trips were blanks but the lake was getting busier and still Paddle hadn't been banked. As you can imagine, it would only get worse the longer she went uncaught. I had seen most of the stock in those two trips, which was great, but I had no sightings of Paddle yet, she was keeping a low profile. Mind you, it was busy and the longer it went on the bigger she would get.

On the way home from one session I decided to go and have a look round Fen. It was busy, so I decided to go have a mooch round Swavesey. As I parked up in the bottom corner, where the wind was blowing, I noticed a black shape gliding along the shelf. It looked like a linear of 30lb plus. As I watched, I saw several others in the slight ripple that was pushing into the corner. It was late in the evening so I got straight into fishing mode; hooks were checked and fresh red fishmeal hook baits were tied on. I had already clocked that the shelf was covered in silkweed, so I could still fish

I managed four twenties off the top in Lake Eight.

my chod rigs over it. I know the carp love this fresh, slimy, green stuff and so do the invertebrates. Before making my way to the area, I made sure I had camo clothing on along with my polarised glasses, so it was harder for them to see me and I could keep an eye on them to determine when it was clear to place a rig.

I soon had four rods spaced out along this small bay and I'd got away with it too, as the fish were still in residence… sweet. I then retired to a safe distance, as I didn't want to spook them away from the traps. I set my brolly up and rung Matiz to tell him I was on them. He told me that I had a very good chance but informed me that the wind was going to change direction before midnight and blow really hard for the night, before calming off by the morning. Just on darkness they started to stick their heads out. The problem was that they were doing this just away from the shelf, over 15ft of water. I told myself to leave the rods be as they may well have been showing there, but I felt that they'd feed on the silkweed on the shelf. The wind got up around 10pm and changed direction, like Matiz had predicted. It was now blowing into the opposite corner. I got up and went over there for a look. As I sat down on the grass I heard something that sounded like a show, then another, and another; they had moved and knowing these carp, they love a new wind! It was clearly time to leg it back and get my gear packed up and loaded on the barrow. Around thirty minutes later, I was standing in the corner where these fish were showing. As I got the rods out I could hear them gently pushing out in the darkness. I decided to fan the rods out from the reedy corner into the deep open water in front of me. All the time I was doing this they were still rolling, so I kept the baiting to a minimum, as I didn't want to spook them.

I had four rods fanned out in the area, but I got a shallower, softer drop near the weed in the corner. The traps were set and it was time to get my house up and get some sleep. As I lay on the bedchair I could still hear them. I must have fallen asleep because the next thing I heard was a buzzer screaming. I looked out and could see the blue LED on the left-hander; the rod near the weed! It was absolutely one-toning as I put my head torch on and pushed my feet into my boots. I grabbed the net, which I'd leant against the brolly as I had my rods spaced out. As I made my way towards the screaming buzzer I had to be careful because the cows that live around the lake had made potholes with their hooves in the soft ground. I didn't fancy a broken ankle, so with the head torch on I made my as quickly as possible to the blue LED. I dropped the net, grabbed the rod and lifted into the fish. It just carried on stripping line from the spool. This carp was seriously pissed off, but with steady pressure he started to kite on a long line, heading right, past all the other rods. I had to carefully dodge the potholes as I made my way round the back of the other rods, dropping the net once I was to the right of the right-hand rod. The fish immediately popped up onto the surface and in the dim torchlight I could see a nice common wallowing on the surface, ready for netting. I guess that the run must have exhausted him so I grabbed the net

I was able to watch some of the A-Team in the gap wearing my 3D camo so they couldn't spot me at close quarters.

and scooped him up.
He weighed in at 31lb 12oz and I placed him in the sack until first light. Checking the phone, I could see that it was 2:30am so I texted Matiz as he was fishing Fen. He replied saying he would be with me for first light to do the pictures. As I lay on the bedchair watching the sunrise I heard footsteps, and Matiz poked his head round the brolly. I got up, pulled on my boots and grabbed a coat, as it was a bit chilly after emerging from the warmth of my bag. We chatted as the light levels improved and I picked a nice bramble bush for the backdrop to the pictures. Once the pictures were done, Matiz left and I thanked him for his help and wished him luck on Fen. Many years had passed since I last fished at Swavesey with Marky, mainly because it's hard to make time for it when you have the pull of Fen just down the road! It was soon time to pack up and go to spend some time with my lovely wife Jane, while praying that Paddle would wait for my return.
I knew where I wanted to be on my next trip to Wooly, and that was either Lumpy's or the Last in Five. It was clear that they were visiting this area a lot in the build up to spawning as the days were getting hotter and we were now well into April. By the time that I'd actually arrived at the complex, I had decided to revert to my usual strategy and find some fish to angle for. There were several anglers fishing Five and Six, and the zone I fancied fishing was occupied. As I walked past Lumpy's and looked across, I could see movements in the gap, so I just carried on and didn't talk to anyone. As it

Tucked away behind the reeds that line much of the banks at Wooly.

Fish like these are the carp that my mates and I love to fish for, regardless of the weight.

was hot, I decided to go and have a look around Lake Eight to see if I could find any on the top. I soon hit the jackpot and found a group of fish milling around in the sun up at the top end of the lake. There was no one fishing Lake Eight so I quickly legged it back to the van for my floater kit. I was buzzing at the prospect of being able to fish my own way again and as I made my way up the bank towards where I had seen those fish, I was confident of quick action. I managed four twenties off the top that day, with the biggest going 26lb 12oz, a scaly mirror and ex- Five and Six resident.

The fish disappeared after the floater therapy, so I put the floater kit back in the van and noticed several motors had gone. One of them was definitely the bloke who was fishing in Last in Five, so now I was praying to the carp gods as I loaded my barrow, "Please be free for Uncle Jim!" As I made way along the bottom of Lake Seven my mind was racing. I parked my barrow and grabbed my rods to put in the swim if it was free. I decided to cheat and go up the causeway that separates Lake Six and Seven as I knew if I went this way I would be able to see from Lumpy's if Last in Five was free. As I got closer I was begging the carp gods to make my day, and as I walked behind Lumpy's and looked across I could see the swim was free… sweet. All of a sudden the angler in Lumpy's popped his head up and said hi! I shook his hand and said, "I'm Jim," which he probably knew, and told me that his name was Colin. Not being rude, I stopped and talked for a few minutes and Colin started telling me about all the fish that were about, mind you, I could easily see that for myself! He also informed me that he had caught Twiglet at 29lb 12oz and also lost a powerful fish that morning! As you could imagine, I was gagging to secure the swim opposite, and I was praying no-one would beat me to it. As he talked, I thought, "I've got to get away and get that swim secured now!" "Colin," I said, "I'm going in opposite you, over there. Is it OK if I have a look into the gap from my side?" I told him that I'd be careful not to spook them and as soon as he said it was fine, I was making a fast exit.

I didn't actually stop to have a look in the gap because I had to get that swim secured ASAP! Thinking back, I got lucky as Noc walked into the swim just after me, saying he was going to go in there. "Too late Noc, this swim's mine," I said. Luckily, he hadn't put anything in the swim and I could see he knew he had fcuked up. With Noc standing there deflated, it was time for some more Uncle Jim therapy. "Steve's seen your rigs and says they're shit," I told him. Just as he was trying to deny it, I continued, "Well fella, Steve looked in your bucket…" at that point I could see he knew Steve had looked and it became an ongoing joke as some of us had been giving Noc therapy about the amount of blank nights he had racked up. You could tell he didn't like it! Sorry mate! Therapy dished out, it was time to get my barrow, and as I walked away I had a smile on my face.

Knowing that all these fish were in the zone I was gagging to get my rods out and

Noc had heard the buzzer and I had to confess that I had a mid-twenty common in the net.

fishing. I pushed the barrow into the swim and got straight to work, getting the rods ready while keeping an eye on the zone. It was clear where I needed to cast my chod rigs; the far margin in front of the gap, and the reed line along the island to the left of the swim. The swim was tight for casting, so I would need to get into the water. I put my chesties on and made my way to the edge. Two casts later the first rod was bang on. The lead hit the reeds but I knew that the bait would have settled back up the leader on the cast. I had moved the top bead so it wasn't 8ft up the leader like normal. Instead, it was 4ft above the bottom bead, ensuring that the pop-up would be sitting in the shallow water at the top of the shelf in silkweed. I decided to only fish two rods and flicked the other one into the gap itself. The third was ready to go and I planned to put that one out to the left in deep water that evening, as I guessed that some carp would probably move out into deep water for the night. The next job was to go round and to bait up from next to the gap, as it would be easy to get all the baits on top of the shelf along with a few broken ones for added attractiveness. I watched from the gap with full 3D camo clothing on so they couldn't see me, and there were loads about. I saw the Carving and Cluster about but still no Paddle. I really hoped that Colin hadn't lost her, as she was being a right bitch and I hadn't even seen her yet, although a few had. All I knew was, the longer she went uncaught, the bigger she would be prior to spawning. I had to pin her down and fast. She definitely seemed to like the gap area; in fact, she seemed to love shallow water in general, going on the evidence of past captures.

Before too long, I'd seen enough and was time to get back on the rods and get my house set up for the night. As I got back into the swim I had a single bleep. "Here we go," I thought. I knew I was close; all they had to do was suck it and see! Everything was set up in rapidly and it was now time to play the waiting game. However, it wasn't to be a long wait because, suddenly, the bobbin pulled up tight and the buzzer screamed into life. I scrambled into my chesties before picking the rod up. The huge bow-wave was accompanied by the screaming clutch as this angry carp legged it way, way left down the lake. The sheer power of this animal had me thinking I had hooked Cluster again. Before I knew it, the fish had made the middle gap along the island and I was forced to follow, picking my way along the silty reed line. He was miles to the left and the power transmitting up the rod was immense. All of a sudden, I became aware of my situation. I could see Noc down in the corner, and I didn't want him seeing me playing a fish, so I edged back into the reeds for cover. I looked up and Colin was in his bivvy and hadn't seen me in the water yet. I was trying to keep it quiet so I didn't have people move in next door.

The fish then kited out from the island margin and swung across the lake, deep down. He had slowed right up by now, and I had him under more control. He carried on kiting towards my margin and I guided him in front of me on a long line making ground all the time. I think this fish knew he was nailed as I soon had him chugging up and down the margin, as he wasn't really doing much. The next thing I knew, he was wallowing on the top and I could see that it was an awesome-looking mirror covered in scales. I pushed the net out and he went in first time. With the fish secured, I peered

My mind was racing, Paddle hadn't been out yet and I prayed that I'd be the one to catch her.

round the reeds and Noc was setting his bivvy up. I couldn't see Colin opposite, so I had reason to hope that no-one had seen me playing the fish. I unhooked him in the net and pushed the net handle into the soft bottom, grabbed the rod and made my way back to the swim. I put the rod up against the reeds and looked over to Colin's swim. He was now sitting in his bivvy, but I was sure that he hadn't seen me with the fish yet. I got all the bits ready for self-takes, as I didn't want to ask someone to do the pictures after to going to such lengths to keep it secret.

Once things were sorted and Colin was out of view, I headed back into the water to fetch my prize. As I broke the net down his scales lit up silver along his body, like he was covered in armour plating. He then thrashed the water to a foam and covered me in spray; he sure weren't happy with his mistake. "Easy tiger," I whispered, as I wrapped the mesh around the net arms. Noc couldn't see me, but as I made my way back to the swim I kept an eye out to see if Colin was watching. He was preoccupied doing something, so I took my chance and carried on out of the water. I gently laid my prize down on the mat and as I unwrapped the mesh I was blown away at the first sight of this stunning fish. Before me lay one of the loveliest-looking carp that I had ever caught.

I poured some cool lake water over him, and readied the sling and scales. Hoisting him, the scales recorded a weight of 28lb 12oz, which seemed particularly irrelevant with this fish. As you can see, he is an awesome beast and these are the quintessential old English carp that my mates and I fish for. After the self-takes were done, it was time to slip him back. I was going to release him in the next swim up, The Stench, so no-one saw me in the water. As I lowered the cradle into the edge, I cupped my hand and covered him in water before I dropped the front of the mat to release him. This is a moment I savour; watching them glide back into the darkness. Still no-one knew either, sweet, time to hide the wet gear from view.

As I looked out, carp were still milling around the shelf, so I quickly tied on a new rig and a fresh hook bait. It landed bang on, first cast. I carefully sunk the line and placed the rod on the rest before clipping the bobbin on and making sure that everything was hanging slack. I then went round to the gap and fired out some more broken boilies. I didn't put whole baits out as they make much more noise. As you can imagine, my confidence was on the up. It had been five weeks since I had caught Willy and things were now happening again, with the capture of the Swavesey common, and the four twenties I had caught earlier on that day from Lake Eight.

It was getting late and the sun was now starting to set and I started to notice less carpy activity in the area. I expected this to happen anyway, let alone after I'd just nailed one. I flicked the third rod into the deeper water for a chance of a night bite and retired to bed. The odd carp rolled to my left in the night, but I left everything where it was as I was hoping that they would be back in the gap by morning. Not long after waking, I was looking out across the misty surface when the same rod screamed off. I jumped up and pulled my chesties on before pulling into another carp that immediately dropped into the deeper water off the shelf. I played this one from the bank for a while and led it in with no real problems. As he got close, the fish went left forcing me to follow it, throwing the net out into the water in front of me. This one didn't have much fight in him though, and I

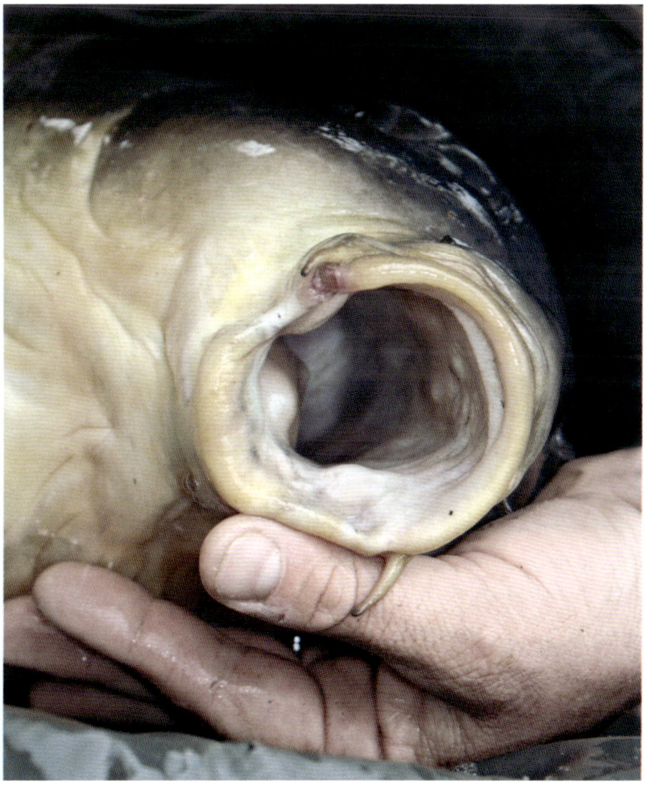

Guess who?

soon had a light-coloured common in the net. I secured the fish in the net and went back to prepare the kit. As I was sorting this out Noc appeared. "Shit," I said to myself, "No more secrets." "Hi Noc..." He'd heard the buzzer and I had to confess that I had a mid-twenty common in the net. The fish was a very pale-coloured carp in perfect condition. I later found out from Andy that it's one that doesn't visit the bank much, another rare beauty to add to my ever-increasing list of babes!

That's one angry carp coming ashore!

After the pictures were done, I thanked Noc and told him not to say anything and joked that if he did, he wouldn't get the Fen ticket that he was after for the next year! Before he left, he told me that he had seen several carp down in the corner to the left of the point in the night, so I knew they had legged it. I was lucky to have caught another, as there now weren't any carpy signs in front of me. I decided to pack up, ready for a quick exit by 10am as there was no signs of carp in the area. On the drive home my mind was racing, thinking about Paddle and how she hadn't been banked yet and praying that she wouldn't

Andy takes the strain as we carefully prepare for the photo session.

He even brought me some champagne down – what a gent.

get caught before my return.

When I got home I text Andy, asking him to let me know if she came out. This fish obsessed me and I just couldn't stop thinking about her. I heard nothing before my next session, which was a good sign, and on the drive down there I was wondering who would be where. When I pulled through the gate, I was surprised to see that there weren't many cars in the car park. For a change, I went a different route, going to Lake Five first and as I got near I could see that someone was in First in Five. Closer inspection revealed a mate of mine called Sam. He's a lovely lad and I'm always winding him up about how nice he is! As we talked, he told me what he had seen and also informed me that he was the only angler on the lake as far as he knew. After a few minutes I wished him good luck and headed off to find myself some carp.

From the information he gave me, it seemed that the carp were up at the opposite end of Lake Five to where I had caught. I was in hunting mode and after a few laps the only fish I had seen were near Sam. There was no way I was going sheep him up though, although I knew he was going the next evening so I reserved the swim just in case. It was colder than the previous week so these fish would be on the munch, plus a northerly was blowing down to Sam's end of the lake. Trust me, for small-water carp these fish love any new wind that comes. I knew I had to be in Lake Five, on this wind, so by the evening I had decided that the middle swim on Lake Five offered the best chance of a bite. Lake Five is the bigger of the two lakes, so they had plenty of room to

The queen of the lake was mine!

move about, and there was only Sam and I there, and Lake Six was empty.

I knew this area fairly well as I had caught The Carving and co from the swim to my left, The Point. Halfway out to the island there was a bar, and I was going to position two rods near it, with one rod short of the bar and the other just over the back in the soft silt. The third rod would be fished to the right, close in, just off the marginal drop off. When I felt this rod down I got a funny drop, so I reeled it in and discovered fresh strands of weed on the lead; this would be a natural food larder. So, I recast the rod back to the area and baited it up with my salty squids. I had got Gary Bayes to add rock salt to my bait. It's something I use a lot but have shied away from talking about over the years. Carp crave salt in their diet (they're naturally sodium deficient) and it's one of the main minerals that they are on the hunt for in its many forms. I think that they can get it from clay, crustacean shells and, of course, anglers' bait. It's a big edge when used correctly, and at certain times of the year, like spring and after spawning, they're on the lookout for it, big time. I even have my hook baits soaking in a salty glug for added pull.

With the rods sorted, it was time to get the house up and give Sam some Uncle Jim text therapy! I sat up until late but didn't hear anything until the birds started to sing, just before first light. I opened my eyes and looked out over the misty lake. I wasn't in any hurry to leave the warmth of my bag, so I just watched the lake from the comfort of my bed.

All of a sudden, I saw some ripples coming out from the left. I jumped up and went to investigate, pulling my coat on before I lost my warmth. "Bosh!" This time it was to the right and as I got to the edge of my swim, I could see the disturbance was emanating from just ten yards behind my left-hand rod. I watched a big plume of bubbles hit the surface and followed them as they got nearer to the rod, sweet, I was on them! I looked across at Sam's swim and saw no signs of life, then a big common pushed out up to the wrist in front of me, 30 yards out. I was 100 per cent sure that it was Paddle. It then came up again, going well right of the swim, looking like it was on its way up to the gap. I legged it round to the gap for a quick look to see if she came in, and sure enough, I could make out a carp coming towards me on the surface. The glare was in my face as the sun was well above the trees now, and I didn't have my glasses with me, but as I watched, straining my eyes to see which one it was, this huge carp came into view. I knew in my heart which one it was and as it entered the gap there was my target fish beneath me, in three feet of water. Trust me, I was in awe of the beast that was so close to me, beneath the very tree I was watching from. She looked big, bigger than I had ever seen her. She was filled out around her tiny, stubby pecs and as she swam over a clearing of sand in the gap, she stopped and did a 360-degree turn, circled the zone and put her head down quickly before making her away into Lake Six. She swam along the island reed line and disappeared from view.

I rang Steve Allcott, telling him what I had just witnessed. When I told him about the way she acted over the sandy spot in the gap, he laughed and said he had salted the zone, big time, when he was last there. I decided to pack up and fish the gap side of Lumpy's. I kept an eye from the tree, but only saw a mirror. It was still colder than normal and I knew there was now a good chance that she would come out in the next few days. I fished the shallow areas of the swim for most of the day, but it just looked dead. Later that evening, I parked up and left my barrow and went for a look.

Sam and I were still the only anglers fishing Five and Six, which is unreal when you think about it. Mind you, I wasn't complaining! As I got near Sam's swim, I could see him up the tree, looking. He hadn't heard me approach and I whispered up to him, "Is she there?" "Yeah mate," came the reply. God, she was on a mission, getting about the lake. Sam climbed down and said to me he was now staying until the early hours. "Good move," I said, continuing, "I'm going on The Point, as I saw some show there this morning." Sam then told me that he'd heard them going mental there in the early hours the previous night. I hadn't heard them, but I'd gone to bed at 11pm. I left him to it after that, wishing him luck before departing. I carried on round Lake Five and placed my glasses on the ground to secure The Point while on the way round to the barrow.

I was going to fish two rods to the right, where I had seen the carp show over the fresh weed growth, and the third slightly left, 20 yards out. I had a cast around, looking for a nice soft drop. I was particularly happy with the left-hander, as it felt really smooth, like it was being worked by carp. When I pulled the lead back, it just pulled through it with ease… this had to be the zone! I had all three rods rocking on the spots as darkness approached. With the house now set up, it was time to cook some dinner, which was to be a rib-eye steak with onions, tomatoes and of course, big open mushrooms. I planned to wash the lot down with a couple of glasses of red wine. I phoned Steve up and told him about the events of the day, chasing Paddle about and I remember saying to Steve that I didn't feel any closer to her. I got my head down early but woke to a single bleep in the early hours. It was really misty, and I heard one go over. After thirty minutes I'd heard several more, they were out there and I stood a good chance of getting a bite.

I must have drifted off because I woke to several bleeps from the buzzer. I jumped up and there was a mother duck and half a dozen ducklings pecking at my indicators! Before getting back into the bag, I threw some crumbed-up boilies into the edge for them. Christ, it was cold, time to get back into the warm bag. I turned my head to face the back of the brolly and drifted off. The next thing I knew, there were several bleeps again. "Piss off," I thought, imagining that the ducks were back. Thankfully, it went quiet, briefly. The buzzer just started screaming and I just shouted, "Piss off!" but the alarm seemed pretty insistent! As I turned round, I could see that the rod was bent down, "Bloody hell, I'm in!" I uttered, jumping up and pulling my chesties on. As I picked the rod up it was thumped down by a massive surge of power. The fish set off towards Sam's swim, stripping fifty to sixty yards of line off the reel. Next, a huge bow-wave pushed up before stopping, just as suddenly. I saw a big shape on the top then it went deep and kited right coming closer. The fish then swung left and I knew that I'd have to follow it. I picked up the net, threw it out into the water and made my way out

Fifty pounds of English common, a very rare creature indeed!

into the lake. The water was still well down and I didn't want to pull it into shallower water and risk a hook pull if it panicked and bolted.

This fish wasn't fighting anymore; I was now just leading it towards the net. All of a sudden, it was on the surface and I could see that it was a big common. I thought that it was The Long Common and as I pushed the net out it went in at the first attempt. At that point it didn't even register it could be Paddle. I just wouldn't allow myself the thought that it was Paddle. I bit the line and pushed the landing handle into the silt while I went and got the bits sorted. When I went back and had another look, I think it began to hit me what might be in the net, as it was clearly massive! I broke the net down, wrapped the mesh around the arms and made my way to the swim. The carp behaved like a baby and when I went to pull her from the water I thought, "'Kin hell, that's heavy!" I looked down and then I saw her stubby pecs, "Christ, it's Paddle!" I couldn't believe it, she was finally mine! I laid her down on the mat and she filled it! Oh my God, it was just her and me and I had finally caught my dream. Before I weighed her, I removed the hook from her mouth and I noticed a fresh tear in the corner of her mouth. The only loss I knew of was Colin's the previous week! I carefully put her in Marky Mark's weigh sling and his scales were already zeroed. I lifted her up and the needle passed the magical 50lb barrier settling on 51lb 4oz. Fifty pounds of English common, a very rare creature indeed!

I still couldn't believe what had happened and quickly popped her into the sack before ringing Rich Stewart, as he was on his way over to do some magazine work. After congratulating me, Rich promised to be with me in half an hour. I went to check on Paddle and she was fine. While I was out at the water's edge, a fish pushed out in front! Even though I had the main prize in the sack, I still wanted that rod back out there, so I tied on a new rig and bait and fuzzed it back out towards where the fish had shown. I put the rod back on the rest and slackened the line off, not even bothering to clip on the bobbin. It was time to send out loads of texts to my mates and then phone Jane and tell her the good news. "Guess what darling," I said, "I've got her and she weighs 51lb 4oz!" I promised her that I'd be home that evening, after we'd sorted the magazine work. Incredibly, the rod that I had just cast back out suddenly buckled over in the rest (I had forgot to turn the buzzer back on) and I coaxed another decent common into the net. It turned out to be Clover again, this time at 33lb 12oz. I sacked her up next to Paddle and again checked she that was OK. Andy was soon on the phone, congratulating me on the capture. I told him I had her sacked up but didn't tell him about Clover, I'd leave that one as a surprise!

I told him that Rich was twenty minutes away and Andy promised to be over shortly. A short while later I was standing in front of the swim when Andy arrived with a posse in tow comprising Mark, Noc and Alan. Andy came up to me, shook my hand and said, "Well done mate… err, what's that other sack?" I just laughed and explained what had happened, telling him that it was only a 'small' one, Clover at 33lb 12oz. Rich arrived and we did a few pictures of Clover first. Next, it was the queen's turn and as I got hold of the sack, I checked that her stubby pecs were laying along her body. As I lifted her up she went mental, thrashing the water to a foam. I passed her to Andy and he placed her into the mat and we both walked her to the very same spot I'd photographed The Carving in the year before.

I'm very funny about others taking pictures on their cameras because they can end up anywhere in this digital era. Plus, those pictures aren't my copyright, so I only let Andy take some on his camera as a back up, letting Rich use my camera and his work one. She was well behaved on the bank and as you can see from the pictures, she sure is a beast in perfect condition. When I held her up for the cameras I was buzzing, in complete awe of the unique carp I was holding. We did a few returners and, as it was now time to let her free, I lowered her into the water and I gently whispered to her, thanking her for the moment. I tickled the underside of her chest and she responded by surging off and disappearing back into her home. I just punched the sky and shouted, "Yessss!"

Later that day Andy popped back with a bottle of Champagne to toast the capture. Thanks Andy, you're a gent! As you can imagine, my phone went into meltdown and as I drove home I had a big smile on my face. I was going to take Jane out to celebrate in true Uncle Jim style.